VISTAS

Pocket Dictionary
&
Language Guide

VISTA
HIGHER LEARNING

Vista Higher Learning
Boston, Massachusetts • Auburn, California

ISBN 1-931100-08-X

Library of Congress Control Number: 2001087342

3 4 5 6 7 8 9 B 05 04 03 02

CONTENTS

Introduction

The **VISTAS Pocket Dictionary & Language Guide** was created to complement **VISTAS: Introducción a la lengua española**. This dictionary contains all the active words and expressions taught in **VISTAS** plus several thousand additional words, expressions, and idioms chosen because of their high frequency and their usefulness to students who are using **VISTAS** to learn Spanish.

The Spanish-English and English-Spanish dictionaries are followed by *Expresiones útiles,* a storehouse of contextualized sentences illustrating new vocabulary, idioms, and grammatical structures which can help you make your Spanish more natural and expressive. These sentences are related to the themes of each lesson of **VISTAS**.

Verb conjugation charts containing all the verbs taught in **VISTAS** follow the *Expresiones útiles,* section.

At the back of the dictionary you will find a reference section containing lists of specialized vocabulary on a variety of topics, such as country names, adjectives of nationality, academic subjects, foods, numbers, sayings, false friends, and so forth.

These features make the **VISTAS Pocket Dictionary & Language Guide** a resource that will be useful for the duration of your study of Spanish and beyond.

Note on Alphabetization

For purposes of alphabetization, the Spanish language contains one more letter, ñ, than English. Ñ follows n; therefore, the word **dañar**, for example, appears after **danzar**.

Abbreviations Used in This Dictionary

adj.	adjective
adv.	adverb
aux.	auxiliary
conj.	conjunction
dem.	demonstrative
d.o.	direct object
f.	feminine
fam.	familiar
form.	formal
i.	intransitive
impers.	impersonal
interj.	interjection
i.o.	indirect object
irreg.	irregular
L.A.	Latin America
loc.	set expression
m.	masculine
n.	noun
obj.	object
p.p.	past participle
pl.	plural
poss.	possessive
prep.	preposition
pron.	pronoun/pronominal
recip.	reciprocal
refl.	reflexive
sing.	singular
subj.	subject/subjunctive
t.	transitive
v.	verb

Español-Inglés
Spanish–English

A

a *prep.* at; to
  a la(s) + (*time*) at + (*time*)
abadía *f.* abbey
abajo *adv.* down
  ¡Abajo! Down (with it/him/her/them)!
abatido/a *adj.* dejected
abeja *f.* bee
abeto *m.* fir tree
abierto *p.p. of* **abrir** opened;
  abierto/a *adj.* open
abogado/a *m. f.* lawyer
abonar *v.t. (soil)* to fertilize
abono *m.* fertilizer
abortar *v.i.* to have a miscarriage
  abortar de manera provocada to have an abortion
aborto *m. (espontáneo)* miscarriage; *(provocado)* abortion
abrazar *v.t.* to hug; to embrace
abrazarse *v. pron. (recip.)* to hug; to embrace each other
abrazo *m.* hug; embrace
abrebotellas *m.* bottle opener
abrelatas *m. sing.* can opener
abreviar *v.t.* to abbreviate
abreviatura *f.* abbreviation
abridor *m.* opener
abrigo *m.* coat; overcoat
abril *m.* April
abrillantador (para pisos/suelos) *m.* (floor) polish

abrillantar *v.t.* to polish
abrir *v.t.* to open
abrirse *v. pron.* to open
  La ventana se abrió de golpe. The window opened suddenly.
absorbente *adj.* absorbent
absorber *v.t.* to absorb
absurdo/a *adj.* absurd
abuelo/a *m.* grandfather; *f.* grandmother
abuelos *m., pl.* grandparents
aburrido/a *adj.* bored; boring
aburrir *v.t.* to bore
  Este libro me aburre. This book bores me.
aburrirse *v. pron.* to get bored
  Espero que hoy no se aburran. I hope you don't get bored today.
acá *adv.* here
  ¡Ven acá! Come here!
acabar *v.t.* to finish
  Acabé la tarea. I'm done with my homework.
acabar de (+ *inf.*) *v.i.* to have just *(done something)*
  Acabo de limpiar. I've just finished cleaning.
acampada *f.* camp; camping
  ir de acampada to go camping
acampar *v.i.* to camp
acantilado *m.* cliff
acariciar *v.t.* to caress; *(hair, pet)* to stroke, to pet
acaso: por si acaso *loc.* just in case
accesorio *m.* accessory
accidentado/a *adj. (terrain)* rugged; *(person)* hurt, injured

accidente *m.* accident
accidente laboral industrial
accident
acción *f.* action
accionar *v.t.* (*machine*) to
operate; to activate
aceite *m.* oil
aceite de oliva olive oil
aceituna *f.* olive
acelerador *m.* accelerator
(pedal)
acelerar *v.t.* to accelerate
¡Acelera! Hurry up!
aceptar *v.t.* to accept
acera *f.* sidewalk
acerca de *prep.* about
**Leí un artículo acerca de
Sevilla.** I read an article
about Seville.
acercarse (a) *v. pron.* to
approach, to come closer
(to)
acero *m.* steel
acero inoxidable stainless
steel
ácido *m.* acid
ácido fólico folic acid
ácido/a *adj.* acid; (*flavor*) tart,
tangy
acogedor(a) *adj.* cosy
acolchado/a *adj.* padded
acompañar *v.t.* to go with, to
accompany
acondicionado *adj.*
conditioned
aconsejar *v.t.* to advise
acontecimiento *m.* event
acordar (o:ue) *v.t.* to agree
acordarse (de) (o:ue) *v. pron.*
to remember

acostarse (o:ue) *v. pron.* to go
to bed
acostumbrarse (a) *v. pron.* to
be accustomed to
acrobacia *f.* acrobatics
acróbata *m., f.* acrobat
activar *v.t.* to activate
actividad *f.* activity
activo/a *adj.* active
acto *m.* act
en el acto *loc.* immediately,
right away
acto seguido *adv.*
immediately after
actor *m.* actor
actriz *f.* actor
actual *adj.* current, present
actualidades *f., pl.* news;
current events
acuarela *f.* watercolor
(painting)
acuario *m.* aquarium
acuático/a *adj.* aquatic
acuerdo *m.* agreement
de acuerdo con according to
llegar a un acuerdo to reach
an agreement
adaptación *f.* adaptation
adaptarse (a) *v. pron.* to adapt;
to adjust
adelantar (a un vehículo) *v.t.*
to pass (a vehicle)
adelante *adv.* forward, ahead
**La librería Porté está un
poco más adelante.** The
Porté Bookshop is a little
farther ahead.
adelgazar *v.i.* to lose weight; to
slim down
además (de) *adv.* furthermore;

besides; in addition (to)

adentro *adv.* inside

aderezar *v.t.* (*food*) to season; (*salad*) to dress

aderezo *m.* seasoning; dressing

adicción *f.* addiction

adicional *adj.* additional

adicto/a *m., f.* addict; *adj.* addicted

adiós *m.* good-bye

aditivo *m.* additive

adivinanza *f.* riddle

adivinar *v.t.* to guess

adjetivo *m.* adjective

administración *f.* management, administration

  administración de empresas business administration

administrar *v.t.* (*business*) to manage; to run

adolescencia *f.* adolescence

adolescente *m., f.* teenager, adolescent

¿adónde? *adv.* (*destination*) where?

adornar *v.t.* to decorate; (*food*) to garnish

adorno *m.* ornament, decoration

  de adorno for decoration

  Se puso un lazo de adorno en el pelo. She wore a ribbon on her hair for decoration.

adquirir (i:ie) *v.t.* to acquire

adquisición *f.* acquisition

adrede *adv.* intentionally, on purpose

aduana *f.* customs

adulación *f.* flattery

adulador(a) *m., f.* flatterer

adular *v.t.* to flatter

advertencia *f.* warning

advertir (i:ie) *v.t.* to warn; to notice

  Por fin alguien advirtió mi presencia. Finally someone noticed I was there.

aéreo/a *adj.* air

  correo aéreo air mail

aeróbico/a *adj.* aerobic

aerolínea *f.* airline

aeroplano *m.* airplane

aeropuerto *m.* airport

afectado/a *adj.* affected

afectar *v.t.* to affect

afeitarse *v. pron.* to shave (*oneself*)

afición *f.* hobby

aficionado/a *adj.* fan

aficionarse (a) *v. pron.* to become a fan (of); (*hobby*) to take up

afinar *v.t.* (*musical instrument*) to tune

afirmativo/a *adj.* affirmative

africano/a *adj./m., f.* African

afuera *adv.* outside

afueras *f., pl.* suburbs; outskirts

agachar *v.t.* (*head*) lower

agacharse *v. pron.* to squat

agencia *f.* office; agency

  agencia de viajes travel agency

agente *m., f.* agent

  agente de viajes travel agent

agosto *m.* August

agotado/a *adj.* (*person, supplies*) exhausted; (*commerce*) out of stock; (*tickets*) sold out

agotamiento *m.* exhaustion

agotarse *v. pron.* (*provisions, supplies*) to run out

agradable *adj.* (*person*) pleasant, nice; (*situation*) enjoyable

agradecer (c:zc) *v.t.* to thank, to be grateful
Te agradezco tu ayuda. Thank you for your help.

agradecido/a *adj.* grateful

agrícola *adj.* agricultural
labor agrícola farm labor

agricultor(a) *m., f.* farmer

agricultura *f.* agriculture, farming

agridulce *adj.* bittersweet

agrio/a *adj.* sour

agrupar *v.t.* to group

agruparse *v. pron.* to get into groups

agua (el) *f.* water
agua bendita holy water
agua dulce fresh water
agua mineral mineral water
agua potable drinking water
agua salada salt water

aguacate *m.* avocado

aguafiestas *m., f.* party pooper

aguantar *v.t.* to endure, to put up with; (*Spain*) to hold

aguante *m.* endurance

águila (el) *f.* eagle

aguja *f.* needle

agujerear *v.t.* (*material*) to make holes; (*ear*) to pierce

agujero *m.* hole

ahijado/a *m.* godson; *f.* goddaughter

ahogado/a *adj.* drowned

ahogar *v.t.* to drown
Ahoga sus dudas leyendo. He drowns his doubts by reading.
Ahoga sus penas trabajando. She drowns her sorrow with work.

ahogarse *v. pron.* to drown
Se ahogó en el río. He drowned in the river.

ahora *adv.* now
ahora mismo right now
de ahora en adelante from now on

ahorrador(a) *adj.* frugal

ahorrar *v.t.* to save

ahorros *m.* savings

aire *m.* air
aire acondicionado air conditioning
al aire libre in the open air

aislante *adj.* insulating

aislar *v.t.* to isolate; to insulate

ajedrecista *m., f.* chess player

ajedrez *m.* chess

ajo *m.* garlic

al (*contraction of* a + el) to the, at the

al (*+ inf.*) upon, on
Al llegar a San Juan, fuimos a la playa. Upon arriving in San Juan, we went to the beach.

ala (el) *f.* wing
ala delta (*vehicle*) hang glider; (*sport*) hang gliding

practicar el ala delta to hang glide

alardear (de) *v.i.* (*Spain*) to boast (about)

Alardeaba de haber ganado. He was boasting about having won.

alarmante *adj.* alarming

albahaca *f.* basil

albañil *m.* builder; bricklayer

albañilería *f.* (*profession*) building; bricklaying

albaricoque *m.* apricot

alberca *f.* (*Mexico*) swimming pool

albergue *m.* hostel

albergue juvenil youth hostel

alcachofa *f.* artichoke

alcalde, alcaldesa *m., f.* mayor

alcaldía *f.* city hall

alcoba *f.* (*L.A.*) bedroom

alcohol *m.* alcohol

alcohólico/a *adj.* alcoholic

aldea *f.* village

alegrarse (de) *v. pron.* to be happy (about)

alegre *adj.* happy; joyful

alegría *f.* joy

alejado/a *adj.* remote

alemán *m.* (*language*) German

alemán, alemana *adj./m., f.* German

alérgico/a *adj.* allergic

aleta *f.* (*fish*) fin; (*swiming*) flipper

alfabeto *m.* alphabet

alfombra *f.* carpet; rug

alga (el) *f.* seaweed

algarabía *f.* rejoicing, jubilation; noisy commotion

algo *pron.* something; anything

algodón *m.* cotton

de algodón (made of) cotton

alguien *pron.* someone; somebody; anyone

algún, alguno/a(s) *adj.* any; some

aliento *m.* breath

dar aliento to encourage

alimentar *v.t.* to feed

alimentarse *v. pron.* to feed oneself

alimento *m.* food

aliñar *v.t.* (*food*) to season; (*salad*) to dress

aliño *m.* seasoning; dressing

aliviar *v.t.* to ease; alleviate; (*pain*) to relieve

aliviar el estrés/la tensión to relieve stress/tension

aliviarse *v. pron.* (*pain*) to let up; (*person*) to get better

alivio *m.* relief

allí *adv.* there

allí mismo right there

alma (el) *f.* soul

almacén *m.* department store

almacenamiento *m.* storage

almacenar *v.t.* to store

almeja *f.* clam

almendra *f.* almond

almendro *m.* almond tree

almíbar *m.* syrup

almohada *f.* pillow

almorzar (o:ue) *v.i.* to have lunch

almuerzo *m.* lunch

¿Aló? *interj.* Hello? (*on the telephone*)

alojado/a *adj.* guest

alojamiento *m.* lodging

alojar (a alguien) *v.t.* to lodge, to put up

alojarse *v. pron.* (*hotel*) to stay

alpinismo *m.* (mountain) climbing

alpinista *m., f.* (mountain) climber

alquilar *v.t.* to rent

alquiler *m.* rent

alrededor (de) *prep.* around
  Hay una muralla alrededor de la ciudad vieja. There is a wall around the old city.

alrededor *adv.* around
  una mesa con cuatro sillas alrededor a table with four chairs around it

alrededores *m., pl.* outskirts, surrounding area
  en los alrededores de Barcelona on the outskirts of Barcelona

altavoz *m.* loudspeaker

alternador *m.* alternator

alternativa *f.* alternative

altillo *m.* attic

alto/a *adj.* tall

alto *m.* halt, stop
  señal de alto stop (sign)

altura *f.* height

aluminio *m.* aluminum
  de aluminio (made of) aluminum

alumno/a *m., f.* (*elementary school*) pupil, student

ama (el) de casa *f.* housekeeper; caretaker; housewife

amable *adj.* nice; friendly

amanecer *m.* dawn
  al amanecer at dawn

amanecer (c:zc) *v. impers.* to dawn; (*person*) to wake up (*in the morning*)
  Amanecí con dolor de cabeza. I woke up with a headache.

amapola *f.* poppy

amante *m., f.* lover; fan; *adj.* loving
  amantes del jazz jazz lovers
  su amante esposa his loving wife
  amante de la buena conversación fond of good conversation

amar *v.t.* to love

amargo/a *adj.* bitter

amarillento/a *adj.* yellowish

amarillo/a yellow

amarse *v. pron.* (*recip.*) to love each other

ambición *f.* ambition

ambicionar *v.t.* to aspire to

ambicioso/a *adj.* ambitious

ambientador *m.* air freshener

ambiente *m.* (*natural*) environment; (*created by people, decoration*) atmosphere

ambos/as *adj.* both
  Sujetó la pelota con ambas manos. He held down the ball with both hands.

ambulancia *f.* ambulance

amenaza *f.* threat

amenazar *v.t.* to threaten

amígdala *f.* tonsil

amigo/a *m., f.* friend

hacer amigos to make friends

amistad *f.* friendship

amistades *m., pl.* friends
Martina tiene muchas amistades en Cartagena. Martina has lots of friends in Cartagena.

amistoso/a *adj.* friendly

amor *m.* love

amortiguador *m.* shock absorber

amueblado/a *adj.* furnished

amueblar *v.t.* to furnish

analfabeto/a *m., f.* illiterate person; *adj.* illiterate

anaranjado/a *adj.* (*color*) orange

anarquía *f.* anarchy

anárquico/a *adj.* anarchic

anatomía *f.* anatomy

anatómico/a *adj.* anatomical

ancho/a *adj.* wide

anchoa *f.* anchovy

anciano/a *adj.* elderly; *m.* elderly man; *f.* elderly woman

anestesia *f.* anesthesia

anestesiar *v.t.* to anesthetize

anestesista *m., f.* anesthetist

anfitrión *m.* host

anfitriona *f.* hostess

anglosajón, anglosajona *adj./m., f.* Anglo-Saxon

anguila *f.* eel

ángulo *m.* angle

anillo *m.* ring
anillo de bodas wedding ring
anillo de compromiso engagement ring

animado/a *adj.* (*person*) in good spirits; (*party*) lively

animal *m.* animal

animar *v.t.* to cheer up; to encourage

animarse *v. pron.* to cheer up

aniversario (de bodas) *m.* (wedding) anniversary

anoche *adv.* last night

anormal *adj.* abnormal

ansia *f.* longing

ansiar *v.t.* to crave for, to long for

anteayer *adv.* the day before yesterday

antepasado/a *m., f.* ancestor

antes *adv.* before
antes (de) que *conj.* before
antes de *prep.* before

antibiótico *m.* antibiotic

anticipación *f.* anticipation; (*business*) advance
con anticipación ahead of time; before hand

anticonceptivo *m.* contraceptive

anticuado/a *adj.* old-fashioned

antideportivo *adj.* unsportsmanlike

antídoto *m.* antidote

antifaz *m.* mask

antigüedades *f., pl.* antiques; antiquities

antiguo/a *adj.* old; ancient

antipatía *f.* dislike

antipático/a *adj.* unpleasant

antojo *m.* whim

antología *f.* anthology

antorcha *f.* torch

anular *v.t.* to cancel

anunciar *v.t.* to announce; to advertise

anuncio *m.* (*newspaper*) advertisement

anzuelo *m.* hook
  morder el anzuelo (*loc.*) to swallow the bait; to bite

añil *adj.* indigo

año *m.* year

añoranza *f.* yearning

añorar (a alguien) *v.t.* to long for (someone); to miss (someone)

apagar *v.t.* (*TV, radio*) to turn off; (*fire*) to put out, to extinguish

apagón *m.* power failure, blackout

aparato *m.* appliance
  aparato circulatorio circulatory system
  aparato digestivo digestive system
  aparato doméstico household appliance
  aparato respiratorio respiratory system

aparecer (c:zc) *v.i.* to appear

apartamento *m.* apartment

apellido *m.* last name

apenas *adv.* hardly; scarcely; barely; just
  Apenas le conozco. I barely know him.
  Apenas te oigo. I can hardly hear you.

aperitivo *m.* appetizer

apilar *v.t.* to stack

apio *m.* celery

aplaudir *v.t./v.i.* to applaud, to clap

aplauso *m.* applause

aplazamiento *m.* postponement

aplazar *v.t.* to postpone, to put off

apodo *m.* nickname

apoyar *v.t.* to support

apoyo *m.* support

apreciar *v.t.* to appreciate

aprecio *m.* esteem

aprender *v.t.* to learn

apresurarse *v. pron.* to hurry

aprobado *m.* passing grade, C

aprobar (o:ue) *v.i.* to pass

aprovechar *v.t.* to make good use of

aprovecharse (de) *v. pron.* to take advantage (of)

aptitud *f.* aptitude, competence

apto/a *adj.* fit (*to practice a profession*); suitable
  No es apto para ejercer la psicología. He's not fit to practice psychology.

apuñalar (a alguien) *v.t.* to stab (somebody)

apurarse *v. pron.* to hurry; to rush

aquel, aquella, aquellos/as *dem. adj.* that (over there); those (over there)

aquél, aquélla, aquéllos/as *dem. pron.* that (over there); those (over there)

aquello *dem. neuter pron.* that; that thing; that fact

aquí *adv.* here
  aquí está here (he/she/it) is
  aquí estamos en... here we

are in . . .
aquí mismo right here
árabe *m.* (*language*) Arabic
árabe *adj.* Arabian; *m., f.* Arab
araña *f.* spider; (*light*) chandelier
árbitro/a *m.* referee; umpire
árbol *m.* tree
  árbol frutal fruit tree
  árbol genealógico family tree
arboleda *f.* grove
arbusto *m.* shrub, bush
archipiélago *m.* archipelago
archivar *v.t.* to file
archivo *m.* file
arcilla *f.* clay
arco *m.* arch; (*sport*) bow
  arco iris *m.* rainbow
ardilla *f.* squirrel
arena *f.* sand
arete *m.* (*L.A.*) earring
argumentar *v.t.* to argue
argumento *m.* (*reasoning*) argument; (*literature, film*) plot
arisco/a *adj.* unfriendly
aristocracia *f.* aristocracy
aristócrata *m., f.* aristocrat
arma (el) *f.* weapon, arm
armario *m.* closet
aroma *m.* scent
arqueólogo/a *m., f.* archaeologist
arquitecto/a *m., f.* architect
arrancar *v.t.* (*car*) to start; (*sheet of paper*) to tear out
arrastrar *v.t.* to drag
arrastrarse (por el piso/suelo) *v. pron.* to crawl (on the ground)

arrecife *m.* reef
arreglar *v.t.* to fix
  El profesor arregló la situación. The professor fixed the situation.
  La modista me arregló el vestido. My dressmaker fixed my dress.
arreglarse *v. pron.* to do oneself up; to get ready
  Tarda mucho en arreglarse. He/She takes forever getting ready.
arrepentido/a *adj.* repentant, feeling sorry
arrepentirse *v. pron.* to be sorry; to regret
arrestado/a *adj.* arrested; under arrest
  estar arrestado/a to be under arrest
arrestar *v.t.* to arrest
arresto *m.* arrest
arriba *adv.* up
  ¡Manos arriba! Hands up!
  Me miró de arriba abajo. He/She looked me up and down.
arriesgarse *v. pron.* to take the risk
arrogante *adj.* arrogant
arroz *m.* rice
arte *m.* art
arteria *f.* artery
artes *f., pl.* arts
  artes marciales martial arts
artesanía *f.* craftsmanship; crafts
articulación *f.* joint, articulation
artículo *m.* article; item

artículos *m., pl.* (*business*) goods
  artículos de cocina kitchenware
  artículos de deporte sporting goods
  artículos de piel leather goods
  artículos de punto knitwear
artista *m., f.* artist
artístico/a *adj.* artistic
arveja *m.* pea
asa (el) *f.* (*cup, serving dish*) handle
asado *m.* roast
  asado de cordero roast lamb
asado *p.p. of* asar roasted; **asado/a** *adj.* roast(ed)
  castañas asadas roasted chestnuts
asar *v.t.* to roast
ascender *v.t.* (*temperature, prices*) to rise; *v.i.* (*employee*) to be promoted
ascenso *m.* rise; (*at work*) promotion
ascensor *m.* elevator
asco *m.* nausea
  ¡Qué asco! How revolting! How disgusting!
asegurar *v.t.* to assure, to guarantee
asegurarse *v. pron.* to make sure
asesinato *m.* murder; assassination
asesino/a *adj./m., f.* murderer; assassin
asfalto *m.* asphalt
así *adv.* thus; so (*in such a way*)

Debe hacerse así. It must be done like this.
  así así so-so
asiático/a *adj.* Asiatic; *m., f.* Asian
asiduo/a *m., f.* (*client*) regular; *adj.* frequent
asiento *m.* seat
  asiento delantero front seat
  asiento trasero rear seat
asignación *f.* (*Mexico*) homework
asistencia *f.* assistance
  asistencia médica health care
asistir (a) *v.i.* to attend
asociación *f.* association
asociar *v.t.* (*ideas, words*) to associate
asociarse (con) *v. pron.* to go into partnership (with)
asombroso/a *adj.* amazing, astonishing
aspecto *m.* appearance
áspero/a *adj.* (*surface, skin*) rough
aspiradora *f.* vacuum cleaner
aspirante *m., f.* candidate
aspirina *f.* aspirin
asqueroso/a *adj.* (*food, smell*) disgusting, revolting; (*place*) filthy
  Esta cocina está asquerosa. This kitchen is filthy.
astrología *f.* astrology
astrólogo/a *m., f.* astrologist
astronauta *m., f.* astronaut
astronomía *f.* astronomy
astrónomo/a *m., f.* astronomer
astuto/a *adj.* shrewd

asumir *v.t.* to assume

atajo *m.* short cut

ataque *m.* attack

  ataque al corazón heart attack

  ataque cardíaco heart attack

  ataque de nervios panic attack

atardecer *m.* dusk

  al atardecer at dusk, at twilight

ataúd *m.* coffin

ateísmo *m.* atheism

atención *f.* attention; care

atender *v.i.* to pay attention

atentado *m.* assault, attack; crime

  atentado terrorista terrorist attack; assassination attempt

atentar (contra) *v.t.* to attempt to assassinate (*somebody*); to attack (*something*)

ateo/a *adj.* atheistic; *m., f.* atheist

aterrizaje *m.* landing

aterrizar *v.i.* to land

atleta *m., f.* athlete

atlético/a *adj.* athletic

atletismo *m.* athletics; track and field

atontado/a *adj.* stunned, dazed

atracar *v.t.* (*bank*) to hold up; (*person*) to mug

atracción *f.* attraction

atraco *m.* robbery, holdup

atractivo/a *adj.* attractive

atractivo *m.* attraction; appeal, charm

  No entiendo su atractivo. I don't understand his appeal.

atraer *v.t. irreg.* (**yo atraigo**) to attract

atragantarse *v. pron.* to choke

atravesar *v.t.* to cross

atreverse *v. pron.* to dare

atrevido/a *adj.* (*dress*) daring, provocative; (*person*) brave; daring, cheeky.

  ¿No te da miedo viajar sola? Eres muy atrevida.
  You're not afraid of traveling all by yourself? You're really brave.

atrevimiento *m.* nerve

atropellar (a alguien con un vehículo) *v.t.* to run over (someone with a vehicle)

atroz *adj.* atrocious, awful

atún *m.* tuna

audición *f.* hearing; (*test*) audition

auditorio *m.* auditorium; audience

auge *m.* peak

  estar en auge to be on the increase

aula *f.* classroom; lecture hall

  aula magna main lecture hall

aumentar *v.t.* to increase

  aumentar de peso to gain weight

aumento *m.* increase

  aumento de sueldo pay raise

aunque *conj.* although, even though

auricular *m.* headphone; (*telephone*) receiver

ausencia *f.* absence

ausentarse *v. pron.* to go away

ausente *adj.* absent
australiano/a *adj./m., f.* Australian
auténtico/a *adj.* real
autobús *m.* bus
autodidacta *m., f.* self-taught person; autodidact
auto(e)stop *m.* hitchhiking
 hacer auto(e)stop to hitchhike
auto(e)stopista *m., f.* hitchhiker
autógrafo *m.* autograph
automático/a *adj.* automatic
automóvil *m.* automobile
automovilismo *m.* motor racing
automovilista *m., f.* motorist
autonomía *f.* autonomy
autónomo/a *adj.* (*government*) autonomous; *m., f.* (*work*) self-employed worker, freelancer
autopista *f.* highway
autor(a) *m., f.* author
 autor intelectual *(L.A.)* mastermind (*of a crime*)
autoritario/a *adj.* authoritarian
autoritarismo *m.* authoritarianism
autorretrato *m.* self-portrait
auxiliar *v.t.* to help
 ¡Auxilio! *interj.* Help!
avance *m.* advance
avanzado/a *adj.* advanzed
avanzar *v.i.* to advance; to move forward
avaricia *f.* avarice
avaricioso/a *adj.* greedy, avaricious
avaro/a *m., f.* miser
ave (el) *f.* bird

avellana *f.* hazelnut
avellano *m.* hazel tree
avenida *f.* avenue
aventura *f.* adventure
aventurero/a *adj.* adventurous; *m., f.* adventurer
avergonzado/a *adj.* embarrassed
avergonzar (o:ue) *v.t.* to shame, to embarrass
avergonzarse (o:ue) *v. pron.* to be ashamed
avería *f.* (*Spain*) (*automobile, mechanical*) breakdown
averiado/a *adj.* (*Spain*) broken down, out of order
averiarse *v. pron.* (*Spain*) to break down
averiguar *v.t.* to find out; to check
aversión *f.* aversion, dislike
avestruz *m.* ostrich
avión *m.* airplane
 viajar en avión to travel by plane
avioneta *f.* light aircraft
avisar *v.t.* to warn, to inform
aviso *m.* warning, notice
avispa *f.* wasp
axila *f.* armpit
¡Ay! *interj.* Oh!, Ouch!, Yikes!
 ¡Ay, qué dolor! Ouch, it hurts!
ayer *adv.* yesterday
ayudar (a) *v.t.* to help (to)
ayudarse *v. pron.* (*recip.*) to help each other
ayunar *v.i.* to fast
ayuno *m.* fast
ayunas: salir en ayunas to go

out without breakfast

ayuntamiento *m.* city hall

azafato/a *m., f.* flight attendant

azafrán *m.* saffron

azar *m.* chance; coincidence

  al azar at random, randomly

azúcar *m.* sugar

azucarero *m.* sugar bowl

azul *adj./m.* blue

  azul celeste sky blue

  azul marino navy blue

azulado/a *adj.* bluish

azulejo *m.* (*ceramic*) tile

B

babero *m.* bib

bacalao *m.* cod, codfish

bahía *f.* bay

bailar *v.t.* to dance

bailarín, bailarina *m., f.* dancer

baile *m.* dance

bajar *v.i.* to go down

bajarse (de un vehículo) *v. pron.* to get off/out of (a vehicle)

bajo/a *adj.* (*person*) short; (*volume, light, temperature*) low

  Por favor, hablen más bajo. Please speak quietly.

bajo/a *prep.* under

  bajo cero below zero

  bajo ningún pretexto under no circumstances

  bajo juramento under oath

balanza *f.* (*for weighing*) scales

balcón *m.* balcony

baldosa *f.* (*floor*) tile

ballena *f.* whale

ballet *m.* ballet

balneario *m.* spa, resort

baloncesto *m.* basketball

balonmano *m.* handball

banana *f.* banana

bañarse *v. pron. (refl.)* to bathe; to take a bath

banco *m.* bank; bench

banda *f.* (*music*) band

  banda sonora sound track

bandera *f.* flag

banquero/a *m., f.* banker

bañera *f.* bathtub

baño *m.* bathroom

baraja (de cartas/naipes) *f.* deck (of cards)

barato/a *adj.* cheap

barba *f.* beard

barbero *m.* barber

barbudo/a *adj.* bearded

barco *m.* ship

barra (de pan) *f.* (*Spain*) loaf (of bread)

barrer (el suelo/el piso) *v.t.* to sweep the floor

barriga *f.* stomach

barrio *m.* neighborhood

barro *m.* mud

barroco/a *adj.* baroque

báscula *f.* scales

bastante *adj.* enough; sufficient

bastar *v.i.* to be enough

  Con esto basta y sobra. This is more than enough.

  Con ocho basta. Eight is enough.

  Dos semanas no bastan para completarlo. Two weeks are not enough to finish it.

bastón *m.* walking stick
basurero *m.* garbage dump; garbage can
basurero/a *m., f.* garbage collector
basura *f.* trash
bata *f.* robe
  bata de baño bathrobe
batidor *m.* whisk
batidora *f.* (*Spain*) blender, mixer
batir *v.t.* to whisk; to beat
  batir un récord mundial to break a world record
baúl *m.* trunk
bautizar *v.t.* to baptize; to name
bautizo *m.* baptism
bazo *m.* spleen
beber *v.t./v.i.* to drink
bebida *f.* drink
beca *f.* grant; scholarship
béisbol *m.* baseball
belleza *f.* beauty
bello/a *adj.* beautiful
  bellas artes *f., pl.* fine arts
bendecir *v.t. irreg.* (**yo bendigo**) to bless
bendición *f.* blessing
beneficiarse *v.t.* to benefit
beneficio *m.* benefit
beneficioso/a *adj.* beneficial
benigno *adj.* benign
berenjena *f.* eggplant
bermellón *m.* vermilion
besar *v.t.* to kiss
besarse *v. pron.* (*recip.*) to kiss (each other)
beso *m.* kiss
betabel *f.* (*Mexico*) (sugar) beet

biblioteca *f.* library
bibliotecario/a *m., f.* librarian
bicarbonato *m.* baking soda
bicicleta *f.* bicycle
bien *adj.* good; well
bienestar *m.* well-being
bienvenida *f.* welcome
  dar la bienvenida to welcome
bienvenido/a *adj.* welcome
bigote(s) *m.* (*pl.*) mustache
bilingüe *adj.* bilingual
bilingüismo *m.* bilingualism
billete *m.* (*Spain*) ticket; paper money
  billete de ida y vuelta round-trip ticket
  Vale muchos billetes. It costs a lot of money.
billón *m.* trillion
  Un billón es un millón de millones. One trillion is a million millions.
biodiversidad *f.* biodiversity
biogenética *f.* genetic engineering
biografía *f.* biography
biográfico/a *adj.* biographical
biología *f.* biology
biólogo/a *m., f.* biologist
biosfera *f.* biosphere
bisabuelo/a *m.* great-grandfather; *f.* great-grandmother
bisagra *f.* hinge
bisnieto/a *m.* great-grandson; *f.* great-granddaughter
bistec *m.* steak
bisturí *m.* scalpel
blanco/a *adj.* white

bluejeans *m., pl.* (*L.A.*) jeans
blusa *f.* blouse
boca *f.* mouth
  boca abajo face-down
  boca arriba face-up
bocina *f.* (*automobile*) horn
boda *f.* wedding
  boda concertada arranged marriage
bodega *f.* (*house*) cellar; (*store*) winecellar
boina *f.* beret
boletín *m.* bulletin, report
  boletín de notas school report
  boletín informativo newsletter
boleto *m.* (*L.A.*) ticket
bolígrafo *m.* pen
bolsa *f.* purse; bag
  la Bolsa the stock market
bolsillo *m.* pocket
  libro de bolsillo paperback book
bolsista *m., f.* stock broker
bolsita *f.* (*diminutive*) small bag
  bolsita de té teabag
bolso *m.* shoulder bag
bomba *f.* bomb
bombero/a *m., f.* firefighter
bonito/a *adj.* pretty
bordar *v.t.* to embroider
bordo: a bordo aboard, on board
  ¡Todos a bordo! All aboard!
borracho/a *adj.* drunk
borrador *m.* eraser
borrar *v.t.* to erase
bosque *m.* forest
  bosque nuboso cloud forest

bosque tropical tropical forest; rainforest
bota *f.* boot
  botas de agua rubber boots
  botas de montar riding boots
botánica *f.* botany
botánico/a *m., f.* botanist; *adj.* botanical
botar *v.t.* (*L.A.*) to throw away
botella *f.* botella
  botella de vino bottle of wine
botiquín *m.* medicine cabinet
  botiquín de primeros auxilios first-aid kit
botón *m.* button
  botón de rebobinado rewind button
botones *m., sing.* bellhop
boxeador(a) *m., f.* boxer
boxear *v.i.* to box
boxeo *m.* boxing
bragas *f., pl.* (*Spain*) panties
brasier *m.* (*L.A.*) bra
brazo *m.* arm
  Es su brazo derecho. He's her right-hand man.
breve *adj.* brief; short
  en breve *adv.* shortly, soon
brevedad *f.* brevity
brillar *v.i.* to shine
brillo (para zapatos) *m.* (shoe) polish
brindar *v.t.* to toast
brindis *m.* toast
brisa *f.* breeze
brócoli *m.* broccoli
broma *f.* joke
  broma pesada practical joke
  bromas aparte joking aside
  en broma in jest, as a joke

hacer bromas to make jokes
bromista *m., f.* joker
bronce *m.* bronze
bronceado/a *adj.* suntanned
bronceador *m.* suntan lotion
broncear *v.t.* to tan
broncearse *v. pron.* to (get a) tan
buceador(a) *m., f.* (*underwater*) diver
bucear *v.i.* to dive
budista *adj./m., f.* Buddhist
bueno *adv.* well
bueno/a, buen *adj.* good
Buenos días. Good morning.
¿Bueno? Hello? (*on telephone*)
Buen viaje. Have a good trip.
Buenas noches. Good evening.; Good night.
Buenas tardes. Good afternoon.
(No) Es bueno que (+ *subj.*)
(No) Es bueno que corras. It's (not) good that you run.
buenísimo/a *adj.* (*superlative*) extremely good
bufanda *f.* scarf
búho *m.* owl
buitre *m.* vulture
bujía *f.* spark plug
bulevar *m.* boulevard
bulto *m.* bundle, package
buque *m.* boat, ship
burbuja *f.* bubble
buscar *v.t.* to look for
búsqueda *f.* search
buzón *m.* mailbox

C

caballero *m.* gentleman
caballo *m.* horse
montado/a a caballo on horseback
cabaña *f.* cabin
cabello *m.* hair
caber *v.i. irreg.* (**yo quepo**) to fit
Esta mesa no cabe aquí. This table doesn't fit here.
Esta falda no me cabe. This skirt doesn't fit me.
no cabe duda que (+ *inf.*) there's no doubt that . . .
cabeza *f.* head
cable *m.* cable
echarle un cable a alguien *idiom.* to help somebody out
cada *adj.* each
cadáver *m.* corpse
cadena *f.* chain
cadena perpétua life imprisonment; life sentence
cadena *f.* channel (TV)
cadera *f.* hip
caer *v.t. irreg.* (**yo caigo**) to fall
caerse *v. pron. irreg.* (**yo me caigo**) to fall (down)
café *m.* (*place*) café; (*drink*) coffee; (*color*) brown
cafetera *f.* coffee maker
cafetería *f.* cafeteria
caída *f.* fall
caída libre free fall
caído *p.p. of* **caer** fallen; **caído/a** *adj.* fallen
caja *f.* box; cash register
caja de música music box
caja fuerte safe
cajero/a *m., f.* cashier

cajero automático automatic teller machine (ATM)

calabaza f. pumpkin

calamar m. squid

calavera m. skull

calcetín m. sock

calculadora f. calculator

calcular v.t. to calculate, to work out

cálculo m. calculation, estimate

caldo m. broth, soup
  caldo de patas (Ecuador) beef soup
  caldo de gallina chicken soup
  caldo de res beef soup

calefacción f. heating

calendario m. calendar

calentador m. heater

calentar (e:ie) v.t. to heat

calentarse (e:ie) v. pron. to warm up

calidad f. quality

caliente adj. hot

calificación f. grade

calificar v.t. to grade

calificarse v. pron. to qualify

callado/a adj. (person) quiet

calle m. street

callejón m. alley
  callejón sin salida dead end, blind alley

calor m. heat

caloría f. calorie

calvo/a adj. bald

calzado m. shoes

calzar v.t. to take size . . . shoes
  Calzo un 38. I take size 38.

calzarse v. pron. to put one's shoes on

calzoncillos m., pl. men's underwear
  calzoncillos largos long underwear

cama f. bed

cámara f. camera
  cámara de video videocamera

camarero/a m. waiter; f. waitress

camarón m. shrimp

camarote m. (ship) cabin

cambiar (de) v.t. to change
  cambiar de casa to move
  cambiar de marcha to shift gears

cambio m. change; exchange rate
  a cambio de in exchange for
  cambio de marchas gearshift
  cambio de moneda currency exchange
  cambio de velocidades gearshift
  en cambio on the other hand

camello m. camel

camerino m. (theater) dressing room

camilla f. stretcher

caminar v.i. to walk

camino m. road, path
  De camino a casa, me perdí. On my way home, I got lost.

camión m. truck

camionero/a m., f. truck driver

camioneta f. pickup truck

camisa f. shirt

camiseta f. T-shirt

campana f. bell

campeón, campeona *m., f.* champion
campeonato *m.* championship
campestre *adj.* rural
campo *m.* countryside; field
  la gente del campo country people
  campo de fútbol soccer field
  campo de golf golf course
cana *f.* gray hair
  echar una cana al aire *idiom.* to let one's hair down
canadiense *adj./m., f.* Canadian
canal *m.* channel (TV)
canario *m.* canary
canción *f.* song
candidato/a *m., f.* candidate
  candidato a la presidencia presidential candidate
canela *f.* cinnamon
cangrejo *m.* crab
canguro *m.* kangaroo
cansado/a (*de + inf.*) *adj.* tired (of + *gerund*)
  Estoy cansado de esperar. I'm tired of waiting.
cansancio *m.* tiredness
cansarse *v. pron.* to tire oneself out
cantante *m., f.* singer
cantar *v.t.* to sing
cantidad *f.* amount
cantimplora *f.* water bottle, canteen
caña *f.* cane
  caña de azúcar sugar cane
  caña de pescar fishing rod
cañería *f.* pipe
capilla *f.* chapel

capital *m.* (*finance*) capital
capital *f.* capital (city)
capítulo *m.* chapter
capó *m.* (*car*) hood
capricho *m.* whim
cápsula *f.* capsule
capturar *v.t.* to capture
cara *f.* face
  cara a cara face to face
¡Caramba! *interj.* Darn! Shoot! Gosh!
caracol *m.* snail
caradura *adj./m., f.* cheeky (person)
  ¡Qué cara más dura tienes! You've got some nerve!
caravana *f.* trailer
carbohidrato *m.* carbohydrate
carbón *m.* coal
carburador *m.* carburator
cárcel *f.* prison, jail
cardiología *f.* cardiology
carencia *f.* lack, (*supplies, food*) shortage
caribeño/a *adj./m., f.* Caribbean (person)
caricia *f.* caress
caries *f.* (*sing. or pl.*) cavity, cavities
cariño *m.* affection
cariñoso/a *adj.* affectionate, loving
carisma *m.* charisma
carne *f.* meat
  carne de res beef
  carne picada/molida ground beef
carnicería *f.* butcher shop
carnicero/a *m., f.* butcher
carnívoro/a *adj.* carnivorous;

m., f. carnivore

caro/a *adj.* expensive

carpeta *f.* folder

carpintería *f.* carpenter's workshop; (*activity*) carpentry

carpintero/a *m., f.* carpenter

carrera *f.* (*profession*) career; (*sports*) race
  a la carrera on the run
  carrera ciclista bicycle race
  carrera contra reloj time trial
  carrera de caballos horse race
  carrera de fondo long-distance race
  carrera de obstáculos steeplechase
  carrera de relevos relay race
  carrera pedestre footrace
  Está en la cima de su carrera. She's at the peak of her career.

carretera *f.* highway

carretilla *f.* wheelbarrow

carril *m.* (*highway*) lane

carro *m.* (*Spain*) cart; (*L.A.*) automobile, car
  carro de bomberos fire engine
  carro de carreras racecar
  carro deportivo sports car

carroza *f.* (*carnival*) float

carta *f.* letter; (*playing*) card

cartel *m.* poster

cartera *f.* wallet

cartero/a *m., f.* mail carrier

casa *f.* house; home
  casa de apartamentos apartment building

  en casa at home

casado/a *adj.* married

casar *v.t.* to marry

casarse (con) *v. pron.* to get married (to)

cascanueces *m., sing.* nutcracker

casco *m.* helmet

casero/a *adj.* (*meal*) homemade, home style

casi *adv.* almost

caso *m.* case
  el caso es que the thing is that
  en caso de in case of

caspa *f.* dandruff

castaña *f.* chestnut

castaño/a *adj.* (*hair, eyes*) brown

castellano *m.* (*language*) Spanish, Castilian

castellano/a *adj./m., f.* Castilian

castigar *v.t.* to punish

castigo *m.* punishment

castillo *m.* castle

casualidad *f.* chance, coincidence
  por (pura) casualidad by (sheer) chance
  ¡Qué casualidad! What a coincidence!

catarata *f.* waterfall

catarro *m.* cold

catástrofe *f.* catastrophe

catastrófico/a *adj.* catastrophic

catedral *f.* cathedral
  como una catedral (*fam.*) huge, enormous

una mentira como una catedral a whopper of a lie

catedrático/a *m., f.* professor; department head

categoría *f.* category

de categoría fine, first-rate, excellent

un restaurante de categoría a first-rate restaurant

un escritor de poca categoría a second-rate writer

católico/a *adj./m., f.* Catholic

catorce fourteen

cava *m.* sparkling wine

caverna *f.* cavern

cavernícola *adj./m., f.* cave dweller; caveman

caza *f.* (*sport*) hunting

cazador(a) *m., f.* hunter

cazar *v.t.* to hunt

cazuela *f.* casserole

cebolla *f.* onion

cebra *f.* zebra

paso cebra (*Spain*) crosswalk

ceder *v.t.* to give in; to give way

ceder el paso to yield (the right of way)

Discutieron hasta que el más sensato cedió. They argued until the most sensible one gave in.

cedro *m.* cedar

ceja *f.* eyebrow

celebrar *v.t.* to celebrate

celos *m., pl.* jealousy

Tiene celos de su hermanita. She is jealous of her little sister.

celoso/a *adj.* jealous

célula *f.* cell

celular *adj.* (*phone*) cellular

celulitis *f.* cellulite

cementerio *m.* cemetery

cemento *m.* cement

cena *f.* dinner

cenar *v.i.* to have dinner

¿Qué hay para cenar? What's for dinner?

cenicero *m.* ashtray

ceniza *f.* ash

censo *m.* census

censura *f.* censorship; censure

censurar *v.t.* to censor; to censure

centro *m.* center; (*city*) downtown

centro comercial shopping mall

centro de gravedad center of gravity

centro de atención center of attention

cepillar *v.t.* to brush

cepillarse *v. pron.* (*hair, teeth*) to brush one's hair/teeth

cepillo *m.* brush

cepillo de dientes toothbrush

cepillo de pelo hairbrush

cera *f.* wax

cerámica *f.* pottery

ceramista *m., f.* ceramist

cerca de *adv.* near

cercano/a *adj.* near; (*relative*) close

Cercano Oriente Near East

cerdo *m.* (*animal*) pig; (*meat*) pork

cereales *m., pl.* cereal; grains
cerebro *m.* brain
cereza *f.* cherry
cerezo *m.* cherry tree
cerilla *f.* match
cero *m.* zero
cerrado *p.p. of* **cerrar** closed;
  cerrado/a *adj.* closed
cerrajero/a *m., f.* locksmith
cerrajería *f.* locksmith's shop
cerrar (e:ie) *v.t.* to close
cerrarse (e:ie) *v. pron.* to close
  **La puerta se cerró
  lentamente.** The door closed
  slowly.
cerrojo *m.* (*lock*) bolt
  correr/echar el cerrojo to
  bolt the door
certeza *f.* certainty
cerveza *f.* beer
césped *m.* grass
cesta *f.* basket
ceviche *m.* marinated fish dish
  ceviche de camarón
  marinated shrimp
chal *m.* shawl
chaleco *m.* vest
champiñón *m.* mushroom
champú *m.* shampoo
chantaje *m.* blackmail
chantajear *v.t.* to blackmail
chantajista *m., f.* blackmailer
chaqueta *f.* jacket
charlatán, charlatana *m., f.*
  chatterbox; *adj.* talkative
chau *fam.* bye
cheque *m.* (bank) check
  cheque de viajero traveler's
  check
  cheque en blanco blank
  check

chequeo (médico) *m.* (*L.A.*)
  physical exam
chévere *adj., fam.* terrific,
  great, cool
chicle *m.* chewing gum
chino *m.* (*language*) Chinese
chino/a *adj./m., f.* Chinese
chismes *m., pl.* gossip
chiste *m.* joke
chistoso/a *adj.* funny, amusing
chocar (con, contra) *v.i.* to
  crash, to collide
chocolate *m.* chocolate
chofer/chófer *m.* chauffeur,
  driver
choque *m.* collision
chuleta *f.* (*food*) chop
  chuleta de cerdo pork chop
cicatriz *f.* scar
cicatrizar *v.i.* to cicatrize, to
  form a scar, to heal
ciclismo *m.* cycling
ciclista *m., f.* cyclist
ciego/a *adj.* blind
  a ciegas *adv.* blindly
cielo *m.* sky; heaven
  ¡Cielos! Good heavens!
cien(to) one hundred
  cientos de miles hundreds
  of thousands
  por ciento per cent
  Es cien por cien(to) algodón.
  It's pure cotton.
ciénaga *f.* swamp
ciencia *f.* science
  ciencia ficción science
  fiction

ciencias exactas exact sciences

científico/a *adj.* scientific; *m., f.* scientist

cierto/a *adj.* certain; true
por cierto by the way

ciervo *m.* deer

cifra *f.* (*arithmetic*) figure, number

cigüeña *f.* stork

cilindro *m.* cylinder

cima *f.* top, summit; peak

cimientos *m., pl.* (*house, building*) foundations

cinco five

cincuenta fifty

cine *m.* movie theater
cine mudo silent movies
cine negro film noir

cineasta *m., f.* filmmaker, director

cinta *f.* (*audio*) tape; ribbon
Siempre lleva una cinta en el pelo. She always wears a ribbon in her hair.

cintura *f.* waist

cinturón *m.* belt
cinturón de seguridad seat belt

ciprés *m.* cypress

circo *m.* circus

circuito *m.* (*electric*) circuit
circuito en serie series circuit
circuito cerrado closed circuit

circulación *f.* circulation; traffic
circulación sanguínea blood circulation

círculo *m.* circle

ciruela *f.* plum

cirugía *f.* surgery

cirujano/a *m., f.* surgeon

cisne *m.* swan

cita *f.* date; appointment

cítrico/a *adj.* citrus

ciudad *f.* city
ciudad natal hometown

ciudadanía *f.* citizenship

ciudadano/a *m., f.* citizen

civilización *f.* civilization

civilizado/a *adj.* civilized

claro/a *adj.* clear; (*color*) light
¡Claro! *interj.* Of course.
¡Claro que sí! (*fam.*) Of course.

clase *f.* class
clase de ejercicios aeróbicos aerobics class
clase alta/baja upper/lower class
clase media middle class
clase trabajadora working class

clásico/a *adj.* classical

clausura *f.* closing
ceremonia de clausura closing ceremony

clavado *m.* (*L.A.*) (high) dive

clavel *m.* carnation

clavícula *f.* clavicle

clavo *m.* nail
dar en el clavo *idiom.* to hit the nail on the head

cliente *m., f.* customer

clientela *f.* clientele, customers

clima *m.* climate

climatizado/a *adj.* (*place,*

climatología *f.* climatology
clínica *f.* clinic
cloaca *f.* sewer
cloro *m.* chlorine
clorofila *f.* chlorophyll
coartada *f.* alibi
cobarde *adj.* coward
cobardía *f.* cowardice
cobertizo *m.* shed
cobija *f.* (*L.A.*) blanket
cobrar *v.t.* (*check*) to cash; (*rent*) to charge for; (*salary*) to earn
   El dueño de mi casa no me cobra la electricidad. My landlord doesn't charge me for electricity.
   Cobro una miseria. I earn a pittance.
cobre *m.* copper
cocer (o:ue) (c:z) *v.t.* to boil, to cook
   cocer a fuego lento to simmer
coche *m.* (*Spain*) car
   coche bomba car bomb
   coche cama sleeper, sleeping car
cocina *f.* kitchen; (*Spain*) stove
cocinar *v.t.* to cook
cocinero/a *m., f.* cook; chef
coco *m.* coconut
codo *m.* elbow
codorniz *f.* quail
cohete *m.* rocket
   cohete espacial space rocket
coincidencia *f.* coincidence
   ¡Qué coincidencia! What a coincidence!
coincidir *v.i.* to coincide, to match up
cojín *m.* cushion
cojo/a *adj.* (*person*) lame
col *f.* (*Spain*) cabbage
cola *f.* line; (*animal*) tail
   cola de caballo pony tail
   hacer cola to line up; to stand in line
colaboración *f.* collaboration
colaborar *v.i.* to collaborate
colador *m.* colander
colar (o:ue) *v.t.* to strain, to drain; **colar café** (*L.A.*) to make coffee
colarse (o:ue) (**en una fiesta**) *v. pron.* to crash (a party)
colchón *m.* mattress
   colchón de agua water bed
   colchón de muelles spring mattress
coleccionar *v.t.* to collect (*as hobby*)
coleccionismo *m.* collecting
coleccionista *m., f.* collector
colesterol *m.* cholesterol
colgar (o:ue) *v.t.* to hang
colibrí *m.* humming bird
cólico *m.* colic
collar *m.* necklace
colmillo *m.* fang; (*in humans*) eye tooth
colmo: ¡Esto es el colmo! *loc.* That's the last straw!
colocación *f.* placing; arrangement
colocar *v.t.* to place, to put; to arrange
colonia *f.* cologne

colonización *f.* colonization, settling

colonizar *v.t.* to colonize

colono *m.* colonist; settler

coloquio *m.* discussion, talk

color *m.* color

columna *f.* column
  columna vertebral spinal column, spine

combustible *m.* fuel

comedia *f.* comedy

comedor *m.* dining room

comenzar (e:ie) *v.t./v.i.* to begin

comer *v.t./v.i.* to eat

comercial *adj.* (*movie*) commercial; (*district, operation*) business-related; *m.* (*L.A.*) commercial, advertisement

comestible *adj.* edible

comestibles *m., pl.* groceries

cometa *f.* kite; *m.* comet

comida *f.* food; meal
  comida basura junk food
  comida rápida fast food

comienzo *m.* beginning
  a comienzos de at the beginning of
  al comienzo at first, in the beginning

comisaría (de policía) *f.* police station

como *prep.* like, as
  Anda despacio como una tortuga. She walks as slowly as a turtle.
  Es tan alto como su padre. He's as tall as his father.
  Quiero un carro como el tuyo. I want a car like yours.

¿cómo? *adv.* how?; what?
  ¿Cómo es...? What's . . . like?
  ¿Cómo está Ud.? *form.* How are you?
  ¿Cómo estás? *fam.* How are you?
  ¿Cómo les fue...? *pl.* How did . . . go for you?
  ¿Cómo se llama (Ud.)? (*form.*) What's your name?
  ¿Cómo te llamas (tú)? (*fam.*) What's your name?

cómoda *f.* chest of drawers

cómodo/a *adj.* comfortable

compañerismo *m.* camaraderie

compañero/a *m., f.* companion; partner; mate
  compañero/a de clase classmate
  compañero/a de cuarto roommate

compañía *f.* company; firm
  El perro me hace compañía. My dog keeps me company.

comparación *f.* comparison
  en comparación con compared to/with

comparar *v.t.* to compare

compartir *v.t.* to share

compás *m.* (*tool*) compass; (*music*) beat, rhythm

competencia *f.* (*L.A.*) competition, contest

competidor(a) *m., f.* competitor

competir (e:i) *v.i.* to compete

competitivo/a *adj.* competitive

complejo/a *adj.* complex

completamente *adv.* completely

complicar *v.t.* to complicate, to

make difficult
cómplice *m., f.* accomplice
comportamiento *m.* behavior
comportarse *v. pron.* to behave oneself
compositor(a) *m., f.* composer
compra *f.* buy, purchase
  ir de compras to go shopping
  la lista de la compra the shopping list
  una buena/mala compra a good/bad buy
comprar *v.t.* to buy
comprender *v.t.* to understand
comprensión *f.* understanding
comprobar *v.t.* **(o:ue)** to check
comprometerse (a) *v. pron.* to promise (to); to get engaged (to)
  Se comprometió a limpiar todas las ventanas. He promised to clean all the windows.
compromiso *m.* commitment; engagement
computación *f.* computer science
computadora *f.* computer
  computadora portátil portable computer; laptop
común *adj.* common, shared
comunicación *f.* communication
comunicar *v.t.* to communicate
comunicarse (con) *v. pron.* to communicate (with)
con *prep.* with
  Con él/ella habla. This is he/she. (*on the telephone*)
  con tal (de) que provided (that)

conciencia *f.* conscience
  a conciencia *adv.* conscientiously
concierto *m.* concert
concordar (con) *v.i.* to agree (with)
concreto *m.* (*L.A.*) concrete
concursar *v.i.* (*contest*) to participate, to take part
concurso *m.* contest; game show
condensar *v.t.* to condense
conducir (c:zc) *v.i.* to drive
conducta *f.* conduct, behavior
conductor(a) *m., f.* chauffeur; driver
conejo *m.* rabbit
conferencia *f.* lecture
confiado/a *adj.* (*person*) trusting
confianza *f.* confidence; trust
  en confianza *adv.* in confidence
  No le tengo mucha confianza. I don't trust him much.
  Es una persona de confianza. She's a trustworthy/reliable person.
confiar (en alguien) *v.t.* to trust (somebody)
  Confía en mí. Trust me.
confirmación *f.* confirmation
confirmar *v.t.* to confirm
  confirmar la reservación to confirm the reservation
confort *m.* comfort
confortable *adj.* comfortable
confundir *v.t.* to confuse

27

confusión *f.* confusion

confuso/a *adj.* (*idea, text*) confused, hazy
Su explicación fue muy confusa. His explanation was very confused.

congelador *m.* freezer

congestionado/a *adj.* (*medicine*) congested; stuffed-up

congreso *m.* conference

conmemoración *f.* commemoration, remembrance
en conmemoración de in memory of

conmemorar *v.t.* to commemorate

conmigo with me

conocer (c:zc) *v.t.* to know; to be acquainted with

conocido/a *adj.* (well-)known; familiar

conquista *f.* conquest

conquistador(a) *m., f.* conqueror

conquistar *v.t.* to conquer

consecuencia *f.* consequence
en consecuencia *adv.* consequently, as a result, therefore; (*to act*) accordingly

conseguir (e:i) *v.t.* to get; to obtain

consejero/a *m., f.* counselor; advisor

consejo *m.* advice
dar consejos to give advice

consenso *m.* consensus

consentimiento *m.* consent, permission

consentir (e:ie) *v.t.* to consent to, to permit

conserje *m., f.* (*hotel*) receptionist

conservación *f.* (*culinary*) preserving; (*environment*) conservation, protection

conservador(a) *adj./m., f.* conservative

conservar *v.t.* (*culinary*) to preserve; to conserve

considerado/a *adj.* (*person*) considerate

constelación *f.* constellation

constitución *f.* constitution

constructor(a) (de obras) *m., f.* builder, building contractor

construir (y) *v.t.* to build

consulado *m.* consulate

consultar *v.t.* (*dictionary, facts*) to look up

consultorio *m.* doctor's office

consumidor(a) *m., f.* consumer

consumir *v.t.* consume

consumo *m.* consumption, intake

contabilidad *f.* accounting

contador(a) *m., f.* accountant

contagiar *v.t.* (*disease*) to pass on

contagio *m.* contagion

contagioso/a *adj.* contagious

contaminación *f.* pollution; contamination
contaminación del aire/del agua air/water pollution

contaminado/a *m., f.* polluted

contaminar *v.t.* to pollute

contar (con) *v.* to count (on)

Contamos contigo. We count on you.

contemplar *v.t.* to contemplate, to gaze at

contemporáneo/a *adj.* contemporary

contentarse (con) *v. pron.* to be pleased (with), to be happy (with)

contento/a *adj.* happy; content

contestadora *f.* answering machine

contestar *v.t.* to answer

contigo with you

Contigo o sin ti. With or without you.

continuar *v.t.* (**yo continúo**) to continue

La novela continúa en el segundo tomo. The novel continues in the second volume.

contra *prep.* against

dos contra uno two against one

Estoy totalmente en contra. I'm totally against it.

Chocó contra un árbol. He crashed into a tree.

contradecir (a alguien) *v.t. irreg.* (**yo contradigo**) to contradict (somebody)

contradecirse *v. pron. irreg.* (**yo me contradigo**) to contradict oneself

contradicción *f.* contradiction

contraponer *v.t. irreg.* (**yo contrapongo**) to contrast

contrario *m.* contrary, opposite; *adj.* opposite

al contrario *adv.* on the contrary, quite the opposite

contrarreloj *adj.* timed

a contrarreloj against the clock

contraseña *f.* password

contrato *m.* contract; lease

contrincante *m., f.* opponent

control *m.* control

control de natalidad birth control

control remoto remote control

controlar *v.t.* to control

convencer (c:z) *v.t.* to convince

convento *m.* convent

conversar *v.i.* to talk

convertirse (e:ie) (en) *v. pron.* to become; to turn into

convertirse en rana to turn into a frog

convertirse en realidad to come true

convicción *f.* conviction

convincente *adj.* convincing

convivencia *f.* coexistence

convivir *v.i.* (*people*) to live together; (*ideas, ideologies*) to coexist

copa *f.* glass; goblet

copa de vino wineglass

copiar *v.t.* to copy

coqueta *f.* flirt, coquette

coquetear *v.i.* to flirt

corazón *m.* heart

corbata *f.* tie

corcho *m.* cork

cordero *m.* lamb

cordillera (montañosa) *f.* (mountain) range

cordón *m.* shoelace

coro *m.* choir, chorus

corpulento/a *adj.* (*person*) hefty

correa *m.* belt

corrección *f.* correction; correctness

correcto/a *adj.* correct

corregir (e:i) (g:j) *v.t.* to correct

correo *m.* post office; mail
  correo electrónico e-mail

correr *v.i.* to run; to jog

correspondencia *f.* mail

corrido *p.p. of* **correr** run

corrida (de toros) *f.* bullfights

corriente *f.* (*electricity*) current
  corriente alterna alternating current, AC
  corriente continua direct current, DC
  corriente eléctrica electric current
  contra corriente aginst the tide
  estar al corriente to be up to date
  ponerse al corriente to catch up
  seguirle la corriente (a alguien) to humor (somebody), to play along with (somebody)

cortacésped *f.* lawnmower

cortar *v.t.* to chop; to slice; to cut; (*lawn*) to mow

corte *f.* cut; (*L.A.*) court (of law)
  corte longitudinal lengthwise section
  Corte Suprema Supreme Court

corte transversal cross section

cortés *adj.* courteous

cortesía *f.* courtesy

cortina *f.* curtain
  correr las cortinas to draw the curtains

corto/a *adj.* short (*in length*)

cortocircuito *m.* short circuit

cosa *f.* thing

cosecha *f.* harvest

cosechar *v.t.* to harvest

coser *v.t.* to sew

costa *f.* coastline, coast

costar (o:ue) *f.* to cost
  costar un ojo de la cara *idiom* to cost an arm and a leg

costero/a *adj.* coastal

costilla *f.* rib

costumbre *f.* habit, custom

cotillear *v.i.* (*Spain*) to gossip

cotilleo *m.* (*Spain*) gossip

cráneo *m.* skull

cráter *m.* crater

creador(a) *m., f.* creator

crear *v.t.* to create

creativo/a *adj.* creative

crecer (c:zc) *v.i.* to grow

creciente *adj.* increasing, growing

crecimiento *m.* growth

crédito *m.* credit

creer (en) *v.t.* to believe (in); to think
  Creo que no. I don't think so.

creído *p.p. of* **creer** believed

crema *f.* cream
  crema antiarrugas anti-wrinkle cream

crema de afeitar shaving cream

crema hidratante moisturizer

cremallera *f.* zipper

cremoso/a *adj.* creamy

crepúsculo *m.* (*evening*) twilight; (*morning*) dawn

criar *v.t.* (*children*) to raise, to bring up

crimen *m.* crime

crisis *f.* crisis

crisis de los cuarenta midlife crisis

crisis nerviosa nervous breakdown

crisis respiratoria respiratory failure

cristal *m.* crystal; glass

cristalería *f.* glassware

cristiano/a *adj./m., f.* Christian

criticar *v.t.* to criticize

crítico/a *m., f.* critic

crítico de arte art critic

cronometrar *v.t.* to time

cronómetro *m.* chronometer; stopwatch

cruce *m.* crossroads

crucero *m.* cruise

crucigrama *m.* crossword

cruda *f.* (*Mexico*) hangover

tener cruda to have a hangover

crudo/a *adj.* (*food*) raw

crujiente *adj.* crunchy; (*bread*) crusty

cruz *f.* cross

Cruz Roja Red Cross

cruzar *v.t.* to cross

cuaderno *m.* notebook

cuadra *f.* city block

cuadrado *m.* square

cuadrilátero *m.* (*boxing*) ring; (*baseball*) home run

cuadro *m.* picture

una falda de cuadros a plaid skirt

¿cuál(es)? *pron.* which one(s)?; what?

¿Cuál te gusta más? Which one do you like best?

¿Cuál es la fecha de hoy? What's today's date?

cuando *conj.* when

Cuando estoy triste, canto. When I'm sad, I sing.

de cuando en cuando *loc.* every so often

de vez en cuando *loc.* now and then

¿cuándo? *adv.* when?

¿Cuándo terminas? When do you finish?

No sé cuándo termina. I don't know when he finishes.

cuanto: cuanto antes as soon as possible

Envíemela cuanto antes. Send it to me as soon as possible.

¿cuánto/a? *adv.* how much?

¿Cuánto cuesta? How much does it cost?

¿Cuánto tiempo hace que esperas? How long have you been waiting?

¿cuántos/as? *adv.* how many?

¿Cuántos años tienes? How old are you?

cuarenta forty

31

cuarto *m.* room
  cuarto de baño bathroom
cuarto/a *adj., m.* fourth
cuatro four
cuatrocientos/as four hundred
cubertería *f.* cutlery
cubierto *p.p. of* **cubrir** covered
cubiertos *m., pl.* silverware
cubrir *v.t.* to cover
cucaracha *f.* cockroach
cuchara *f.* tablespoon
cucharita *f.* teaspoon
cucharón *m.* ladle
cuchillo *m.* knife
cuello *m.* neck
cuenta *f.* bill; account
  a fin de cuentas all things considered, after all
  A fin de cuentas, es mejor esperar que irse. All things considered, it's better to wait than to leave.
  A fin de cuentas, ¿a quién le importa? After all, who cares?
  cuenta corriente checking account
  cuenta de ahorros savings account
  en resumidas cuentas to make a long story short
  por mi cuenta on my own
cuentakilómetros *m., sing.* odometer, speedometer
cuento *m.* story
cuerda *f.* rope
cuero *m.* leather
cuerpo *m.* body
cuestión *f.* issue, matter
  Es un experto en cuestiones de historia medieval. He's an expert in matters of medieval history.
cuestionar *v.t.* to question
cuestionarse *v. pron.* to ask oneself
  Tenemos que cuestionarnos si es válida la conclusión. We have to ask ourselves if the conclusion is valid.
cuidado *m.* care; *interj.* Watch out!
cuidar *v.t.* to take care of
cuidarse *v. pron.* to take care of oneself
culpa *f.* fault
  echar la culpa a alguien to blame someone
  tener la culpa to be to blame
culpable *adj.* guilty; *m., f.* guilty person
culpar *v.t.* to blame
cultivar *v.t.* to grow
cultura *f.* culture
  Tiene mucha cultura. She's a highly educated person.
culturismo *m.* bodybuilding
cumpleaños *m., sing.* birthday
cumplir (años) *v.t.* to have a birthday
  ¿Cuántos años cumples?
cumplir (con) *v.i. (duty)* to carry out
  Cumplí con mi deber. I did my duty.
cuna *f.* cradle
cuñado/a *m.* brother-in-law; *f.* sister-in-law
cura *f.* cure; *m.* priest
curar *v.t.* to cure

curita *f.* adhesive bandage
currículum *m.* (*Spain*) résumé; curriculum vitae
curso *m.* course
curva *f.* curve, bend
  curva peligrosa sharp bend
custodiar *v.t.* to guard
cutis *m.* skin, complexion
  limpieza de cutis skin cleansing

D

dados *m., pl.* (*game*) dice
dama *f.* lady
damas *f., pl.* (*game*) checkers
danza *f.* dance
dañar *v.t.* to damage; to harm
dañarse *v. pron.* to get damaged; (*food*) to go bad
dañino/a *adj.* harmful
daño *m.* damage, harm
dar *v.t. irreg.* (**yo doy**) to give
  dar a luz (a) to give birth (to)
  dar en el clavo *idiom* to hit the nail on the head
  dar lo mismo to not matter
  Me da lo mismo si vienes o no. It doesn't matter to me if you come or not.
  dar un consejo to give advice
dardos *m., pl.* (*game*) darts
darse (con) *v. pron. irreg.* to bump into; to run into
  darse cuenta de (que) to realize, to become aware of
  Gustavo se dio cuenta de que tenía que salir por la puerta de atrás. Gustavo realized he would have to leave by the back door.

darse prisa to hurry up
de *prep.* of; from
  ¿De dónde eres (tú)? *fam.* Where are you from?
  ¿De dónde es (Ud.)? *form.* Where are you from?
  ¿De parte de quién? Who is calling? (*on telephone*)
debajo de *prep.* below; under
debate *m.* debate
debatir *v.t.* to debate
deber (**+ inf.**) *v. aux.* to have to; should; must
  Deberías salir más temprano. You should leave earlier.
deber *m.* responsibility; obligation; duty
  Tu deber es esperar aquí. Your duty is to wait here.
deberes *m., pl.* homework
debido *adj.* appropriate
  a su debido tiempo in due course
  con el debido respeto with all due respect
  debido a (que) *loc.* due to, owing to (the fact that); because of
  No hubo partido debido a la lluvia. There was no match because of the rain.
débil *adj.* weak
década *f.* decade
  la década de los sesenta the sixties
decadencia *f.* decadence; decline
decaer *v. irreg.* (**yo decaigo**) to decay, to decline; to deteriorate

decano/a *m., f.* (*university*) dean

decepcionado/a *adj.* disappointed

decepcionarse *v.t.* to be disappointed

decidido *p.p. of* **decidir** decided

decidido/a *adj.* (*person*) determined

decidir *v.t.* to decide

decidirse *v. pron.* to make up one's mind

¡Decídete de una vez! Come on, make up your mind!

décimo/a *adj.* tenth

decir *m.* a saying

Es sólo un decir. It's just a manner of speaking.

decir *v.t. irreg.* (**yo digo**) to say; to tell

¿Diga? Hello? (*on the telephone*)

No me diga(s). You don't say.

decisión *f.* decision

tomar una decisión to make a decision

declarar *v.t.* to declare; to say

decorado *m.* (*theater*) set

decorar *v.t.* to decorate; (*food*) to garnish

dedicación *f.* dedication

dedicar *v.t.* to dedicate

dedicatoria *f.* dedication

dedo *m.* finger; (*del pie*) toe

defecto *m.* fault, defect

defectuoso/a *adj.* faulty, defective

defender *v.t.* to defend, to protect

defensa *f.* defense

defensa personal self-defense

deficiencia *f.* deficiency, shortcoming

déficit *m.* deficit

definición *f.* definition

definir *v.t.* to define

deforestación *f.* deforestation

defunción *f.* death

dejar *v.t.* to let; to quit; to leave behind

dejar una propina to leave a tip

dejar de (+ *inf.*) *v.i.* to stop (*doing something*)

del (*contraction of* de + el) of the; from the

delantal *m.* apron

delante de *prep.* in front of

deleite *m.* delight

delfín *m.* dolphin

delgado/a *adj.* thin; slender

delicioso/a *adj.* delicious

diligencia *f.* errand

hacer diligencias to do errands

delincuencia *f.* crime, delinquency

delincuente *m., f.* criminal

delineante *m.* draftsman, *f.* draftswoman

delinear *v.t.* to deliniate; to outline

delito *m.* crime, offense

demás (lo/los/las) *pron.* the rest

demasiado *adv.* too much

democracia *f.* democracy

demócrata *m., f.* democrat

democrático/a *adj.* democratic
demostración *f.* proof
demostrar *v.t.* to prove
densidad *f.* density
dentadura *f.* teeth
  dentadura postiza false teeth
  tener buena/mala dentadura to have good/bad teeth
dentista *m., f.* dentist
dentro *adv.* (*space*) inside; (*time*) within
  Llámame dentro de dos horas. Call me within two hours.
denuncia *f.* report
denunciar *v.t.* (*crime*) to report
departamento *m.* department
depender (de) *v.t.* to depend (on)
  Eso no depende de mí. That doesn't depend on me.
dependiente/a *m., f.* clerk
depilarse *v.t.* (*eyebrows*) to pluck; (*legs*) to shave, to wax
deporte *m.* sport
deportista *m., f.* sports person
deportivo/a *adj.* sports-loving, sports-related
depositar *v.t.* to deposit
depósito *m.* tank
  depósito de gasolina gas tank
depredador(a) *adj.* predatory
depredador *m.* predator
depresión *f.* depression
deprimido/a *adj.* depressed
deprimirse *v. pron.* to get depressed
derecha *f.* right
  a la derecha (de) to the right of

derecho/a *adj.* straight
  (todo) derecho straight ahead
  Siga (todo) derecho. Keep on going straight.
derechos *m., pl.* rights
deriva *f.* drift
  a la deriva adrift
dermatólogo/a *m., f.* dermatologist
derramar *v.t.* (*liquid*) to spill
derramarse *v. pron.* (*liquid*) to spill over, to run over
derrame *m.* spillage; (*medical*) hemorrhage
derretir *v.t.* to melt
  El calor derritirá la mantequilla. The heat will melt the butter
derretirse *v. pron.* to melt
  El helado se derritió. The ice cream melted.
derrota *f.* defeat
derrotar *v.t.* to defeat, to beat (*an opponent*)
desactivar *v.t.* to defuse
desafiar *v.t.* to challenge
desafinado/a *adj.* out of tune
desafío *m.* challenge
desafortunadamente *adv.* unfortunately
desagradecido/a *adj.* ungrateful
desagüe *m.* wastepipe, drainpipe
desanimado/a *adj.* downhearted
desaparecer *v.t.* to disappear
desaparecido/a *adj.* missing

desaparición *f.* disappearance
desarreglado/a *adj.* unkempt, messy
desarrollar *v.t.* to develop
desarrollo *m.* development
desastre *m.* disaster
  desastre natural natural disaster
desastroso/a *adj.* disastrous
desatascar *v.t.* to unblock, to clear
desayunar *v.t.* to have breakfast
desayuno *m.* breakfast
descafeinado/a *adj.* decaffeinated
descalificación *f.* (*sports*) disqualification
descalificar *v.* (*sports*) to disqualify
descalzarse *v. pron.* to take off one's shoes
descampado *m.* open ground
  en un descampado in/on open ground
descansar *v.i.* to rest
descapotable *adj./m.* (*automobile*) convertible
descarga *f.* (*electricity*) discharge
  descarga eléctrica electric shock
descarrilamiento *m.* derailment
descarrilar *v.t.* to derail
descender *v.i.* to descend
descendiente *m., f.* descendant
descenso *m.* descend; (*temperatures, prices*) fall, decline, decrease

descifrar *v.t.* to decipher, to decode
descompuesto/a *adj.* (*L.A.*) not working; out of order
desconfiado/a *adj.* distrustful
desconfiar (de alguien) *v.i.* distrust
descontar *v.t.* to discount; to give a discount
descremado/a *adj.* (*dairy products*) skimmed
describir *v.t.* to describe
descubierto *p.p. of* **descubrir** discovered
descubrimiento *m.* discovery
descubrir *v.t.* to discover
descuento *m.* discount
desde *prep.* from; *conj.* since
  Les llamé desde Japón. I called them from Japan.
  ¿Desde cuándo lo sabes? Since when have you known it?
desear *v.t.* to wish, to desire
desechable *adj.* disposable
desechar *v.t.* (*leftovers*) to throw away
desembocadura *f.* (*river*) mouth
desempacar *v.t./intrans.* to unpack
desempleo *m.* unemployment
desengañar *v.t.* to disillusion
desengaño *m.* disappointment
desenvolver (o:ue) *v.t.* to unwrap
deseo *m.* desire, wish
desértico/a *adj.* pertaining to the desert, desert-like

desesperación f. desperation

desesperado/a adj. desperate

desesperanza f. despair

desesperar v.t. to exasperate
La lentitud del tren le desesperó. The slowness of the train exasperated him.

desesperarse v. pron. to despair, to give up hope
No te desesperes; todo saldrá bien. Don't give up hope; everything will be fine.

desfavorable adj. unfavorable

desfile m. parade

desgraciado/a adj. unhappy, unfortunate; m., f. wretch

desgracia f. misfortune

desgraciadamente adv. unfortunately

deshelar (e:ie) v.t. to defrost

deshelarse (e:ie) v. pron. (ice) to melt; (river, lake) to thaw

deshidratar v.t. to dehydrate

deshielo m. thaw

desierto m. desert

desigualdad f. inequality

desinfectante adj./m. disinfectant

desinfectar v.t. to disinfect

desintoxicación f. detoxification

desintoxicar v.t. to detoxify

desmayarse v. pron. to faint

desnatado/a adj. (dairy products) skimmed

desodorante m. deodorant

desordenado/a adj. disorderly

despacio adv. slowly

despedida f. farewell; good-bye

despedirse (e:i) (de) v. pron. to say good-bye (to)

despegar v.i. (airplane, rocket) to take off

despegue m. (airplane, rocket) takeoff

despeinado/a adj. disheveled, unkempt

despejado/a adj. (sky) clear

despensa f. pantry

despertador m. alarm clock

despertarse (e:ie) v. pron. to wake up

despistado/a adj. absent-minded, forgetful; m., f. scatterbrain

desplazamiento m. movement; trip

desplazarse v. pron. to move (from one place to another); to travel

después adv. afterwards; then
después de after

destacar v.t. to emphasize, to stress

destino m. destination, destiny

destornillador m. screwdriver

destrucción f. destrucction

destruir (y) v.t. to destroy

desventaja f. disadvantage

desvestirse (e:i) v. pron. to get undressed, to undress

detalle m. detail

detallista adj./m., f. perfectionist

detención f. arrest

detener v.t. irreg. (yo detengo) (vehicle) to stop; (person) to arrest

detenido *p.p. of* **detener** arrested

detenido/a *adj.* detained; under arrest

estar detenido to be under arrest

detractor(a) *m., f.* detractor; critic

detrás de *adv.* behind

devolución f. (*purchase*) return; (*money*) refund

devolver (o:ue) *v.t.* to take back

día *m.* day

día de fiesta holiday

día laborable work day

diabetes *f.* diabetes

diabético/a *adj./m., f.* diabetic

diagnosticar *v.t.* to diagnose

diagnóstico *m.* diagnostic

diálogo *m.* dialogue

diamante *m.* diamond

diapositiva *f.* slide

diario *m.* diary; newspaper

diario/a *adj.* daily

diarrea *f.* diarrhea

dibujar *v.t.* to draw

dibujo *m.* drawing

dibujos animados *m., pl.* (*animated*) cartoons

diccionario *m.* dictionary

dicho *m.* saying

dicho *p.p. of* **decir** said

diciembre *m.* December

dictador(a) *m., f.* dictator

dictadura *f.* dictatorship

diecinueve nineteen

dieciocho eighteen

dieciséis sixteen

diecisiete seventeen

diente *m.* tooth

dieta *f.* diet

a dieta on a diet

dieta equilibrada balanced diet

diez ten

diferencia *f.* difference

a diferencia de in contrast to, unlike

diferente *adj.* different

difícil *adj.* hard; difficult

dificultad *f.* difficulty, hardship

dificultar *v.t.* to make difficult

difunto/a *m., f.* deceased (person)

diligencia *f.* errand

dimisión *f.* resignation

dimitir *v.i.* to resign

dinamita *f.* dynamite

dinamitar *v.t.* to dynamite

dinastía *f.* dynasty

dinero *m.* money

dinosaurio *m.* dinosaur

Dios *m.* God

¡Dios me libre! *loc.* Heaven forbid!

diplomático/a *adj.* diplomatic, tactful; *m., f.* diplomat

dirección *f.* address

direcciones *f., pl.* directions

directo *adj.* (*fly*) direct, nonstop

en directo *adv.* (*radio, TV*) live

director(a) *m., f.* director; (*orchestra*) conductor

disciplina *f.* discipline; (*university*) subject

disco *m.* (computer) disk

disco compacto compact

disc; CD
discoteca *f.* discoteque
discreto/a *adj.* discreet
discriminación *f.* discrimination
disculpa *f.* apology
pedir disculpas to apologize
disculpar *v.t.* to excuse
disculparse (por) *v. pron.* to apologize for
discurso *m.* speech
discusión *f.* argument
discutir *v.t.* to argue
diseñador(a) *m., f.* designer
diseño *m.* design
disfraz *m.* costume
disfrutar (de) *v.t.* to enjoy; to reap the benefits (of)
disfunción *f.* dysfunction
disgusto: a disgusto *adv.* against one's will
Fui, pero a disgusto. I went, but against my will.
disimular *v.t.* to hide; to conceal; to pretend
disminución *f.* decrease
disminuir (y) *v.i.* (*number*) to decrease; *v.t.* (*price, speed*) to reduce
Ha disminuido el número de parados. The number of unemployed people has drecreased.
Debes disminuir la velocidad. You have to reduce your speed.
disparar *v.t./v.i.* to shoot, to fire
disparo *m.* shot, gunshot
disponibilidad *f.* availability
disponible *adj.* available

distancia *f.* distance
distinguido/a *adj.* distinguished
distinguir *v.t.* (**yo distingo**) to distinguish
distribución *f.* distribution
distribuir (y) *v.t.* to distribute
divergencia *f.* difference
divergente *adj.* (*opinions*) differing
divergir (e:i) (g:j) *v.i.* to differ
diversión *f.* fun activity
divertido/a *adj.* fun
divertir (e:ie) *v.t.* to entertain
Pepe nos divirtió con sus historias. Pepe entertained us with his stories.
divertirse (e:ie) *v. pron.* to have fun
divisar *v.t.* to sight
divorciado/a *adj.* divorced
divorciarse (de) *v. pron.* to get divorced (from)
divorcio *m.* divorce
divulgación *f.* spreading
divulgar *v.t.* (*news, information*) to spread
El chismoso divulgó la noticia por toda la universidad. The gossip spread the news around the whole university.
doblar *v.t.* (*paper, clothes*) to fold; (*corner*) to turn; (*movie*) to dub
doble *adj.* double
doce twelve
docena *f.* dozen
doctor(a) *m., f.* doctor
doctorado *m.* doctorate; Ph.D.

documental *m.* documentary

documentar *v.t.* to document; to provide evidence for
Estos artículos no documentan nada. These do not provide any evidence.

documentarse *v. pron.* to do research
Tuve que documentarme muy bien para escribir la tesis. I had to do a lot of research to write the thesis.

documento *m.* document
documentos de viaje travel documents

dólar *f.* dollar

doler (o:ue) *v.i.* to hurt
Me duele mucho. It hurts a lot.

dolor *m.* ache; pain
dolor de cabeza headache

doméstico/a *adj.* domestic

dominar *v.t.* to dominate; to master
Aún no domino muy bien el español. I haven't quite mastered Spanish yet.

dominarse *v. pron.* to restrain, to control oneself

domingo *m.* Sunday

dominó *m.* (*game*) dominoes; (*game piece*) domino

don/doña *title of respect used with a person's first name*

donante *m., f.* donor

donde *conj.* where
Están donde las dejaste. They are where you left them.
¿dónde? *adv.* where

¿Dónde están las llaves? Where are the keys?

donjuán *m.* womanizer

dorado/a *adj.* gold, golden

dormir (o:ue) *v.i.* to sleep

dormirse (o:ue) *v. pron.* to go to sleep; to fall asleep; to oversleep
Llego un poco tarde; me dormí. I'm a bit late; I overslept.

dos two

doscientos/as two hundred

drama *m.* drama; play

dramático/a *adj.* dramatic

dramaturgo/a *m., f.* playwright

droga *f.* drug

drogadicto/a *adj.* drug-addicted; *m., f.* drug addict

ducha *f.* shower

ducharse *v. pron.* to shower; to take a shower

duda *f.* doubt
poner en duda to question, to doubt
Nadie pone en duda su talento. Nobody questions his talent.
sin duda undoubtedly, without a doubt

dudar *v.t.* to doubt

dueño/a *m., f.* owner; landlord

dulce *adj.* sweet

dulces *m., pl.* sweets; candy

duna *f.* dune

duradero/a *adj.* lasting

durante *prep.* during

durar *v.i.* to last
¿Cuánto dura la película? How long is the movie?

El dinero no duró mucho.
The money didn't last long.
¿Dura más la piel? Does
leather last longer?
durazno m. (L.A.) peach
duro/a adj. hard

E

e conj. (used instead of **y**
before words beginning with
i and **hi**) and
Javier e Inés Javier and Inés
masaje e hidratación
massage and moisturizing
ebrio/a adj. inebriated, drunk
echar v.t. to throw
echar chispas idiom to be
hopping mad
echar la casa por la ventana
loc. to go overboard, to pull
out all the stops
echar una carta al buzón to
put a letter in the mailbox
echarle flores a alguien
idiom to flatter someone
eclipse m. eclipse
ecología f. ecology
ecológico/a adj. ecological;
(food) organic
ecologista m., f.
environmentalist, ecologist
economía f. economics
ecosistema m. ecosystem
ecoturismo m. ecotourism
ecuador m. equator
¿Cruzar el ecuador? To cross
the equator?
ecuatoriano/a adj. Ecuadorian
edad f. age
edad de piedra Stone Age

edad media Middle Ages
No nos dijo su edad. He
didn't tell us his age.
edificio m. building
educado/a adj. polite, well-
mannered
efectivo m. (money) cash
en efectivo in cash
efecto m. effect
bajo los efectos del alcohol
under the influence of
alcohol
efectos especiales special
effects
efecto invernadero
greenhouse effect
efecto secundario side
effect
en efecto in fact
eficacia f. effectiveness
eficaz adj. effective
eficiencia f. efficiency
eficiente adj. efficient
egoísmo m. selfishness
egoísta adj. selfish
ejemplo m. example
ejercicio m. exercise
ejercicios aeróbicos aerobic
exercises
ejercicios de estiramiento
stretching exercises
ejercicios de portugués
Portuguese exercises
hacer ejercicio to exercise,
to work out
ejército m. army
el art. m., sing. the
él pron. m. sing. he; him
elástico/a adj. elastic
elección f. election

electorado *m.* electorate
electricista *m., f.* electrician
electrocutarse *v. pron.* to be electrocuted
electrólisis *f.* electrolysis
electrónica *f.* electronics
elefante *m.* elephant
elegante *adj.* elegant
elegir (e:i) (g:j) *v.t.* to elect
elemental *adj.* (*course, level*) elementary
  Elemental, amigo Watson. Elementary, my dear Watson.
elevado/a *adj.* (*quantity*) large; (*price*) high
  un elevado número de personas a large number of people
  un precio elevado a high price
eliminación *f.* elimination
eliminar *v.t.* to eliminate
ella *pron. fem. sing.* she; her
ellos/as *pron. m., f. pl.* them
  Dáselo a ellos. Give it to them.
elocuencia *f.* eloquence
elocuente *adj.* eloquent
elogiar *v.t.* to praise
elogio *m.* praise
embajada *f.* embassy
embalse *m.* reservoir
embarazada *adj.* pregnant
embarcadero *m.* jetty, wharf
embarcar *v.i.* (*passengers*) to board (*a ship*)
embargo: sin embargo however; yet
embotellamiento (de tráfico) *m.* (*Spain*) traffic jam

embrague *m.* clutch (pedal)
embriagado/a *adj.* inebriated, drunk
embudo *m.* funnel
emergencia *f.* emergency
emigración *f.* emigration
emigrante *m., f.* emigrant
emigrar *v.i.* emigrate
emitir *v.t.* to broadcast
emocionante *adj.* exciting
empacar *v.t.* to pack
empacharse *v. pron.* to get an upset stomach
empatar *v.i.* (*sports*) to tie
empate *m.* (*sports*) tie
empeorar *v.t.* to get worse; to make worse
  Esto empeora la situación. This makes the situation worse.
empezar (e:ie) *v.t.* to begin
  para empezar to begin
empleado/a *m., f.* employee
empleo *m.* job, employment
empobrecer (c:zc) *v.t.* to impoverish, to make poor
  Las guerras empobrecen los países. Wars impoverish countries.
empobrecerse (c:zc) *v. pron.* to become impoverished, poor
empresa *f.* company; firm
empresario/a *m., f.* entrepreneur
empujar *v.t.* to push
en *prep.* in; on
  en caso (de) que in case (that)
  ¡En marcha! Forward ho!
  ¿En qué puedo servirles?

How may I help you?

en resumidas cuentas *loc.* to make a long story short, in short

en un dos por tres *idiom* in a jiffy

enamorado/a *adj.* in love; beloved

enamorarse (de) *v. pron.* to fall in love (with)

encantado/a *adj.* delighted; pleased to meet you

encantador(a) *adj.* charming

encantar *v.t.* to like very much; (*inanimate things*) to love

encanto *m.* charm

encarcelar *v.t.* to imprison, to jail

encargar *v.t.* to order

encargo *m.* order

encendedor *m.* lighter

encender *v.t.* to light, to turn on

encerar *v.t.* to polish, to wax

encía *f.* (*dental*) gum

encima de *adv.* on top of

por encima *adv.* (*read*) superficially

encontrar (o:ue) *v.t.* to find

encontrar(se) (o:ue) *v. pron.* to meet (each other); to find (each other)

encuesta *f.* poll; survey

energía *f.* energy

enero *m.* January

énfasis *m.* emphasis

enfatizar *v.t.* to emphasize

enfermarse *v. pron.* to get sick

enfermedad *f.* illness

enfermero/a *m., f.* nurse

enfermo/a *adj.* sick

enfocar *v.t.* (*a topic*) to focus on, to look at

El programa enfoca el problema de la falta de vivienda. The program looks at the problem of homelessness.

enfoque *m.* approach

enfrentamiento *m.* clash

enfrentar *v.t.* to confront, to face

Hay que enfrentar la realidad. It's necessary to face reality.

enfrentarse (con) *v. pron.* to confront

El ejército se enfrentará con el enemigo. The army will confront the enemy.

enfrente de *adv.* opposite; facing

El ayuntamiento está enfrente de la catedral. The town hall is opposite the cathedral.

enfriar *v.t.* to chill

engañar *v.t.* to decieve, to cheat on

engaño *m.* deception

engordar *v.i.* to gain weight

que no engorda *adj.* non-fattening

engreído/a *adj.* conceited

enigma *m.* enigma, mystery

enigmático/a *adj.* enigmatic, mysterious

enloquecer (c:zc) *v.i.* to go crazy

ennegrecer (c:zc) *v.t.* to blacken

ennegrecerse (c:zc) *v. pron.* to go black, (*sky, clouds*) to darken

enojado/a *adj.* mad; angry

enojar *v.t.* to annoy, to make angry

enojarse (con) *v. pron.* to get angry (with)

enredadera *f.* climbing plant

enriquecer (c:zc) *v.t.* to enrich, to make rich
La lectura enriquece la imaginación. Reading enriches imagination.

enriquecerse (c:zc) *v. pron.* to get rich

ensalada *f.* salad

ensaladera *f.* salad bowl

ensayar *v.t.* to rehearse

ensayo *m.* essay; rehearsal

enseguida *adv.* right away

enseñanza *f.* learning

enseñar *v.t.* to teach

ensuciar *v.t.* to dirty; to get dirty

entender (e:ie) *v.t.* to understand

entierro *m.* burial

entonces *adv.* then

entrada *f.* entrance; (*Spain*) ticket

entrar (en) *v.i.* to enter, to come in

entre *prep.* between; among
entre tú y yo between you and me
entre la multitud among the crowd

entregar *v.t.* to turn in, to deliver

entremeses *m., pl.* hors d'oeuvres; appetizers

entrenador(a) *m., f.* coach

entrenamiento *m.* coaching; training
El boxeo requiere mucho entrenamiento. Boxing requires a lot of training.
El entrenamiento duró seis horas. The training lasted six hours.

entrenarse *v. pron.* to practice; to train

entretener *v.t. irreg.* (yo entretengo) to entertain

entretenerse *v. pron. irreg.* (yo me entretengo) to amuse oneself; to hang about
No te entretengas camino a la escuela. Don't mess around on the way to school.

entretenido/a *adj.* entertaining

entrevista *f.* interview

entrevistador(a) *m., f.* interviewer

entrevistar *v.t.* to interview

entusiasmado/a *adj.* enthusiastic

entusiasmo *m.* enthusiasm

envase *m.* container

envejecer (c:zc) *v.i.* to age, to grow old

envejecimiento *m.* aging

enviar *v.t.* to send; to mail
Te enviaré los libros por correo. I'll mail you the books.

envidioso/a *adj.* envious, jealous

envolver (o:ue) *v.t.* to wrap

papel de envolver wrapping paper

enyesar *v.t.* (*medicine*) to put in a cast

El médico me enyesó el brazo. The doctor put my arm in a cast.

Tengo el brazo enyesado. My arm is in a cast.

equilibrado/a *adj.* balanced

equipado/a *adj.* equipped

equipaje *m.* luggage

equipo *m.* team

equipo local home team

equipo visitante visiting team

equipo de técnicos team of technicians

equitación *f.* (horse) riding

equivalencia *f.* equivalence

equivaler *v.i.* to be equivalent to

equivocación *f.* mistake

equivocado/a *adj.* mistaken; wrong

equivocarse *v. pron.* to make a mistake, to be mistaken

¿Me equivoco al pensar que mientes? Am I mistaken in thinking you're lying?

Nos equivocamos de camino. We went the wrong way.

ermita *f.* chapel

ermitaño/a *m., f.* hermit

eructar *v.i.* to belch, to burp

eructo *m.* belch, burp

erupción *f.* eruption

hacer erupción (*volcano*) to erupt

escalada *f.* (*mountaineering*) climb, ascent

escalador(a) *m., f.* (*mountaineering*) climber

escalar *v.t.* to climb

escalar montañas to climb mountains

escalera *f.* stairs; stairway

escalera de incendios fire escape

escalera mecánica escalator

escalofrío *m.* shiver

tener escalofríos to be shivering; to have the chills

escalón *m.* step, stair

escandaloso/a *adj.* loud; outrageous

escapada *f.* getaway

escaparate *m.* (*Spain*) shop window

escarcha *f.* frost

escayola *f.* (*Spain*) plaster cast

escayolar *v.* (*Spain*) *trans.* to put in a cast

escenario *m.* stage

escoba *f.* broom

escoger (g:j) *v.t.* choose

esconder *v.t.* to hide

escorpión *m.* scorpion

escribir *v.t./v.i.* to write

escribir a máquina to type

escribir un mensaje electrónico to write an e-mail message

escribir una (tarjeta) postal to write a postcard

escribir una carta to write a letter

escrito *p.p. of* **escribir** written

por escrito *adv.* in writing
escritor(a) *m., f.* writer
escritorio *m.* desk
escuchar *v.t.* to listen to
  escuchar la radio to listen to
  the radio
  escuchar música to listen to
  music
escuela *f.* school
esculpir *v.t.* to sculpt
escultor(a) *m., f.* sculptor
escultura *f.* sculpture
escurrir *v.t.* (*dishes*) to drain;
  (*clothes*) to wring out
ese, esa, esos, esas *dem. adj.*
  that (by you); those (by you)
ése, ésa, ésos, ésas *dem.* that
  (one by you); those (by you)
esfera *f.* sphere
esforzarse (o:ue) *v. pron.* to try
  hard
  Debes esforzarte más. You
  must try harder.
esfuerzo *m.* effort
esgrima *f.* (*sport*) fencing
esgrimidor(a) *m., f.* fencer
esmeralda *f.* emerald
esnob *adj.* snobbish; *m., f.* snob
esnobismo *m.* snobbery
esnórkel *m.* snorkel
eso *dem. pron. neuter.* that (by
  you)
esófago *m.* esophagus
espacio *m.* space
espalda *f.* back
  **No me importa que hablen a
  mis espaldas.** I don't mind
  them talking behind my back.
España *f.* Spain
español *m.* (*language*) Spanish

español(a) *adj./m., f.* Spanish
espárrago *m.* asparagus
espátula *f.* spatula
especialista *m., f.* specialist
especialización *f.* major field
  of study or interest;
  specialization
especializarse *v. pron.* to
  specialize
especie *f.* (*biology*) species;
  type
  **especie en peligro de
  extinción** endangered
  species
  especie protegida protected
  species
espectacular *adj.* spectacular
espectáculo *m.* show
espectador(a) *m., f.* spectator
espejo *m.* mirror
esperanza *f.* hope
  esperanza de vida life
  expectancy
esperar *v.t.* to wait for; to hope;
  to wish
espina *f.* (*fish*) bone; (*plant*)
  thorn
espinaca *f.* spinach
espolvorear *v.t.* (*sugar*) to
  sprinkle
esponja *f.* sponge
esponjoso/a *adj.* (*pastry*)
  spongy, soft; (*fabric*) fluffy
espontáneo/a *adj.*
  spontaneous
esposo/a *m., f.* husband/wife;
  spouse
espuma *f.* foam
esqueleto *m.* skeleton
esquema *m.* outline

esquí (acuático) *m.* (water) skiing

esquiador(a) *m., f.* skier

esquiar *v.i.* to ski

esquina *f.* (*outside*) corner

establecer (c:zc) *v.t.* to establish

establecer una marca mundial to set a world record

establo *m.* stable

estación *f.* station; season

estación de autobuses bus station

estación del metro subway station

estacionamiento *m.* parking; parking space; parking lot

estacionar *v.t.* to park

estacionarse *v. pron.* to park

estadio *m.* stadium

estado *m.* state

estado civil marital status

Estados Unidos *m. pl.* (EE.UU.; E.U.) United States

estadounidense *adj./m., f.* from the United States

estafador(a) *m., f.* fraudster, con artist

estafar *v.t.* to defraud

estampado/a *adj.* printed, patterned

estampilla *f.* stamp

estancia *f.* stay

Nuestra estancia en La Coruña fue magnífica. Our stay in La Coruña was magnificent.

estanque *m.* pond (*man-made*)

estante *m.* bookcase; bookshelf

estar *v.i.* to be

(no) está nada mal it's not at all bad

estar a (veinte kilómetros) de aquí to be (twenty kilometers) from here

estar a dieta to be on a diet

estar a régimen to be on a diet

estar aburrido/a to be bored

estar afectado/a por to be affected by

estar bajo control to be under control

estar cansado/a to be tired

estar contaminado/a to be polluted

estar de acuerdo (con) to be in agreement with

estar de acuerdo to agree

no estar de acuerdo to disagree

estar de moda to be in fashion

estar de vacaciones *f., pl.* to be on vacation

estar de vuelta to be back

estar en buena forma to be in good shape

estar en las nubes to be daydreaming

estar enfermo/a to be sick

estar perdido/a to be lost

estar roto/a to be broken

estar seguro/a to be sure

estar torcido/a to be twisted; to be sprained

estatua *f.* statue

este *m.* east

al este to the east

este, esta, estos, estas *dem. adj.* this; these

éste, ésta, éstos, éstas *dem. pron.* this (one); these

Éste es don Pedro. This is don Pedro.

estéreo *m.* stereo

estéril *adj.* sterile

esterilizar *v.t.* to sterilize

esteticista *m., f.* beautician

estetoscopio *m.* stethoscope

estiércol *m.* manure

estilo *m.* style; (*swimming*) stroke, style

 algo por el estilo something like that

 estilo braza (*Spain*) breaststroke

 estilo espalda backstroke

 estilo libre freestyle

 estilo mariposa butterfly

 estilo pecho (*L.A.*) breaststroke

estiramiento *m.* stretching

estirar *v.t.* to stretch

esto *dem. pron. neuter* this; this thing

estómago *m.* stomach

estornudar *v.i.* to sneeze

estos *dem. adj. m., pl.* these

éstos *dem. pron. m., pl.* these

estrecho/a *adj.* narrow, tight

estrella *f.* star

 estrella *m., f.* **de cine** movie star

 estrella fugaz shooting star

estrellado/a *adj.* starry

estrenar *v.t.* to wear for the first time; to début

estreno *m.* (*film, play*) premiere

estreñido/a *adj.* constipated

estreñimiento *m.* constipation

estrés *m.* stress

estresado/a adj. under stress

estresante *adj.* (*situation*) stressful

estropear *v.t.* to damage

estropearse *v. pron.* (*automobile*) to break down

estudiante *m., f.* student

estudiantil *adj.* student

estudiar *v.t.* to study

estudioso/a *adj.* studious

estufa *f.* (*L.A.*) stove

estupendo/a *adj.* stupendous

etapa *f.* stage; step

ética *f.* ethics

ético/a *adj.* ethical

euforia *f.* euphoria, elation

eufórico/a *adj.* euphoric

Europa *f.* Europe

europeo/a *adj.* European

evadir *v.t.* (*danger, problem*) to avoid; (*taxes*) to evade

evadirse *v. pron.* (*responsibility, prison*) to escape

 Luis se evadió de la responsabilidad. Luis escaped responsibility.

evaluación *f.* assessment; test

evaluar *v.t.* to assess; to test

evasión *f.* escape

evitar *v.t.* to avoid

evolución *f.* evolution

evolucionar *v.i.* to evolve

exageración *f.* exaggeration

exagerar *v.t.* to exaggerate

 No exageres el valor de las cosas. Do not exaggerate the value of things.

examen *m.* test; examination

excavadora *f.* power shovel, excavator

excavar *v.t.* to dig, to excavate

excelente *adj.* excellent

exceso *m.* excess; too much
  en exceso in excess, too much

excursión *f.* hike; tour; excursion
  Vamos de excursión. We're going hiking.

excursionista *m., f.* hiker

exigir (g:j) *v.t.* to demand

éxito *m.* success
  tener éxito to succeed

éxodo *m.* exodus

experiencia *f.* experience

experimentar *v.t.* to experiment; to try out

expiración *f.* expiration

expirar *v.t.* (*time period, contract*) to expire

explicar *v.t.* to explain

explorar *v.t.* to explore
  explorar un pueblo to explore a town
  explorar una ciudad to explore a city

explosivo/a *adj.* explosive

exponer *v.t. irreg.* **(yo expongo)** (*art*) to exhibit

exportación *f.* exportation

exportar *v.t.* to export

exposición *f.* exhibition

expresión *f.* expression

expresivo/a *adj.* expressive

exprimidor *m.* juicer

expulsar *v.t.* to expel

expulsión *m.* expulsion

extinción *f.* extinction

extinguir *v.t.* **(yo extingo)** (*fire*) to extinguish, to put out
  Los bomberos extinguieron el incendio. The firefighters put out the blaze.

extinguirse *v. pron.* **(yo me extingo)** to become extinct; to die out
  Su entusiasmo se está extinguiendo poco a poco. Her enthusiasm is dying little by little.

extranjero/a *adj.* foreign; *m., f.* foreigner
  en el extranjero abroad

extrañar (algo o a alguien) *v.t.* to miss

extrañarse (de) *v. pron.* to be surprised, to find strange
  Me extraña que no te hayas quejado. I'm surprised that you haven't complained.

extraño/a *adj.* strange, odd
  Es extraño que (+ *subj.*) It's strange that…
  Es extraño que tosas tanto. It's strange that you cough so much.

extravagante *adj.* flamboyant

extremidades *f., pl.* (*anatomy*) extremities

F

fábrica *f.* factory

fabricación *f.* manufacture
  fabricación en serie mass production

fabricante *m., f.* manufacturer

fabricar *v.t.* to manufacture, to produce
  fabricar en serie to mass produce
fabuloso/a *adj.* fabulous
fachada *f.* facade
fácil *adj.* easy
facilitar *v.t.* to facilitate, to make easier
faisán *m.* pheasant
falda *f.* skirt
fallecer (c:zc) *v.i.* to pass away
fallecido/a *m., f.* deceased
fallecimiento *m.* death
falta *f.* lack; (*spelling*) mistake
  falta de recursos lack of resources
  falta de ortografía spelling mistake
faltar *v.t.* to lack; to need
familia *f.* family
familiar *adj.* family; (*known*) familiar
  Este lugar me resulta familiar. This place looks familiar.
famoso/a *adj.* famous; *m., f.* famous person, celebrity
fango *m.* mud
faringe *f.* pharynx
farmacia *f.* pharmacy
  farmacia de guardia 24-hour pharmacy
faro *m.* (*automobile*) headlight
fascinar *v.t.* to fascinate
fatigado/a *adj.* weary
fatigarse *v. pron.* to wear oneself out
favorable *adj.* favorable
favorito/a *adj.* favorite

fax *m.* fax (machine)
fe *f.* faith
febrero *m.* February
fecha *f.* date
  fecha de caducidad expiration date
fecundación *f.* fertilization
fecundar *v.t.* to fertilize
felicidad *f.* happiness
  ¡Felicidades! Congratulations! (*for an event such as a birthday or anniversary*)
felicitar *v.t.* to congratulate
  ¡Felicitaciones! Congratulations! (*for an event such as an engagement or a good grade on a test*)
feliz *adj.* happy
  ¡Feliz cumpleaños! Happy birthday!
fenomenal *adj.* fantastic, great
fenómeno *m.* phenomenon
feo/a *adj.* ugly
ferrocarril *m.* railroad
fértil *adj.* fertile
fertilidad *f.* fertility
fertilizante *m.* fertilizer
festejar *v.t.* to celebrate
festejo *m.* celebration
festival *m.* festival
fiambre *m.* cold cut
fiambrera *f.* (*Spain*) lunch box
fianza *f.* bail
ficha *f.* (*game*) counter, game piece
fidelidad *f.* fidelity; faithfulness
fiebre *f.* fever
fiel *adj.* faithful; loyal

fiesta *f.* party
  dar una fiesta to throw a party
fijo/a *adj.* set; fixed; permanent
  precio fijo fixed price
  trabajo fijo permanent job
fila *f.* row
filatelia *f.* philately, stamp collecting
filmoteca *f.* film library
filología *f.* philology
filólogo/a *m., f.* philologist
filosofar *v.i.* to philosophize
filosofía *f.* philosophy
filósofo/a *m., f.* philosopher
fin *m.* end
  fin de semana weekend
  a fin de *conj.* in order to
  a fines de at the end of
  al fin *loc.* at last
  al fin y al cabo *loc.* after all
  por fin *adv.* at last
final *m.* end
  al final at the end
  a finales de at/toward the end of
finalmente *adv.* finally
financiar *v.t.* to finance
fingir (g:j) *v.t.* to pretend
  Fingía no saberlo. She pretended not to know it.
firma *f.* signature
firmar *v.t.* to sign (*a document*)
física *f.* physics
físico/a *m., f.* physicist
flaco/a *adj.* skinny
flamenco/a *adj., m.* (*music*) flamenco
flan *m.* baked custard
flecha *f.* arrow

flexible *adj.* flexible
flexionar *v.t.* to flex
flor *f.* flower
florería *f.* (*L.A.*) flower shop
florero *m.* vase
florero/a *m., f.* (*L.A.*) florist
florista *m., f.* (*Spain*) florist
floristería *f.* (*Spain*) flower shop
flotar *v.i.* to float
fluir (y) *v.i.* to flow
foca *f.* seal
folklórico/a *adj.* folk; folkloric
folleto *m.* brochure
fondo *m.* (*street, corridor*) end; (*sea*) bottom
  a fondo *adv.* completely
  al fondo *adv.* at the end
fondos *m., pl.* (*money*) funds
fonética *f.* phonetics
fonología *f.* phonology
fontanería *f.* (*Spain*) *f.* plumbing
fontanero/a *m., f.* (*Spain*) plumber
forense *m., f.* forensic scientist
forma *f.* shape
  estar en buena/mala forma to be in good/bad shape
formación *f.* training
  formación profesional vocational training
formar *v.t.* to train
formulario *m.* form
  (re)llenar el formulario fill out the form
fortaleza *f.* fortress
fortuna *f.* fortune
  por fortuna *adv.* fortunately
fósforo *m.* match

fósil *m.* fossil

fosilizarse *v. pron.* to fossilize, to become fossilized

fotografía *f.* photograph

fotocopiadora *f.* photocopier

fotocopiar *v.t.* to photocopy

fotosíntesis *f.* photosynthesis

fracasado/a *adj.* failed, unsuccessful

fracasar *v.i.* to fail

fracaso *m.* failure

frambuesa *f.* raspberry

francés *m.* (*language*) French

francés, francesa *adj./m., f.* French

Francia *f.* France

frase *f.* phrase; sentence

frazada *f.* (*L.A.*) blanket

frecuencia *f.* frequency
con (mucha) frecuencia frequently, regularly

frecuentemente *adv.* frequently

fregadero (de la cocina) *m.* (kitchen) sink

fregar *v.* (*Spain*) *trans.* to mop

fregona *f.* (*Spain*) mop

frenar *v.i.* to brake

freno *m.* brake
freno de mano handbrake

frente *f.* (*anatomy*) forehead

fresa *f.* strawberry

fresco/a *adj.* cool

frijol *m.* bean

frío/a *adj.* cold; chilled
Sírvase frío. Serve chilled.

fritada *f.* fried dish (*pork, fish, etc.*)

frito/a *adj.* fried

frontera *f.* border, frontier

fronterizo/a *adj.* border

fruta *f.* fruit

frutería *f.* fruit store

frutilla *f.* (*L.A.*) strawberry

fucsia *adj.* fuchsia

fuego *m.* fire
fuegos artificiales *m., pl.* fireworks

fuente *f.* platter, serving dish; fountain
fuente de fritada platter of fried food

fuera *adv.* outside

fuerte *adj.* strong

fuga *f.* (*prison*) escape; (*gas, water*) leak

fugarse *v. pron.* to escape, to flee, to run away

fugitivo/a *m., f.* fugitive

fumar *v.t.* to smoke
Prohibido fumar. No smoking.

función *f.* show, function

funcionar *v.i.* to work; to function
Funciona a la perfección. It works perfectly.

funeral *m.* funeral

furioso/a *adj.* furious

fusible *m.* (*electricity*) fuse

fútbol *m.* soccer
fútbol americano football

futbolista *m., f.* soccer player; football player

futuro/a *adj./m.* future
en el futuro cercano in the near future
futura mamá mother-to-be
un trabajo sin futuro a job with no prospects

G

gacela f. gazelle

gafas (oscuras) f. pl. (sun)glasses

galardón m. award, prize

galardonado/a m., f. award-winner

galardonar v.t. to award

galaxia f. galaxy

galería f. gallery

galleta f. cookie

gallo m. rooster

gana f. desire
  de buena/mala gana adv. willingly/unwillingly

ganadería f. ranching, cattle raising

ganadero/a m., f. rancher, cattle farmer

ganar v.t. to win; (money) to earn
  ganarse la vida idiom to make a living, to earn one's living **Mario se gana la vida escribiendo guiones de telenovela.** Mario makes his living writing soap opera scripts.

ganga f. bargain

garaje m. garage

garantía f. guarantee, warranty

garantizar v.t. to guarantee

garbanzo m. chickpea

gardenia f. gardenia

garganta f. throat

gas m. gas
  gas lacrimógeno tear gas

gasolina f. gasoline

gasolinera f. gas station

gastar v.t. (money) to spend

gasto m. expense

gastronomía f. gastronomy

gatillo m. (firearm) trigger
  apretar el gatillo to pull the trigger

gato/a m., f. cat

géiser m. geyser

gelatina f. gelatine

generoso/a adj. generous

genética f. genetics

genético/a adj. genetic

gente f. people
  buena gente idiom nice person, nice guy, nice gal

geografía f. geography

geólogo/a m., f. geologist

geometría f. geometry

geométrico/a adj. geometric(al)

geranio m. geranium

gerente m., f. manager

gimnasia f. gymnastics
  gimnasia rítmica rhythmic gymnastics

gimnasio m. gymnasium

gimnasta m., f. gymnast

ginecólogo/a m., f. gynecologist

girar v.t./intrans. to turn
  Gire a la izquierda en la próxima esquina. Turn left at the next corner.
  No gires la cabeza. Don't turn your head.

girasol m. sunflower

giro m. turn
  giro bancario bank draft
  giro postal money order

globo m. balloon

glotón, glotona adj. gluttonous; greedy

gobernar (e:ie) *v.t.* to govern, to rule

gobierno *m.* government

golf *m.* golf

golfista *m., f.* golfer

golpe *m.* blow; coup
Dio unos golpes en la mesa. He pounded on the table several times.
de golpe *adv.* suddenly
Ocurrió de golpe. It happened suddenly.

goma *f.* (*pencil*) eraser
de goma (made of) rubber

gordo/a *adj.* fat

gorra *f.* cap (*with a visor*)
gorra de béisbol baseball cap

gorrión *m.* sparrow

gorro *m.* cap (*without a visor*)
gorro de lana wool cap, ski cap

gota *f.* drop

gótico/a *adj.* Gothic

gozar (de) *v.t.* to enjoy
Mi padre goza de una salud de hierro. My father has a strong constitution.

grabadora *f.* tape recorder

gracias *f., pl.* thank you; thanks
Gracias por todo. Thanks for everything.
Gracias una vez más. Thanks again.
(Muchas) gracias. Thank you (very much). Thanks (a lot).

graduación *f.* graduation

graduar *v.t.* (*temperature, etc.*) to adjust, to regulate

graduarse *v. pron.* (*university*) to graduate

gran, grande *adj.* big; great
Es un gran amigo. He's a great friend.

granada *f.* (*fruit*) pomegranate; (*military*) grenade

granero *m.* barn

grano *m.* grain, seed, bean; (*medical*) blemish, pimple
ir al grano *idiom* to get to the point

grasa *f.* fat

gratis *adj.* free of charge

grave *adj.* (*illness, wound, problem*) serious

gravedad *f.* gravity

gravísimo/a *adj.* (*superlative*) extremely serious

griego *m.* (*language*) Greek

griego *adj./m., f.* Greek

grifo *m.* faucet

grillo *m.* cricket

gripe *f.* flu

gris *adj./m.* gray

gritar *v.i.* to scream

grito *m.* yell, shout

grosero/a *adj.* rude, ill-mannered

grúa *f.* (*machinery*) crane

grupo *m.* group

guagua *f.* bus

guantes *m., pl.* gloves

guapo/a *adj.* handsome; good-looking

guarda forestal *m., f.* ranger

guardabarros *m.* (*automobile*) fender

guardar *v.t.* to save (on a computer)

guardería *f.* nursery school,

day-care center
guardia *m., f.* guard, police
officer
estar de guardia (*doctor*) to
be on duty, to be on call
guardia de seguridad
security guard
guerra *f.* war
guía *m., f.* guide
guía de teléfonos phone
book
Lo puedo usar de guía. I can
use it as a guide.
guiñar (el ojo) *v.t.* to wink
guión *m.* script, screenplay
guionista *m., f.* scriptwriter,
screenwriter
guisante *m.* pea
guisar *v.i. (Spain)* to cook
guiso *m.* stew
gusano *m.* worm
gustar *v.i.* to be pleasing to; to
like
Me gusta. I like it.
Me gustaría. I would like it.
¿Te gusta(n)…? Do you
like…?
¿Te gustaría (+ *inf.*)…?
Would you like to…?
gusto *m.* pleasure; (*senses*)
taste
El gusto es mío. The
pleasure is mine.
Gusto de (+ *inf.*)… It's a
pleasure to . . .

H

haber *v. impers. irreg.* **hay**
sing. there is; *pl.* there are
Hay (mucha) contaminación.

It's (very) smoggy.
Hay (mucha) niebla. It's
(very) foggy.
hay que it is necessary (that)
**Hay que pensar antes de
hablar.** Think before you
speak.
No hay de qué. You're
welcome.
haber *v. aux. irreg.* (*in
compound verbs*) to have
Yo no lo he hecho. I haven't
done it.
hábil *adj.* skillful
habilidad *f.* skill
habitación *f.* room
habitación doble double
room
habitación individual single
room
hablar *v.i.* to talk; to speak
hacer *v.t. irreg.* (**yo hago**) to do;
to make
hacer amigos to make
friends
hacer cola to stand in line
hacer diligencias to do
errands; to run errands
hacer ejercicio to exercise,
to work out
hacer ejercicios aeróbicos
to do aerobics
**hacer ejercicios de
estiramiento** to do stretching
exercises
hacer el papel to play a role
hacer gimnasia to exercise,
to work out
hacer juego (con) (*clothing*)
to match, to go well with

hacer la cama to make the bed

hacer las maletas to pack (the suitcases)

hacer quehaceres domésticos to do household chores

hacer turismo to go sightseeing

hacer un viaje to go on a trip

hacer una excursión to go on a hike; to go on a tour

hacer v. impers. (weather)

Hace buen tiempo. The weather is good. It's good weather.

Hace calor. It's hot.

Hace fresco. It's cool.

Hace frío. It's cold.

Hace mal tiempo. The weather is bad. It's bad weather.

Hace (mucho) viento. It's (very) windy.

Hace sol. It's sunny.

hacer v. impers. (time)

hace dos semanas two weeks ago

hacerse v. pron. irreg. (yo me hago) to become

hacerse el sordo to pretend not to hear

hacerse rico to become rich

hacha (el) f. ax

hacia prep. toward

hada (el) f. fairy

hada madrina fairy godmother

hallar v.t. to find

hallazgo m. find, discovery

Aquel restaurante fue un verdadero hallazgo. That restaurant was a real find.

halterofilia f. (sport) weightlifting

hamaca f. hammock

hambre (el) f. hunger

hambriento/a adj. hungry

hamburguesa f. hamburger

harina f. flour

harina de otro costal idiom another kettle of fish

hartarse v. pron. to get fed up; (food) to fill oneself

hasta prep. until, toward

Hasta la vista. See you later.

Hasta luego. See you later.

Hasta mañana. See you tomorrow.

Hasta pronto. See you soon.

hasta que conj. until

hasta que lleguen until they arrive

hebreo m. (language) Hebrew

hebreo adj./m., f. Hebrew

hecho p.p. of **hacer** done

de hecho in fact

heladería f. ice cream shop

helado m. ice cream

helado/a adj. iced

helicóptero m. helicopter

hembra f. female

hemisferio m. hemisphere

hemorragia f. hemorrhage

herbívoro/a adj. herbivorous; m., f. herbivore

heredar v.t. to inherit

heredera f. heiress

heredero m. heir

hereditario/a adj. hereditary

herencia *f.* inheritance
herida *f.* wound
herido/a *adj./m., f.* injured
 Hubo un herido de gravedad.
 One person was seriously
 injured.
hermanastro/a *m.* stepbrother;
 f. stepsister
hermano/a *m.* brother, *f.* sister
 hermano/a mayor/menor
 older/younger brother/sister
hermanos *m., pl.* brothers and
 sisters
hermético/a *adj.* airtight
hermoso/a *adj.* beautiful
héroe *m.* hero
heroína *f.* heroine
herramienta *f.* tool
hervido/a *adj.* boiled
hervir (e:ie) *v.t.* to boil
hidráulico/a *adj.* hydraulic
hiedra *f.* ivy
hielo *m.* ice
 quebrar/romper el hielo *loc.*
 break the ice
hierba *f.* grass
hierbas *f., pl.* herbs
hierro *m.* iron
hígado *m.* liver
higo *m.* fig
higuera *f.* fig tree
hijastro/a *m.* stepson; *f.*
 stepdaughter
hijo/a *m.* son; *f.* daughter
 hijo/a único/a only child
hijos *m., pl.* children
hilera *f.* row
hilo *m.* thread
 de hilo (made of) linen
 hilo dental dental floss

hindú *adj./m., f.* Hindu
hipérbole *f.* hyperbole
hípica *f.* equestrian sports
hipo *m.* hiccups
hipódromo *m.* hippodrome
hipoteca *f.* mortgage
hipotecar *v.t.* to mortgage
hipótesis *f.* hypothesis
hipotético/a *adj.* hypothetical
hispano/a *adj./m., f.* Hispanic
historia *f.* history; story
historiador(a) *m., f.* historian
hockey *m.* hockey
 hockey sobre césped (*L.A.*)
 field hockey
 hockey sobre hielo ice
 hockey
 hockey sobre hierba (*Spain*)
 field hockey
hoguera *f.* bonfire
hoja *f.* (*plant*) leaf; (*paper*)
 sheet
 hoja de vida (*Colombia*)
 résumé
hola *interj.* hello; hi
hombre *m.* man
 hombre de negocios
 businessman
 hombre del tiempo
 weatherman
 hombre lobo werewolf
 hombre rana frogman, diver
hombrera *f.* shoulder pad
hombro *m.* shoulder
homenaje *m.* tribute, homage
homenajear *v.t.* to pay homage
hora *f.* hour
 ¿A qué hora…? At what
 time…?
horario *m.* schedule

horizonte *m.* horizon
hormiga *f.* ant
hormigón *m.* (*Spain*) concrete
hormona *f.* hormone
hornear *v.t.* to bake
  pan recién horneado freshly baked bread
hornillo *m.* portable electric stove
horno *m.* oven
  horno de microondas microwave oven
horror *m.* horror
hortensia *f.* hydrangea
horticultor(a) *m., f.* horticulturalist
horticultura *f.* horticulture
hospedar *v.t.* to provide accommodation
hospital *m.* hospital
hospitalario/a *adj.* hospitable
hospitalidad *f.* hospitality
hostal *m.* inn; hostel
hotel *m.* hotel
hoy *adv.* today
  hoy día *adv.* nowadays
  Hoy es... Today is . . .
huelga *f.* strike
huelguista *m., f.* striker
huella *f.* footprint; mark
  huella dactilar fingerprint
huerta *f.* orchard
huerto *m.* vegetable garden
hueso *m.* bone; (*fruit*) pit
huésped *m., f.* guest
huevo *m.* egg
huida *f.* escape
huir (y) *v.i.* to flee, to escape
  Huir de la injusticia. Escape injustice.

humanidades *f., pl.* humanities
humanismo *m.* humanism
humanista *m., f.* humanist
humectante *m.* moisturizer
humedad *f.* humidity
húmedo *adj.* humid; damp
humilde *adj.* humble
  en mi humilde opinión in my humble opinion
humillado/a *adj.* humiliated
humo *m.* smoke
huracán *m.* hurricane

I

iceberg *m.* iceberg
ida *f.* (*travel*) one way
  boleto/billete de ida one way ticket
idea *f.* idea
idioma *m.* language
iglesia *f.* church
ignorancia *f.* ignorance
ignorante *adj.* ignorant
igual *adj.* equal, same, like
  dos y dos igual a cuatro two and two equals four
  Es igual que su madre. She's like her mother.
  Son las dos iguales. They are both the same.
  ¿Blanco o negro? –Me da igual. ¿Black or white? – It's all the same to me.
igualdad *f.* equality
igualmente *adv.* likewise
  ¡Que te diviertas! –Igualmente. Have fun! –Likewise.
ilegible *adj.* illegible
ilusionado/a *adj.* thrilled

ilustrar *v.t.* to illustrate
imaginar *v.t.* to imagine
imaginarse *v. pron.* to imagine
imán *m.* magnet
imitación *f.* imitation
imitar *v.t.* to imitate
impaciencia *f.* impatience
impacientarse *v. pron.* to get impatient
   Se impacientó con el retraso del autobús. She got impatient over the delay of the bus.
impaciente *adj.* impatient
impedir (e:i) *v.t.* to prevent
impensable *adj.* unthinkable
imperio *m.* empire
impermeable *adj.* waterproof
impermeable *m.* raincoat
importación *f.* importation
importante *adj.* important
   (No) Es importante que (+ subj.) It's (not) important that…
   Es importante que vengas a clase. It's important that you come to class.
importar *v.i.* to be important to; to matter
   No importa. It doesn't matter.
imposible *adj.* impossible
   (No) Es imposible que (+ subj.) It's (not) impossible that…
   Es imposible que tenga sed. It's impossible that she's thirsty.
impostor(a) *m., f.* impostor
imprenta *f.* print shop
impresora *f.* printer

imprimir *v.t.* to print
improbable *adj.* improbable
   (No) Es improbable que (+ subj.) It's (not) improbable that…
   Es improbable que llueva. It probably won't rain.
impuesto *m.* tax
inadvertido/a *adj.* unnoticed
inauguración *f.* inauguration
inaugurar *v.t.* to inaugurate
incendio *m.* fire
incertidumbre *f.* uncertainty
incógnito *adj.* unknown
   de incógnito *adv.* incognito
incomprensible *adj.* incomprehensible
incomprensión *f.* lack of understanding
inconcebible *adj.* inconceivable
inconveniente *m.* drawback
increíble *adj.* incredible
incremento *m.* increase
independiente *adj.* independent
independizarse *v. pron.* to become independent
indicar *v.t.* to indicate, to show
índice *m.* rate
   índice de mortalidad mortality rate
   índice de natalidad birth rate
indicio *m.* evidence
indígena *adj.* indigenous, native
indiscreto/a *adj.* indiscreet, tactless
individual *adj.* individual; *m.* (*sport*) singles

individualidad *f.* individuality

inefable *adj.* indescribable

inesperado/a *adj.* unexpected

inexplicable *adj.* inexplicable

infarto *m.* heart attack

infección *f.* infection

influir (en) (y) *v.i.* to influence
Los poemas de Darío influyeron en otros poetas. Darío's poems influenced other poets.

informar *v.t.* to inform

informarse *v. pron.* to get information

informe *m.* report; (*written work*) paper

infusión (de hierbas) *f.* herbal tea

ingeniero/a *m., f.* engineer

ingerir (e:ie) *v.t.* to ingest

ingestión *f.* ingestion

Inglaterra *f.* England

ingle *f.* groin

inglés *m.* (*language*) English

inglés, inglesa *adj./m., f.* English

ingrávido/a *adj.* weightless

injusto/a *adj.* unfair

inmaduro/a *adj.* (*person*) immature

inmediatamente *adv.* immediately

inmigración *f.* immigration

inmigrante *m., f.* immigrant

inmigrar *v.i.* to immigrate

inmunizar (a alguien contra algo) *v.t.* to immunize

inmunológico/a *adj.* immunological

innovación *f.* innovation

innovador(a) *adj.* innovative; *m., f.* innovator

innovar *v.t.* to innovate

inolvidable *adj.* unforgettable

inquietante *adj.* worrying

inquietar(se) *v. pron.* to worry

inquieto/a *adj.* worried

inscribirse *v. pron.* to register, to enroll
Quiere inscribirse en la clase de astronomía. She intends to register for the astronomy class.

inscripción *f.* registration, enrollment

insecto *m.* insect

insípido/a *adj.* (*food*) bland; (*person, work*) insipid

insistencia *f.* insistence

insistir (en) *v.i.* to insist (on)
(insistir en +*inf.*) Insistió en invitarme. He insisted on inviting me.
(insistir en que + *subj.*) Insiste en que vayamos todos. He insists on all of us going.

insociable *adj.* unsociable

insólito/a *adj.* unusual

insomnio *m.* insomnia

insoportable *adj.* unbearable

inspector(a) *m., f.* inspector
inspector de aduanas customs inspector

inspirar *v.t.* to inspire

instalación *f.* installation
instalaciones deportivas sports facilities

instalar *v.t.* (*equipment*) to install

instalarse *v. pron.* to settle, install oneself
   Se instaló delante de la tele y no se movió. He settled in front of the TV and didn't budge.
institución *f.* institution
instrumento *m.* (*medical, musical*) instrument
insulina *f.* insulin
inteligente *adj.* intelligent
intentar *v.* to try
intento *m.* attempt; try
intercambiar *v.t.* exchange
intercambio *m.* exchange
interés *m.* interest
interesante *adj.* interesting
interesar *v.i.* to be interesting to; to interest
interesarse (en) *v. pron.* to take an interest (in)
   Siempre se interesa en los resultados. He's always interested in the results.
intermedio *adj.* intermediate
intermitente *m.* (*automobile*) turn signal
internacional *adj.* international
Internet *m.* Internet
interpretación *f.* (*oral translation*) interpreting
interpretar *v.t.* to play (a role), to perform
intérprete *m., f.* interpreter
interrumpir *v.t.* to interrupt
intervención *f.* intervention, participation
   intervención quirúrgica operation
intestino *m.* intestine

intestino delgado small intestine
intestino grueso large intestine
intimar (con alguien) *v.i.* to get close (to someone)
intimidad *f.* privacy
intolerante *adj.* intolerant
intriga *f.* intrigue
intrigado/a *adj.* intrigued, in suspense
inundación *f.* flood
inundar *v.t.* to flood
inútil *adj.* useless
inválido/a *adj.* (*person*) disabled
invernadero *m.* greenhouse
inverosímil *adj.* unlikely, improbable; unrealistic
invertebrado/a *adj./m.* invertebrate
invertir (i:ie) *v.t.* to invest
investigador(a) *m., f.* researcher
investigar *v.t.* to research
invierno *m.* winter
invitado/a *m., f.* guest
invitar *v.t.* to invite
involuntario *adj.* involuntary
inyección *f.* injection
inyectar *v.t.* to inject
ir *v.i. irreg.* to go
   ir a (+ *inf.*) to be going to (do something) **Voy a leer un rato.** I'm going to read for a while.
   ir de compras to go shopping
   ir de excursión (a las montañas) to go for a hike (in the mountains)

ir de pesca to go fishing
ir de vacaciones to go on vacation
ir en auto(móvil) to go by auto(mobile); to go by car
ir en autobús to go by bus
ir en avión to go by plane
ir en barco to go by ship
ir en metro to go by subway
ir en motocicleta to go by motorcycle
ir en taxi to go by taxi
ir en tren to go by train
¡Vamos! Let's go!; Come on!
ironía *f.* irony
irónico/a *adj.* ironic
irse *v. pron. irreg.* to go away; to leave **No te vayas, aún es temprano.** Don't leave; it's still early.
  irse de pinta (*idiom*) (*Mexico*) to play hooky
italiano *m.* (*language*) Italian
italiano/a *adj./m., f.* Italian
itinerario *m.* itinerary
izquierdo/a *adj.* left
  a la izquierda (de) to the left (of)

J

jabón *m.* soap
jabonera *f.* soap dish
jamás *adv.* never; not ever
jamón *m.* ham
Januká *m.* Chanukah
japonés *m.* (*language*) Japanese
japonés, japonesa *adj./m., f.* Japanese
jardín *m.* garden, yard

jardinería *f.* gardening
jardinero/a *m., f.* gardener
jarra *f.* pitcher
jarrón *m.* vase
jefe/a *m., f.* boss
jerarquía *f.* hierarchy
jerárquico/a *adj.* hierarchical
jerarquizado/a *adj.* hierarchical
jerez *m.* (*wine*) sherry
jeringa *f.* syringe
jirafa *f.* giraffe
joroba *f.* hump
jorobado/a *adj.* hunchbacked
jota *f.* (*playing cards*) jack
joven *adj.* young; *m., f.* youth, young person
joyas *f.* jewels
joyería *f.* jewelry store
joyero/a *m., f.* jeweler; *m.* jewelry box
jubilado/a *m., f.* retired person
jubilarse *v. pron.* to retire (from work)
judío/a *adj.* Jewish; *m., f.* Jew
juego *m.* game
  juego limpio/sucio fair/foul play
juegos *m. pl.* games
  juegos de azar gambling
  juegos de mesa board games
  Juegos Olímpicos Olympic Games
  Juegos Paralímpicos Paralympics
jueves *m., sing.* Thursday
juez *m., f.* judge
jugador(a) *m., f.* player; gambler

jugar (u:ue) *v.t./v.i.* to play
  jugar a las cartas to play cards
jugo *m.* juice
  jugo de fruta fruit juice
jugoso/a *adj.* juicy
juguete *m.* toy
juguetería *f.* toy store
juicio *m.* judgment; trial
julio *m.* July
junio *m.* June
junta *f.* board, committee
  junta directiva board of directors
juntos/as *adj./adv.* together
jurado *m.* jury
jurar *v.i.* to swear
justicia *f.* justice
justo/a *adj.* fair
juvenil *adj.* youthful
juventud *f.* youth
juzgar *v.t.* to judge

K

kilo(gramo) *m.* kilo(gram)
kilómetro *m.* kilometer

L

la *art. f., sing.* the
la *d.o. pron. f., sing.* her, it, you
labio *m.* lip
laboratorio *m.* laboratory
lacio/a *adj.* (*hair*) straight
ladera *f.* hillside, mountainside, slope
  El primer grupo subió por la ladera norte. The first group ascended the northern slope.
lado *m.* side
  al lado de beside
  por un lado…, por otro

lado… on (the) one hand . . . , on the other hand . . .
ladrar *v.i.* to bark
ladrido *m.* bark
ladrillo *m.* brick
ladrón, ladrona *m., f.* thief; robber; burglar
lagarto *m.* lizard
lago *m.* lake
lágrima *f.* tear
lamentar *v.t.* to regret
lámpara *f.* lamp
lana *f.* wool
  de lana (made of) wool
lancha *f.* motorboat
langosta *f.* lobster
langostino *m.* prawn
lanzado *p.p. of* **lanzar** thrown
lanzado/a *adj.* (*person*) impulsive, impetuous
lanzamiento *m.* launch, throw
  lanzamiento de bala (*L. A.*) shot put
  lanzamiento de disco discus throw
  lanzamiento de jabalina javelin throw
  lanzamiento de peso (*Spain*) shot put
lanzar *v.t.* to throw; to launch
  La NASA lanzó un cohete a Saturno. NASA launched a rocket to Saturn.
lápiz *m.* pencil
  lápiz labial lipstick
largo/a *adj.* long
  a la larga in the long run
laringe *f.* larynx
larva *f.* larva
las *art. f., pl.* the
las *d.o. pron. f., pl.* them

lástima f. shame, pity
Es una lástima que (+ subj.) It's too bad that...
Es una lástima que no te puedas quedar. It's a pity that you can't stay.
lastimar v.t. to hurt
lastimarse v. pron. to injure oneself
lastimarse el pie to injure one's foot
lata f. (tin) can
¡Qué lata! loc. What a drag!
latido m. heartbeat
latín m. (language) Latin
latino/a adj./m., f. Latin
latir v.i. (heart) to beat
lavabo m. sink
lavadora f. washing machine
lavandería f. laundromat
lavaplatos m., sing. dishwasher
lavar v.t. to wash
lavarse v. pron. to wash (oneself)
lavarse la cara to wash one's face
lavarse las manos to wash one's hands
lazo m. bow; ribbon
lazos m., pl. ties
lazos familiares family ties
le i.o. pron. sing. to/for him, her, form. you
lección f. lesson
leche f. milk
lechuga f. lettuce
lector m., f. reader
leer v.t. to read
leer el correo electrónico to read e-mail

leer el periódico to read the newspaper
leer la revista to read the magazine
legado m. legacy
legal adj. legal
legalizar v.t. to legalize
leído p.p. of **leer** read
lejano/a adj. distant; remote; far-off
un pariente lejano a distant relative
lejía f. bleach
lejos de adv. far from
lengua f. tongue; language
lenguas extranjeras f., pl. foreign languages
lentamente adv. slowly
lenteja f. lentil
lentes m., pl. eyeglasses, lenses
lentes de contacto contact lenses
lentes de sol/oscuros/negros sunglasses
lento/a adj. slow
leña f. firewood
leño m. log
león m. lion
leopardo m. leopard
les i.o. pron. pl. to/for them, form you
letra f. (alphabet) letter; handwriting; (song) lyrics
Tienes una letra ilegible. Your handwriting is illegible.
letra de imprenta printing
Escriba su nombre completo en letra de imprenta. Print your full name.

letra mayúscula capital letter

letra minúscula lowercase letter

letrero *m.* sign

levadura *f.* yeast

levantar *v.t.* to lift

levantar pesas to lift weights

levantarse *v. pron.* to get up

ley *f.* law

la ley del más fuerte the survival of the fittest

leyenda *f.* legend

liberación *f.* liberation

liberal *adj./m., f.* liberal

liberar *v.t.* to free, to release

libertad *f.* liberty, freedom

la Estatua de la Libertad the Statue of Liberty

libertad condicional parole

libertad de expresión freedom of speech

libra *f.* pound

libre *adj.* free

librería *f.* bookstore

libro *m.* book

libro de bolsillo paperback

libro de consulta reference book

licencia *f.* license

licencia de conducir/manejar driver's license

licor *m.* liqueur, liquor

licuadora *f.* (*L.A.*) blender

licuar *v.t.* to blend

líder *m., f.* leader

liderar *v.t.* to lead

liderazgo *m.* leadership

ligar *v.i.* (*Spain*) to pick up boys/girls

ligero/a *adj.* (*weight/food*) light

lima *f.* (*tool*) file; nail file

limitar *v.t.* to limit; to restrict

límite *m.* limit

limón *m.* lemon, lime

limonero *m.* lemon tree

limosna *f.* alms, charity

vivir de limosnas to live by begging

limpiaparabrisas *m. sing.* windshield wiper

limpiar *v.t.* to clean

limpiar la casa to clean the house

limpio/a *adj.* clean

limusina *f.* limousine

lindo/a *adj.* pretty

línea *f.* line

línea discontinua broken line

lingüista *m., f.* linguist

lingüística *f.* linguistics

lingüístico/a *adj.* linguistic

linterna *f.* flashlight

líquido/a *adj./m.* liquid

lirio *m.* lily

lista *f.* list

lista de espera waiting list

lista de éxitos best-seller list

pasar lista to call roll

listo/a *adj.* smart; ready

estar listo/a to be ready

ser listo/a to be smart

literal *adj.* literal

Es una traducción demasiado literal; no suena natural. It's too literal a translation; it doesn't sound natural.

literario/a *adj.* literary

literatura *f.* literature

litro *m.* liter

liviano/a *adj.* light
llamada *f.* call
  llamada telefónica
  telephone call
llamar (a alguien) *v.t.* to call
  (somebody)
  llamar a cobro revertido to
  call collect
  llamar la atención (a) to
  attract attention (to)
  llamar por teléfono to call on
  the phone
llamarse *v. pron.* to be called;
  to be named
llanta *f.* tire
llanura *f.* prairie
llave *f.* key
  llave maestra master key
llavero *m.* key chain
llegada *f.* arrival
llegar *v.i.* to arrive
  llegar a ser to become
  llegar tarde to be late
llenar *v.t.* to fill; (*form*) (*L.A.*) to
  fill out
  llenar el tanque to fill the
  tank
  llenar un formulario to fill
  out a form
lleno/a *adj.* full
llevar *v.t.* to carry, to take;
  (*clothes*) to wear **¿Qué es
  eso que llevas puesto?**
  What's that you're wearing?
  llevar una vida sana to lead
  a healthy lifestyle
llevarse *v. pron.* to take
  Puedes llevártelo. You can
  take it.
  llevarse bien/mal con to get
  along well/badly with

llorar *v.i.* to cry
lloriquear *v.i.* to whine
llorón, llorona *adj./m., f.*
  crybaby
llover (o:ue) *v. impers.* to rain
  llover a cántaros *idiom* to
  pour, to rain cats and dogs
  Llueve. It's raining.
lluvia *f.* rain
  lluvia ácida acid rain
lo *d.o. pron.* it, him, *form.* you
  Dilo. Say it.
  Díselo. Say it to him.
lobo *m.* wolf
loco/a *adj.* crazy
  loco de remate stark raving
  mad
locomotora *f.* locomotive
locura *f.* madness
locutor(a) *m., f.* (*TV, radio*)
  announcer
lograr *v.t.* to achieve
logro *m.* achievement
lombriz *f.* earthworm
lomo *m.* flank steak
  lomo a la plancha grilled
  flank steak
lona *f.* canvas
lonchera *f.* (*L.A.*) lunch box
longevidad *f.* longevity
loro *m.* parrot
los *d.o. pron. m. pl.* them, *form.*
  you
los *art. m., pl.* the
lucha *f.* fight, struggle
luchar (por) *v.i.* to fight, to
  struggle (for)
lucir (c:zc) *v.* to look good
luego *adv.* afterwards, then;
  later
  desde luego *idiom* of course

¡**Hasta luego!** See you later.
Y luego qué. And then what?
lugar *m.* place
lujo *m.* luxury
lujoso/a *adj.* luxurious
luna *f.* moon
  luna de miel honeymoon
lunar *m.* mole, beauty mark;
  polka dot
  una corbata de lunares a
  polka-dot tie
lunes *m., sing.* Monday
lupa *f.* magnifying glass
luz *f.* light, electricity
  Apaga la luz. Turn out the
  light.
  la luz del sol sunlight

M

maceta *f.* flower pot
macho *m.* male
madera *f.* wood
madrastra *f.* stepmother
madre *f.* mother
madrina *f.* godmother
madrugada *f.* early morning
madrugar *v.i.* to get up early
madurez *f.* maturity; middle
  age
maduro/a *adj.* (*person*) mature;
  (*fruit*) ripe
maestría *f.* (*L.A.*) master's
  degree
maestro/a *m., f.* (*elementary
  school*) teacher
magia *f.* magic
mágico/a *adj.* magical
magma *m.* magma
magnesio *m.* magnesium
magnífico/a *adj.* magnificent
mago/a *m., f.* magician

maíz *m.* corn
maleducado/a *adj.* rude, bad-
  mannered
maleta *f.* suitcase
maletero *m.* (*Spain*)
  (*automobile*) trunk
malgastar *v.t.* to waste
  **No malgastes tu tiempo en
  tonterías.** Don't waste your
  time with stupid little things.
maligno *adj.* (*tumor*) malignant
malo/a *adj.* bad; mean
  estar de mal humor to be in
  a bad mood
  ¡Mala suerte! Unlucky!
  ¡Qué película más mala!
  What a terrible movie!
  (No) Es malo que (+ *subj.*)
  It's (not) bad that…
  No es malo que lo digas. It's
  not bad that you say it.
mamá *f.* mom
mami *f.* mom
mamífero *m.* mammal
manantial *m.* (*water*) spring
mandar *v.t.* to order; to send
mandarina *f.* tangerine
manejar *v.i.* to drive
manera *f.* way
  de ninguna manera by no
  means; no way
manga *f.* sleeve
manguera *f.* hose
manicomio *m.* mental hospital
manicura *f.* manicure
manifestación *f.* demonstration
manifestante *m., f.*
  demonstrator
manillar *m.* (*Spain*) (*bike*)
  handlebars
maniquí *m.* mannequin

mano *f.* hand

manta *f.* blanket

mantel *m.* tablecloth

mantener (e:ie) *v.t. irreg.* **(yo mantengo)** to maintain, to support; to keep
   Mantengan la calma. Keep calm.
   Mantener las apariencias. Keeping up appearances.
   ¿Quién va a mantener a la familia? Who's going to support the family?

mantenerse (en forma) (e:ie) *v. pron. irreg.* **(yo me mantengo)** to stay (in shape)

mantequilla *f.* butter

manzana *f.* apple

mañana *f.* morning, A.M.; *adv.* tomorrow
   a las dos de la mañana at two in the morning, at two A.M.

mapa *m.* map
   mapa de carreteras road map

maquillador(a) *m., f.* makeup artist

maquillaje *m.* makeup

maquillar *v.t.* to apply makeup

maquillarse *v. pron.* to put on one's makeup

máquina *f.* machine
   máquina de afeitar razor
   máquina de coser sewing machine
   máquina de escribir typewriter

mar *m.* sea, ocean
   en alta mar on the high sea

maratón *m.* marathon

maravillosamente *adv.* marvelously

maravilloso/a *adj.* marvelous

marca *f.* mark; (*commerce*) brand, brand name; (*sport*) record
   Es una marca de prestigio. It's a well-known brand.
   Superó su marca. She beat her own record.

marcador *m.* (*sports*) scoreboard

marcapasos *m., sing.* pacemaker

marcar *v.t.* (*telephone*) to dial; (*sports*) to score
   Marca el 007. Dial 007.
   ¿Quién marcó el gol de la victoria? Who scored the winning goal?

marea *f.* tide
   marea alta/baja high/low tide
   marea negra oil slick

mareado/a *adj.* dizzy; nauseated

marearse *v. pron.* to get dizzy
   ¿Te mareas en barco? Do you get seasick?

maremoto *m.* seaquake; tidal wave

margarina *f.* margarine

margarita *f.* daisy

marinero *m.* sailor

mariposa *f.* butterfly

mariscada *f.* assorted seafood

mariscos *m., pl.* shellfish

mármol *m.* marble

marrón *adj./m.* brown

martes *m., sing.* Tuesday

martillo *m.* hammer

marzo *m.* March

más *adv./ pron.* more ¿**Quieres más?** Would you like some more?

  mas de (+ *number*) more than **Hay más de diez personas.** There are more than ten people.

  más… que more… than **más grande que una casa** bigger than a house

  más tarde later

masa *f.* dough

masaje *m.* massage

masajista *m.* masseur; *f.* masseuse

máscara *f.* mask

mascarilla *f.* mask

masticar *v.t.* to chew

matar *v.t.* to kill

  matar dos pájaros de un tiro *loc.* to kill two birds with one stone

matarse *v. pron.* to kill oneself **Se mata estudiando.** She studies like crazy.

matemáticas *f., pl.* mathematics

matemático/a *m., f.* mathematician

materia *f.* matter; (*school*) subject

  materia inorgánica inorganic matter

  ¿Qué materia enseña la Srta. López? What subject does Miss López teach?

materno/a *adj.* (*relative*) maternal

matrícula *f.* (*education*) registration, matriculation; (*automobile*) registration number, license plate

  matrícula de honor (*grade*) distinction, magna cum laude

matricularse *v. pron.* (*education*) to register, to enroll

matrimonio *m.* marriage

máximo/a *m.* maximum, top

mayo *m.* May

mayonesa *f.* mayonnaise

mayor *adj.* older

  el/la mayor the oldest

mayordomo *m.* butler

mayoría *f.* majority

me *pron.* me

  Dámelo. Give it to me.

mecánico/a *m., f.* mechanic

mecanismo *m.* mechanism

mecanógrafo/a *m., f.* typist

mecedora *f.* rocking chair

mecer (c:z) *v.t.* to rock

medalla *f.* medal

mediano/a *adj.* medium

medianoche *f.* midnight

medias *f., pl.* pantyhose, stockings

medicamento *m.* medication

medicina *f.* medicine

medición *f.* measurement

médico/a *m., f.* doctor; *adj.* medical

  médico de cabecera family doctor

  médico de familia family doctor

  médico/a de guardia doctor on call, doctor on duty

tratamiento médico medical treatment

medida *f.* measurement, size

medio/a *m.* half

medio ambiente *m.* environment

medio/a hermano/a *m.* half-brother; *f.* half-sister

mediocre *adj.* mediocre

mediodía *m.* noon, midday

medios *m., pl.* means; resources

los medios de comunicación the media

medir (e:i) *v.t.* to measure

meditación *f.* meditation

meditar *v.i.* to meditate

médula *f.* marrow

medusa *f.* jellyfish

megáfono *m.* megaphone

mejilla *f.* cheek

mejillón *m.* mussel

mejor *adj.* better; best

el/la mejor *m., f.* the best

lo mejor the best (thing)

Es mejor que (+ subj.) It's better that…

Es mejor que vayas. It's better that you go.

mejora *f.* improvement

mejorar *v.t.* to improve

mejorarse *v. pron.* to get better

mellizo/a *m., f.* twin

melocotón *m.* (*Spain*) peach

melón *m.* melon

membrana *f.* membrane

memoria *f.* memory

de memoria *adv.* by heart

Se sabe el poema de memoria. He knows the

poem by heart.

memorizar *v.t.* to memorize

mendigo/a *m., f.* beggar

menopausia *f.* menopause

menor *adj.* younger

el/la menor *m., f.* the youngest

menos *adv.* less

a menos que (+ subj.) *conj.* unless **Iré a menos que lluvia.** I'll go unless it rains.

menos cuarto/quince quarter to/of **Son las dos menos cuarto/quince.** It's a quarter to/of two.

menos de (+ number) less than **Tengo menos de una hora.** I have less than an hour.

menos… que less… than **¿Qué es menos interesante que hablar?** What's less interesting than talking?

por lo menos at least

mensaje *m.* message

mensaje electrónico e-mail message

mensualidad *f.* (*monthly payment*) installment

menta *f.* mint

mentalidad *f.* mentality

mentir (e:ie) *v.i.* to lie

mentira *f.* lie

parecer mentira *idiom* to be hard to believe; to be incredible

Aunque parezca mentira, sólo tiene diez años. It's hard to believe, but he's only ten.

mentiroso/a *adj.* liar

menú *m.* menu
menudo/a *adj.* tiny, minute
  a menudo *adv.* frequently, often
mercadillo *m.* street market
mercado *m.* market
  mercado al aire libre open-air market
mercurio *m.* mercury
merecer (c:zc) *v.t.* to deserve
merendar (e:ie) *v.i.* to have a snack in the afternoon
merienda *f.* afternoon snack
mérito *m.* merit
merluza *f.* (*fish*) hake
mermelada *f.* jam
mes *m.* month
mesa *f.* table
mesero/a *m.* waiter; *f.* waitress
meseta *f.* plateau
mesita *f.* end table
  mesita de noche night stand
meta *f.* objective, goal
metabolismo *m.* metabolism
metabolizar *v.t.* to metabolize
metáfora *f.* metaphor
metafórico/a *adj.* metaphoric
metal *m.* metal
metamorfosis *f.* metamorphosis
meteorito *m.* meteorite
meteorólogo/a *m., f.* meteorologist
meter *v.t.* to put (into)
  meter la pata put one's foot in one's mouth
metereología *f.* meteorology
metódico/a *adj.* methodical
método *m.* method
metro *m.* meter; subway

mexicano/a *adj./m., f.* Mexican
mí *pron.* me
  ¿Para mí? For me?
mezclar *v.t.* to mix, to toss
mezquita *f.* mosque
mi(s) *poss.* my
micrófono *m.* microphone
microonda *f.* microwave
microscopio *m.* microscope
miedo *m.* fear
  No tengas miedo. Don't be afraid.
miel *f.* honey
miembro *m.* member; (*body*) limb
mientras *adv.* while
  mientras tanto meanwhile
miércoles *m., sing.* Wednesday
mil *m.* one thousand
  a las mil y una very late
  Anoche llegó a las mil y una. Last night he arrived very late.
  Mil perdones. I'm extremely sorry.
milagro *m.* miracle
milla *f.* mile
millón *m.* million
  mil millones a billion (US)
mimbre *m.* wicker
mina *f.* mine
mineral *m.* mineral
minería *f.* mining industry
minero/a *m., f.* miner
minifalda *f.* miniskirt
mínimo/a *adj./m.* minimum
  como mínimo at least
ministro/a *m., f.* (*government*) minister

minoría f. minority
minúsculo/a adj. minute, tiny
minuto m. minute
mío/a(s) poss. my, (of) mine
miope adj. myopic
miopía f. myopia
mirar v.t. to watch
  mirar (la) televisión to watch television
misil m. missile
mismo/a adj. same
misterioso/a adj. mysterious
mitad f. half, middle
mitin m. political meeting
mochila f. backpack
moda f. fashion
  ir a la moda v. to be fashionably dressed or trendy
módem m. modem
modernizar v.t. to modernize
moderno/a adj. modern, trendy
modificar v.t. to modify
modista f. dressmaker
modo m. way, manner; (verb tense) mood ¿**el modo subjuntivo o el indicativo?** ¿the subjunctive or the indicative mood?
  de ningún modo by no means
  de todos modos anyway; in any case
moho m. mold
mojado/a adj. wet
mojar v.t. to wet, to get wet
mojarse v. pron. to get (oneself) wet
  Salí sin paraguas y me mojé toda. I went out without an umbrella and I got all wet.
molestar v.t. to bother, to annoy; to disturb
  No le molestes, está estudiando. Don't disturb him, he's studying.
  Deja de molestarme, estoy pensando. Stop bothering me, I'm thinking.
  Este ruido me molesta. This noise annoys me.
molestia f. inconvenience, bother
  No es ninguna molestia. It's no bother at all.
molino m. (machine, factory) mill
monarca m., f. monarch
monarquía f. monarchy
monasterio m. monastery
mondadientes m. toothpick
moneda f. coin
monedero m. coin purse
monitor m. (computer) monitor
monitor(a) m., f. trainer, coach, instructor
  monitor de esquí ski instructor
monja f. nun
monje m. monk
mono m. monkey
monólogo m. monologue
montacargas m. forklift
montaña f. mountain
montar v.t. (horse, bike) to ride; (machine, furniture) to assemble
  ¿Aún no has montado el escritorio? You still haven't assembled the desk?

monumento *m.* monument

mora *f.* blackberry

morado/a *adj.* purple

moral *f.* moral

moralidad *f.* morality

morder (o:ue) *v.t.* to bite

mordisco *m.* bite

moreno/a *adj.* brunet(te)

morfología *f.* morphology

moribundo/a *adj.* moribund, dying

morir (o:ue) *v.i.* to die
  Me muero por ir. I'm dying to go.
  Me muero por un beso. I'm dying for a kiss.

mortalidad *f.* mortality

mosca *f.* fly

mosquitero *m.* mosquito net

mostaza *f.* mustard

mostrar (o:ue) *v.t.* to show

moto *f.* motorcycle

motocicleta *f.* motorcycle

motociclismo *m.* motorcycling

motociclista *m., f.* motorcyclist

motor *m.* motor, engine

móvil *adj.* mobile

movilidad *f.* mobility

mozo/a *(L.A.) m.* waiter; *f.* waitress

muchacho/a *m., f.* boy, girl

muchísimo/a *adj. (superlative)* very much
  Muchísimas gracias. Thank you very much.

mucho/a *adj.* many; a lot of; much; *adv.* a lot
  muchas veces many times
  Mucho gusto. Pleased to meet you.

mudanza *f.* move

mudar *v.t.* to move, to change
  Las serpientes mudan de piel cada año. Snakes change their skin each year.

mudarse *v. pron.* to move (from one house to another)
  ¿Cuántas veces te has mudado este año? How many times have you moved this year?

mudo/a *adj.* mute

muebles *m., pl.* furniture

muela *f.* molar, back tooth; *(generic)* tooth **Me sacaron una muela.** I had a tooth pulled.
  muela del juicio wisdom tooth

muelle *m.* spring

muerte *f.* death

muerto/a *p.p. of* **morir** died; *adj.* dead
  Estoy muerto de hambre. I'm starving.

muestra *f.* sample

mujer *f.* woman
  mujer de negocios businesswoman
  mujer policía female police officer

mujeriego *m.* womanizer

multa *f.* fine

multitud *f.* crowd

mundial *adj.* worldwide

mundo *m.* world

municipal *m.* municipal

muñeca *f.* doll; wrist

muralla *f.* wall

murciélago *m. (animal)* bat

muro *m.* wall
músculo *m.* muscle
musculoso/a *adj.* muscular
museo *m.* museum
música *f.* music
musical *adj.* musical
músico/a *m., f.* musician
muslo *m.* thigh
musulmán, musulmana *adj./m., f.* Muslim
muy *adv.* very
  Muy amable. That's very kind of you.
  Muy bien, gracias. Very well, thank you.

N

nacer (c:zc) *v.i.* to be born
nacimiento *m.* birth
nación *f.* nation
  Naciones Unidas United Nations **Ése es el edificio de las Naciones Unidas.** That's the UN building.
nacional *adj.* national
nacionalidad *f.* nationality
nacionalismo *m.* nationalism
nacionalista *adj.* nationalist
nada *pron./adv.* nothing
  De nada. You're welcome.
  No está nada mal. It's not bad at all.
  No me gustan nada. I don't like them at all.
nadador(a) *m., f.* swimmer
nadar *v.i.* to swim
nadie *pron.* no one, nobody, not anyone
  No lo sabe nadie. Nobody knows it.

naipe *m.* playing card
naranja *f.* orange
naranjo *m.* orange tree
nariz *f.* nose
narrador(a) *m., f.* narrator
nata *f.* (*Spain*) cream; (*on boiled milk*) skin
natación *f.* swimming
  natación sincronizada synchronized swimming
natalidad *f.* birthrate
natural *adj.* natural
naturaleza *f.* nature
naturalmente *adv.* naturally; of course
navaja *f.* jackknife, penknife
navegar *v.i.* to sail
  navegar en la Red to surf the Web
Navidad *f.* Christmas
necesario/a *adj.* necessary
  (No) Es necesario que (+ subj.) It's (not) necessary that…
  No es necesario que te quedes. It's not necessary that you stay.
neceser *m.* toilet kit
necesidad *f.* necessity
necesitar *v.t.* to need
nectarina *f.* nectarine
negación *f.* refusal
negar (e:ie) *v.t.* to deny
negarse (e:ie) *v. pron.* to refuse
negativo/a *m.* negative
negocios *m., pl.* business, commerce
negro/a *adj./m.* (*color*) black
nervio *m.* nerve

nervioso/a *adj.* nervous
neumático *m.* tire
neurona *f.* neuron
nevar (e:ie) *v. impers.* to snow
  Nieva. It's snowing.
ni *conj.* nor
  Ni tú ni yo. Neither you nor I.
niebla *f.* fog
nieto/a *m.* grandson; *f.*
  granddaughter
nieve *f.* snow
ningún, ninguno/a(s) *adj.* no;
  none; not any
  ningún problema no problem
niñez *f.* childhood
niño/a *m., f.* child
  de niño/a as a child
  niño/a mimado/a spoiled
  child, brat
nitrógeno *m.* nitrogen
nivel *m.* level
no *adv.* no; not
  No, no vengo. No, I'm not
  coming.
  Vienes, ¿no? You're coming,
  right?
  ¿Vienes o no? Are you
  coming or not?
noche *f.* night
  de la noche in the evening,
  at night, P.M. **a las diez de la**
  noche at ten P.M.
  por la noche at night
nogal *m.* walnut tree
nombre *m.* name
  en mi nombre in my name
  en nombre de on behalf of, in
  the name of
  nombre de pila first name
nórdico/a *adj.* Nordic; *m., f.*

  Northern European
norte *m.* north
  al norte to the north
norteamericano/a *adj./m., f.*
  (North) American
nos *pron.* us, ourselves, each
  other
  Nos vemos. See you.
nosotros/as *pron.* we, us
  entre nosotros/as between
  us; off the record
nota *f.* (*school*) grade, mark
notar *v.t.* to notice
noticias *f., pl.* news
noticiero *m.* newscast
novatada *f.* practical joke
  hacer una novatada (a
  alguien) *v.* to haze
  (somebody)
novato/a *adj.* inexperienced,
  new
novecientos/as nine hundred
noveno/a *adj./m.* ninth
noventa ninety
noviembre *m.* November
novillo *m.* steer
  hacer novillos (*Spain*) to play
  hooky
novio/a *m., f.* boyfriend,
  girlfriend
nube *f.* cloud
nublado/a *adj.* cloudy
  Está muy nublado. It's very
  cloudy.
núcleo *m.* nucleus
nuera *f.* daughter-in-law
nuestro/a(s) *poss.* our
nueve nine
nuevo/a *adj.* new
  de nuevo again

nuez *f.* walnut
número *m.* number, (*shoe*) size
nunca *adv.* never; not ever
nutrición *f.* nutrition
nutricionista *m., f.* nutritionist

Ñ

ñame *m.* yam

O

o *conj.* or
  O te quedas o te vas. Either you stay or you go.
obedecer (c:zc) *v.t.* to obey
obesidad *f.* obesity
obeso/a *adj.* obese
objetivo/a *m.* objective; aim, goal
objeto *m.* object; purpose
  ¿Cuál es el objeto de esta discusión? What's the purpose of this argument?
obligar *v.t.* to force, to oblige; to make
  (a alguien a + *inf.*)
  No le obligues a estudiar. Don't force him to study.
  (a alguien a que + *subj.*)
  No me obligues a que lo diga. Don't make me say it.
obra *f.* (*of art, literature, music, etc.*) work
  obra maestra masterpiece
observación *f.* observation
observador(a) *adj.* observant
observatorio *m.* observatory
observar *v.t.* to observe
obtener (e:ie) *v.t. irreg.* **(yo obtengo)** to obtain; to get
océano *m.* ocean; sea

ochenta eighty
ocho eight
ochocientos/as eight hundred
ocio *m.* leisure time
ocioso/a *adj.* idle
ocre *m.* ocher
octavo/a *adj./m.* eighth
octubre *m.* October
oculista *m., f.* optician
ocupación *f.* occupation
ocupado/a *adj.* busy
ocurrir *v. impers.* to occur; to happen
  Ocurrió lo inesperado. The unexpected happened.
odiar *v.t.* to hate
oeste *m.* west
  al oeste to the west
ofender *v.t.* to offend
ofenderse *v. pron.* to take offense
ofensa *f.* insult
oferta *f.* offer
oficina *f.* office
oficio *m.* trade
ofrecer (c:zc) *v.t.* to offer
ofrenda *f.* offering
oftalmólogo/a *m., f.* ophthalmologist
oído *m.* sense of hearing; inner ear
oído *p.p. of* **oír** heard
oír (y) *v.t./v.i. irreg.* **(yo oigo)** to hear
  oiga *form., sing.* listen (*in conversation*)
  oír decir que *idiom* to have heard that **He oído decir que te casas.** I've heard that you are getting married.

oye *fam., sing.* listen (*in conversation*)

¡Ojalá! *interj.* I hope so!

Ojalá (que) + *subj.*

Ojalá que vuelva pronto.
I hope he comes back soon.

Ojalá no llueva mañana.
I hope it doesn't rain tomorrow.

ojo *m.* eye

ola *f.* wave

oler (a) *v.i. irreg.* to smell (like)

Huele a humo aquí. It smells like smoke here.

olfato *m.* (*sense*) smell

olimpiada/olimpiadas *f./f., pl.* Olympic Games, Olympics

Olimpiadas Especiales Special Olympics (*athletes with mental retardation*)

olímpico/a *adj.* olympic

olla *f.* cooking pot

olla a presión pressure cooker

olor *m.* smell, odor

el olor de la primavera the smell of spring

olor corporal body odor

olvidar *v.t.* to forget

ombligo *m.* navel

omoplato *m.* scapula

once eleven

oncólogo/a *m., f.* oncologist

onda *f.* (*physics, radio*) wave

onza *f.* ounce

opaco/a *adj.* opaque

ópera *f.* opera

operación *f.* operation

opinar *v.t.* to express an opinion

opinión *f.* opinion

en mi opinión in my opinion

oportunidad *f.* opportunity

optimista *adj./m., f.* optimist

orden *m.* order, sequence; *f.* order, command

A la orden. (*L.A.*) You are welcome.

A sus órdenes. At your service.

ordenado/a *adj.* orderly; well-organized

ordenador *m.* (*Spain*) computer

ordinal *adj.* ordinal

orégano *m.* oregano

oreja *f.* (*outer*) ear

organización *f.* organization; arrangement

organizar *v.t.* to organize; to arrange

órgano *m.* organ

órganos de los sentidos sensory organs

orgullo *m.* pride

orgulloso/a *adj.* proud

original *adj.* original

originalidad *f.* originality

orilla *f.* shore, (river)bank

La casa está a orillas del mar. The house is on the seashore.

orina *f.* urine

orinar *v.i.* to urinate

oro *m.* gold

orquesta *f.* orchestra

ortográfico/a *adj.* spelling

os *fam., pl.* you

¿Os gusta? Do you like it?

osito *m.* teddy bear

oso/a *m., f.* bear
Osa Mayor Big Dipper
Osa Menor Little Dipper
ostra *f.* oyster
otoño *m.* autumn
otro/a *adj.* other; another
otra vez again
oveja *f.* sheep
OVNI (Objeto Volador No Identificado) *m.* UFO (Unidentified Flying Object)
oxidarse *v. pron.* to rust
óxido *m.* rust
oxígeno *m.* oxygen
oyentes *m., pl.* listeners

P

paciencia *f.* patience
paciente *adj./m., f.* patient
pacifista *adj./m., f.* pacifist
padecer de (c:zc) *v.i.* (*disease*) to suffer from
Padece del corazón. He has heart problems.
padecimiento *m.* suffering
padrastro *m.* stepfather
padre *m.* father
padres *m., pl.* parents
padrino *m.* godfather
pagar *v.t.* to pay
pagar a plazos to pay in installments
pagar al contado to pay in cash
pagar en efectivo to pay in cash
pagar la cuenta to pay the bill
página *f.* page
página principal home page

país *m.* country
país desarrollado developed country
país en vías de desarrollo developing country
paisaje *m.* landscape; countryside
pájaro *m.* bird
pala *f.* shovel
palabra *f.* word
palacio *m.* palace
paladar *m.* palate
palanca *f.* lever
paleontología *f.* paleontology
paleontólogo/a *m., f.* paleontologist
pálido/a *adj.* pale, pallid
palmera *f.* palm tree
palo *m.* stick; (*golf*) club
de tal palo, tal astilla *loc.* like father, like son
paloma *f.* dove
pan *m.* bread
pan integral whole-wheat bread
pan tostado toasted bread; toast
panadería *f.* bakery
páncreas *m.* pancreas
pandilla *f.* gang
pandillero/a *m., f.* gang member
pantaletas *f., pl.* (*Venezuela*) panties
pantalla *f.* screen
pantalones *m., pl.* pants
pantalones cortos shorts
pantano *m.* (*natural*) marsh, swamp; (*man-made*) reservoir

pantorrilla *f.* (anatomy) calf
pañuelo *m.* handkerchief
papa *f.* (*L.A.*) potato
  papas fritas fried potatoes;
  french fries
papá *m.* dad
papás *m., pl.* parents
papel *m.* paper; *m.* role
  papel de aluminio tinfoil
  papel higiénico toilet paper
  hacer un buen/mal papel
  idiom to make a good/bad
  impression
papelera *f.* wastebasket
papi *m.* daddy
paquete *m.* package
par *m.* pair
  un par de días a couple of
  days
para *prep.* for; in order to
  para que so that
parabrisas *m., sing.* windshield
paracaídas *m., sing.* parachute
paracaidismo *m.* parachuting
paracaidista *m., f.* parachutist
parachoques *m., sing.* bumper
parada *f.* (*train, bus*) stop
parador *m.* lodging
paraguas *m.* umbrella
paragüero *m.* umbrella stand
parar *v.i.* to stop
pararrayos *m.* lightning rod
parásito *m.* parasite
parecer (c:zc) *v.i.* to seem; to
  appear
  al parecer *adv.* apparently,
  seemingly
**parecerse (c:zc) (a alguien/a
  algo)** *v. pron.* to look like
  (*somebody/something*); to be
  alike

¿A quién se parece? Who
does he/she look like?
pared *f.* wall
pareja *f.* partner; (*married*)
couple
  **¿Cuántas parejas vienen a
  cenar?** How many couples
  are coming for dinner?
parientes *m., pl.* relatives
párpado *m.* eyelid
parque *m.* park
  parque acuático water park
  parque de atracciones
  (*Spain*) amusement park
  parque de diversiones
  (*L.A.*) amusement park
  parque natural nature
  reserve
párrafo *m.* paragraph
parrilla *f.* grill
  a la parrilla grilled, broiled
parte *f.* part
  de parte de on behalf of
participación *f.* participation
participante *m., f.* competitor
participar *v.t.* to participate
partida *f.* departure
partido *m.* (*sports*) game,
match; (*politics*) party
partir *v.t.* to cut; *v.i.* to leave
  a partir de from, starting (on)
pasa *f.* raisin
pasado *p.p. of* **pasar** passed
pasado/a *adj.* last; past
  el pasado lunes last Monday
pasaje *m.* ticket
  pasaje de ida y vuelta
  roundtrip ticket
pasajero/a *m., f.* passenger
pasamanos *m.* handrail,
bannister

79

pasaporte *m.* passport
pasar *v.i.* to go by; to pass
  pasar la aspiradora to vacuum
  pasar por el banco to go by the bank
  pasar por la aduana to go through customs
  pasar tiempo to spend time
  pasarlo bien/mal to have a good/bad time
  pasarlo de película to have a great time
pasatiempo *m.* pastime
pasear *v.i.* to take a walk; to stroll
  pasear en bicicleta to ride a bicycle
paseo *m.* stroll, walk
pasillo *m.* hallway
paso *m.* step; way
  paso a nivel railroad crossing
  paso de peatones (*L.A.*) crosswalk
  ceder el paso to yield (the right of way)
pasta (de dientes) *f.* toothpaste
pastel *m.* cake; pie
  pastel de chocolate chocolate cake
  pastel de cumpleaños birthday cake
pastelería *f.* pastry shop
pastilla *f.* pill; tablet
patata *f.* (*Spain*) potato
  patatas fritas fried potatoes, french fries
  tortilla de patatas potato omelet

paterno/a *adj.* (*relative*) paternal
patilla *f.* sideburn
patinaje *m.* skating
  patinaje artístico figure skating
  patinaje sobre hielo ice skating
  patinaje sobre ruedas roller skating
patinar *v.i.* to skate
  patinar en línea to rollerblade
patio *m.* patio; yard
patrimonio *m.* heritage
patrocinador(a) *m., f.* sponsor
patrocinar *v.t.* to sponsor
patrón *m.* boss, owner
pavo *m.* turkey
payaso/a *m., f.* clown
paz *f.* peace
peatón *m.* pedestrian
peca *f.* freckle
pecho *m.* chest; breast
pechuga (de pollo) *f.* (chicken) breast
pecoso/a *adj.* freckled
pedagogía *f.* pedagogy
pedagógico/a *adj.* pedagogical
pedagogo/a *m., f.* pedagogue
pedal *m.* pedal
  pedal del acelerador gas pedal
  pedal del embrague clutch pedal
  pedal del freno brake pedal
pedante *adj.* pedantic
pedazo *m.* piece
pedicura *f.* pedicure
pedir (e:i) *v.t.* to ask for; to

request; (*food*) to order
pedir prestado to borrow
pedir un préstamo to apply
for a loan
peinado *m.* hairstyle; hairdo
**Su nuevo peinado le sienta
bien.** Her new hairdo suits
her.
peinarse *v. pron.* to comb one's
hair
peine *m.* comb
pelapapas *m.* peeler
pelar *v.t.* to peel
peldaño *m.* step, stair
pelea *f.* quarrel, fight
pelearse *v. pron.* to quarrel, to
fight
**Siempre se pelean por lo
mismo.** They always quarrel
over the same thing.
película *f.* movie
peligro *m.* danger
peligroso/a *adj.* dangerous
pelirrojo/a *adj.* red-headed
pelo *m.* hair
pelota *f.* ball; baseball
peluca *f.* wig
peludo/a *adj.* hairy
peluquería *f.* beauty salon
peluquero/a *m., f.* hairdresser
pena *f.* ache, grief, pity
No vale la pena. It's not
worth the trouble.
pendiente *adj.* (*problem,
matter*) unresolved
estar pendiente to be waiting
**Estoy pendiente de que el
jefe me llame.** I'm waiting for
the boss to call me.
tener (un asunto) pendiente

to have (an) unfinished
(matter)
pendientes *m.* (*Spain*) earrings
penicilina *f.* penicillin
península *f.* peninsula
penitenciaría *f.* penitentiary
pensar (e:ie) (en) *v.t.* to think
(about)
pensar + *inf.* to intend to (*do
something*)
Pienso llamarle mañana. I
intend to call him tomorrow.
pensión *f.* boardinghouse;
retirement pension
pensionista *m., f.* pensioner,
retired person
peor *adj.* worse; worst
el/la peor the worst
lo peor the worst (thing)
pepino *m.* cucumber
pequeño/a *adj.* small
pera *f.* pear
percha *f.* hanger
perchero *m.* coat hanger
perder (e:ie) *v.t.* to lose
perdido *p.p. of* perder lost;
perdido/a *adj.* lost
Perdón. Pardon me; Excuse
me.
perdonar *v.t.* to forgive
peregrinación *f.* pilgrimage
peregrino/a *m., f.* pilgrim
perejil *m.* parsley
pereza *f.* laziness
perezoso/a *adj.* lazy
perfecto/a *adj.* perfect
perfil *m.* profile
perforadora *f.* (*tool*) drill
perforar *v.t.* to drill; to
perforate

perfume *m.* perfume
perfumería *f.* perfumery
perico *m.* parakeet
perímetro *m.* perimeter
periódico *m.* newspaper
periodismo *m.* journalism
periodista *m., f.* journalist
periquito *m.* parakeet
permanecer (c:zc) *v.i.* to remain; to stay
permiso *m.* permission
 Con permiso. Pardon me., Excuse me.
 Con su permiso, tengo que irme. If you'll excuse me, I have to leave.
 permiso de trabajo work permit
permitir *v.t.* to permit, to allow
pero *conj.* but
perro *m.* dog
perseguir (e:i) *v.t. irreg.* **(yo persigo)** to pursue; to chase
persiana *f.* blind
persistente *adj.* persistent
persistir *v.i.* to persist
persona *f.* person
personaje *m.* character
 personaje principal main character
personalidad *f.* personality
pertenecer (c:zc) (a) *v.t.* to belong to
pertenencias *f., pl.* belongings
pesa *f.* weight
pesadilla *f.* nightmare
pesado/a *adj.* heavy; annoying
pesar *m.* sorrow
 a pesar de despite, in spite of

pesar *v.t.* to weigh
pesarse *v. pron.* to weigh oneself
pesca *f.* fishing
pescadería *f.* fish market
pescado *m.* (*cooked*) fish
pescador *m.* fisherman
pescar *v.i.* to fish
pesimista *adj.* pessimist
peso *m.* weight
pestaña *f.* eyelash
pesticida *m.* pesticide
pétalo *m.* petal
petrificado/a *adj.* petrified
pez *m.* (*live*) fish
 pez gordo big shot
picante *adj.* spicy
pico *m.* beak
pie *m.* foot
piedra *f.* stone
piel *f.* skin
 de piel (made of) leather
pierna *f.* leg
píldora *f.* pill
pimienta *f.* black pepper
pimiento *m.* bell pepper
pinacoteca *f.* art gallery
pinar *m.* pine forest
pinchar *v.t.* (*tire*) to go flat
pingüino *m.* penguin
pino *m.* pine tree
pintada *f.* graffiti
 Hay pintadas de pandillas en la pared. There is gang graffiti on the wall.
pintalabios *m.* lipstick
pintar *v.t.* to paint
pintor(a) *m., f.* painter
pintoresco/a *adj.* picturesque
pintura *f.* painting

piña f. pineapple

piragua f. canoe

piragüismo m. (sport) canoeing

piragüista m., f. canoeist

pirámide f. pyramid

piropear v.t. to make flattering comments

piropo m. flattering comment

piscina f. swimming pool
  piscina climatizada indoor pool

piso m. (of a building) floor, story; (L.A.) floor; (Spain) apartment

pista f. track; clue
  Dame una pista. Give me a clue.
  pista cubierta indoor track
  pista de aterrizaje landing strip
  pista de atletismo sports track
  pista de baile dance floor
  pista de esquí ski slope
  pista de hielo ice rink
  pista de hierba grass court
  pista de patinaje skating rink
  pista de tenis tennis court
  pista de tierra batida clay court

pizarra f. blackboard

pizca f. (quantity) pinch, little bit

placa (de matrícula) f. license plate

placer m. pleasure; delight
  Ha sido un placer. It's been a pleasure

plagiar v.t. to plagiarize

plagio m. plagiarism

plancha f. (appliance) iron; griddle
  a la plancha grilled

planchar v.t. (clothes) to iron

plan m. plan

planeta m. planet

planetario m. planetarium

plano m. (architecture) blueprint; city map

plano/a adj. (surface) flat

planta f. plant; (building) floor
  planta baja ground floor

plantado/a: dejar plantado/a (a alguien) to stand (somebody) up

plástico m. plastic
  de plástico (made of) plastic

plata f. silver

plátano m. banana; plantain

plateado/a adj. silver

plato m. plate; (meal) dish, course
  plato principal main dish/main course

playa f. beach

plaza f. (city) square
  plaza de toros bullring
  plaza mayor town square

plazo m. (time) period, (payments) installment

plegable adj. folding

plegar v.t. to fold

plomería f. (L.A.) plumbing

plomero/a m., f. (L.A.) plumber

plomo m. lead

pluma f. pen; feather

pluralidad f. plurality

pluralismo m. plurarism

población f. population

poblar (o:ue) v.t. to populate

pobre *adj.* poor
pobreza *f.* poverty
poco/a *adj.* little; few
poder (o:ue) *v. aux.* to be able to; can
poderoso/a *adj.* powerful
podio *m.* podium
poema *m.* poem
poesía *f.* poetry
poeta *m., f.* poet
polémica *f.* controversy
polémico/a *adj.* controversial, polemical
   El aborto es aún un tema polémico. Abortion is still a controversial topic.
polen *m.* pollen
policía *f.* police (force); *m., f.* police officer
polideportivo *m.* sports center
política *f.* politics
político/a *m., f.* politician
pollo *m.* chicken
   pollo asado roast chicken
polvo *m.* dust
pomelo *m.* (*Argentina, Spain*) grapefruit
ponchera *f.* punchbowl
poner *v.t. irreg.* **(yo pongo)** to put; to place; *v.i.* to turn on (*electrical appliances*)
   poner a uno al día/al corriente *idiom* to bring someone up to date
   poner en libertad (a alguien) to release (*somebody*)
   poner la mesa to set the table
   poner una inyección to give an injection

ponerse (+ adj.) *v. pron. irreg.* **(yo me pongo)** to become (+ *adj.*); to put on clothing
   ponerse elegante to dress up
   Te has puesto muy elegante esta noche. You have dressed up tonight.
   ponerse rojo/a to blush
por *prep.* for; for the sake of; for; by; in; through; due to; in exchange
   por aquí around here
   por ejemplo for example
   por eso that's why; therefore
   Por favor. Please.
   por fin finally
   por la mañana in the morning
   por la noche at night
   por la tarde in the afternoon
   por lo menos at least
   por lo visto apparently
   ¿por qué? why?
   por supuesto of course
   por teléfono by phone; on the phone
   por último finally
porcentaje *m.* percentage
porche *m.* porch
porción *f.* serving
porque *conj.* because
portaaviones *m., sing.* aircraft carrier
portarse *v. pron.* to behave oneself
   portarse bien/mal to behave well/badly
portátil *adj.* portable
portavoz *m., f.* spokesperson

portero/a *m., f.* doorman, porter
porvenir *m.* future
poseer *v.t.* to own
posesión *f.* possession
posesivo/a *adj.* possessive
posible *adj.* possible
  lo antes posible as soon as possible
postal *f.* postcard
postre *m.* dessert
potencia *f.* power
pozo *m.* well
práctica *f.* practice
practicar *v.i.* to practice
  practicar deportes to play sports
práctico/a *adj.* handy; useful
precaución *f.* precaution
precio *m.* price
predecir (e:i) *v.t. irreg.* **(yo predigo)** to predict, to foretell
predicción *f.* predicction
  predicción del tiempo weather forecast
prefabricado/a *adj.* prefabricated
prefabricar *v.t.* to prefabricate
preferir (e:ie) *v.t.* to prefer
pregunta *f.* question
preguntar *v.t.* to ask (*a question*)
premiar *v.t.* to award
premio *m.* prize; award
prenda *f.* garment
  Colgaron las prendas en el armario. They hung up the garments in the wardrobe.
prensa *f.* press
preocupado/a *adj.* worried

preocuparse (por) *v. pron.* to worry (about)
  No se/te preocupe(s). Don't worry.
preparar *v.t.* to prepare
prepararse *v. pron.* to get ready
preparativos *m., pl.* preparations
  los preparativos del viaje/para la boda the travel/wedding preparations
preposición *f.* preposition
presa *f.* prey
presentación *f.* introduction
presentador(a) *m., f.* presenter
presentar *v.t.* to introduce; (*performance*) to put on
  Le presento a… *form.* I would like to introduce you to…
presidiario/a *m., f.* convict
presión *f.* pressure
  las presiones de la vida diaria pressures of daily life
  presión sanguínea blood pressure
preso/a *m., f.* prisoner
prestado/a *adj.* borrowed
préstamo *m.* loan
prestar *v.t.* to lend
presumido/a *adj.* vain
presupuesto *m.* budget
pretencioso/a *adj.* pretentious
pretexto *m.* excuse
prevención *f.* prevention
prevenir (e:ie) *v.t. irreg.* **(yo prevengo)** to prevent
primavera *f.* spring

primer, primero/a *adj.* first
  en primer lugar *adv.* firstly
primitivo/a *adj.* primitive
primo/a *m., f.* cousin
primogénito/a *m., f.* firstborn
principal *adj.* main
príncipe *m.* prince
princesa *f.* princess
prisa *f.* haste; hurry
  a toda prisa as fast as
  possible
  ¡De prisa! Hurry!
  sin prisa pero sin pausa
  slowly but surely
prisión *f.* prison
probable *adj.* probable
probador *m.* dressing room
probar (o:ue) *v.t.* to taste; to try
probarse (o:ue) *v. pron.*
  (*clothes*) to try on
problema *m.* problem
prodigio/a *m., f.* prodigy
prodigioso/a *adj.* exceptional
productos *m., pl.* products
  productos alimenticios
  foodstuffs
  productos lácteos dairy
  (products)
profesión *f.* profession
profesor(a) *m., f.* teacher;
  professor
  profesor(a) particular tutor
profundidad *f.* depth
profundo/a *adj.* deep
programa *m.* program
  programa de computación
  software
  programa de entrevistas talk
  show
programador(a) *m., f.*
programmer
prohibido *p.p. of* **prohibir**
prohibited
  prohibido adelantar (*traffic
  sign*) passing prohibited
  prohibido el paso (*traffic
  sign*) no entry
prohibir *v.t.* to prohibit; to
forbid
prolífico/a *adj.* prolific
promedio *m.* average
promesa *f.* promise
prometer *v.t.* to promise
pronombre *m.* pronoun
pronto *adj.* soon
propagar *v.t.* to propagate, to
spread, to disseminate
  **Algunos periódicos
  propagan rumores.** Some
  papers disseminate rumors.
propagarse *v. pron.* to
propagate, to spread
  **El rumor se propagaba
  rápidamente.** The rumor was
  propagating rapidly.
propenso/a a *adj.* prone to
propiedad *f.* property
propietario/a *m., f.* owner,
proprietor
propina *f.* tip
propio/a *adj.* own
proponer *v.t. irreg.* **(yo
propongo)** to propose
propósito *m.* intention; purpose
  a propósito *adv.* on purpose,
  deliberately
  a propósito by the way
  buenos propósitos good
  intentions
propuesta *f.* proposal

protección *f.* protection
proteger (g:j) *v.t.* to protect
proteína *f.* protein
protesta *f.* protest
protestante *adj./m., f.* Protestant
protestar *v.i.* to protest
provecho *m.* benefit
  ¡Buen provecho! Enjoy your meal!
provisiones *f., pl.* provisions, supplies
provocación *f.* provocation
provocado/a *adj.* induced
provocar *v.t.* to cause; to provoke
próximo/a *adj.* next
proyección *f.* projection
proyectar *v.t.* to project
proyectil *m.* missile
proyecto *m.* project
prueba *f.* test; quiz
  prueba de aptitud aptitude test
  prueba de la alcoholemia sobriety test
  prueba de nivel placement test
psicología *f.* psychology
psicólogo/a *m., f.* psychologist
psiquiatra *m., f.* psychiatrist
pubertad *f.* puberty
publicar *v.t.* to publish
público *m.* audience
pueblo *m.* town
puente *m.* bridge
  puente colgante suspension bridge
puerta *f.* door
  puerta principal front door

puerta trasera back door
puerto *m.* port, harbor
Puerto Rico *m.* Puerto Rico
puertorriqueño/a *adj./m., f.* Puerto Rican
pues *conj.* well; *adv.* then
puesto *m.* position; job; *p.p. of* **poner** put
puesta *f.* **de sol** sunset
pulgar *m.* thumb
pulmón *m.* lung
pulpo *m.* octopus
pulsera *f.* bracelet
punto *m.* point, period
  en punto (*time*) on the dot, exactly, sharp
puntual *adj.* punctual
puñal *m.* dagger
puñalada *f.* stab
puño *m.* fist
pupila *f.* pupil
puro/a *adj.* pure; *adv.* sheer; *m.* cigar
  aceite puro de oliva pure olive oil
  pura casualidad sheer coincidence

Q

que *pron.* that; who; *conj.* that; (*in exclamations*) what; how
  ¡Qué alto eres! How tall you are!
  ¡Qué dolor! What pain!
  ¡Qué extraño! How strange!
  ¡Qué grande! How big!
  ¡Qué gusto (+ inf.)! What a pleasure to . . . !
  ¡Qué lata! *loc.* What a drag!

¡Qué ropa más bonita! What pretty clothes!

¡Qué sorpresa! What a surprise!

¿qué? *adv.* what?

¿Qué día es hoy? What day is it?

¿Qué hay de nuevo? What's new?

¿Qué hora es? What time is it?

¿Qué les parece? What do you (*pl.*) think?

¿Qué pasa? What's happening?; What's going on?

¿Qué pasó? What happened?; What's wrong?

¿Qué precio tiene? What is the price?

¿Qué tal? How are you?; How is it going?

¿Qué tal...? How is/are . . . ?

¿Qué talla lleva/usa? What size do you take?

¿Qué tiempo hace? What's the weather like?

quedar *v.i.* to be left over; (*clothing*) to fit; to be located

Ese vestido te queda muy bien. That dress fits you nicely.

¿Dónde queda la panadería? Where's the bakery (located)?

quedarse *v. pron.* to stay; to remain

¡Quédate! Stay!

quedarse calvo to go bald

quedarse embarazada to get pregnant

quedarse soltero/a to stay single

quedarse viudo/a to be widowed

quehaceres *m., pl.* chores

quehaceres domésticos household chores

queja *f.* complaint

quejarse (de) *v. pron.* to complain (about)

quemado/a *adj.* burned; (*figurative*) burned out

quemar *v.t.* to burn

No quemes la ropa vieja. Don't burn old clothes.

querer (e:ie) *v.t.* to want; to love

Quisiera un café. I would like a coffee.

querido/a *adj.* beloved

queso *m.* cheese

quien *pron.* who; whom **Ella es quien me lo dijo.** She's the one who told me.

¿quién(es)? who?; whom?

¿Quién es...? Who is . . . ?

¿Quién habla? Who is speaking? (*telephone*)

química *f.* chemistry

químico/a *adj.* chemical; *m., f.* chemist

quince fifteen

quinceañero/a *m., f.* fifteen-year-old; teenager

fiesta de quinceañera young woman's fifteenth birthday celebration

quincena *f.* two weeks, fortnight

quinientos/as five hundred
quinto/a *adj./m.* fifth
quirófano *m.* operating room
quitar *v.t.* to take away
  El policía me quitó los documentos. The police officer took away my documents.
  quitar la mesa to clear the table
quitarse *v. pron.* (*clothes*) to take off
  Quítate esos zapatos. Take those shoes off.
quizás *adv.* perhaps

R

rábano *m.* radish
rabino/a *m., f.* rabbi
racismo *m.* racism
racista *adj./m., f.* racist
radio *f.* (*medium*) radio; *m.* (*set*) radio
radiografía *f.* X-ray
radioyente *m., f.* radio listener
raíz *f.* root
rallador *m.* grater
rama *f.* branch
rana *f.* frog
rápido/a *adj.* fast; *adv.* quickly
  comida rápida fast food
  ¡Ven rápido! Come quickly!
raqueta *f.* (*sports*) racket
rascacielos *m.* skyscraper
rastrillo *m.* rake
rasuradora *f.* razor
rato *m.* while **Espera un rato, por favor.** Wait a while, please.
  ratos libres *m., pl.* spare time

ratón *m.* mouse
  ratón de biblioteca bookworm
raya *f.* stripe
  de rayas striped
  una camisa de rayas a striped shirt
rayo *m.* lightning bolt
raza *f.* race
razón *f.* reason
  Lo hice por dos razones. I did it for two reasons.
  Tienes razón. You're right.
  No tienes razón. You're wrong.
reacción *f.* reaction
reaccionar *v.i.* to react
real *adj.* royal
realeza *f.* royalty
realizar *v.t.* to carry out; to make
rebaja *f.* sale
  de rebaja reduced
rebanada *f.* slice
  una rebanada de pan a slice of bread
rebobinar *v.t.* to rewind
  Apriete el botón de rebobinar. Push the rewind button.
recado *m.* (*phone*) message
  dejar un recado to leave a message
recaudar (fondos) *v.t.* to raise (money)
receloso/a *adj.* distrustful
recepción *f.* front desk
receta *f.* prescription; (*cooking*) recipe

recetar *v.t.* (*medication*) to prescribe

rechazar *v.t.* to reject

rechazo *m.* rejection

recibir *v.t.* to receive; to get

recibo *m.* receipt; bill
  el recibo del teléfono the phone bill

reciclaje *m.* recycling

reciclar *v.t.* to recycle

recién *adv.* just
  recién casado/a newlywed
  recién nacido/a newborn (baby)
  recién pintado/a wet paint

recipiente *m.* container

recital *m.* (*music, poetry*) recital

recoger (g:j) *v.t.* to pick up

recomendable *adj.* advisable

recomendar (e:ie) *v.t.* to recommend

reconocer (c:zc) *v.t.* to recognize

reconocimiento *m.* recognition

récord *m.* (*sports*) record

recordar (o:ue) *v.t.* to remember

recorrer *v.t.* to tour around an area

recreo *m.* recess

rectángulo *m.* rectangle

rectificar *v.t.* to rectify

recuerdo *m.* souvenir

recuerdos *m., pl.* regards

recurso *m.* resource
  recurso natural natural resource

red *f.* net; network; Internet

reducir (c:zc) *v.t.* to reduce

reemplazar *v.t.* to replace

reflexionar *v.i.* to reflect

reforma *f.* reform

reformar *v.t.* to reform

reforzar (o:ue) *v.t.* to reinforce

refrán *m.* saying

refrescante *adj.* refreshing

refresco *m.* soft drink

refrigerador *m.* refrigerator

refrigerar *v.t.* to refrigerate

refuerzo *m.* reinforcement

regadera *f.* watering can

regalar *v.t.* to give (*as a gift*)

regalo *m.* gift, present

regar *v.t.* (*plants*) to water

regatear *v.i.* to bargain

régimen *m.* diet
  Está a régimen. She's on a diet.

región *f.* region; area

regla *f.* rule; ruler

regresar *v.i.* to return

regular *adj.* regular; so-so; OK

regular *v.t.* to regulate

regularización *f.* regularization

reído *p.p.* of **reír** laughed

reina *f.* queen

reinar *v.i.* to reign

reino *m.* kingdom

reírse (e:i) *v.i.* (**yo río**) to laugh

reírse (e:i) (de) *v. pron.* (**yo me río**) to laugh (about)

rejuvenecer (c:zc) *v.t.* to rejuvenate

rejuvenecimiento *m.* rejuvenation

relación *f.* relationship

relajación *f.* relaxation

relajarse *v. pron.* to relax

relámpago *m.* lightning bolt

religión *f.* religion
religioso/a *adj.* religious
rellenar *v.t.* (*culinary*) to stuff; (*document*) (*Spain*) to fill out
relleno *m.* stuffing
relleno/a (de) *adj.* stuffed (with)
  Me encantan los chiles rellenos de queso rallado. I love chilies stuffed with grated cheese.
reloj *m.* clock; watch
remar *v.i.* to row
remedio *m.* remedy
remero/a *m., f.* rower
remo *m.* oar
remolacha *f.* beet
remolino *m.* whirlpool; whirlwind
remover (o:ue) *v.t.* to stir
renacentista *adj.* Renaissance
renacimiento *m.* Renaissance
rencor *m.* grudge, resentment, hard feelings
  Todavía siente rencor por lo que le hicieron. She still resents what they did to her.
rencoroso/a *adj.* resentful
renglón *m.* line
  papel con renglones lined paper
renovación *f.* renewal, updating, renovation
renovar (o:ue) *v.t.* to renew, to change, to renovate
renunciar (a) *v.t.* to resign (from)
repelente *m.* (*for insects*) repellent
repente: de repente *adv.* suddenly
repetir (e:i) *v.t.* to repeat
repollo *m.* (*L.A.*) cabbage
reportaje *m.* report
reportero/a *m., f.* reporter; journalist
reposar *v.i.* to rest
  Tenía que reposar por varias semanas después de la operación. He had to rest for several weeks after the operation.
reposo *m.* rest
represa *f.* dam
represión *f.* repression
reprimir *v.t.* to repress
  Tuvo que reprimir la emoción. He had to repress his emotion.
reprimirse *v. pron. (refl.)* to control oneself
reproducir (c:zc) *v.t.* to repeat, to reproduce
  Es difícil reproducir los resultados. It's difficult to reproduce the results.
reproducirse (c:zc) *v. pron. (biology)* to reproduce; to happen again
  Es improbable que se reproduzcan tales circunstancias. It's unlikely that such circumstances will happen again.
reptil *m.* reptile
resaca *f.* (*Spain*) hangover
  tener resaca to have a hangover
rescatar *v.t.* to rescue
rescate *m.* rescue

reservación *f.* reservation
  hacer una reservación to
  book
reservado/a *adj.* reserved
resfriado *m.* cold
residencia *f.* residence
  residencia de ancianos
  home for the elderly
  residencia estudiantil
  dormitory
residente *adj./m., f.* resident
residir *v.i.* to live, to reside
resistencia *f.* resistance
resistir *v.t.* to resist
resolución *f.* (*problem*)
  solution; (*conflict*) settlement
resolver (o:ue) *v.t.* to resolve;
  to solve
respaldar *v.t.* (*person,
  decision*) to back, to support
respecto: con respecto a with
  regard to, regarding
respetar *v.t.* to respect
respeto *m.* respect
respiración *f.* breathing,
  respiration
  respiración boca a boca
  mouth-to-mouth
  resuscitation
respirar *v.i.* to breathe
responder *v.t.* to respond, to
  answer
respuesta *f.* answer
restaurante *m.* restaurant
restaurar *v.t.* to restore
restos *m., pl.* leftovers
resuelto *p.p. of* **resolver**
  resolved
resultado *m.* result
resumen *m.* summary

en resumen in summary
resumir *v.t.* to summarize
  resumiendo summarizing
retar (a alguien a + *inf.*) *v.t.*
  to challenge (somebody to
  + *inf.*)
  Me retó a imitarle. He
  challenged me to imitate him.
reto *m.* challenge
  **El gran reto de nuestro siglo
  es acabar con la pobreza.**
  The great challenge of our
  century is to end poverty.
retórica *f.* rhetoric
retórico/a *adj.* rhetorical
retraído/a *adj.* withdrawn
retrasarse *v.i.* to be late
retraso *m.* delay
retrato *m.* portrait, photograph
  of people
retrovisor *m.* rearview mirror
reumatismo *m.* rheumatism
reunión *f.* meeting
revelar *v.t.* to reveal;
  (*photography*) to develop
revés: al revés *adv.* the other
  way around; backward(s)
revisar *v.t.* to check
  revisar el aceite to check
  the oil
revisión *f.* (*Spain*) (medical)
  checkup
revista *f.* magazine
rey *m.* king
rezar *v.i.* to pray
riachuelo *m.* stream, brook
rico/a *adj.* rich; (*food*) tasty,
  delicious
ridículo/a *adj.* ridiculous
  Es ridículo que (+ *subj.*) It's

ridiculous that…
Es ridículo que llores. It's ridiculous that you cry.
rincón *m.* (*inside*) corner
rinoceronte *m.* rhinoceros
riñón *m.* kidney
río *m.* river
riquísimo/a *adj.* (*superlative*) extremely delicious
risa *f.* laughter
　morirse/partirse de risa to die laughing
robar *v.t.* to rob; to steal
roble *m.* oak tree
robo *m.* robbery; theft
rocío *m.* dew
rodaja *f.* slice
　hamburguesa con queso y rodajas de cebolla a hamburger with cheese and sliced onions
rodaje *m.* (*cinema*) filming, shooting
rodar *v.t.* (*cinema*) to shoot, to film
rodilla *f.* knee
rogar (o:ue) *v.t.* to beg; to plead
rojizo/a *adj.* reddish
rojo/a *adj./m.* red
　al rojo vivo red-hot
　La situación está al rojo vivo. The situation is at the boiling point.
románico/a *adj.* Romanesque
romano/a *adj./m., f.* Roman
romanticismo *m.* Romanticism
romántico/a *adj./m., f.* romantic
romero *m.* rosemary
rompecabezas *m., sing.* puzzle
rompeolas *m.* breakwater

romper *v.t./v.i.* to break; to break up
　romper el hielo *loc.* break the ice
　¿Han roto? Have they broken up?
romperse *v. pron.* to break
　Se rompió la pierna. He broke his leg.
ron *m.* rum
roncar *v.i.* to snore
ronquido *m.* snore
ropa *f.* clothing; clothes
　ropa deportiva sportswear
　ropa interior underwear
ropero *m.* wardrobe
rosa *f.* rose
rosado/a *adj./m.* pink
rosal *m.* rosebush
roto/a *adj.* broken
rubí *m.* ruby
rubio/a *m., f.* blond(e)
rueda *f.* wheel
　rueda de recambio spare tire
　rueda de repuesto spare tire
rugido *m.* roar
rugir (g:j) *v.i.* to roar
ruido *m.* noise
ruidoso/a *adj.* noisy
ruleta *f.* roulette
rumor *m.* rumor
ruta *f.* route
rutina *f.* routine
　rutina diaria daily routine

S

sábado *m.* Saturday
sábana *f.* sheet

saber *v.t. irreg.* **(yo sé)** to know; to know how to; *m.* knowledge
  saber (a) to taste like
  Sabe a limón. It tastes like lemon.
sabiduría *f.* wisdom
sabihondo/a *adj./m., f.* know-it-all
sabio/a *adj.* learned, wise; *m., f.* wise person
sabor *m.* flavor
sabrosísimo/a *adj.* (*superlative*) extremely delicious
sabroso/a *adj.* tasty; delicious
sacacorchos *m.* corkscrew
sacar *v.t.* to take out
  sacar fotos to take pictures
  sacar la basura to take out the trash
  sacar una muela to extract a tooth; to pull a tooth
saco *m.* bag, sack
  saco de dormir sleeping bag
sacudir *v.t.* to shake; to dust
  sacudir el polvo to dust
  sacudir los muebles to dust the furniture
saga *f.* saga
sagrado/a *adj.* sacred
sal *f.* salt
sala *f.* living room; room
  sala de emergencia emergency room
salado/a *adj.* salty
salario *m.* salary
salchicha *f.* sausage
salero *m.* salt shaker
salida *f.* departure; exit

callejón sin salida dead-end street
  salida del sol sunrise
salir *v.i. irreg.* **(yo salgo)** to leave; to go out
  salir con to go out with; to date (*someone*)
  salir de to leave from
  salir para to leave for (*a place*)
salmón *m.* salmon
salón *m.* hall; salon; classroom
  salón de actos auditorium
  salón de belleza beauty salon
salsa *f.* sauce
saltar *v.i.* to jump
saltear *v.t.* to sauté
salto *m.* jump
  salto alto (*L.A.*) high jump
  salto de altura (*Spain*) high jump
  salto de longitud (*Spain*) long jump
  salto largo (*L.A.*) long jump
  salto mortal somersault
salud *f.* health
saludable *adj.* healthy
saludar *v.t.* to greet, to say hello
saludarse *v. pron.* to greet (each other), to say hello (to each other)
  ¿No se saludan? They don't say hello to each other?
saludo *m.* greeting
  Saludos. (*in a letter*) Best wishes.
  Saludos a tu padre. Give my regards to your father.

salvaje *adj.* (*animal, flower*) wild
salvamento *m.* rescue
salvar *v.t.* to save
salvavidas *m., f.* lifeguard; *m.* life jacket
salvia *f.* sage
sandalia *f.* sandal
sandía *m.* watermelon
sándwich *m.* sandwich
sangre *f.* blood
sanguíneo/a *adj.* blood
sano/a *adj.* healthy
sapo *m.* toad
sarampión *m.* measles
sardina *f.* sardine
sartén *f.* frying pan
sastre *m.* tailor
satisfecho/a *adj.* satisfied
sauna *f.* sauna
savia *f.* (*botany*) sap
se *pron.* himself, herself, itself, *form.* yourself, themselves, yourselves
se one; on one; on us
  Se pueden comprar boletos aquí. One can buy tickets here.
  Se nos dañó el auto. The car broke down on us.
  Se nos pinchó una llanta. We had a flat tire.
secador *m.* hairdryer
secadora *f.* clothes dryer
secar *v.t.* to dry
sección *f.* section
  sección de (no) fumadores *f.* (no) smoking section
seco/a *adj.* dry
secretario/a *m., f.* secretary

secuencia *f.* sequence
secuestrar *v.t.* (*person*) to kidnap; (*airplane*) to hijack
secuestro *m.* kidnapping; hijack
sed *f.* thirst
seda *f.* silk
  de seda (made of) silk
sedentario/a *adj.* sedentary; related to sitting
sediento/a *adj.* thirsty
sedimentación *f.* sedimentation
sedimento *m.* sediment
seducir (c:zc) *v.t.* to seduce; to captivate
seductor(a) *adj.* seductive; *m.* seducer, *f.* seductress
seguir (e:i) *v.t.* (**yo sigo**) to follow; to continue
según *prep.* according to
segundo/a *adj./m.* second
  en segundo lugar *adv.* secondly
seguro *m.* insurance
  seguro médico medical insurance
seguro/a *adj.* sure; safe
  (No) Es seguro que (+ *subj.*) It's (not) sure that…
  No es seguro que lo tenga. He may not have it.
seis six
seiscientos/as six hundred
seleccionar *v.t.* to select
selecto/a *adj.* select
sello *m.* stamp
selva *f.* jungle
semáforo *m.* traffic signal

95

semana *f.* week
  semana entrante/que viene next week
  Semana Santa Holy Week
semántica *f.* semantics
semejante *adj.* similar
semestre *m.* semester
semilla *f.* seed
seminario *m.* seminar
senado *m.* senate
sencillo/a *adj.* simple; (*person*) modest
sendero *m.* trail; trailhead
sensatez *f.* good sense
sensato/a *adj.* sensible
sensibilidad *f.* sensitivity
sensible *adj.* sensitive
sentar (e:ie) *v.i.* (*clothes*) to suit
  Esa chaqueta te sienta bien. That jacket suits you.
sentarse (e:ie) *v. pron.* to sit down
sentido *m.* sense
  sentido común common sense
  sentido del orden sense of order
sentimental *adj.* sentimental
sentir (e:ie) *v.t.* to feel
  Lo siento. I'm sorry.
sentirse (e:ie) *v. pron.* to feel
  Me siento bien/mal. I feel good/bad.
señal *f.* sign
  señal de alto stop sign
  señal de tráfico traffic sign
señor (Sr.) *m.* Mr.; sir
señora (Sra.) *f.* Mrs.; ma'am
señorita (Srta.) *f.* Miss

separar *v.t.* to separate
separarse (de) *v. pron.* to separate (from)
septiembre *m.* September
séptimo/a *adj./m.* seventh
sequía *f.* drought
ser *m.* being
  ser humano human being
  ser vivo living being
ser *v. irreg.* to be
  sea lo que sea *loc.* be that as it may
  ser aficionado/a (a) to be a fan (of)
  ser alérgico/a (a) to be allergic (to)
  ser gratis to be free of charge
serio/a *adj.* serious
serpentina *f.* streamer
serpiente *f.* snake
  serpiente de cascabel rattlesnake
serrar *v.t.* to saw
servicio *m.* service
servilleta *f.* napkin
servir (e:i) *v.i.* to serve; to help
sesenta sixty
setecientos/as seven hundred
setenta seventy
seto *m.* hedge
seudónimo *m.* pseudonym, pen name
sexismo *m.* sexism
sexto/a *adj./m.* sixth
sí *adv.* yes
si *(conj.)* if
SIDA (síndrome de inmunodeficiencia adquirida) *m.* AIDS

sido *p.p. of* **ser** been

sidra *f.* cider

siempre *adv.* always
siempre que (+ *subj.*) whenever **Voy siempre que puedo.** I go whenever I can.
siempre y cuando (+ *subj.*) provided (that) **Iré siempre y cuando vengas conmigo.** I'll go provided you come with me.

sien *f.* (*anatomy*) temple

sierra *f.* saw

siesta *f.* afternoon nap

siete seven

siglo *m.* century

significar *v.t.* to mean

siguiente *adj.* next, following

silbar *v.i.* to whistle

silbato *m.* whistle

silenciador *m.* (*automobile*) muffler

silencio *m.* silence

silla *f.* seat
silla de ruedas wheel chair

sillón *m.* armchair

silvestre *adj.* (*flower, plant*) wild

simbiosis *f.* symbiosis

simbolizar *v.t.* symbolize

similar *adj.* similar

simpático/a *adj.* (*person*) nice; likeable

sin *prep.* without
sin (+ *inf.*) without (+ *-ing*)
sin hablar without talking
sin que *conj.* without
sin ton ni son *adv.* without rhyme or reason

sinagoga *f.* sinagogue

sinfín *m.* a great many, a lot
Aún tiene un sinfín de cosas que hacer. He still has a lot of things to do.

sinfonía *f.* symphony

sinfónica *f.* symphony orchestra

sinfónico/a *adj.* symphonic

sino *conj.* but
No una sino dos. Not one but two.

sinónimo/a *m.* synonym; *adj.* synonymous

sintaxis *f.* syntax

síntoma *m.* symptom

sinvergüenza *m., f.* shameless person; scoundrel

sistema *m.* system
sistema inmunológico immune system

sitio *m.* place; site; Web site

situado/a *p.p. of* **situar** located

sobrar *v.t.* to be left over
Sobró mucho dinero. There was a lot of money left over.

sobras *m., pl.* leftovers

sobre *m.* envelope; *prep.* on; over

sobreestimar *v.t.* overestimate

sobrehumano/a *adj.* superhuman

sobrenombre *m.* nickname

sobresaliente *adj.* outstanding; *m.* (*grade*) excellent

sobresalir *v.i. irreg.* **(yo sobresalgo)** to excel, to stand out

sobrevalorar *v.t.* to overvalue; to overrate

sobrino/a *m.* nephew; *f.* niece

sobrio/a *adj.* sober
sociable *adj.* sociable
socializar *v.i.* to socialize
sociedad *f.* society
sociología *f.* sociology
sociólogo/a *m., f.* sociologist
socorrer *v.t.* to help
socorro *m.* help; *interj.* Help!
sodio *m.* sodium
sofá *m.* couch; sofa
sofocar *v.t.* (*fire*) to suffocate, to put out; (*weather*) to be stifling
 El calor me sofoca. The heat is stifling.
sofoco *m.* suffocation
sol *m.* sun
solamente *adv.* only
solario *m.* solarium
soldadura *f.* weld
soldar (o:ue) *v.t.* to weld
soleado/a *adj.* sunny
soler (o:ue) + inf. *v.i.* usually; to be accustomed to
 Suelo desayunar sólo café con leche. I usually just have coffee with milk for breakfast.
 Suelo ir los domingos. I usually go on Sundays.
solicitar *v.t.* to apply (*for a job*)
solicitud (de trabajo) *f.* (job) application
sollozar *v.i.* to sob
sollozo *m.* sob
solo *adj.* alone
sólo *adv.* only
 Sólo sé que estoy solo. I only know that I'm alone.
soltar (o:ue) *v.t.* to release; to let go

soltero/a *adj.* single; unmarried
soltura *f.* ease, agility
solución *f.* solution
solucionar *v.t.* to solve
sombra *f.* shade, shadow
sombrero *m.* hat
sombrilla *f.* sunshade, beach umbrella
someterse a *v. pron.* (*test, examination*) to undergo
sonar (o:ue) *v.t.* to ring; (*alarm*) to go off
sonreído *p.p.* of **sonreír** smiled
sonreír (e:i) *v.i.* to smile
sonrisa *f.* smile
soñar (o:ue) *v.t.* to dream; *v.i.*
 soñar con algo to dream about something
 soñar despierto to daydream
sopa *f.* soup
soportar *v.t.* to support, to withstand, to endure
 No lo soporto más. I can't take it any more.
soprano *m., f.* soprano
sorbete *m.* sorbet
sorbo *m.* sip
sordo/a *adj.* deaf
sorprender *v.t.* to surprise
sorprenderse *v. pron.* to be surprised
 Se sorprendió al verme. He was surprised to see me.
sorpresa *f.* surprise
 por sorpresa *adv.* by surprise
sortija *f.* ring
soso/a *adj.* (*culinary*) bland, tasteless; (*person*) boring, dull

sospecha *f.* suspicion
sospechar (algo) *v.t.;* **(de alguien)** *v.i.* to suspect
sospechoso/a *adj.* suspicious
sostener (e:ie) *v.t. irreg.* **(yo sostengo)** support
sótano *m.* basement; cellar
su(s) *poss.* his; her; *form.* your; their
suave *adj.* (*to the touch*) soft; (*taste*) mild
subir *v.t.* to go up; to get on/in (*a vehicle*)
subjetivo/a *adj.* subjective
submarino *m.* submarine
subrayado *adj.* underlined
subrayar *v.t.* to underline
subterráneo/a *adj.* underground, subterranean
sucesivamente *adv.* successively
y así sucesivamente and so forth
sucio/a *adj.* dirty
sucre *m.* Ecuadorian currency
sudado/a *adj.* sweaty
sudamericano/a *adj./m., f.* South American
sudar *v.i.* to sweat
suegro/a *m.* father-in-law; *f.* mother-in-law
sueldo *m.* salary
suelo *m.* floor
sueño *m.* sleep
suerte *f.* luck
suéter *m.* sweater
sufrir *v.t.* to suffer **Sufre muchas presiones.** He's under a lot of pressure.
sufrir una enfermedad to suffer from an illness **Sufre una grave enfermedad.** He has a serious illness.
sugerencia *f.* suggestion
sugerir (e:ie) *v.t.* to suggest
suicidarse *v. pron.* to commit suicide
suicidio *m.* suicide
sujetador *m.* (*Spain*) *m.* bra
sumamente *adv.* extremely
suministrador(a) *m., f.* supplier
suministrar *v.t.* to supply
suministro *m.* supply; *m., pl.* supplies
suntuoso/a *adj.* sumptuous
superar *v.t.* to exceed, to go beyond; to overcome **La realidad supera la ficción.** Truth is stranger than fiction.
superarse *v. pron.* to better oneself
supermercado *m.* supermarket
superstición *f.* superstition
supersticioso/a *adj.* superstitious
supervisar *v.t.* to supervise
supervivencia *f.* survival
superviviente *m., f.* survivor
suponer *v.t. irreg.* **(yo supongo)** to suppose; to assume
sur *m.* south
al sur to the south
surtido *m.* assortment; variety
suspender *v.t.* (*examination*) to fail; (*performance*) to cancel
suspenso *m.* (*grade*) fail, F
sustancia *f.* substance
sustantivo *m.* noun
sustituir (y) *v.t.* to replace

Sustituyeron el azúcar por la miel. They replaced the sugar with honey.

sustituto/a *m., f.* substitute

suyo/a(s) *adj./pron. poss.* (of) his; her; (of) hers; (of) its; *form.* your, (of) yours; their (of)

T

tabaco *m.* tobacco

tablero *m.* blackboard; board
  tablero de anuncios bulletin board
  tablero de control control panel

taburete *m.* stool

tacaño/a *adj.* stingy

tachadura *f.* crossing out, correction

tachar *v.t.* to cross out, to delete

tacto *m.* (*sense*) touch

tal *adv.* such **Nunca te dije tal cosa.** I never told you any such thing.
  Son tal para cual. They are two of a kind.
  tal vez *adv.* maybe
  tales como such as

talentoso/a *adj.* talented

talla *f.* size
  talla grande large

tallar *v.t.* (*wood, stone*) to carve

taller *m.* workshop
  taller de mecánica mechanic's workshop

talón *m.* heel

tamaño *m.* size

también *adv.* also; too

tampoco *adv.* neither; not either

tan *adv.* so
  tan pronto como as soon as
  tan... como as . . . as

tanque *m.* tank

tanto *adv.* so much
  No es para tanto. It's no big deal.
  por lo tanto therefore
  tanto... como as much . . . as
  tantos/as... como as many . . . as

tapa *f.* lid; (*Spain*) bar snack
  ir de tapas (*Spain*) to go out and have a snack in a bar

tapar *v.t.* to cover

tapete (verde) *m.* (*games*) card table

tapiz *m.* tapestry

taquilla *f.* box office, ticket office

tardar (en) *v.i.* to be late (in) **El autobús tardó en llegar.** The bus was late (in arriving).
  a más tardar at the very latest **Llévamelo el jueves a más tardar.** Bring it to me on Thursday at the very latest.

tarde *adv.* late

tarde *f.* afternoon; evening; P.M.
  a las tres de la tarde at three in the afternoon, at three P.M.

tarea *f.* homework

tarjeta *f.* card
  tarjeta de crédito credit card
  tarjeta de invitación

invitation

tarjeta de Navidad Christmas card

tarjeta postal postcard

tartamudear *v.i.* to stutter, to stammer

tatarabuelo/a *m.* great-great grandfather; *f.* great-great grandmother

tauromaquia *f.* bullfighting

taxi *m.* taxi(cab)

taza *f.* cup; mug

tazón *m.* bowl

te *pron. fam.* you

Te presento a... Let me introduce you to . . .

té *m.* tea

té helado iced tea

teatro *m.* theater

techo *m.* (*L.A.*) roof, ceiling; (*Spain*) ceiling

teclado *m.* keyboard

técnico/a *m., f.* technician

teja *f.* (*roof*) tile

tejado *m.* (*Spain*) roof

tejido *m.* weaving; (*anatomy*) tissue

tela *f.* fabric

tela metálica wire netting

telaraña *f.* spiderweb

teleadicto/a *m., f.* couch potato

teléfono (celular) *m.* (cellular) telephone

telenovela *f.* soap opera

telescopio *m.* telescope

teletrabajo *m.* telecommuting

televisión *f.* television

televisión por cable cable television

televisor *m.* television set

tema *m.* subject; theme

temática *f.* subject matter

temático/a *adj.* thematic, according to subject

temer *v.t.* to fear

temperamento *m.* temperament

temperatura *f.* temperature

templo *m.* temple

temporada *f.* season

temprano *adj.* early

tenazas *f., pl.* tongs

tendedero *m.* clothesline

colgar la ropa en el tendedero to hang clothes on the line

tendencia *f.* tendency

tender (e:ie) *v.t.* (*clothes*) to hang out

tendón *m.* tendon

tenedor *m.* fork

tener (e:ie) *v.t. irreg.* (**yo tengo**) to have

tener algo en la punta de la lengua *loc.* to have something on the tip of one's tongue

tener calor to be hot

tener cuidado to be careful

tener en cuenta to keep in mind

tener éxito to be successful

tener fama de to be well-known for, to have a reputation for

tener buena/mala fama to have a good/bad reputation

tener fiebre to have a fever

tener frío to be cold

tener ganas de (+ *inf.*) to feel like (*doing something*); would like to **Tengo ganas de visitar Diamantina.** I would like to visit Diamantina.

tener hambre to be hungry

tener malas pulgas *idiom* to be bad tempered

tener miedo de to be afraid of, to be scared of

tener miedo (de) que to be afraid that

tener planes to have plans

tener prisa to be in a hurry

tener razón to be right

tener sed to be thirsty

tener sueño to be sleepy

tener suerte to be lucky

tener una cita to have a date, an appointment

tener... años to be ... years old

Tengo... años. I'm ... years old.

tener (e:ie) *v.aux. irreg.* **(yo tengo)** to have

tener que (+ *inf.*) to have to (*do something*) **Tengo que irme.** I have to go.

tener que ver con *loc.* to have to do with **La carta no tiene nada que ver con el problema.** The letter doesn't have anything to do with the problem.

tenis *m.* tennis

tenista *m., f.* tennis player

tenor *m.* tenor

tensión *f.* tension

tentáculo *m.* tentacle

teñir (e:i) *v.t.* to dye

teoría *f.* theory

teorizar (sobre algo) *v.i.* to theorize (about something)

terapeútico/a *adj.* therapeutic

terapia *f.* therapy

tercer, tercero/a *adj.* third

en tercer lugar *adv.* thirdly

tercio *m.* third

terciopelo *m.* velvet

terminar *v.t.* to end; to finish

terminar de (+*inf.*) *v.i.* to finish (*doing something*)

¿Has terminado de leer el libro? Have you finished reading the book?

termostato *m.* thermostat

ternera *f.* veal

terraza *f.* terrace

terremoto *m.* earthquake

terreno *m.* plot of land, lot; terrain

terrible *adj.* terrible

Es terrible que (+ *subj.*) It's terrible that...

Es terrible que diga eso. It's terrible that he says that.

terrorista *adj./m., f.* terrorist

tertulia *f.* gathering (*to discuss literature, politics, etc.*)

tesis *f.* thesis

tesoro *m.* treasure

testarudo/a *adj.* stubborn

testigo *m., f.* witness; *m.* (*relay race*) baton

tetera *f.* teapot

ti *obj. of prep., fam.* you

tiburón *m.* shark

tiempo *m.* time; weather

a tiempo on time

buen tiempo nice weather
tiempo libre free time
tienda *f.* shop, store
tienda de campaña tent
tierno/a *adj.* tender; (*person*) affectionate
tierra *f.* land; ground; soil; Earth
tigre *m.* tiger
tijeras *f., pl.* scissors
timbre *m.* doorbell
tímido/a *adj.* timid, shy
timón *m.* (*ship*) rudder
tina *f.* (*L.A.*) bathtub
tinta *f.* ink
tinto *m.* red (wine)
tío/a *m.* uncle; *f.* aunt
tíos *m. pl.* aunts and uncles
típico/a *adj.* typical, traditional
tipo *m.* type, kind, sort; (*person*) figure
No es mi tipo. He's not my type.
¿Qué tipo de música te gusta? What kind of music do you like?
Tiene muy buen tipo. She has a lovely figure.
tirantes *m., pl.* suspenders
tirar *v.t.* to throw
tiro *m.* shot
tiro al blanco target shooting
tiro al plato trapshooting
tiro con arco archery
título *m.* title
tiza *f.* chalk
toalla *f.* towel
toallero *m.* towel bar
tobillo *m.* ankle
tobogán *m.* (*child's toy*) slide
tocadiscos compacto *m., sing.*

compact-disc player
tocar *v.t.* to touch; (*musical instrument*) to play
todavía *adv.* yet; still
todo *m.* everything
Todo está bajo control. Everything is under control.
todo/a *adj.* whole, entire; all
del todo *adv.* entirely **No está del todo equivocada.** She is not entirely mistaken.
por todo el mundo all over the world
todo el mundo the whole world
todos los días every day
todos *m., pl.* all of us; everybody; everyone
tolerancia *f.* tolerance
tolerante *adj.* tolerant
tolerar *v.t.* to tolerate
tomar *v.t.* to take; to drink
algo de tomar something to drink
tomar clases to take classes
tomar el sol to sunbathe
tomar en cuenta take into account
tomar fotos to take photos
tomar la temperatura to take someone's temperature
tomarle el pelo a alguien *idiom* to pull someone's leg, to kid someone
tomate *m.* tomato
tomillo *m.* thyme
tonto/a *adj.* silly; foolish
torcer (o:ue) (c:z) *v.t.* to twist
torcerse (o:ue) (c:z) (el tobillo) *v. pron.* to sprain (one's ankle)

103

torcido/a *adj.* twisted; sprained
torero/a *m., f.* bullfighter
tormenta *f.* storm
tornado *m.* tornado
tornillo *m.* screw
toro *m.* bull
toronja *f.* (*L.A.*) grapefruit
torpe *adj.* clumsy, awkward
torre *f.* tower
  torre de control control tower
tortilla *f.* (*egg*) omelet; (*corn*) kind of flat bread
  tortilla de maíz flat bread made of corn flour
  tortilla de patatas potato omelet
tortuga *f.* turtle
tos *f., sing.* cough
toser *v.i.* to cough
tostado/a *adj.* toasted
tostadora *f.* toaster
trabajador(a) *m., f.* hard-working person
trabajar *v.i.* to work
trabajo *m.* job; work; (*paper*) written work
tradición *f.* tradition
traducción *f.* translation
traducir (c:zc) *v.t.* to translate
traductor(a) *m., f.* translator
traer *v.t. irreg.* (**yo traigo**) to bring
traficante *m., f.* (*arms, drugs*) dealer
traficar (en/con) *v.i.* to traffic in
tragaluz *m.* skylight
tragaperras *f., sing.* slot machine
tragar *v.t.* to swallow

tragedia *f.* tragedy
trágico/a *adj.* tragic
traición *f.* treason, betrayal, treachery
traicionar (algo o a alguien) *v.t.* to betray (something or someone)
traicionero/a *adj.* treacherous
traído *p.p. of* **traer** brought
traje *m.* suit
  traje de baño bathing suit
traidor(a) *m., f.* traitor; *adj.* treacherous
tramar *v.t.* to plot, to scheme
trampa *f.* trap; trick; catch
  ¿Cuál es la trampa? What's the catch?
  hacer trampa(s) to cheat
trampolín *m.* diving board
tranquilidad *f.* calm, tranquility
tranquilizar *v.t.* to calm down
tranquilizarse *v. pron.* to calm down
tranquilo/a *adj.* (*person*) easygoing; quiet; calm
  ¡Tranquilo! Stay calm!
transatlántico *m.* ocean liner
transbordador *m.* ferry; (*space*) shuttle
transeúnte *m., f.* passer-by; non-resident
transferencia *f.* transfer
transfusión *f.* transfusion
transmitir *v.t.* to broadcast
transparente *adj.* transparent; see-through
transpiración *f.* perspiration
transpirar *v.i.* to perspire
transplante *m.* transplant
transportar *v.t.* to transport; to

carry

transporte *m.* transportation

trapeador *m.* (*L.A.*) mop

trapear *v.t.* (*L.A.*) to mop

trapo *m.* dishcloth

trasnochar *v.i.* to stay up all night

trastorno *m.* (*medicine*) disorder

  trastorno estomacal stomach disorder

  trastorno mental mental disorder

trasvasar *v.t.* (*computer*) to download

tratar *v.i.* to try

  tratar de (+ *inf.*) to try to (+ *inf.*)

  Trata de resolverlo. Try to solve it.

trato *m.* deal

  Trato hecho. It's a deal.

travesura *f.* prank

travieso/a *adj.* naughty, mischievous

trayectoria *f.* (*rocket, ball*) path, trajectory

trece thirteen

treinta thirty

tren *m.* train

  tren de alta velocidad high-speed train

trenza *f.* braid

tres three

trescientos/as three hundred

triángulo *m.* triangle

tribunal *m.* (*Spain*) court

  Tribunal Supremo (*Spain*) Supreme Court

triciclo *m.* tricycle

trigo *m.* wheat

trigonometría *f.* trigonometry

trimestre *m.* trimester; quarter

  El año tiene cuatro trimestres. The year has four quarters.

trípode *m.* tripod

triste *adj.* sad

  Es triste que (+ *subj.*) It's sad that…

  Es triste que esté tan enfermo. It's sad that he's so sick.

tristeza *f.* sadness

triturar *v.t.* to crush

  triturador de basura garbage disposal

triunfar *v.t.* to succeed; to win

trivialidad *f.* triviality

trivializar *v.t.* to trivialize

tronco *m.* (*living tree*) trunk; (*lumber*) log

  dormir como un tronco *idiom.* to sleep like a log

tropezar (e:ie) *v.i.* to stumble

tropezarse (e:ie) (con alguien) *v. pron.* to run/bump into (*somebody*)

trozo *m.* piece, bit, slice

trucha *f.* trout

trueno *m.* thunder

tú *pron. fam.* you

  Tú eres… You are . . .

tu(s) *poss. fam.* your

tuberculosis *f.* tuberculosis

tubería *f.* pipe

tubo *m.* tube

  tubo de ensayo test tube

  tubo de escape exhaust pipe

tulipán *m.* tulip

tumbarse *v. pron.* to lie down
  tumbarse al sol lie down in the sun, sunbathe
tumbona *f.* lounge chair, deck chair
túnel *m.* tunnel
turbina *f.* turbine
turismo *m.* tourism
turista *m., f.* tourist
turístico/a *adj.* touristic
turno *m.* turn; (*work*) shift
turquesa *f.* turquoise
tuyo/a(s) *poss. fam.* your; (of) yours

U

Ud. *pron. form. sing.* you
Uds. *pron. form. pl.* you
último/a *adj.* last
  por último *adv.* finally
un, uno/a *art.* a; one
único/a *adj.* only
  …y ese es el único problema …and that's the only problem
unido/a *adj.* close
  una familia muy unida a close family
universidad *f.* university; college
universo *m.* universe
unos/as *pron.* some
untar *v.t.* to spread (*butter, honey*)
  untar pan con mantequilla to butter a piece of bread
uña *f.* (*finger, toe*) nail
urbanización *f.* (housing) development
urgente *adj.* urgent

(No) Es urgente que (+ *subj.*) It's (not) urgent that…
  Es urgente que termines. It's urgent that you finish.
usar *v.t.* to use; to wear
  Esta camisa está sin usar. This shirt hasn't been worn.
usted *pron. form. sing.* you
ustedes *pron. form. pl.* you
utensilio *m.* utensil
útero *m.* womb, uterus
útil *adj.* useful
uva *f.* grape

V

vaca *f.* cow
vacaciones *f., pl.* vacation
vacío/a *adj.* empty
vainilla *f.* vanilla
vajilla *f.* dishes, crockery, china
vale *interj.* (*Spain*) okay
  Ven a la una, ¿vale? Come at one o'clock, okay?
  ¡Sí, vale! Yes, sure!
valentía *f.* bravery, courage
valer *v.t. irreg.* (**yo valgo**) to be worth, to cost
  No vale la pena. It's not worth the trouble.
valiente *adj.* brave
valla *f.* fence
vallas *f., pl.* (*sport*) hurdles
valle *m.* valley
valor *m.* value; courage
valorar *v.t.* to value
vapor *m.* vapor, steam
vaquero/a *m.* cowboy; *f.* cowgirl
  una película de vaqueros

a western (movie)
variación *f.* variation
variado/a *adj.* varied, diverse
variar *v.t./v.i.* **(yo varío)** to vary
varios/as *pron.* several
  Irán varios de ustedes.
  Several of you will go.
vaso *m.* glass
vecino/a *m., f.* neighbor
vegetación *f.* vegetation
vehículo *m.* vehicle
  vehículos pesados heavy
  vehicles
veinte twenty
veinticinco twenty-five
veinticuatro twenty-four
veintidós twenty-two
veintinueve twenty-nine
veintiocho twenty-eight
veintiséis twenty-six
veintisiete twenty-seven
veintitrés twenty-three
veintiún, veintiuno/a twenty-
  one
vejez *f.* old age
vejiga *f.* bladder
vela *f.* (*ship*) sail; (*sport*)
  sailing; candle
velero *m.* sailboat
velocidad *f.* speed
  velocidad máxima speed
  limit
velódromo *m.* velodrome
vena *f.* vein
venda *f.* bandage
vendaje *m.* dressing
vendar *v.t.* to bandage
vendedor(a) *m., f.* salesperson
vender *v.t.* to sell
venido *p.p. of* **venir** come;
  arrived

venir (e:ie) *v.i. irreg.* **(yo vengo)**
  to come
  venir al mundo to be born; to
  come into the world
ventaja *f.* advantage
ventana *f.* window
ventilador *m.* fan
ver *v.t./v.i. irreg.* **(yo veo)** to see
  ¡A ver! Let's see!
veraneante *m., f.* summer
  vacationer
veranear *v.i.* to spend the
  summer
  Veraneo en las montañas.
  I summer in the mountains.
verano *m.* summer
veras: de veras *loc.* really
verbena *f.* festival; open-air
  dance
verbo *m.* verb
verdad *f.* truth
  Es cierto, ¿verdad? It's true,
  right?
  Es verdad que (+ ind.) It's
  true that… **¿Es verdad que
  eres millonario?** Is it true
  that you're a millionaire?
verdadero/a *adj.* true
verde *adj./m.* green
  verde claro light green
  verde oscuro dark green
verduras *f., pl.* vegetables
vergonzoso/a *adj.* disgraceful;
  shameful
vergüenza *f.* embarrassment;
  shame
verosímil *adj.* credible;
  realistic, true-to-life
  **Sus personajes no son
  verosímiles.** His characters
  aren't realistic.

verruga *f.* wart
versátil *adj.* versatile
vértebra *f.* vertebra
vertebrado/a *adj./m.* vertebrate
vertedero *m.* garbage dump
vesícula (biliar) *f.* gall bladder
vestido *m.* dress
vestirse (e:i) *v. pron.* to get dressed
vestuario *m.* locker room
veterinaria *f.* veterinary science
veterinario/a *m., f.* veterinarian
vez *f.* time
  a veces sometimes
  dos veces twice
  en vez de instead of
  tres veces three times
  una vez once; one time
  una vez más one more time
vía *f.* (railroad) track
  Vía Láctea Milky Way
viajar *v.i.* to travel
viaje *m.* trip
viajero/a *m., f.* traveler
vibración *f.* vibration
vibrar *v.i.* to vibrate
vicio *m.* vice
  El trabajo es su único vicio. Work is his only vice.
vicioso/a *m., f.* dissolute person
vid *f.* (grape) vine
vida *f.* life
video(casete) *m.* video (cassette)
videocasetera *f.* VCR
videoconferencia *f.* teleconference; video conference

vidrio *m.* glass
  de vidrio (made of) glass
vieira *f.* scallop
viejo/a *adj.* old
viento *m.* wind
viernes *m., sing.* Friday
vinagre *m.* vinegar
vínculo *m.* tie, bond
vino *m.* wine
  vino blanco white wine
  vino tinto red wine
violencia *f.* violence
viruela *f.* smallpox
visera *f.* eyeshade
visitante *m., f.* visitor
visitar *v.t.* to visit
  visitar monumentos to visit monuments
vista *f.* (*senses*) sight; view
  amor a primera vista love at first sight
  habitación con vistas a room with a view
  Hasta la vista. See you.
  Tener vista de águila. To have eyes like a hawk.
  Tierra a la vista. Land ho!
visto/a *p.p. of* **ver** seen
  por lo visto *adv.* apparently
vitamina *f.* vitamin
vitrina *f.* (*L.A.*) shop window
viudo/a *m.* widower; *f.* widow
víveres *m., pl.* provisions, supplies
vivienda *f.* housing
vivir *v.i.* to live
vivo/a *adj.* bright; lively; living
volante *m.* steering wheel
volar (o:ue) *v.i.* to fly
volcán *m.* volcano

voleibol *m.* volleyball
voltear *v.t.* (*L.A.*) to turn (over)
volumen *m.* volume
voluntario *adj.* voluntary; *m., f.* volunteer
volver (o:ue) *v.i.* to return
  volver a ver(te, lo, la) to see (you/him/her) again
  ¿Cuándo te volveré a ver? When will I see you again?
vomitar *v.t./v.i.* to vomit
vos (*Argentina*) *pron.* you
vosotros/as *pron. fam. pl.* you
votar *v.t./v.i.* to vote (for)
voto *m.* vote
voz *f.* voice
vuelta *f.* lap
vuelta *f.* return trip; (*sports*) lap
  de vuelta back
  Estará de vuelta a la una. She will be back at one.
vuelto *p.p. of* **volver** returned
vuestro/a(s) *poss. fam.* your

W

walkman *m.* walkman

X

xenofobia *f.* xenophobia
xenófobo/a *adj.* xenophobic; *m., f.* xenophobe

Y

y *conj.* and
  y cuarto quarter after/past (time)
  y media half-past (time)
  y quince quarter after/past (time)
  y treinta thirty (minutes past the hour)
ya *adv.* already
  Ya fui. I already went.
yerno *m.* son-in-law
yeso *f.* (*L.A.*) plaster cast
yo *pron.* I
  Yo soy... I'm . . .
yoga *m.* yoga
yogur *m.* yogurt

Z

zanahoria *f.* carrot
zapatería *f.* shoe store
zapatilla *f.* slipper
  zapatillas de deporte tennis shoes
zapato *m.* shoe
  zapato de tacón alto high-heeled shoe
  zapatos de tenis tennis shoes
zona *f.* area
  zona verde green space
zoológico *m.* zoo
zoólogo/a *m., f.* zoologist
zorro *m.* fox
zueco *m.* clog
zumo *m.* (*Spain*) juice

English-Spanish
Inglés-Español

A

A.M. en la mañana, de la mañana
abbey *n.* abadía *f.*
abbreviate *v.t.* abreviar
abbreviation *n.* abreviatura *f.*
able: be able to poder (o:ue)
abnormal *adj.* anormal
aboard *adv.* a bordo
  All aboard! ¡Todos a bordo!
abortion *n.* aborto *m.* provocado
  have an abortion abortar de manera provocada
abroad *adv.* en el extranjero
absence *n.* ausencia *f.*
absent *adj.* ausente
absorb *v.t.* absorber
absorbent *adj.* absorbente
absurd *adj.* absurdo/a
accelerate *v.t.* acelerar
accelerator (pedal) *n.* acelerador *m.*
accept *v.t.* aceptar
accessory *n.* accesorio *m.*
accident *n.* accidente *m.*
  industrial accident accidente laboral
accommodation: provide accommodation hospedar
accompany *v.t.* acompañar
according to *prep.* de acuerdo a; según
account *n.* cuenta *f.*
  checking account cuenta corriente
  take into account tomar en cuenta
accountant *n.* contador(a) *m., f.*
accounting *n.* contabilidad *f.*
accustomed *adj.* acostumbrado/a
  be accustomed to acostumbrarse (a)
ache *n.* dolor *m.*
achieve *v.t.* lograr
achievement *n.* logro *m.*
acid *n.* ácido *m.*; ácido/a *adj.*
  acid rain lluvia *f.* ácida
acquainted: be acquainted with conocer
acquire *v.t.* adquirir
acquisition *n.* adquisición *f.*
acrobat *n.* acróbata *m., f.*
acrobatics *n.* acrobacia *f.*
action *n.* acción *f.*
activate *v.t.* activar
active *adj.* activo/a
activity *n.* actividad *f.*
actor *n.* actor *m.*, actriz *f.*
adapt *v.i.* adaptarse
adaptation *n.* adaptación *f.*
addict *n.* adicto/a *m., f.*
  drug addict drogadicto/a
addicted *adj.* adicto/a
  drug-addicted drogadicto/a
addiction *n.* adicción *f.*
additional *adj.* adicional
additive *n.* aditivo *m.*
address *n.* dirección *f.*
adhesive bandage *n.* curita *f.*
adjective *n.* adjetivo *m.*
adjust *v.t. (temperature, etc.)* graduar; *v.i.* adaptarse
administration *n.* administración *f.*

adolescence n. adolescencia f.

adolescent n. adolescente m., f.

advance n. avance m.

advance v.i. avanzar

advanced adj. avanzado/a

advantage n. ventaja f.

adventure n. aventura f.

adventurer n. aventurero/a m., f.

adventurous adj. aventurero/a

advertise v.t. anunciar

advertisement n. anuncio m.

advice n. consejo m.
  give advice dar un consejo

advisable adj. aconsejable, recomendable

advise v.t. aconsejar; recomendar

advisor n. consejero/a m., f.

aerobic adj. aeróbico/a
  aerobic exercises n., pl. ejercicios m., pl. aeróbicos
  do aerobics hacer ejercicios aeróbicos
  aerobics class n. clase f. de ejercicios aeróbicos

affected adj. afectado/a
  be affected by estar afectado/a por

affectionate adj. cariñoso/a, tierno/a

affirmative adj. afirmativo/a

afraid: be afraid (of) tener miedo (de); **be afraid that** tener miedo (de) que

African n., adj. africano/a m., f.

after prep. después de

afternoon n. tarde f.

in the afternoon de la tarde; por la tarde

afterward adv. después; luego

again adv. otra vez

age n. edad f.

age v.i. envejecer

agility n. soltura f.

aging n. envejecimiento m.

agree (about) v. concordar (con), estar de acuerdo (sobre)

agreement n. acuerdo m.
  be in agreement with estar de acuerdo (con)
  reach an agreement llegar a un acuerdo

agricultural adj. agrícola

agriculture n. agricultura f.

AIDS (Acquired Immune Deficiency Syndrome) n. SIDA m. (Síndrome de Inmunodeficiencia Adquirida)

aim n. objetivo m., meta f.

air n. aire m.

air-conditioned adj. climatizado/a

air conditioning n. aire acondicionado

air freshener n. ambientador m.

air pollution n. contaminación f. del aire

aircraft carrier n. portaaviones m., sing.

airline n. aerolínea f.

airplane n. aeroplano m.; avión m.
  by plane en avión
  go by plane ir en avión

airport *n.* aeropuerto *m.*
airtight *adj.* hermético/a
alarm *n.* alarma *f.*
alarming *adj.* alarmante
alcohol *n.* alcohol *m.*
alcoholic *adj.* alcohólico/a
all *adj.* todo/a
  all of us *n.* todos *m., pl.*
  all over the world en todo el
  mundo
allergic *adj.* alérgico/a
  be allergic (to) ser alérgico/a
  (a)
alleviate *v.t.* aliviar
alley *n.* callejón *m.*
almond *n.* almendra *f.*
almond tree *n.* almendro *m.*
almost *adv.* casi
alms *n.* limosna *f.*
alone *adj.* solo/a
along *prep.* por
alphabet *n.* alfabeto *m.*,
  abecedario *m.*
already *adv.* ya
also *adv.* también
alternating current: AC
  corriente *f.* alterna
alternative *n.* alternativa *f.*
alternator *n.* alternador *m.*
although *conj.* aunque
aluminum *n.* aluminio *m.*
  made of aluminum de
  aluminio
always *adv.* siempre
amazing *adj.* asombroso/a
ambition *n.* ambición *f.*
ambitious *adj.* ambicioso/a
ambulance *n.* ambulancia *f.*
American *n., adj.*
  norteamericano/a, *m., f.;*

estadounidense *m., f.*
among *prep.* entre
amount *n.* cantidad *f.*
amuse oneself *v.* entretenerse
amusement park *n.* parque *m.*
  de atracciones *(Spain);*
  parque de diversiones *(L.A.)*
amusing *adj.* chistoso/a,
  gracioso/a, divertido/a
anarchic *adj.* anárquico/a
anarchy *n.* anarquía *f.*
anatomy *n.* anatomía *f.*
ancestor *n.* antepasado/a *m., f.*
anchovy *n.* anchoa *f.*
and *conj.* y *(e before words
  beginning with* i *or* hi*)*
  and so forth y así
  sucesivamente
anesthesia *n.* anestesia *f.*
anesthetist *n.* anestesista *m., f.*
anesthetize *v.t.* anestesiar
angle *n.* ángulo *m.*
Anglo-Saxon *n,. adj.*
  anglosajón *m.,* anglosajona *f.*
angry *adj.* enojado/a
  get angry (with) enojarse
  (con)
animal *n.* animal *m.*
ankle *n.* tobillo *m.*
anniversary *n.* aniversario *m.;*
  (wedding) aniversario de
  bodas
announce *v.t.* anunciar
announcer *n. (TV/radio)*
  locutor(a) *m., f.*
annoy *v.t.* molestar
  The noise is annoying me.
  Me molesta el ruido.
another *adj.* otro/a
answer *n.* respuesta *f.*

answer *v.t.* contestar
ant *n.* hormiga *f.*
anthology *n.* antología *f.*
antibiotic *n.* antibiótico *m.*
anticipation *n.* expectativa *f.*
antidote *n.* antídoto *m.*
antiques *n., pl.* antigüedades *f., pl.*
antiquities *n., pl.* antigüedades *f., pl.*
any *adj.* algún, alguno/a(s)
anyone *pron.* alguien
anything *pron.* algo
apartment *n.* apartamento *m.*
apartment building *n.* casa *f./*edificio *m.* de apartamentos
apologize *v.i.* disculparse
apology *n.* disculpa *f.*
apparently *adv.* por lo visto
appear *v.i. (come into view)* aparecer; *(seem)* parecer
appearance *n. (looks)* aspecto *m.*
appetizers *n., pl.* aperitivos *m., pl.;* entremeses *(Spain) m., pl.*
applaud *v.t./v.i.* aplaudir
applause *n.* aplauso *m.*
apple *n.* manzana *f.*
appliance *n.* aparato *m.*
household appliance aparato doméstico
application *n.* solicitud *f.*
apply *v.t. (for a job)* solicitar, *(for a loan)* pedir un préstamo; *(oneself)* aplicarse
appointment *n.* cita *f.*
have an appointment tener una cita
appreciate *v.t.* apreciar

approach *n.* enfoque *m.*
apricot *n.* albaricoque *m.*
April *n.* abril *m.*
apron *n.* delantal *m.*
aptitude test *n.* prueba *f.* de aptitud
aquarium *n.* acuario *m.*
aquatic *adj.* acuático/a
Arab *n.* árabe *m., f.; (language)* árabe
Arabic *adj.* árabe
archaeologist *n.* arqueólogo/a *m., f.*
archery *n.* tiro *m.* con arco
archipelago *n.* archipiélago *m.*
architect *n.* arquitecto/a *m., f.*
area *n.* región *f.;* zona *f.*
argue *v.t.* discutir; argumentar
argument *n. (reasoning)* argumento *m.; (dispute)* discusión *f.*
aristocracy *n.* aristocracia *f.*
aristocrat *n.* aristócrata *m., f.*
arm *n. (limb)* brazo *m.; (weapon)* arma (el) *f.*
armchair *n.* sillón *m.*
armpit *n.* axila *f.*
army *n.* ejército *m.*
around *prep.* alrededor (de)
There is a wall around the old city. Hay una muralla alrededor de la ciudad vieja. *adv.* alrededor **a table with four chairs around it** una mesa con cuatro sillas alrededor
around here por aquí
arrange *v.t.* colocar; organizar
arranged marriage *n.* boda *f.* concertada

arrangement n. (position) colocación f.

arrest n. detención f., arresto m.

arrest v.t. arrestar
under arrest detenido/a; arrestado/a
be under arrest estar arrestado; estar detenido

arrested p.p. arrestado (of arrestar)

arrival n. llegada f.

arrive v.i. llegar

arrogant adj. arrogante

arrow n. flecha f.

art n. arte m.; las artes f., pl.

artery n. arteria f.

artichoke n. alcachofa f.

article n. artículo m.

artist n. artista m., f.

artistic adj. artístico/a

arts n., pl. artes f., pl.

as como
as . . . as tan… como
as a child de niño
as many . . . as tantos/as… como
as much . . . as tanto… como
as soon as en cuanto; tan pronto como

ascent n. (hill, mountain) escalada f.

ash n. ceniza f.

ashamed: be ashamed avergonzarse

ashtray n. cenicero m.

Asian n., adj. asiático/a m., f.

ask v.t. (a question) preguntar
ask for pedir (e:i)
ask oneself v.ref. preguntarse; cuestionarse; **We have to ask ourselves if the conclusion is valid.** Tenemos que cuestionarnos si es válida la conclusión.

asparagus n. espárrago m.

asphalt n. asfalto m.

aspire (to) v.i. ambicionar

aspirin n. aspirina f.

assassin n. asesino/a m., f.

assassination n. asesinato m.

assess v.t. evaluar

assessment n. evaluación f.

assistance n. asistencia f.

association n. asociación f.

assortment n. surtido m.

assume v.t. asumir; suponer

assure v.t. asegurar

astonishing adj. asombroso/a

astrologist n. astrólogo/a m., f.

astrology n. astrología f.

astronaut n. astronauta m., f.

astronomer n. astrónomo/a m., f.

astronomy n. astronomía f.

at prep. a
at + time a la(s) + time
At what time . . . ? ¿A qué hora…?
At your service. A sus órdenes.

atheism n. ateísmo m.

atheist n. ateo/a m., f.

atheistic adj. ateo/a

athlete n. atleta m., f.

athletic adj. atlético/a

atmosphere n. (created by people, decoration) ambiente m. (metheorology) atmósfera f.

atrocious *adj.* atroz
attack *n.* ataque *m.*
attack *v.t.* atacar
attempt *n.* intento *m.*
  assassination attempt atentado *m.* terrorista
attempt to assassinate *v.t.* atentar (contra)
attend *v.t.* asistir (a)
attention *n.* atención *f.*
attic *n.* altillo *m.*
attract *v.t.* atraer
attraction *n.* atracción *f.*
attractive *adj.* atractivo/a
audience *n.* público *m.*
audiotape *n.* cinta *f.*
audition *n.* *(try-out)* audición *f.*
auditorium *n.* auditorio *m.;* salón *m.* de actos
August *n.* agosto *m.*
aunt *n.* tía *f.*
aunts and uncles *n., pl.* tíos *m., pl.*
Australian *n., adj.* australiano/a *m., f.*
author *n.* autor(a) *m., f.*
authoritarian *adj.* autoritario/a
authoritarianism *n.* autoritarismo *m.*
autograph *n.* autógrafo *m.*
automatic *adj.* automático/a
  automatic teller machine *n.* **(ATM)** cajero *m.* automático
automobile *n.* automóvil *m.;* carro *m.*
  auto racing *n.* automovilismo *m.*
autonomous *adj.* autónomo/a
autonomy *n.* autonomía *f.*
autumn *n.* otoño *m.*

availability *n.* disponibilidad *f.*
available *adj.* disponible
avarice *n.* avaricia *f.*
avaricious *adj.* avaricioso/a
avenue *n.* avenida *f.*
average *n.* promedio *m.*
aversion *n.* aversión *f.*
avocado *n.* aguacate *m.*
avoid *v.t.* evitar; *(danger, problem)* evadir
award *n.* premio *m.;* galardón *m.*
award *v.t.* galardonar; premiar
award-winner *n.* galardonado/a *m., f.*
aware: become aware of darse cuenta de
awful *adj.* atroz, horrible
awkward *adj.* torpe
ax *n.* hacha (el) *f.*

B

back *n.* espalda *f.*
back *v.t.* respaldar
  be back estar de vuelta
backpack *n.* mochila *f.*
backseat *n.* asiento *m.* trasero
backstroke *n.* estilo *m.* espalda
bad *adj.* mal, malo/a
  It's bad that . . . Es malo que (+ *subj.*)
  It's not at all bad. No está nada mal.
bad-mannered *adj.* maleducado/a
bad-tempered: be bad-tempered *idiom* tener malas pulgas
bag *n.* bolsa *f.*
bail *n.* fianza *f.*

115

bake *v.t.* hornear
bakery *n.* panadería *f.*
baking soda *n.* bicarbonato *m.*
balanced *adj.* equilibrado/a
balcony *n.* balcón *m.*
bald *adj.* calvo/a
ball *n.* pelota *f.;* bola *f.*
ballet *n.* ballet *m.*
balloon *n.* globo *m.*
banana *n.* banana *f.;* plátano *m.*
band *n.* banda *f.*
bandage *n.* venda *f.*
bandage *v.t.* vendar
bank *n.* banco *m.*
  bank draft *n.* giro *m.* bancario
banker *n.* banquero/a *m., f.*
banister *n.* pasamanos *m., sing.*
baptism *n.* bautizo *m.*
baptize *v.t.* bautizar
barber *n.* barbero *m.*
bargain *n.* ganga *f.*
bargain *v.i.* regatear
bark *n.* ladrido *m.*
bark *v.i.* ladrar
barn *n.* granero *m.*
baroque *adj.* barroco/a
baseball *n. (sport)* béisbol *m.; (ball)* pelota *f.*
basement *n.* sótano *m.*
basil *n.* albahaca *f.*
basketball *n. (sport)* baloncesto *m.*
bat *n. (sport)* bate *m.; (animal)* murciélago *m.*
bath *n.* baño *m.*
  take a bath bañarse
bathe *v.i.* bañarse

bathing suit *n.* traje *m.* de baño
bathrobe *n.* bata *f.* de baño
bathroom *n.* baño *m.;* cuarto *m.* de baño
bathtub *n.* bañera *f.;* tina *(L.A.) f.*
baton *n. (sport)* testigo *m.*
bay *n.* bahía *f.*
be *v.* ser; estar
  He/She/It is from . . . Es de…
  be that as it may *loc.* sea lo que sea
beach *n.* playa *f.*
beach umbrella *n.* sombrilla *f.*
beak *n.* pico *m.*
bean *n. (coffee)* grano *m.;* frijol *m.*
bear *n.* oso/a *m., f.*
beard *n.* barba *f.*
bearded *adj.* barbudo/a
beat *n. (music)* compás *m.*
beat *v.t.* batir; *(an opponent)* derrotar; *(heart)* latir
beautician *n.* esteticista *m., f.*
beautiful *adj.* hermoso/a
beauty *n.* belleza *f.*
beauty salon *n.* peluquería *f.;* salón *m.* de belleza
because *conj.* porque
because of *prep.* debido a
become *v.i.* hacerse **He became famous.** Se hizo famoso.; llegar a ser **She wants to become president.** Ella quiere llegar a ser presidente.; ponerse (+ *adj.*) **He becomes sad sometimes.** A veces él se pone triste.; convertirse (en) **The church became a museum.** La

iglesia se convirtió en
museo.
bed *n.* cama *f.*
  go to bed acostarse (o:ue)
  make the bed hacer la cama
bedroom *n.* alcoba *f.;*
  recámara *f.;* cuarto *m.;*
  dormitorio
bee *n.* abeja *f.*
beef *n.* carne *f.* de res
been *p.p.* sido (*of* ser)
beer *n.* cerveza *f.*
beet *n.* remolacha *f.;* betabel
  (Mexico.) f.
before *adv., conj., prep.* antes;
  antes (de) que; antes de
beg *v.t.* rogar (o:ue)
beggar *n.* mendigo/a *m., f.*
begin *v.t.* comenzar (e:ie);
  empezar (e:ie)
behalf: on behalf of de parte
  de; en nombre de
behave (oneself) *v.* portarse,
  comportarse
  behave well/badly portarse
  bien/mal
behavior *n.* comportamiento
  m., conducta *f.*
behind *prep.* detrás de
being *n.* ser *m.*
belch *v.i.* eructar
belch *n.* eructo *m.*
believe (in) *v.t.* creer (en)
  be hard to believe parecer
  mentira **It's hard to believe,**
  but he's only ten. Aunque
  parezca mentira, tiene sólo
  diez años.
bellhop *n.* botones *m., sing.*
belly *n.* barriga *f.,* vientre *m.*

belong to *v.t.* pertenecer (a)
belongings *n., pl.* pertenencias
  f., pl.
beloved *adj.* querido/a
below *adv., prep.* abajo;
  debajo de
belt *n.* correa *f.;* cinturón *m.*
bench *n.* banco *m.*
bend *n.* curva *f.*
beneficial *adj.* beneficioso/a
benefit *n.* beneficio *m.*
benefit *v.i.* beneficiarse
benign *adj.* benigno
beret *n.* boina *f.*
beside *prep.* al lado de
best *adj.* mejor
  the best *n.* el/la mejor *m., f.;*
  (neuter) lo mejor
betray *v.t.* traicionar
betrayal *n.* traición *f.*
better *adj.* mejor
  It's better that . . . Es mejor
  que…
  get better mejorarse; *(health)*
  aliviarse
better (oneself) *v.t.* superarse
  Better late than never. *loc.*
  Más vale tarde que nunca.
between *prep.* entre
bib *n.* babero *m.*
bicycle *n.* bicicleta *f.*
  ride a bicycle pasear/montar
  en bicicleta
big *adj.* gran, grande
Big Dipper *n.* Osa *f.* Mayor
big shot *n.* pez *m.* gordo
bill *n.* cuenta *f.;* factura *f.*
billion *n.* mil *m.* millones (de)
biodiversity *n.* biodiversidad *f.*
biographical *adj.* biográfico/a

biography *n.* biografía *f.*
biologist *n.* biólogo/a *m., f.*
biology *n.* biología *f.*
biosphere *n.* biosfera *f.*
bird *n.* ave (el) *f.,* pájaro *m.*
birth *n.* nacimiento *m.*
birth control *n.* control *m.* de natalidad
birthday *n.* cumpleaños *m., sing.*
  Happy birthday! ¡Feliz cumpleaños!
  have a birthday cumplir años
  birthday cake pastel *m.* de cumpleaños
birthrate *n.* (índice *m.* de) natalidad *f.*
bite *n.* mordisco *m.*
bite *v.t.* morder
bitter *adj.* amargo/a
bittersweet *adj.* agridulce
black *n., adj.* negro/a
blackberry *n.* mora *f.*
blackboard *n.* pizarra *f.; m.* pizarrón
blackout *n.* apagón *m.*
bladder *n.* vejiga *f.*
bland *adj.* insípido/a; soso/a
blanket *n.* cobija *(L.A.) f.;* frazada *(L.A.) f.;* manta *f.*
bleach *n.* lejía *f.*
blend *v.t.* licuar
blender *n.* licuadora *(L.A.) f.;* batidora *(Spain) f.*
bless *v.t.* bendecir
blind *adj.* ciego/a
blind *n.* persiana *f.*
block *n.* *(city)* cuadra *(L.A.) f.;* manzana *(Spain)*
blond(e) *adj.* rubio/a

blood *n.* sangre *f.*
blood circulation *n.* circulación *f.* (sanguínea)
blood pressure *n.* presión *f.* sanguínea
blouse *n.* blusa *f.*
blue *n., adj.* azul
blueprint *n.* plano *m.*
bluish *adj.* azulado/a
blush *v.i.* ponerse rojo/a, sonrojarse
board *n.* *(organizational)* junta *f.;* tablero *m.*
board *v.i.* *(ship)* embarcar
board games *n., pl.* juegos *m., pl.* de mesa
board of directors *n.* junta *f.* directiva
boardinghouse *n.* pensión *f.*
boast (about) *v.t.* alardear (de) *(Spain)*
  He was boasting about having won. Alardeaba de haber ganado.
body *n.* cuerpo *m.*
boil *v.t.* hervir
boiled *adj.* hervido/a
bolt *n.* *(lock)* cerrojo *m.*
bolt (the door) *v.t.* correr el cerrojo
bomb *n.* bomba *f.*
bond *n.* vínculo *m.*
bone *n.* hueso *m.; (fish)* espina *f.*
bonfire *n.* hoguera *f.*
book *n.* libro *m.*
book *v.t.* hacer una reservación
bookcase *n.* estantería *f.*
bookstore *n.* librería *f.*

bookworm n. ratón m. de biblioteca

boot n. bota f.
   rubber boot bota de agua

bore v.t. aburrir

bored adj. aburrido/a
   be bored estar aburrido/a
   get bored aburrirse

boring adj. aburrido/a; soso/a

born: be born nacer

borrow v.t. pedir prestado

borrowed adj. prestado/a

boss n. jefe m., jefa f.

botanical adj. botánico/a

botanist n. botánico/a m., f.

botany n. botánica f.

bother v.t. molestar **Does the music bother you?** ¿Te molesta la música?

bottle n. botella f.

bottle opener n. abrebotellas m., sing.

bottom n. fondo m.

boulevard n. bulevar m.

bow n. lazo m.; (sport) arco m.

bowl n. tazón m.

box v.i. boxear

boxer n. boxeador(a) m., f.

boxer shorts n., pl. calzoncillos m., pl.

boxing n. boxeo m.

boy n. chico m.; muchacho m.

boyfriend n. novio m.

bra n. sostén m.; sujetador (Spain) m.; brasier (L.A.) m.

braid n. trenza f.

brain n. cerebro m.

brake v.i. frenar

brake n. freno m.
   brake pedal n. pedal m. del freno

branch n. rama f.

brand (name) n. marca f.
   It's a well-known brand. Es una marca de prestigio.

brat n. niño/a m., f. mimado/a

brave adj. valiente

bravery n. valentía f.

bread n. pan m.
   freshly-baked bread pan recién horneado

break v.t. romper **She breaks the glass.** Ella rompe el vaso.; romperse **He broke his leg.** Se rompió la pierna.
   break a world record batir un récord mundial

break down v.i. (auto) descomponerse (L.A.), dañarse (L.A.); averiarse (Spain); estropearse, sufrir una avería
   The . . . broke down on us. Se nos dañó el/la…
   break the ice loc. romper el hielo

break up (with) v.i. romper (con)

breakdown n. (mechanical) avería (Spain) f.

breakfast n. desayuno m.
   have breakfast desayunar

breakwater n. rompeolas m., sing.

breast n. pecho m.
   chicken breast pechuga f. (de pollo)

breaststroke n. estilo m. braza (Spain); estilo m. pecho (L.A.)

breath n. aliento m.

breathe *v.i.* respirar
breathing *n.* respiración *f.*
breeze *n.* brisa *f.*
brick *n.* ladrillo *m.*
bricklayer *n.* albañil *m.*
bricklaying *n.* albañilería *f.*
bridge *n.* puente *m.*
bright *adj. (color)* vivo/a
bring *v.t.* traer
bring up *v.t. (children)* criar
broadcast *v.t.* transmitir; emitir
broccoli *n.* brócoli *m.*
brochure *n.* folleto *m.*
broiled *adj.* a la parrilla
broken *adj.* roto/a
  be broken estar roto/a
broken down *adj.* averiado/a
  (Spain)
bronze *n.* bronce *m.*
brook *n.* riachuelo *m.*
broom *n.* escoba *f.*
broth *n.* caldo *m.*
brother *n.* hermano *m*
  brothers and sisters *n., pl.*
  hermanos *m., pl.*
  younger brother *n.* hermano
  m. menor
brother-in-law *n.* cuñado *m.*
brought *p.p.* traído *(of* traer)
brown *n., adj. (color)* café;
  marrón; *(eyes, hair)*
  castaño/a
brunet(te) *adj.* moreno/a
brush *n.* cepillo *m.*
brush *v.t.* cepillar
  brush one's hair cepillarse el
  pelo
  brush one's teeth cepillarse
  los dientes
bubble *n.* burbuja *f.*

Buddhist *n., adj.* budista *m., f.*
build *v.t.* construir
builder *n.* albañil *m.;*
  constructor(a) *m., f.* (de
  obras)
building *n.* edificio *m.;*
  (profession) albañilería *f.*
  apartment building casa *f.*
  de apartamentos/edificio *m.*
  de apartamentos
  building contractor *n.*
  constructor(a) *m., f.* (de
  obras)
bull *n.* toro *m.*
bulletin *n.* boletín *m.*
bulletin board *n.* tablero *m.* de
  anuncios
bullfight *n.* corrida *f.* de toros
bullfighter *n.* torero/a *m., f.*
bullfighting *n.* tauromaquia *f.*
bullring *n.* plaza *f.* de toros
bump into *v. (meet*
  accidentally) darse con
bumper *n.* parachoques *m.,*
  sing.
burglar *n.* ladrón *m.,* ladrona *f.*
burial *n.* entierro *m.*
burn *v.t.* quemar
burned (out) *adj.* quemado/a
burp *n.* eructo *m.*
burp *v.i.* eructar
bus *n.* autobús *m.;* camión *m.*
  (Mexico)
  go by bus ir en autobús
bus station *n.* estación *f.* de
  autobuses
bush *n.* arbusto *m.*
business *n.* negocios *m., pl.*
business administration *n.*
  administración *f.* de

empresas

businessman *n.* hombre *m.* de negocios

business-related *adj.* comercial

businesswoman *n.* mujer *f.* de negocios

busy *adj.* ocupado/a

but *conj.* pero; (*in negative sentences*) sino

butcher shop *n.* carnicería *f.*

butler *n.* mayordomo *m.*

butter *n.* mantequilla *f.*

  butter a piece of toast untar una tostada con mantequilla

butterfly *n.* mariposa *f.*

butterfly stroke *n.* estilo *m.* mariposa

button *n.* botón *m.*

buy *v.t.* comprar

by *prep.* por

  by the way a propósito, por cierto

bye *fam.* chau; adiós

C

cabbage *n.* col *(Spain) f.*; repollo *(L.A.) m.*

cabin *n.* cabaña *f.*

cable *n.* cable *m.*

  cable television *n.* televisión *f.* por cable

café *n.* café *m.*

cafeteria *n.* cafetería *f.*

cake *n.* pastel *m.*

calculate *v.t.* calcular

calculation *n.* cálculo *m.*

calculator *n.* calculadora *f.*

calendar *n.* calendario *m.*

calf *n.* (*anat.*) pantorrilla *f.*

call *v.t.* llamar

  be called llamarse

  be on call estar de guardia

  call on the phone llamar por teléfono

calm *n., adj.* tranquilidad *f.*; tranquilo/a

  Stay calm! ¡Tranquilo/a!

calm down *v.* tranquilizarse

calorie *n.* caloría *f.*

camaraderie *n.* compañerismo *m.*

camel *n.* camello *m.*

camera *n.* cámara *f.*

camp *n.* acampada *f.*

camp *v.i.* acampar

  go camping ir de acampada

can *n.* lata *f.*

  can opener *n.* abrelatas *m., sing.*

can *v.aux.* poder (o:ue)

  I can't take it any more! *loc.* ¡No puedo más!/¡No soporto más!

Canadian *n., adj.* canadiense *m., f.*

canary *n.* canario *m.*

cancel *v.t.* cancelar; anular; (*performance*) suspender

candidate *n.* aspirante *m., f.*; candidato/a *m., f.*

candle *n.* vela *f.*

candy *n.* dulces *m., pl.*

cane *n.* caña *f.*

canoe *n.* piragua *f.*

canoeing *n.* piragüismo *m.*

canoeist *n.* piragüista *m., f.*

canvas *n.* lona *f.*

cap *n.* (*with a visor*) gorra *f.*; (*without a visor*) gorro *m.*

capital *n.* capital *f.*
  capital letter *n.* mayúscula *f.*
capsule *n.* cápsula *f.*
capture *v.t.* capturar
car *n.* carro *(L.A.) m.;* coche *(Spain) m.;* automóvil *m.*
  go by car ir en auto(móvil)
carbohydrate *n.* carbohidrato *m.*
carburator *n.* carburador *m.*
card *n.* tarjeta *f.; (playing)* carta *f.,* naipe *m.*
card table *n.* tapete (verde) *m.*
cardiology *n.* cardiología *f.*
care *n.* cuidado *m.,* atención *f.*
  take care of cuidar
  take care of oneself cuidarse
  be careful tener cuidado; ¡Cuidado!
career *n.* carrera *f.*
Caribbean *adj.* caribeño/a
carnation *n.* clavel *m.*
carnivore *n.* carnívoro/a *m., f.*
carnivorous *adj.* carnívoro/a
carpenter *n.* carpintero/a *m., f.*
carpet *n.* alfombra *f.*
carrot *n.* zanahoria *f.*
carry *v.t.* llevar; transportar
cart *n.* carro *(Spain) m.*
cartoons *n., pl. (animated)* dibujos *m., pl.* animados; *(political)* caricaturas *f., pl.* (políticas)
carve *v.t.* tallar
case *n.* caso *m.*
  in case (of) en caso (de) que
cash (a check) *v.t.* cobrar
cash *n.* efectivo *m.*
cash register *n.* caja *f.*

cashier *n.* cajero/a *m., f.*
casserole *n.* cazuela *f.*
cast *n.* yeso *(L.A.) m.;* escayola *(Spain) f.*
castle *n.* castillo *m.*
cat *n.* gato/a *m., f.*
catastrophe *n.* catástrofe *f.*
catastrophic *adj.* catastrófico/a
catch *v.t. (illness)* pegar
category *n.* categoría *f.*
cathedral *n.* catedral *f.*
Catholic *n., adj.* católico/a *m., f.*
cattle *n.* ganado *m.*
cattle farmer *n.* ganadero/a *m., f.*
cattle raising *n.* ganadería *f.*
cause *v.t.* causar; provocar
cavern *n.* caverna *f.*
cedar *n.* cedro *m.*
celebrate *v.t.* celebrar; festejar
celebration *n.* festejo *m.*
celery *n.* apio *m.*
cell *n.* célula *f.*
cellar *n.* sótano *m.; (wine)* bodega *f.*
cement *n.* cemento *m.*
cemetery *n.* cementerio *m.*
censor *v.t.* censurar
censorship *n.* censura *f.*
censure *n.* censura *f.*
censure *v.t.* censurar
census *n.* censo *m.*
century *n.* siglo *m.*
cereal *n.* cereales *m., pl.*
certain *adj.* cierto/a
certainty *n.* certeza *f.*
chain *n.* cadena *f.*
chalk *n.* tiza *f.*

challenge n. reto m.; desafío m.
challenge v.t. desafiar; retar
champion n. campeón m., campeona f.
championship n. campeonato m.
chance n. azar m.
chandelier n. araña f. (de luces)
change v.t. cambiar (de); renovar
change n. cambio m.
change purse n. monedero m.
channel n. (TV, radio) cadena f.; canal m.
Chanukah n. Januká m.
chapel n. capilla f.; ermita f.
character n. carácter m.; (fictional) personaje m.
  main character personaje principal
charisma n. carisma m.
charity n. caridad f.; (money) limosna f.; (organization) sociedad f. benéfica
charm n. encanto m.
charming adj. encantador(a)
chase v.t. perseguir
chatterbox n. charlatán m., charlatana f.
chauffeur n. conductor(a) m., f.
cheap adj. barato/a
cheat v.i. hacer trampa(s); (money) engañar
cheat on v.t. (relationship) engañar
check n. (bank) cheque m.
check v.t. comprobar; revisar; averiguar

check the oil revisar el aceite
checkers n., pl. (game) damas f., pl.
checkup n. revisión (Spain) f.; chequeo (médico) (L.A.) m.
cheek n. mejilla f.
cheeky adj. caradura
cheeky person n. caradura m., f.
cheer up v. animar(se)
cheese n. queso m.
chef n. cocinero/a m., f.
chemical adj. químico/a
chemist n. químico/a m., f.
chemistry n. química f.
cherry n. cereza f.
cherry tree n. cerezo m.
chess n. ajedrez m.
chess player n. ajedrecista m., f.
chest n. (anatomy) pecho m.
chest of drawers n. cómoda f.
chew v.t. masticar
chicken n. pollo m.
chickpea n. garbanzo m.
child n. niño/a m., f. (son, daughter) hijo/a m., f.
  only child hijo/a único/a
childhood n. niñez f.
children n., pl. (sons and daughters) hijos m., pl.
chill v.t. enfriar
chilled adj. frío/a
chimney n. chimenea f.
china n. (fine) porcelana f.
Chinese n., adj. chino/a m., f.; (language) chino
chlorine n. cloro m.
chlorophyll n. clorofila f.

chocolate *n.* chocolate *m.*
chocolate cake *n.* pastel *m.* de chocolate
choir *n.* coro *m.*
choke *v.i.* atragantarse
cholesterol *n.* colesterol *m.*
choose *v.t.* escoger
chop *n. (meat)* chuleta *f.*
chop *v.t.* cortar
chores *n., pl.* quehaceres *m., pl.*
  household chores quehaceres domésticos
  do household chores hacer quehaceres domésticos
chorus *n.* coro *m.*
Christian *n., adj.* cristiano/a *m., f.*
Christmas *n.* Navidad *f.*
  Christmas card *n.* tarjeta *f.* de Navidad
cider *n.* sidra *f.*
cinnamon *n.* canela *f.*
circle *n.* círculo *m.*
circuit *n. (electric)* circuito *m.*
circus *n.* circo *m.*
citizen *n.* ciudadano/a *m., f.*
citrus *adj.* cítrico/a
city *n.* ciudad *f.*
  city hall *n.* ayuntamiento *m.*
clam *n.* almeja *f.*
clap *v.t./v.i.* aplaudir
clash *n.* enfrentamiento *m.*
class *n.* clase *f.*
  take classes tomar clases
classical *adj.* clásico/a
classmate *n.* compañero/a *m., f.* de clase
classroom *n.* aula *f.;* salón *m.*
clavicle *n.* clavícula *f.*

clay *n.* arcilla *f.*
clean *adj.* limpio/a
clean *v.t.* limpiar
clear *adj.* claro/a; *(weather)* despejado/a
  It's (very) clear. *(weather)* Está (muy) despejado.
clear *v.t. (pipes)* desatascar
  clear the table quitar la mesa
clerk *n.* dependiente/a *m., f.*
cliff *n.* acantilado *m.*
climate *n.* clima *m.*
climatology *n.* climatología *f.*
climb *n. (mountain)* escalada *f.*
climb *v.t.* escalar
  climb mountains escalar montañas
climber *n. (mountain)* alpinista *m., f.,* escalador(a) *m., f.*
climbing *n. (mountain)* alpinismo *m.*
clinic *n.* clínica *f.*
clock *n.* reloj *m.*
  alarm clock despertador *m.*
clog *n.* zueco *m.*
close *adj. (relative)* cercano/a; *(people)* unido/a
  get close (to someone) intimar (con alguien)
close *v.t.* cerrar (e:ie)
closed *adj.* cerrado/a
closet *n.* armario *m.*
closing *n.* clausura *f.*
clothes *n., pl.* ropa *f.*
  What pretty clothes! ¡Qué ropa más bonita!
  clothes dryer *n.* secadora *f.*
clothesline *n.* tendedero *m.*
cloud *n.* nube *f.*

have one's head in the clouds estar en las nubes
cloudy *adj.* nublado/a
 It's (very) cloudy. Está (muy) nublado.
clown *n.* payaso/a *m., f.*
clue *n.* pista *f.*
 Give me a clue. Dame una pista.
clumsy *adj.* torpe
clutch *n.* embrague *m.*
 clutch pedal *n.* pedal *m.* del embrague
coach *n.* entrenador(a) *m., f.*
coaching *n.* entrenamiento *m.*
coal *n.* carbón *m.*
coast *n.* costa *f.*
coastal *adj.* costero/a
coastline *n.* costa *f.*
coat *n.* abrigo *m.*
 coat hanger *n.* perchero *m.*
cockroach *n.* cucaracha *f.*
coconut *n.* coco *m.*
cod *n.* bacalao *m.*
coffee *n.* café *m.*
 coffee maker *n.* cafetera *f.*
coffin *n.* ataúd *m.*
coincide *v.i.* coincidir
coincidence *n.* azar *m.;* coincidencia *f.*
colander *n.* colador *m.*
cold *n. (temperature)* frío *m.;* *(illness)* catarro *m.,* resfriado *m.*
 be (feel) cold tener frío
 It's cold. *(weather)* Hace frío.
collaborate *v.i.* colaborar
collaboration *n.* colaboración *f.*
collect *v.t.* coleccionar

collecting *n.* coleccionismo *m.*
collector *n.* coleccionista *m., f.*
college *n.* universidad *f.*
collision *n.* choque *m.*
cologne *n.* colonia *f.*
colonist *n.* colono *m.*
colonization *n.* colonización *f.*
colonize *v.t.* colonizar
colony *n.* colonia *f.*
color *n.* color *m.*
column *n.* columna *f.*
comb *n.* peine *m.*
comb one's hair *v. refl.* peinarse
come *v.i.* venir
comedy *n.* comedia *f.*
comfort *n.* confort *m.*
comfortable *adj.* confortable; cómodo/a
comic strip *n.* tira *f.* cómica, historieta *f.*
commemorate *v.t.* conmemorar
commemoration *n.* conmemoración *f.*
commerce *n.* negocios *m., pl.*
commercial *adj.* comercial
committee *n.* junta *f.*
common *adj.* común
communicate *v.t.* comunicar *(speak with)* comunicarse (con)
communication *n.* comunicación *f.*
compact disc (CD) *n.* disco *m.* compacto
compact disc player *n.* tocadiscos *m., sing.* compacto
companion *n.* compañero/a *m., f.*

125

company n. compañía f.; empresa f.

comparison n. comparación f.

compete v.i. competir

competence n. aptitud f.

competition n. competencia (L.A.) f.; competición (Spain) f.

competitive adj. competitivo/a

competitor n. competidor(a) m., f.; participante m., f.

complain v.i. quejarse

complaint n. queja f.

completely adv. completamente; a fondo

complex adj. complejo

complexion n. cutis m.

complicate v.t. complicar

composer n. compositor(a) m., f.

computer n. computadora f.

computer disk n. disco m.

computer monitor n. monitor m.

computer science n. computación f.

con artist n. estafador(a) m., f.

conceal v.t. disimular

conceited adj. engreído/a

concert n. concierto m.

concrete n. concreto (L.A.) m.; hormigón (Spain) m.

condense v.t. condensar

conditioned adj. acondicionado/a

conduct n. conducta f.

conductor n. (music) director(a) m., f.

conference n. congreso m.

confirm v.t. confirmar

confirm the reservation confirmar la reservación

confirmation n. confirmación f.

confront v.t. enfrentar; enfrentarse (con)

The army will confront the enemy. El ejército se enfrentará con el enemigo.

confuse v.t. confundir

confusion n. confusión f.

congested adj. congestionado/a

congratulate v.t. felicitar

Congratulations! (for an event such as a birthday or anniversary) ¡Felicidades! f., pl.; (for an event such as an engagement or a good grade on a test) ¡Felicitaciones! f., pl.

conquer v.t. conquistar

conqueror n. conquistador(a) m., f.

conquest n. conquista f.

conscience n. conciencia f.

consensus n. consenso m.

consent n. consentimiento m.

consent to v. consentir

conservative n., adj. conservador(a) m., f.

conserve v.t. conservar

considerate adj. considerado/a

constellation n. constelación f.

constipated adj. estreñido/a

constipation n. estreñimiento m.

constitution n. constitución f.

consume v.t. consumir

consumer n. consumidor(a) m., f.

consumption *n.* consumo *m.*

contact lenses *n., pl.* lentes *m., pl.* de contacto

contagion *n.* contagio *m.*

contagious *adj.* contagioso/a

container *n.* recipiente *m.*; envase *m.*

contamination *n.* contaminación *f.*

content *adj.* contento/a

contest *n.* competencia *(L.A.) f.*; concurso *m.*

continue *v.t.* seguir (e:i)

contraceptive *n.* anticonceptivo *m.*

contract *n.* contrato *m.*

contradict *v.t.* contradecir

contradiction *n.* contradicción *f.*

contrast *v.t.* contraponer

control *n.* control *m.*

  control panel *n.* tablero *m.* de control

  control tower *n.* torre *f.* de control

control *v.t.* controlar

  be under control estar bajo control

control oneself *v.* dominarse

controversial *adj.* polémico/a

controversy *n.* polémica *f.*

convent *n.* convento *m.*

convertible *n., adj. (car)* descapotable *m.*

convict *n.* presidiario/a *m., f.*

conviction *n.* convicción *f.*

convince *v.t.* convencer

convincing *adj.* convincente

cook *n.* cocinero/a *m., f.*

cook *v.t./v.i.* cocinar

cookie *n.* galleta *f.*

cool *adj.* fresco/a; *(slang)* chévere

  It's cool. *(weather)* Hace fresco.

copper *n.* cobre *m.*

copy *v.t.* copiar

cork *n.* corcho *m.*

corkscrew *n.* sacacorchos *m, sing.*

corn *n.* maíz *m.*

corner *n.* esquina *m.*

corpse *n.* cadáver *m.*

correct *v.t.* corregir

correction *n.* corrección *f.*

correctness *n.* corrección *f.*

cost *v.t.* costar (o:ue)

  cost an arm and a leg *idiom.* costar un ojo de la cara

costume *n.* disfraz *m.*

cosy *adj.* acogedor(a)

cotton *n.* algodón *m.*

  made of cotton de algoldón

couch *n.* sofá *m.*

  couch potato *n.* teleadicto/a *m., f.*

cough *n.* tos *f.*

cough *v.i.* toser

counselor *n.* consejero/a *m., f.*

count (on) *v.t.* contar (con)

counter *n. (game)* ficha *f.*

country *n. (nation)* país *m.*; *(rural)* campo *m.*

  developed country país desarrollado

  developing country país en vías de desarrollo

countryside *n.* campo *m.*; paisaje *m.*

couple *n.* pareja *f.*

a couple of days un par de días
courage *n.* valentía *f.*; valor *m.*
course *n.* curso *m.*; materia *f.*
court *n. (of law)* corte *(L.A.) f.*, tribunal *(Spain) m.*; *(sport)* cancha *f.*
  clay court pista *f.* de tierra batida
  grass court pista *f.* de hierba
courtesy *n.* cortesía *f.*
cousin *n.* primo/a *m., f.*
cover *v.t.* cubrir; *(container, pan)* tapar
covered *p.p.* cubierto *(of cubrir)*
cow *n.* vaca *f.*
coward *adj.* cobarde
cowardice *n.* cobardía *f.*
cowboy *n.* vaquero *m.*
cowgirl *n.* vaquera *f.*
crab *n.* cangrejo *m.*
cracker *n.* galleta *f.* (salada)
cradle *n.* cuna *f.*
crafts *n.* artesanía *f.*
craftsmanship *n.* artesanía *f.*
crane *n. (machinery)* grúa *f.*
crash (into sthg.) *v.i.* chocar (contra algo)
  crash a party colarse en una fiesta
crater *n.* cráter *m.*
crave *v.t.* ansiar
crawl *v.i.* arrastrarse (por el suelo)
crazy *adj.* loco/a
cream *n.* crema *f.*; *(dairy)* nata *f.*
  anti-wrinkle cream crema antiarrugas

creamy *adj.* cremoso/a
create *v.t.* crear
creative *adj.* creativo/a
creator *n.* creador(a) *m., f.*
credible *adj.* verosímil
credit *n.* crédito *m.*
  credit card *n.* tarjeta *f.* de crédito
cricket *n.* grillo *m.*
crime *n.* crimen *m.*; delincuencia *f.*
criminal *n.* delincuente *m., f.*
crisis *n.* crisis *f.*
  mid-life crisis crisis de los cuarenta
critic *n.* detractor(a) *m., f.*
crockery *n.* vajilla *f.*
cross *v.t.* cruzar; atravesar
cross section *n. (Tech.)* corte *m.* transversal
crossroads *n., pl.* cruce *m.*
crosswalk *n.* paso *m.* de peatones
crossword (puzzle) *n.* crucigrama *m.*
cruise *n.* crucero *m.*
crunchy *adj.* crujiente
crusty *adj. (bread)* crujiente
cry *v.i.* llorar
crybaby *n.* llorón *m.*, llorona *f.*
crystal *n.* cristal *m.*
cucumber *n.* pepino *m.*
culture *n.* cultura *f.*
cup *n.* taza *f.*
cure *n.* cura *f.*
cure *v.t.* curar
currency exchange *n.* cambio *m.* de moneda
current *n.* corriente *f.*
  alternating current (AC)

corriente alterna
direct current (CD) corriente continua
current events *n., pl.* actualidades *f., pl.*
curriculum vitae *n.* currículum *m.*
curtain *n.* cortina *f.*
curve *n.* curva *f.*
cushion *n.* cojín *m.*
custard *n. (baked)* flan *m.;* natillas *f., pl.*
custom *n.* costumbre *f.*
customer *n.* cliente *m., f.*
customs *n.* aduana *f.*
  go through customs pasar por la aduana
  customs inspector *n.* inspector(a) *m., f.* de aduanas
cut *n.* corte *f.*
cut *v.t.* cortar
  cut class *idiom* irse de pinta *(Mexico);* hacer novillos *(Spain)*
cutlery *n.* cubertería *f.*
cycling *n.* ciclismo *m.*
cycling race *n.* carrera *f.* ciclista
cyclist *n.* ciclista *m., f.*
cylinder *n.* cilindro *m.*
cypress *n.* ciprés *m.*

D

dad *n.* papá *m.*
daily *adj.* diario/a
daily routine *n.* rutina *f.* diaria
dairy *n.* productos *m., pl.* lácteos
daisy *n.* margarita *f.*

dam *n.* represa *f.*
damage *v.t.* dañar; estropear
damp *adj.* húmedo/a
dance *n.* baile *m.;* danza *f.*
dance *v.t.* bailar
dance floor *n.* pista *f.* de baile
dancer *n.* bailarín *m.,* bailarina *f.*
danger *n.* peligro *m.*
dangerous *adj.* peligroso/a
dare (to + *inf.*) *v.t.* atreverse (a + *inf.*)
daring *adj.* atrevido/a
darken *v.t. (sky, clouds)* ennegrecerse
darts *n., pl. (game)* dardos *m., pl.*
date (someone) *v.t.* salir con (alguien)
date *n. (appointment)* cita *f.; (calendar)* fecha *f.*
  have a date tener una cita
  What is the date (today)? ¿Cuál es la fecha (de hoy)?
daughter *n.* hija *f.*
daughter-in-law *n.* nuera *f.*
dawn *n.* amanecer *m.*
dawn *v.i.* amanecer
day *n.* día *m.*
  What day is it? ¿Qué día es hoy?
day before yesterday *adv.* anteayer
day-care center *n.* guardería *f.*
daydream *v.i.* soñar despierto
dazed *adj.* atontado/a
dead-end street *n.* callejón *m.* sin salida
deaf *adj.* sordo/a
deal *n.* trato *m.*

It's a deal. Trato hecho.
It's no big deal. No es para tanto.
dealer *n.* *(arms, drugs)* traficante *m., f.*
dean *n.* *(university)* decano/a *m., f.*
death *n.* muerte *f.;* defunción *f.;* fallecimiento *m.*
debate *n.* debate *m.*
debate *v.t.* debatir
debut *v.t.* *(movie, play)* estrenar
decadence *n.* decadencia *f.*
decaffeinated *adj.* descafeinado/a
deceased *n., adj.* fallecido/a *m., f.,* difunto/a *m., f.*
deceive *v.t.* engañar
December *n.* diciembre *m.*
deception *n.* engaño *m.*
decide *v.t.* decidir
decided *adj.* decidido/a
decipher *v.t.* descifrar
decision *n.* decisión *f.*
  make a decision tomar una decisión
deck (of cards) *n.* baraja *f.* (de cartas/naipes)
deck chair *n.* tumbona *f.*
declare *v.t.* declarar
decline *n.* descenso *m.;* decadencia *f.*
decode *v.t.* descifrar
decorate *v.t.* decorar; adornar
decrease *n.* descenso *m.;* disminución *f.*
decrease *v.t.* disminuir
dedicate *v.t.* dedicar
dedication *n.* dedicación; dedicatoria *f.*

deer *n.* ciervo *m.*
defeat *n.* derrota *f.*
defeat *v.t.* derrotar
deficiency *n.* deficiencia *f.*
deficit *n.* déficit *m.*
define *v.t.* definir
definition *n.* definición *f.*
deforestation *n.* deforestación *f.*
defraud *v.t.* estafar
defuse *v.t.* desactivar
dejected *adj.* abatido/a
delay *n.* retraso *m.,* atraso *m.*
delicious *adj.* delicioso/a, rico/a, sabroso/a
  be delicious *loc.* estar para chuparse los dedos
delight *n.* deleite *m.,* placer *m.*
delighted *adj.* encantado/a
delineate *v.t.* delinear
delinquency *n.* delincuencia *f.*
democracy *n.* democracia *f.*
democrat *n.* demócrata *m., f.*
democratic *adj.* democrático/a
demonstrate *v.i.* manifestarse
demonstration *n.* manifestación *f.*
demonstrator *n.* manifestante *m., f.*
density *n.* densidad *f.*
dental floss *n.* hilo *m.* dental
dentist *n.* dentista *m., f.*
deny *v.t.* negar (e:ie)
deodorant *n.* desodorante *m.*
department *n.* departamento *m.*
department head *n.* catedrático/a *m., f.*
department store *n.* almacén *m.*

departure *n.* partida *f.*; salida *f.*
deposit *v.t.* depositar
depressed *adj.* deprimido/a
depression *n.* depresión *f.*
depth *n.* profundidad *f.*
derail *v.t.* descarrilar
derailment *n.* descarrilamiento *m.*
dermatologist *n.* dermatólogo/a *m., f.*
descend *v.i.* descender
descendant *n.* descendiente *m., f.*
descent *n.* descenso *m.*
describe *v.t.* describir
desert *n., adj.* desierto *m.*; desértico/a
deserve *v.t.* merecer
design *n.* diseño *m.*
designer *n.* diseñador(a) *m., f.*
desire *n.* deseo *m.*
desire *v.t.* desear
desk *n.* escritorio *m.*
despair *n.* desesperanza *f.*
despair *v.i.* desesperar(se); perder las esperanzas
desperate *adj.* desesperado/a
desperation *n.* desesperación *f.*
dessert *n.* postre *m.*
destroy *v.t.* destruir
destruction *n.* destrucción *f.*
detail *n.* detalle *m.*
detained *adj.* detenido/a
deteriorate *v.* decaer
determined *adj.* condicionado/a
detoxification *n.* desintoxicación *f.*
detoxify *v.t.* desintoxicar

detractor *n.* detractor(a) *m., f.*
develop *v.t.* desarrollar
development *n.* desarrollo *m.*; *(housing)* urbanización *f.*
dew *n.* rocío *m.*
diabetes *n.* diabetes *f.*
diabetic *n., adj.* diabético/a *m., f.*
diagnose *v.t.* diagnosticar
diagnostic *n.* diagnóstico *m.*
dial (the number) *v.t.* marcar (el número)
dialogue *n.* diálogo *m.*
diamond *n.* diamante *m.*
diarrhea *n.* diarrea *f.*
diary *n.* diario *m.*
dice *n., pl.* dados *m., pl.*
dictator *n.* dictador(a) *m., f.*
dictatorship *n.* dictadura *f.*
dictionary *n.* diccionario *m.*
die out *v.t.* extinguirse
die *v.i.* morir (o:ue)
died *p.p.* muerto (*of* morir)
diet *n.* dieta *f.*
  balanced diet dieta equilibrada
  be on a diet estar a dieta
differ *v.i.* divergir
difference *n.* diferencia *f.*, divergencia *f.*
differing *adj. (opinions)* divergente
difficult *adj.* difícil
  make difficult dificultar; complicar
difficulty *n.* dificultad *f.*
dig *v.t.* excavar
dining room *n.* comedor *m.*
dinner *n.* cena *f.*
  have dinner cenar

dinosaur n. dinosaurio m.
diplomat n. diplomático/a m., f.
diplomatic adj. diplomático/a
directions n., pl. direcciones f.,
  pl. indicaciones (Spain) f., pl.
  give directions dar
  direcciones
director n. director(a) m., f.
dirty adj. sucio/a
dirty v.t. ensuciar
  get dirty ensuciar
disabled adj. (person)
  inválido/a
disadvantage n. desventaja f.
disagree v.i. no estar de
  acuerdo
disappear v.i. desaparecer
disappearance n. desaparición
  f.
disappointed adj.
  decepcionado/a
  be disappointed
  decepcionarse
disaster n. desastre m.
  natural disaster desastre
  natural
disastrous adj. desastroso/a
discipline n. disciplina f.
discoteque n. discoteca f.
discount n. descuento m.
discount v.t. descontar
  give a discount descontar
discover v.t. descubrir
discovered p.p. descubierto
  (of descubrir)
discovery n. descubrimiento
  m.; hallazgo m.
discreet adj. discreto/a
discrimination n.
  discriminación f.

discus throw n. lanzamiento m.
  de disco
disgraceful adj. vergonzoso/a
disgusting adj. asqueroso/a
dish n. plato m.
  main dish plato principal
  serving dish fuente f.
dishcloth n. trapo m.
dishes (set) n., pl. vajilla f.
disheveled adj. despeinado/a
dishwasher n. lavaplatos m.,
  sing.
disinfect v.t. desinfectar
disinfectant n., adj.
  desinfectante
disk n. disco m.
dislike n. antipatía f.; aversión
  f.
disorder n. desorden m.;
  (medical) trastorno m.
disorderly adj. desordenado/a
disposable adj. desechable
disqualification n. (sport)
  descalificación f.
disqualify v.t. (sports)
  descalificar
disseminate v.t. propagar
distant adj. lejano/a
distinction n. (grade) matrícula
  f. de honor
distinguish v.t. distinguir
distinguished adj.
  distinguido/a
distribute v.t. distribuir
distribution n. distribución f.
distrustful adj. receloso/a
dive n. salto m.; clavado (L.A.)
  m.
dive v.i. (underwater) bucear
diving board n. trampolín m.

diver *n.* *(scuba)* buceador(a) *m., f.*
diverse *adj.* variado/a
divorce *n.* divorcio *m.*
divorced *adj.* divorciado/a
  get divorced (from) divorciarse (de)
dizzy *adj.* mareado/a
  feel dizzy marearse
do *v.t.* hacer
do oneself up *v.* arreglarse
doctor *n.* doctor(a) *m., f.;* médico/a *m., f.*
  doctor on call/duty médico/a de guardia
doctorate *n.* doctorado *m.*
document *n.* documento *m.*
document *v.t.* documentar
documentary *n.* documental *m.*
dog *n.* perro/a *m., f.*
doll *n.* muñeca *f.*
dolphin *n.* delfín *m.*
domestic *adj.* doméstico/a
dominate *v.t.* dominar
domino *n.* dominó *m.*
done *p.p.* hecho *(of* hacer*)*
donor *n.* donante *m., f.*
door *n.* puerta *f.*
  back door puerta trasera
  front door puerta principal
doorbell *n.* timbre *m.*
doorman *n.* portero/a *m., f.*
dormitory *n.* residencia *f.* estudiantil
double *adj.* doble
double room *n.* habitación *f.* doble
doubt *n.* duda *f.*
  There is no doubt that . . . No cabe duda que… ; No hay

duda que…
  without a doubt sin duda
doubt *v.t.* dudar
dough *n.* masa *f.*
dove *n.* paloma *f.*
down *adv.* abajo, debajo (de)
downhearted *adj.* desanimado/a
download *v.t.* *(computer)* trasvasar
downtown *n.* centro *m.*
draftsman *n.* delineante *m.*
draftswoman *n.* delineante *f.*
drag *v.t.* arrastrar
drain *v.t.* colar *(L.A.); (the dishes)* escurrir (los platos)
drainpipe *n.* desagüe *m.*
drama *n.* drama *m.*
dramatic *adj.* dramático/a
draw *v.t.* dibujar
drawback *n.* inconveniente *m.*
drawing *n.* dibujo *m.*
dream *v.i.* soñar
dress *n.* vestido *m.*
dress *v.t.* vestirse (e:i)*; (salad)* aderezar; aliñar
  get dressed vestirse (e:i)
dress up *v.* ponerse elegante
  You have dressed up tonight. Te has puesto muy elegante esta noche.
dressing *n.* *(culinary)* aderezo *m.,* aliño *m.; (medical)* vendaje *m.*
dressing room *n.* probador *m.*
dressmaker *n.* modista *f.*
drill *n.* *(tool)* perforadora *f.*
drill *v.t.* perforar
drink *n.* bebida *f.*
drink *v.t.* beber; tomar

Do you want something to drink? ¿Quieres algo de tomar?

drive *v.t.* conducir *(Spain)*; manejar *(L.A.)*

driver *n.* conductor(a) *m., f.*

driveway *n.* entrada *f.*

drop *n.* gota *f.; (temperature, price)* descenso *m.*

drought *n.* sequía *f.*

drown *v.t.* ahogar **Ahoga sus penas cantando.** She drowns her sorrows by singing. *v.i.* ahogarse **Te ahogas en un vaso de agua.** You get worked up about nothing.

drowned *adj.* ahogado/a

drug *n.* droga *f.*
  drug addict *n., adj.* drogadicto/a *m., f.*

drunk *adj.* borracho/a; ebrio/a; embriagado/a

dry *adj.* seco/a

due to *prep.* debido a; por
  due to the fact that debido a

dull *adj.* sin brillo; *(person)* aburrido/a, soso/a

dune *n.* duna *f.*

during *prep.* durante; por

dusk *n.* atardecer *m.*

dust *n.* polvo *m.*

dust *v.t.* sacudir
  dust the furniture sacudir los muebles

duty: be on duty estar de guardia

dye *v.t.* teñir

dying *adj.* moribundo/a
  I'm dying to/for . . . Me muero por (+ *inf.*)/n. ...

dynamite *n.* dinamita *f.*

dynamite *v.t.* dinamitar

dynasty *n.* dinastía *f.*

dysfunction *n.* disfunción *f.*

E

each *adj.* cada

eagle *n.* águila (el) *f.*

ear *n.* oreja *f.*
  inner ear *n.* oído *m.*

early *adj., adv.* temprano/a
  early morning *n.* madrugada *f.*

earn *v.t.* ganar
  earn one's living *idiom* ganarse la vida

earring *n.* arete *(L.A)* *m.*; pendiente *m. (Spain)*

earth *n.* tierra *f.*

earthquake *n.* terremoto *m.*

earthworm *n.* lombriz *f.*

ease *n.* soltura *f.*

ease *v.t.* aliviar

east *n.* este *m.*
  to the east al este

easy *adj.* fácil
  make easier facilitar
  Easier said than done. *idiom* Del dicho al hecho hay gran trecho.

easygoing *adj.* tranquilo/a

eat *v.t.* comer

eclipse *n.* eclipse *m.*

ecological *adj.* ecológico/a

ecologist *n.* ecologista *m., f.*

ecology *n.* ecología *f.*

economics *n.* economía *f.*

ecosystem *n.* ecosistema *m.*

ecotourism *n.* ecoturismo *m.*

Ecuadorian *n., adj.*

ecuatoriano/a *m., f.*
edible *adj.* comestible
eel *n.* anguila *f.*
effective *adj.* eficaz
effectiveness *n.* eficacia *f.*
efficiency *n.* eficiencia *f.*
efficient *adj.* eficiente, eficaz
effort *n.* esfuerzo *m.*
egg *n.* huevo *m.*
eggplant *n.* berenjena *f.*
eight hundred ochocientos/as
eight ocho
eighteen dieciocho
eighth octavo *m.;* octavo/a
eighty ochenta
either . . . or *conj.* o… o
elastic *adj.* elástico/a
elbow *n.* codo *m.*
elderly *adj.* anciano/a
elect *v.t.* elegir
election *n.* elección *f.*
electorate *n.* electorado *m.*
electric *adj.* eléctrico/a
electric current *n.* corriente *f.* eléctrica
electric shock *n.* descarga *f.* eléctrica
electrician *n.* electricista *m., f.*
electricity *n.* electricidad *f.;* luz *f.*
electrocuted: be electrocuted electrocutarse
electrolysis *n.* electrólisis *f.*
electronics *n.* electrónica *f.*
elegant *adj.* elegante
elementary *adj.* elemental; *(school)* primario/a
elephant *n.* elefante *m.*
elevator *n.* ascensor *m.*
eleven once
eliminate *v.t.* eliminar

elimination *n.* eliminación *f.*
eloquence *n.* elocuencia *f.*
eloquent *adj.* elocuente
e-mail *n.* correo *m.* electrónico
  e-mail message *n.* mensaje *m.* electrónico
embarrass *v.t.* avergonzar
embarrassed *adj.* avergonzado/a
embarrassment *n.* vergüenza *f.*
embrace *v.t.* abrazar; *(each other)* abrazarse
embroider *v.t.* bordar
emerald *n.* esmeralda *f.*
emergency *n.* emergencia *f.*
emergency room *n.* sala *f.* de emergencia
emigrant *n.* emigrante *m., f.*
emigrate *v.i.* emigrar
emigration *n.* emigración *f.*
emphasis *n.* énfasis *m.*
emphasize *v.t.* destacar; enfatizar
empire *n.* imperio *m.*
employee *n.* empleado/a *m., f.*
employment *n.* empleo *m.*
encourage *v.t.* dar aliento; animar
end *n.* fin *m.*
  at the end (of) *(physical location)* al fondo (de); *(month, century)* a fines de
end *v.t.* terminar
end table *n.* mesita *f.*
endangered species *n., pl.* especie(s) *f. (pl.)* en peligro de extinción
endurance *n.* resistencia *f.;* aguante *m.;*
endure *v.t.* soportar; aguantar

energy n. energía f.

engaged: get engaged (to) comprometerse (con)

engagement ring n. anillo m. de compromiso

engineer n. ingeniero/a m., f.

English adj., n. inglés m., inglesa f.; (language) inglés

enigma n. enigma m.

enigmatic adj. enigmático/a

enjoy v.t. disfrutar (de)

enjoyable adj. agradable; divertido/a

enough adj. bastante

enrich v.t. enriquecer

enroll v.i. matricularse; inscribirse

enrollment n. inscripción f.

entertaining adj. entretenido/a

enthusiasm n. entusiasmo m.

enthusiastic adj. entusiasmado/a

entirely adv. totalmente; del todo **He is not entirely mistaken.** No está del todo equivocado.

entrance n. entrada f.

entrance hall n. (residence) recibidor m.

entrepreneur n. empresario/a m., f.

envelope n. sobre m.

envious adj. envidioso/a

environment n. medio ambiente m.; (natural) ambiente m.

environmentalist n. ecologista m., f.

equality n. igualdad f.

equestrian sports n., pl. hípica f.

equipped adj. equipado/a

equivalence n. equivalencia f.

equivalent: be equivalent to equivaler

erase v.t. borrar

eraser n. borrador m.; (pencil) goma f.

errand n. diligencia f. **do/run errands** hacer diligencias

erupt v.i. (volcano) hacer erupción

eruption n. erupción f.

escalator n. escalera f. mecánica

escape n. evasión f.; huida f.; (prison) fuga f.

escape v.i. huir; fugarse; evadirse **Luis escaped responsibility.** Luis se evadió de la responsabilidad.

esophagus n. esófago m.

establish v.t. establecer

esteem n. aprecio m.

estimate n. cálculo m.

ethical adj. ético/a

ethics n. ética f.

euphoria n. euforia f.

euphoric adj. eufórico/a

European n., adj. europeo/a m., f.

evade v.t. evadir

evening n. tarde f. **in the evening** de la noche; por la noche

event n. acontecimiento m.

every adj. cada **every day** cada día, todos los días

everybody n. todos m., pl.

everything n. todo m.

Everything is under control. Todo está bajo control.

evidence *n.* indicio *m.;* pruebas *f., pl.*
  lack of evidence falta *f.* de pruebas

evolution *n.* evolución *f.*

evolve *v.i.* evolucionar

exactly *adv.* exactamente; *(time)* en punto

exaggerate *v.t.* exagerar

exaggeration *n.* exageración *f.*

exam *n.* examen *m.*

example: for example por ejemplo

exasperate *v.t.* desesperar **The slowness of the train exasperated him.** La lentitud del tren le desesperó.

excavate *v.t.* excavar

excavator *n.* excavadora *f.*

exceed *v.t.* superar

excel *v.i.* sobresalir

excellent *adj.* excelente; *(grade)* sobresaliente

exceptional *adj.* prodigioso/a

excess *n.* exceso *m.*
  in excess en exceso

exchange *n.* intercambio *m.*
  in exchange for a cambio de

exchange *v.t.* intercambiar

exciting *adj.* emocionante

excursion *n.* excursión *f.*

excuse *v.t.* disculpar
  Excuse me. *(May I?)* Con permiso.; *(Pardon me.)* Perdón.; *(interrupting)* Disculpe. **Excuse me, can you tell me…** Disculpe, puede decirme…

exercise *n.* ejercicio *m.; v.i.* hacer ejercicio
  do stretching exercises hacer ejercicios de estiramiento

exhaust pipe *n.* tubo *m.* de escape

exhausted *adj.* agotado/a

exhaustion *n.* agotamiento *m.*

exhibit *v.t. (paintings, goods)* exponer; *(skill)* demostrar

exhibition *n.* exposición *f.*

exit *n.* salida *f.*

exodus *n.* éxodo *m.*

expel *v.t.* expulsar

expense *n.* gasto *m.*

expensive *adj.* caro/a

experience *n.* experiencia *f.*

experiment *v.i.* experimentar

expiration *n.* expiración *f.*

expiration date *n.* fecha *f.* de caducidad

expire *v.i.* expirar

explain *v.t.* explicar

explore *v.t.* explorar
  explore a city/town explorar una ciudad/pueblo

explosive *adj.* explosivo/a

export *v.t.* exportar

exportation *n.* exportación *f.*

expression *n.* expresión *f.*

expressive *adj.* expresivo/a

expulsion *n.* expulsión *m.*

extinction *n.* extinción *f.*
  become extinct extinguirse

extinguish *v.t.* extinguir

extremely *adv.* sumamente

extremities *n., pl.* extremidades *f., pl.*

eye *n.* ojo *m.*

eyebrow n. ceja f.
eyelash n. pestaña f.
eyelid n. párpado m.
eyeshade n. visera f.

F

fabric n. tela f.
fabulous adj. fabuloso/a
façade n. fachada f.
face n. cara f.
face v.t. enfrentar **It's necessary to face the problem immediately.** Hay que enfrentar el problema en seguida.
facedown adv. boca abajo
faceup adv. boca arriba
facilitate v.t. facilitar
facing prep. enfrente de
fact n. hecho m.
  in fact de hecho; en efecto
factory n. fábrica f.
fail v.t. (exam) suspender; fracasar
fail n. (grade) suspenso m.
failed adj. fracasado/a
failure n. fracaso m.
fair adj. justo/a
fairy n. hada (el) f.
fairy godmother n. hada madrina
faithful adj. fiel
faithfulness n. fidelidad f.
fall v.i. caer; (down) caerse
fallen p.p. caído (of caer)
familiar adj. conocido/a
family n., adj. familia f.; familiar
family doctor n. médico/a m., f. de cabecera; médico/a de familia

family tree n. árbol m. genealógico
famine n. hambre m.
famous adj. famoso/a
fan n., adj. aficionado/a m., f.; ventilador m.
  be a fan of ser aficionado/a a
fang n. colmillo m.
far from adv. lejos de
farewell n. despedida f.
farmer n. agricultor(a) m., f.
farming n. agricultura f.
far-off adj. lejano/a
fascinate v.t. fascinar
fashion n. moda f.
  be in fashion estar de moda
  be fashionably dressed ir a la moda
fast adj. rápido/a
fast n. ayuno m.
fast v.i. ayunar
fast adj. rápido/a, veloz
  fast food n. comida f. rápida
fat adj. gordo/a
fat n. grasa f.
father n. padre m.
father-in-law n. suegro m.
fatten v.t. engordar
faucet n. grifo m.
favorable adj. favorable
favorite adj. favorito/a
fax n. fax m.
fear n. miedo m.
fear v.t. temer
February n. febrero m.
feed v.t. alimentar
  get fed up hartarse
feel v.t. sentir
  feel like (doing something) tener ganas de (+ inf.)

feeling sorry *adj.* arrepentido/a
female *n.* hembra *f.*
fence *n.* valla *f.*
fencer *n.* esgrimidor(a) *m., f.*
fencing *n. (sport)* esgrima *f.*
fender *n.* guardabarros *m., sing.*
ferry *n.* transbordador *m.*
fertile *adj.* fértil
fertility *n.* fertilidad *f.*
fertilization *n.* fecundación *f.*
fertilize *v.t.* fecundar; *(the soil)* abonar (la tierra)
fertilizer *n.* abono *m.;* fertilizante *m.*
festival *n.* festival *m.;* verbena *f.*
fever *n.* fiebre *f.*
  have a fever tener fiebre
few *adj.* pocos/as
fidelity *n.* fidelidad *f.*
field *n.* campo *m.; (sport)* cancha *f.*
  major field of study *n.* especialización *f.*
field hockey *n.* hockey *m.* sobre césped *(L.A.);* hockey sobre hierba *(Spain)*
fifteen quince
fifth quinto *m.;* quinto/a
fifty cincuenta
fig *n.* higo *m.*
fig tree *n.* higuera *f.*
fight *n.* pelea *f.;* lucha *f.*
fight *v.i.* luchar (por); pelear; pelearse
figure *n.* figura *f.; (number) n.* cifra *f.*
figure skating *n.* patinaje *m.* artístico

file *n.* archivo *m.; (tool)* lima *f.*
file *v.t.* archivar
fill *v.t.* llenar
fill out *v.t. (document)* rellenar *(Spain);* llenar *(L.A.)*
  fill out a form llenar un formulario
  fill the tank llenar el tanque
film *v.t.* rodar
film *n.* película
film library *n.* filmoteca *f.*
filming *n.* rodaje *m.*
filmmaker *n.* cineasta *m., f.*
fin *n.* aleta *f.*
finally *adv.* finalmente; por último; por fin
finance *v.t.* financiar
find *n.* hallazgo *m.* **That restaurant was a real find.** Ese restaurante fue un verdadero hallazgo.
find *v.t.* encontrar (o:ue); *(each other)* encontrarse
  I can't find my shoe. No encuentro el zapato.
  Finally, they found each other. Al fin se encontraron.
find out *v.t.* averiguar
fine *n.* multa *f.*
fine *adj.* bien
  That's fine. Está bien.
fine arts *n., pl.* bellas artes *f., pl.*
finger *n.* dedo *m.* (de la mano)
fingerprint *n.* huella *f.* dactilar
finish *v.t.* terminar; *(doing something)* terminar de *(+ inf.)*
fir tree *n.* abeto *m.*
fire *n.* fuego *m.;* incendio *m.*

fire engine n. carro m. de bomberos

fire escape n. escalera f. de incendios

firefighter n. bombero/a m., f.

fireplace n. chimenea f.

firewood n. leña f.

fireworks n., pl. fuegos m., pl. artificiales

firm n. compañía f.; empresa f.

first adj. primer, primero/a

first name n. nombre m. de pila

first-aid kit n. botiquín m. de primeros auxilios

firstborn n. primogénito/a m., f.

fish n. (food) pescado m.; (live) pez m.

  marinated fish n. ceviche m.

fish market n. pescadería f.

fish v.t. pescar

fisherman n. pescador m.

fishing n. pesca f.

  go fishing ir de pesca

fit adj. (suitable) apto/a **He's not fit to practice psychology.** No es apto para ejercer la psicología.; (physically) en forma

fit v.i. (clothing) quedar **Does it fit me?** ¿Me queda bien?

five cinco

five hundred quinientos/as

fix v.t. (put in working order) arreglar

fixed adj. (set) fijo/a

  fixed price n. precio m. fijo

flag n. bandera f.

flamboyant adj. extravagante

flank steak n. lomo m.

flashlight n. linterna f.; foco m.

flat: go flat v.t. ponchar (Mexico); pinchar **We had a flat tire.** Se nos ponchó una llanta.

flatter v.t. adular

  flatter someone idiom echarle flores a alguien

flatterer n. adulador(a) m., f.

flattery n. adulación f.

flavor n. sabor m.

flee v.i. fugarse; huir

flex v.t. flexionar

flexible adj. flexible

flight n. vuelo m.; (escape) huida f.

flight attendant n. azafato/a m., f.

flipper n. aleta f.

flirt n. coqueta f.

flirt v.i. coquetear

float n. carroza f.

float v.i. flotar

flood n. inundación f.

flood v.t. inundar

floor n. (story in a building) piso m.; (ground) suelo (Spain) m., piso (L.A.) m.

  ground floor planta f. baja

florist n. florista (Spain) m., f.; florero/a (L.A.) m., f.

flour n. harina f.

flow v.i. fluir

flower n. flor f.

flower pot n. maceta f.

flower shop n. florería (L.A.) f.; floristería (Spain) f.

flu n. gripe f.

fluffy adj. (fabric, baked goods) esponjoso/a

fly *n.* mosca *f.*
foam *n.* espuma *f.*
focus on *v.t.* enfocar
fog *n.* niebla *f.*
   It's (very) foggy. Hay (mucha) niebla.
fold *v.t.* plegar
folder *n.* carpeta *f.*
folding *adj.* plegable
folic acid *n.* ácido *m.* fólico
folk *adj.* folklórico/a
follow *v.t.* seguir (e:i)
food *n.* comida *f.;* alimento *m.*
foolish *adj.* tonto/a
foot *n.* pie *m.*
football *n.* fútbol *m.* americano
footprint *n.* huella *f.*
footrace *n.* carrera *f.* pedestre
for *prep.* para; por
forbid *v.t.* prohibir
forehead *n.* frente *f.*
foreign *adj.* extranjero/a
forensic scientist *n.* forense *m., f.*
forest *n.* bosque *m.*
   tropical forest bosque tropical
forget *v.t.* olvidar
forgive *v.t.* perdonar
forgiveness *n.* perdón *m.*
fork *n.* tenedor *m.*
forklift *n.* montacargas *m., sing.*
form *n. (shape)* forma *f.; (document)* formulario *m.*
fortnight *n.* quincena *f.*
fortress *n.* fortaleza *f.*
forty cuarenta
forward *adv.* hacia adelante
fossil *n.* fósil *m.*

fossilize *v.i.* fosilizarse
   become fossilized fosilizarse
foundation *n. (building)* cimientos *m., pl.*
fountain *n.* fuente *f.*
four cuatro
four hundred cuatrocientos/as
fourteen catorce
fourth cuarto *m.;* cuarto/a
fox *n.* zorro *m.*
fraud *n.* estafador(a) *m., f.*
freckle *n.* peca *f.*
freckled *adj.* pecoso/a
free *adj.* libre; *(price)* gratis
   be free of charge ser gratis
free *v.t.* liberar
free fall *n.* caída *f.* libre
free time *n.* tiempo *m.* libre; ratos *m., pl.* libres
freedom *n.* libertad *f.*
freedom of speech *n.* libertad de expresión
freelancer *n.* [trabajador(a)] autónomo/a *m., f.*
freestyle *n.* estilo *m.* libre
freezer *n.* congelador *m.*
French *n., adj.* francés *m.,* francesa *f.; (language)* francés
french fries *n., pl.* papas *f., pl.* fritas
frequently *adv.* frecuentemente; con frecuencia; a menudo
Friday *n.* viernes *m., sing.*
fried *adj.* frito/a
fried food *n.* fritada *f.*
fried potatoes *n., pl.* papas (L.A.) *f., pl.* fritas; patatas *(Spain) f., pl.* fritas

friend n. amigo/a m., f.
  make friends hacer amigos
friendly adj. amable;
  amistoso/a
friendship n. amistad f.
frog n. rana f.
from prep. de; desde
  from the United States
  estadounidense
  from time to time adv. de vez
  en cuando
front desk n. recepción f.
front door n. puerta f. principal
front seat n. asiento m.
  delantero
frost n. escarcha f.
frugal adj. ahorrador(a)
fruit n. fruta f.
fruit store n. frutería f.
fruit tree n. árbol m. frutal
fuchsia adj. fucsia
fuel n. combustible m.
fugitive n. fugitivo/a m., f.
full adj. lleno/a
fun adj. divertido/a
  have fun divertirse (e:ie)
fun activity n. diversión f.
function v.i. funcionar
funds n., pl. (money) fondos m.,
  pl.
funeral n. funeral m.
funnel n. embudo m.
funny adj. chistoso/a
furious adj. furioso/a
furnish v.t. amueblar
furnished adj. amueblado/a
furniture n. muebles m., pl.
furthermore adv. además (de)
fuse n. fusible m.
future n., adj. futuro/a; futuro
  m.; porvenir m.

G

gain v.t. ganar; obtener
  gain weight aumentar de
  peso; engordar
galaxy n. galaxia f.
gallbladder n. vesícula f.
  (biliar)
gallery n. galería f.
  art gallery pinacoteca f.
gambler n. jugador(a) m., f.
gambling n. juegos m., pl. de
  azar
game n. juego m.; (match)
  partido m.
game piece n. ficha f.
game show n. concurso m.
gang n. pandilla f.
gang member n. pandillero/a
  m., f.
garage n. garaje m.
garbage n. basura f.
garbage can n. basurero m.
garbage collector n.
  basurero/a m., f.
garbage disposal n. triturador
  m. de basura
garbage dump n. basurero m.;
  vertedero m.
garden n. jardín m.; huerto m.
  large garden n. huerta f.
gardener n. jardinero/a m., f.
gardenia n. gardenia f.
gardening n. jardinería f.
garlic n. ajo m.
garment n. prenda f.
garnish v.t. decorar; adornar
gas pedal n. pedal m. del
  acelerador
gas station n. gasolinera f.
gas tank n. depósito m. de
  gasolina

gasoline *n.* gasolina *f.*

gastronomy *n.* gastronomía *f.*

gathering *n.* *(to discuss politics, literature, etc.)* tertulia *f.*

gaze at *v.* contemplar

gazelle *n.* gacela *f.*

gearshift *n.* *(car)* cambio *m.* de marchas/velocidades

gelatin *n.* gelatina *f.*

generous *adj.* generoso/a

genetic *adj.* genético/a

genetic engineering *n.* biogenética *f.*

genetics *n.* genética *f.*

geography *n.* geografía *f.*

geologist *n.* geólogo/a *m., f.*

geometric(al) *adj.* geométrico/a

geometry *n.* geometría *f.*

geranium *n.* geranio *m.*

German *n., adj.* alemán *m.,* alemana *f.; (language)* alemán

get *v.t.* conseguir (e:i); obtener

get along well/badly with llevarse bien/mal con

get off (a vehicle) *v.* bajar (de)

get on/in (a vehicle) *v.* subir a

get up *v.* levantarse

get up early madrugar

getaway *n.* escapada *f.*

geyser *n.* géiser *m.*

gift *n.* regalo *m.*

giraffe *n.* jirafa *f.*

girl *n.* chica *f.;* muchacha *f.*

girlfriend *n.* novia *f.*

give *v.t.* dar; *(gift)* regalar

give in *v.* ceder

give up (doing something) *v.* dejar de (+ *inf.*)

give up hope *v.* desesperarse

give way *v.* ceder (el paso)

glass *n.* *(drinking)* vaso *m., (material)* vidrio *m.,* cristal *m.*

made of glass de vidrio

glasses *n., pl.* gafas *f., pl.*

glassware *n.* cristalería *f.*

glove *n.* guante *m.*

gluttonous *adj.* glotón *m.,* glotona *f.*

go *v.i.* ir

Let's go. Vamos.

go shopping ir de compras

go away *v.* irse; ausentarse

go beyond *v.* superar

go by *v.* pasar por

go by the bank pasar por el banco

go down *v.* bajar(se)

go off *v.* *(alarm)* sonar

go out (with) *v.* salir (con)

go out and have a snack in a bar ir de tapas *(Spain)*

go overboard *loc.* echar la casa por la ventana

go up *v.* subir

go with *v.* acompañar

goal *n.* meta *f.;* objetivo *m.*

goblet *n.* copa *f.*

God *n.* Dios *m.*

god *n.* *(deity)* dios *m.*

goddaughter *n.* ahijada *f.*

godfather *n.* padrino *m.*

godmother *n.* madrina *f.*

godson *n.* ahijado *m.*

going to: be going to (do something) ir a (+ *inf.*)

gold *adj.* dorado/a

gold *n.* oro *m.*

golden *adj.* dorado/a
golf *n.* golf *m.*
golf club *n.* palo *m.* de golf
golf course *n.* campo *m.* de golf
golfer *n.* golfista *m., f.*
good *adj.* buen, bueno/a
  I'm good, thanks. Bien, gracias.
  It's good that . . . Es bueno que (+ *subj.*)…
  in good spirits *adj.* animado/a
  Good afternoon. Buenas tardes.
  Good evening. Buenas noches.
  Good morning. Buenos días.
  Good night. Buenas noches.
good sense *n.* sensatez *f.*
good-bye *n.* adiós *m.;* despedida *f.*
  say good-bye despedirse
good-looking *adj.* guapo/a
goods *n.* artículos *m., pl.*
gossip *n.* chismes *m., pl.;* cotilleo *(Spain) m.*
gossip *v.i.* cotillear *(Spain);* chismear
Gothic *adj.* gótico/a
govern *v.t.* gobernar
government *n.* gobierno *m.*
grade *n.* calificación *f.;* nota *f.*
grade *v.t.* calificar
graduate (from, in) *v.i.* graduarse
graduation *n.* graduación *f.*
graffiti *n.* pintada *f.*
  There was gang graffiti on the wall. Había pintadas de pandillas en la pared.
grain *n.* grano *m.*
grains *n., pl.* cereales *m., pl.*
grandchildren *n., pl.* nietos *m., pl.*
granddaughter *n.* nieta *f.*
grandfather *n.* abuelo *m.*
grandmother *n.* abuela *f.*
grandparents *n., pl.* abuelos *m., pl.*
grandson *n.* nieto *m.*
grant *n.* beca *f.*
grape *n.* uva *f.*
grapefruit *n.* pomelo *(Argentina, Spain) m.;* toronja *(L.A.) f.*
grass *n.* césped *m.;* hierba *f.;* pasto *(L.A.) m.*
grateful *adj.* agradecido/a
grater *n.* rallador *m.*
grave *n.* tumba *f.*
gravity *n.* gravedad *f.*
gray *n., adj.* gris *m.*
gray hair *n.* cana *f.*
great *adj.* fenomenal
great-grandchildren *n., pl.* bisnietos *m., pl.*
great-granddaughter *n.* bisnieta *f.*
great-grandfather *n.* bisabuelo *m.*
great-grandmother *n.* bisabuela *f.*
great-grandparents *n., pl.* bisabuelos *m., pl.*
great-grandson *n.* bisnieto *m.*
great-great-grandfather *n.* tatarabuelo *m.*
great-great-grandmother *n.* tatarabuela *f.*

great-great-grandparents *n.,
pl.* tatarabuelos *m., pl.*
greedy *adj.* avaricioso/a
Greek *n., adj.* griego/a *m., f.;
(language)* griego
green *n., adj.* verde *m.*
  dark green verde oscuro
green space *n.* zona *f.* verde
greet *v.t.* saludar **He greets his
friend.** Él saluda a su amigo.;
(each other) saludarse **They
greet each other.** Ellos se
saludan.
greeting *n.* saludo *m.*
  Greetings to . . . Saludos a…
grenade *n. (military)* granada *f.*
grill *n.* parrilla *f.;* plancha *f.*
grilled *adj. (food)* a la plancha;
a la parrilla **grilled flank
steak** lomo a la plancha
groceries *n., pl.* comestibles
m., pl.
group *n.* grupo *m.*
group *v.t.* agrupar
  get into groups agruparse
grove *n.* arboleda *f.*
grow *v.t.* cultivar; *v.i.* crecer
growing *adj.* creciente
growth *n.* crecimiento *m.*
grudge *n.* rencor *m.*
guarantee *n.* garantía *f.*
guarantee *v.t.* garantizar;
asegurar
guard *v.t.* custodiar
guess *v.t.* adivinar
guest *n. (at a house/hotel)*
huésped(a) *m., f.; (at a
function)* invitado/a *m., f.*
guide *n.* guía *m., f.*
gum *n. (chewing)* chicle *m.;*

(anat.) encía *f.*
gunshot *n.* disparo *m.*
gymnasium *n.* gimnasio *m.*
gymnast *n.* gimnasta *m., f.*
gymnastics *n.* gimnasia *f.*
  rhythmic gymnastics
gimnasia rítmica
gynecologist *n.* ginecólogo/a
m., f.

H

hair *n.* pelo *m.;* cabello *m.*
hairbrush *n.* cepillo *m.* de pelo
hairdo *n.* peinado *m.* **Her new
hairdo suits/suited her.** Su
nuevo peinado le sienta/le
sentaba bien.
hairdresser *n.* peluquero/a *m.,
f.*
hairdryer *n.* secador *m.*
hairstyle *n.* peinado *m.*
hairy *adj.* peludo/a
hake *n.* merluza *f.*
half *n., adj.* medio *m.;* medio/a
half-brother *n.* medio hermano
m.
half-past . . . …y media
half-sister *n.* media hermana *f.*
hall *n.* salón *m.*
hallway *n.* pasillo *m.*
ham *n.* jamón *m.*
hamburger *n.* hamburguesa *f.*
hammer *n.* martillo *m.*
hammock *n.* hamaca *f.*
hand *n.* mano *f.*
  Hands up! ¡Manos arriba!
handball *n.* balonmano *m.*
handbrake *n.* freno *m.* de mano
handkerchief *n.* pañuelo *m.*
handle *n.* asa *m.*

handlebars *n., pl.* manillar *(Spain) m.*; manubrio *(L.A.) m.*

handrail *n.* pasamanos *m., sing.*

handsome *adj.* guapo

handy *adj.* práctico/a

hang *v.t.* colgar
   hang clothes on the line colgar la ropa en el tendedero

hang glider *n.* ala (el) *f.* delta

hang gliding *v.* practicar el ala delta

hang out (clothes) *v.* tender (ropa)

hanger *n.* percha *f.*

hangover *n.* resaca *(Spain) f.*; cruda *(Mexico) f.*
   have a hangover tener cruda; tener resaca

happen *v.t.* ocurrir
   What happened? ¿Qué pasó?
   What's happening? ¿Qué pasa?

happy *adj.* alegre; contento/a; feliz
   be happy alegrarse (de)
   be happy (with) contentarse (con)

harbor *n.* puerto *m.*

hard *adj.* difícil; duro/a
   hard to believe *idiom* parece mentira

hard feelings *n., pl.* rencor *m.*

hardly *adv.* apenas

hardship *n.* dificultad *f.*

hard-working *adj.* trabajador(a)

harmful *adj.* dañino/a

harvest *n.* cosecha *f.*

harvest *v.t.* cosechar

haste *n.* prisa *f.*

hat *n.* sombrero *m.*

hate *v.i.* odiar

have *v.t.* tener
   have a good/bad time pasarlo bien/mal
   have something on the tip of one's tongue *loc.* tener algo en la punta de la lengua
   have to (do something) tener que (+ *inf.*); deber (+ *inf.*)
   have to do with *loc.* tener que ver con **The letter doesn't have anything to do with the problem.** La carta no tiene nada que ver con el problema.
   have an unfinished (matter) tener (un asunto) pendiente

haze (someone) *v.t.* hacer una novatada (a alguien)

hazel tree *n.* avellano *m.*

hazelnut *n.* avellana *f.*

head *n.* cabeza *f.*

headache *n.* dolor *m.* de cabeza

headlight *n.* faro *m.*

headphone *n.* auricular *m.*

health *n.* salud *f.*

health care *n.* asistencia *f.* médica

healthful *adj.* saludable

healthy *adj.* sano/a

hear *v.t.* oír

heard *p.p.* oído (*of* oír)
   have heard *idiom* oír decir que
   I've heard that Mapi and Kiko are getting married. He

oído decir que Mapi y Kiko
se van a casar.
hearing: sense of hearing *n.*
oído *m.*
heart *n.* corazón *m.*
by heart de memoria **He
knows the poem by heart.** Se
sabe el poema de memoria.
heart attack *n.* infarto *m.*;
ataque *m.* al corazón; ataque
cardíaco
heartbeat *n.* latido *m.*
heat *n.* calor *m.*
heat *v.t.* calentar
heater *n.* calentador *m.*
heating *n.* calefacción *f.*
heaven *n.* cielo *m.*
Heaven forbid! *loc.* ¡Dios me
libre!
heavy vehicles *n., pl.* vehículos
m., pl. pesados
Hebrew *n., adj.* hebreo/a *m., f;
(language)* hebreo
hedge *n.* seto *m.*
heel *n.* talón *m.*
hefty *adj.* corpulento/a
height *n.* altura *f.*
heir *n.* heredero *m.*
heiress *n.* heredera *f.*
helicopter *n.* helicóptero *m.*
Hello *interj.* Hola.; *(on the
telephone)* ¿Aló?, ¿Bueno?,
¿Diga?
helmet *n.* casco *m.*
help (to) *v.t.* ayudar (a); servir
(e:i); *(each other)* ayudarse
(a)
Help! *interj.* ¡Auxilio!;
¡Socorro!
hemisphere *n.* hemisferio *m.*
hemorrhage *n.* hemorragia *f.*

herbivore *n.* herbívoro/a *m., f.*
herbivorous *adj.* herbívoro/a
herbs *n., pl.* hierbas *f., pl.*
here *adv.* aquí
Here it is. Aquí está.
Here we are in . . . Aquí
estamos en…
hereditary *adj.* hereditario/a
heritage *n.* patrimonio *m.*
hermit *n.* ermitaño/a *m., f.*
hero *n.* héroe *m.*
heroine *n.* heroína *f.*
Hi *interj.* Hola
hiccups *n., pl.* hipo *m.*
hide *v.t.* esconder; disimular
hierarchical *adj.* jerárquico/a;
jerarquizado/a
hierarchy *n.* jerarquía *f.*
high jump *n.* salto *m.* alto
(L.A.); salto *m.* de altura
(Spain)
highway *n.* autopista *f.;*
carretera *f.*
hijack *n.* secuestro *m.*
hijack *v.t (aircraft)* secuestrar
hike *n.* excursión *f.*
**go for a hike (in the
mountains)** ir de excursión (a
las montañas)
go hiking ir de excursión
go on a hike hacer una
excursión
hiker *n.* excursionista *m., f.*
hillside *n.* ladera *f.*
Hindu *n., adj.* hindú *m., f*
hint *n.* consejo *m.;* indicación *f.*
hip *n.* cadera *f.*
hippodrome *n.* hipódromo *m.*
Hispanic *n., adj.* hispano/a *m.,
f.*
historian *n.* historiador(a) *m., f.*

history *n.* historia *f.*
hitchhike *v.i.* hacer auto(e)stop
hitchhiker *n.* auto(e)stopista *m.*, *f.*
hobby *n.* afición *f.*; pasatiempo *m.*
hockey *n.* hockey *m.*
hold *v.t.* aguantar *(Spain)*
hold up *v.t. (bank)* atracar
holdup *n.* atraco *m.*
hole *n.* agujero *m.*; hueco *m.*; *(in the ground)* hoyo
  make holes in agujerear
holiday *n.* día *m.* de fiesta
Holy Week *n.* Semana *f.* Santa
homage *n.* homenaje *m.*
  pay homage to homenajear
home *n.* casa *f.*; hogar *m.*
  at home en casa
  home for the elderly *n.* residencia *f.* de ancianos
homemade *adj.* casero/a
home page *n.* página *f.* principal
home run *n.* cuadrilátero *m.*
home style *adj.* casero/a
home team *n. (sports)* equipo *m.* local
hometown *n.* ciudad *f.* natal; *(my…)* mi pueblo *m.*, mi ciudad *f.*
homework *n.* deberes *m.*, *pl.*; asignación *f.*; tarea *f.*
honey *n.* miel *f.*
honeymoon *n.* luna *f.* de miel
hood *n. (car)* capó *m.*; *(jacket)* capucha *f.*
hope *n.* esperanza *f.*
hope *v.t.* esperar
  I hope (that) *interj.* Ojalá (que)

horizon *n.* horizonte *m.*
hormone *n.* hormona *f.*
horn *n.* cuerno *m.*; *(car)* bocina *f.*
horror *n.* horror *m.*
hors d'oeuvres *n.*, *pl.* entremeses *m.*, *pl.*
horse *n.* caballo *m.*
  ride a horse montar a caballo
horse race *n.* carrera *f.* de caballos
horseback riding *n.* equitación *f.*
horticulturalist *n.* horticultor(a) *m.*, *f.*
horticulture *n.* horticultura *f.*
hose *n.* manguera *f.*
hospitable *adj.* hospitalario/a
hospital *n.* hospital *m.*
hospitality *n.* hospitalidad *f.*
host *n.* anfitrión *m.*
hostel *n.* albergue *m.*; hostal *m.*
hostess *n.* anfitriona *f.*
hot *adj.* caliente
  be hot *(weather)* hacer calor; *(feel)* tener calor
  It's hot. *(weather)* Hace calor.
hotel *n.* hotel *m.*
hour *n.* hora *f.*
house *n.* casa *f.*
housewife *n.* ama *f.* de casa
housing *n.* vivienda *f.*
how *adv.* ¿cómo?
  How are you? *fam.* ¿Cómo estás?; ¿Qué tal? *form.* ¿Cómo está usted?
  How did it go for you . . .? ¿Cómo le/les fue…?

How is it going? ¿Qué tal?
How is/are . . . ? ¿Qué tal...?
How many? ¿Cuánto/a(s)?
How may I help you? ¿En qué puedo servirle(s)?
How much does it cost? ¿Cuánto cuesta…?
How . . . ! ¡Qué…!
How big! ¡Qué grande!
How nice to see you. *loc.* Dichosos los ojos (que te ven).
however *conj.* sin embargo
hug *v.t.* abrazar; (*each other*) abrazarse
human *adj.* humano/a
human being *n.* ser *m.* humano
humanism *n.* humanismo *m.*
humanist *n.* humanista *m., f.*
humanities *n., pl.* humanidades *f., pl.*
humble *adj.* humilde
humid *adj.* húmedo/a
humidity *n.* humedad *f.*
humiliated *adj.* humillado/a
humming bird *n.* colibrí *m.*
hump *n.* joroba *f.*
hunchbacked *adj.* jorobado/a
hunger *n.* hambre *f.*
  be hungry tener hambre
hungry *adj.* hambriento/a
hunt *v.t.* cazar
hunter *n.* cazador(a) *m., f.*
hunting *n.* caza *f.*
hurdles *n., pl. (sport)* vallas *f., pl.*
hurricane *n.* huracán *m.*
hurry *v.i.* apurarse; darse prisa; apresurarse
  be in a hurry tener prisa

hurt *v.t.* doler (o:ue); lastimar
  It hurts me a lot . Me duele mucho.
husband *n.* esposo *m.;* marido *m.*
hydrangea *n.* hortensia *f.*
hydraulic *adj.* hidráulico/a
hyperbole *n.* hipérbole *f.*
hypothesis *n.* hipótesis *f.*
hypothetical *adj.* hipotético/a

I

ice *n.* hielo *m.*
ice cream *n.* helado *m.*
ice-cream shop *n.* heladería *f.*
ice hockey *n.* hockey *m.* sobre hielo
ice rink *n.* pista *f.* de hielo
ice skating *n.* patinaje *m.* sobre hielo
iceberg *n.* iceberg *m.*
iced *adj.* helado/a
iced tea *n.* té *m.* helado
idea *n.* idea *f.*
idle *adj.* ocioso/a
if *conj.* si
ignorance *n.* ignorancia *f.*
ignorant *adj.* ignorante
illiterate (person) *n., adj.* analfabeto/a *m., f.*
ill-mannered *adj.* grosero/a; maleducado/a
illness *n.* enfermedad *f.*
imagine *v.t.* imaginar
imitate *v.t.* imitar
imitation *n.* imitación *f.*
immediately *adv.* inmediatamente; en el acto
immigrant *n., adj.* inmigrante *m., f.*

immigrate *v.i.* inmigrar
immigration *n.* inmigración *f.*
immune system *n.* sistema *m.* inmunológico
immunize *v.t.* inmunizar
immunological *adj.* inmunológico/a
impatience *n.* impaciencia *f.*
impatient *adj.* impaciente
  get impatient impacientarse
  She got impatient over the delay. Se impacientó con el atraso.
impetuous *adj. (person)* lanzado/a, impulsivo/a
import *v.t.* importar
important *adj.* importante
  be important (to) *v.i.* importar
importation *n.* importación *f.*
impossible *adj.* imposible
impostor *n.* impostor(a) *m., f.*
impoverish *v.t.* empobrecer
impression *n.* impresión *f.*
  make a good/bad impression causar una buena/mala impresión
imprison *v.t.* encarcelar
improbable *adj.* improbable; inverosímil
improve *v.t.* mejorar
improvement *n.* mejora *f.*
impulsive *adj.* lanzado/a
in *prep.* en
  in a jiffy *idiom* en un dos por tres; en un santiamén
in front of *prep.* delante de
inaugurate *v.t.* inaugurar
inauguration *n.* inauguración *f.*
incomprehensible *adj.* incomprensible

inconceivable *adj.* inconcebible
inconvenience *n.* molestia *f.*
increase *n.* aumento *m.;* incremento *m.*
  be on the increase estar en auge
increasing *adj.* creciente
incredible *adj.* increíble
independent *adj.* independiente
  become independent independizarse
indescribable *adj.* inefable
indigenous *adj.* indígena
indigo *n., adj.* añil *m.*
individual *n., adj.* individuo *m. (may be pejorative:* **Who's that guy?** ¿Quién es ese individuo?)*; individual
individuality *n.* individualidad *f.*
inebriated *adj.* ebrio/a; embriagado/a
inequality *n.* desigualdad *f.*
inexperienced *adj.* novato/a
inexplicable *adj.* inexplicable
infection *n.* infección *f.*
influence *v.t.* influir en; influenciar
  Darío's poems influenced other poets. Los poemas de Darío influyeron en otros poetas.
inform *v.t.* informar
  inform oneself informarse
ingest *v.t.* ingerir
ingestion *n.* ingestión *f.*
inherit *v.t.* heredar
inheritance *n.* herencia *f.*

inject *v.t.* inyectar
injection *n.* inyección *f.*
  give an injection poner una inyección
injure *v.t. (oneself)* lastimarse
  injure one's (foot) lastimarse el (pie)
injured *n., adj.* herido/a *m., f.*
inn *n.* hostal *m.*
innovate *v.i.* innovar
innovation *n.* innovación *f.*
innovative *adj.* innovador(a)
innovator *n.* innovador(a) *m., f.*
insect *n.* insecto *m.*
insipid *adj.* insípido/a
insist (on + gerund) insistir (en + *inf.*)
  He insists on going. Insiste en ir.
insistence *n.* insistencia *f.*
insomnia *n.* insomnio *m.*
inspire *v.t.* inspirar
install *v.t. (equipment)* instalar
  install oneself instalarse
installment *n. (payment)* plazo *m. (monthly payment)* mensualidad *f.*
  pay in installments pagar a plazos
institution *n.* institución *f.*
instrument *n.* instrumento *m.*
insulate *v.t.* aislar
insulation *n.* aislante *m.*
insulin *n.* insulina *f.*
insult *n.* insulto *m.;* ofensa *f.*
intake *n.* consumo *m.*
intelligent *adj.* inteligente
intend to (+ inf.) *v.* pensar (+ *inf.*)
intentionally *adv.*

intencionalmente, adrede, a propósito
interest *n.* interés *m.*
interest *v.t.* interesar
  take an interest (in) interesarse (en) **He's only interested in the results.** Sólo se interesa en los resultados.
interesting *adj.* interesante
intermediate *adj.* intermedio/a
international *adj.* internacional
Internet *n.* red *f.;* Internet *m.*
interpreter *n.* intérprete *m., f.*
interpreting *n.* interpretación *f.*
interrupt *v.t.* interrumpir
intervention *n.* intervención *f.*
interview *n.* entrevista *f.*
interview *v.t.* entrevistar
interviewer *n.* entrevistador(a) *m., f.*
intestine *n.* intestino *m.*
intolerant *adj.* intolerante
intrigue *n.* intriga *f.*
intrigued *adj.* intrigado/a
introduction *n.* presentación *f.*
invertebrate *n., adj.* invertebrado *m.;* invertebrado/a
invest *v.t.* invertir (i:ie)
invitation *n.* invitación *f.*
invite *v.t.* invitar
involuntary *adj.* involuntario/a
iron *n. (metal)* hierro *m.; (clothes)* plancha *f.*
iron *v.t.* planchar (la ropa)
ironic *adj.* irónico/a
irony *n.* ironía *f.*
isolate *v.t.* aislar
  isolate oneself aislarse

issue *n.* cuestión *f.*
Italian *n., adj.* italiano/a *m., f.;* *(language)* italiano
item *n.* artículo *m.*
itinerary *n.* itinerario *m.*
ivy *n.* hiedra *f.*

J

jack *n. (playing cards)* jota *f.*
jacket *n.* chaqueta *f.*
jackknife *n.* navaja *f.*
jail *n.* cárcel *f.*
jail *v.t.* encarcelar
jam *n.* mermelada *f.*
January *n.* enero *m.*
Japanese *n., adj.* japonés *m.,* japonesa *f.; (language)* japonés
javelin throw *n.* lanzamiento *m.* de jabalina
jealous *adj.* celoso/a; envidioso/a
jealousy *n.* celos *m., pl.*
jeans *n.* bluejeans *(L.A.) m., pl.;* vaqueros, tejanos *(Spain) m., pl.*
jellyfish *n.* medusa *f.*
jest: in jest en broma
jetty *n.* embarcadero *m.*
Jew *n.* judío/a *m., f.*
jeweler *n.* joyero/a *m., f.*
jewelry box *n.* joyero *m.*
jewelry store *n.* joyería *f.*
jewel *n.* joya *f.*
Jewish *adj.* judío/a
job *n.* empleo *m.;* puesto *m.;* trabajo *m.*
job application *n.* solicitud *f.* de trabajo
jog *v.i.* correr

joint *n. (anatomy)* articulación *f.*
joke *n.* broma *f.*
  as a joke en broma
  make jokes hacer bromas
  practical joke broma pesada; novatada *f.*
joker *n.* bromista *m., f.*
journalism *n.* periodismo *m.*
journalist *n.* periodista *m., f.;* reportero/a *m., f.*
joy *n.* alegría *f.*
joyful *adj.* alegre
jubilation *n.* algarabía *f.*
judge *n.* juez *m., f.*
judge *v.t.* juzgar
judgment *n.* juicio *m.*
juice *n.* jugo *(L.A.) m.;* zumo *(Spain) m.*
  fruit juice jugo/zumo de fruta
juicer *n.* exprimidor *m.*
juicy *adj.* jugoso/a
July *n.* julio *m.*
jump *n.* salto *m.*
jump *v.i.* saltar
June *n.* junio *m.*
jungle *n.* selva *f.,* jungla *f.*
jury *n.* jurado *m.*
just *adv.* apenas
  have just *(done something)* acabar de (+ *inf.*)
justice *n.* justicia *f.*

K

kangaroo *n.* canguro *m.*
key *n.* llave *f.*
key chain *n.* llavero *m.*
keyboard *n.* teclado *m.*
kid *n.* niño/a *m., f.*
kid *v.i.* bromear

kid someone *idiom* tomarle el pelo a alguien
kidnap *v.t. (people)* secuestrar
kidnapping *n.* secuestro *m.*
kidney *n.* riñón *m.*
kill *v.t.* matar (a alguien)
  kill two birds with one stone *loc.* matar dos pájaros de un tiro
kilometer *n.* kilómetro *m.*
kind: That's very kind of you. (Eres/Es usted) Muy amable.
kingdom *n.* reino *m.*
kiss *n.* beso *m.*
  give a kiss dar un beso
kiss *v.t.* besar; *(each other)* besarse
kitchen *n.* cocina *f.*
kitchenware *n.* artículos *m., pl.* de cocina
knee *n.* rodilla *f.*
knife *n.* cuchillo *m.*
knit *v.i.* hacer punto
knitted *adj.* de punto
knitwear *n.* artículos *m., pl.* de punto
know *v.t.* saber; conocer
know-it-all *n., adj.* sabihondo/a *m., f.*
known *adj.* conocido/a

L

laboratory *n.* laboratorio *m.*
lack *n.* falta *f.;* carencia *f.*
lack *v.t.* faltar
lack of understanding *n.* incomprensión *f.*
ladle *n.* cucharón *m.*
lake *n.* lago *m.*
lamb *n.* cordero *m.*

lame *adj.* cojo/a
lamp *n.* lámpara *f.*
land *n.* tierra *f.; (parcel)* terreno *m.*
land *v.t.* aterrizar
landing *n.* aterrizaje *m.*
landing strip *n.* pista *f.* de aterrizaje
landlord *n.* dueño/a *m., f.*
landscape *n.* paisaje *m.*
lane *n. (highway)* carril *m.*
language *n.* lengua *f.;* idioma *m.*
  foreign languages *n., pl.* lenguas *f., pl.* extranjeras
lap *n. (sports)* vuelta *f.*
laptop (computer) *n.* computadora *f.* portátil
large *n., adj. (clothing size)* talla *m.* grande; grande, *(quantity)* elevado/a **You notice a large quantity of fat in the food.** Se nota una cantidad elevada de grasa en la comida.
large intestine *n.* intestino *m.* grueso
larva *n.* larva *f.*
larynx *n.* laringe *f.*
last *adj.* pasado/a; último/a
last *v.i.* durar
last night *adv.* anoche
lasting *adj.* duradero/a
late *adv.* tarde
  be late llegar tarde; retrasarse **be late (in)** tardar en **The bus was late (in arriving).** El autobús tardó en llegar.

later *adv.* más tarde
  at the very latest a más tardar **Bring it to me on Thursday at the very latest.** Tráemelo el jueves a más tardar.
Latin *n., adj.* latino/a *m., f.; (language)* latín *m.*
laugh *v.i.* reír, reírse (e:i)
laughed *p.p.* reído *(of* reír)
launch *n.* lanzamiento *m.*
launch *v.t.* lanzar **NASA launched a rocket to Saturn.** La NASA lanzó un cohete a Saturno.
laundromat *n.* lavandería *f.*
law *n.* ley *f.*
lawn mower *n.* cortacésped *f.*
lawyer *n.* abogado/a *m., f.*
laziness *n.* pereza *f.*
lazy *adj.* perezoso/a
lead *n.* plomo *m.* **a lead pipe** un tubo de plomo
lead *v.t.* liderar
leader *n.* líder *m., f.*
leadership *n.* liderazgo *m.*
leaf *n.* hoja *f.*
leak *n. (gas, water)* fuga *f.*
learn *v.t.* aprender
learned *adj.* sabio/a
learning *n.* enseñanza *f.*
lease *n.* contrato *m.*
least: at least por lo menos
leather *n.* piel *f.*
  made of leather de piel
leather goods *n., pl.* artículos *m., pl.* de piel
leave *v.i.* salir; irse; partir; dejar
  leave a message dejar un

mensaje/recado
leave alone dejar
leave behind dejar
leave for *(a place)* salir para…
leave from salir de
lecture *n.* conferencia *f.*
lecture hall *n.* aula (el) *f.*
  main lecture hall aula magna
left *adj., n.* izquierdo/a *m., f.*
  be left over quedar, sobrar
  to the left (of) a la izquierda (de)
leftovers *n., pl.* restos *m., pl.;* sobras *f., pl.*
leg *n.* pierna *f.*
legacy *n.* legado *m.*
legal *adj.* legal
legalize *v.t.* legalizar
legend *n.* leyenda *f.*
leisure time *n.* ocio *m.*
lemon *n.* limón *m.*
lemon tree *n.* limonero *m.*
lend *v.t.* prestar
lengthwise section *n. (Tech.)* corte *m.* longitudinal
lentil *n.* lenteja *f.*
leopard *n.* leopardo *m.*
less *adv.* menos
  less . . . than menos… que
  less than + *(number)* menos de + *(number)*
lesson *n.* lección *f.*
let *v.t.* dejar
  let go soltar
  let up *(pain)* aliviarse
letter *n.* carta *f.; (alphabet)* letra *f.*
  put a letter in the mailbox

echar una carta al buzón
lettuce *n.* lechuga *f.*
level *n.* nivel *m.*
lever *n.* palanca *f.*
liar *n.* mentiroso/a *m., f.*
liberal *n., adj.* liberal *m., f.*
liberation *n.* liberación *f.*
liberty *n.* libertad *f.*
librarian *n.* bibliotecario/a *m., f.*
library *n.* biblioteca *f.*
license *n. (driver's)* licencia *f.* de manejar/conducir
license plate *n.* (placa *f.* de) matrícula *f.*
lid *n.* tapa *f.*
lie *n.* mentira *f.*
lie *v.i.* mentir
lie down (in the sun) *v.* tumbarse (al sol)
life *n.* vida *f.*
life expectancy *n.* esperanza *f.* de vida
life imprisonment *n.* cadena *f.* perpétua
life jacket *n.* salvavidas *m., sing.*
life sentence *n.* cadena *f.* perpétua
lifeguard *n.* salvavidas *m., f., sing.*
lifestyle: lead a healthy lifestyle llevar una vida sana
lift *v.t.* levantar
lift weights levantar pesas
light *n., adj.* luz *f.;* liviano/a
light aircraft *n.* avioneta *f.*
light green *n., adj.* verde *m.* claro
lighter *n.* encendedor *m.*

lightning bolt *n.* rayo *m.;* relámpago *m.*
lightning rod *n.* pararrayos *m., sing.*
like *prep.* como
What's . . . like? ¿Cómo es...?
like *v.t.* gustar
Do you like . . . ? ¿Te gusta(n)...?
I like . . . very much. Me encanta...
would like to tener ganas de (+ *inf.*) **I would like to visit Diamantina.** Tengo ganas de visitar Diamantina.
Would you like to? ¿Te gustaría?
Like father, like son. *loc.* De tal palo, tal astilla.
likeable *adj.* simpático/a
likely: be likely that (*something will happen*) ser probable que (+ *subj.*) **It's likely that they won't arrive on time.** Es probable que no lleguen a tiempo.
likewise *adv.* igualmente
lily *n.* lirio *m.*
limb *n. (body)* miembro *m.*
limit *v.t.* limitar
limousine *n.* limusina *f.*
line *n.* línea *f.;* cola *f.* **There is a long line at the cinema.** Hay una larga cola en el cine.
stand in/on line hacer cola
line up hacer cola
linen *adj.* de hilo
linguist *n.* lingüista *m., f.*
linguistic *adj.* lingüístico/a

linguistics *n.* lingüística *f.*
lion *n.* león *m.*
lipstick *n.* lápiz *m.* labial; pintalabios *m., sing.*
liqueur *n.* licor *m.*
liquid *n., adj.* líquido *m.;* líquido/a
listen to *v.t.* escuchar
  listen to music escuchar música
  listen to the radio escuchar la radio
  Listen! *(command)* ¡Oye! *fam., sing.;* ¡Oigan! *form., pl.*
listener *n.* oyente *m., f.; (radio)* radioyente *m., f.*
literature *n.* literatura *f.*
little *adj.* pequeño/a; poco/a
little bit *n.* pizca *f.*
Little Dipper *n.* Osa *f.* Menor
live *v.i.* vivir; residir
  live by begging vivir de limosnas
lively *adj.* vivo/a
liver *n.* hígado *m.*
living being *n.* ser *m.* vivo
living room *n.* sala *f.*
lizard *n.* lagarto *f.*
loaf (of bread) *n.* barra *f.* (de pan) *(Spain)*
loan *n.* préstamo *m.*
lobster *n.* langosta *f.*
located *adj.* situado/a
  be located quedar
locker room *n.* vestuario *m.*
locomotive *n.* locomotora *f.*
lodge *v.t.* alojar
lodging *n.* alojamiento *m.;* parador *m.*
log *n. (wood)* tronco *m.,* leño *m.*

long *adj.* largo/a
  long-distance race *n.* carrera *f.* de fondo
  long jump *n.* salto *m.* de longitud *(Spain);* salto *m.* largo *(L.A.)*
long for *v.* ansiar
  long for (someone) añorar (a alguien)
longevity *n.* longevidad *f.*
longing *n.* ansia *f.*
look after oneself *v.* cuidarse
look at *v.* mirar; *(a topic)* enfocar **The program looks at the problem of homelessness.** El programa enfoca el problema de la falta de vivienda.
look for *v.* buscar
look good *v.* lucir
look in *v. (reference)* consultar **I'll look in the dictionary.** Consultaré el diccionario.
look up *v. (word)* buscar (en el diccionario)
lose *v.t.* perder (e:ie)
  lose weight adelgazar
lost *adj.* perdido/a
  be lost estar perdido/a
lot *n.* terreno *m.*
lot of, a *adj.* mucho/a
  a lot *n.* sinfín *m.* **She still has a lot of things to do.** Todavía tiene un sinfín de cosas que hacer.
loud *adj.* escandaloso/a
loudspeaker *n.* altavoz *m.*
lounge chair *n.* tumbona *f.*
love *n.* amor *m.*

in love *adj.* enamorado/a
fall in love (with)
enamorarse (de)
love *v.t. (another person)*
querer (e:ie); *(things)*
encantar
loyal *adj.* fiel
luck *n.* suerte *f.*
be lucky tener suerte
luggage *n.* equipaje *m.*
lunch *n.* almuerzo *m.*
have lunch almorzar (o:ue)
lung *n.* pulmón *m.*
luxurious *adj.* lujoso/a
luxury *n.* lujo *m.*
lying *adj.* mentiroso/a

M

ma'am *n.* señora *f.* (Sra.)
machine *n.* máquina *f.*
answering machine
contestadora *f.*
mad *adj.* enojado/a
be hopping mad *idiom* echar
chispas
madness *n.* locura *f.*
magazine *n.* revista *f.*
magic *n.* magia *f.*
magical *adj.* mágico/a
magician *n.* mago/a *m., f.*
magma *n.* magma *m.*
magna cum laude *(grade)*
matrícula de honor
magnesium *n.* magnesio *m.*
magnet *n.* imán *m.*
magnificent *adj.* magnífico/a
magnifying glass *n.* lupa *f.*
mail carrier *n.* cartero/a *m., f.*
mail *n.* correo *m.* **I sent it in
the mail.** Lo mandé por
correo.; correspondencia *f.*

You got a lot of mail.
Recibiste mucha
correspondencia.
mail *v.t.* enviar *or* mandar (por
correo)
mailbox *n.* buzón *m.*
main *adj.* principal
maintain *v.t.* mantener
majority *n.* mayoría *f.*
make *v.t.* hacer; *(coffee)* colar
make a living *idiom* ganarse
la vida **Mario makes his
living writing soap opera
scripts.** Mario se gana la
vida escribiendo guiones de
telenovela.
make a long story short *loc.*
en resumidas cuentas
make one's mouth water
idiom. hacérsele agua la
boca **It smells good. It
makes my mouth water.**
¡Qué bien huele! Se me hace
agua la boca.
make sure *v.* asegurarse
make up *v.* maquillar
make up one's mind *v.*
decidirse
makeup *n.* maquillaje *m.*
put on makeup *v.* maquillarse
makeup artist *n.* maquillador(a)
m., f.
male *n.* macho *m.*
malignant *adj.* maligno/a
mammal *n.* mamífero *m.*
man *n.* hombre *m.*
manage *v.t. (business)*
administrar
management *n.* administración
f.
manager *n.* gerente *m., f.*

manicure *n.* manicura *f.*
mannequin *n.* maniquí *m.*
manufacture *n.* fabricación *f.*
manufacture *v.t.* fabricar
manufacturer *n.* fabricante *m.,*
f.
manure *n.* estiércol *m.*
many *adj.* mucho/a
  a great many *n.* sinfín *m.*
map *n.* mapa *m.*
  city map *n.* plano *m.*
  road map mapa *m.* de
  carreteras
marathon *n.* maratón *m.*
marble *n.* mármol *m.*
March *n.* marzo *m.*
margarine *n.* margarina *f.*
marital status *n.* estado *m.* civil
mark *n.* marca *f.; (imprint)*
  huella *f.; (grade)* nota *f.*
market *n.* mercado *m.*
  street market *n.* mercadillo
  m.
marriage *n.* matrimonio *m.*
married *adj.* casado/a
marrow *n.* médula *f.*
marry: get married (to) *v.*
  casarse (con)
marsh *n.* pantano *m.*
martial arts *n., pl.* artes *f., pl.*
  marciales
marvelous *adj.* maravilloso/a
marvelously *adv.*
  maravillosamente
mask *n.* máscara *f.;* mascarilla
  f.; antifaz *m.*
mass produce *v.t.* fabricar en
  serie
mass production *n.* fabricación
  f. en serie
massage *n.* masaje *m.*

masseur *n.* masajista *m.*
masseuse *n.* masajista *f.*
master *v.t.* dominar
  I am far from mastering
  Spanish. Estoy lejos de
  dominar el español.
master's degree *n.* maestría
  (L.A.) f.
masterpiece *n.* obra *f.* maestra
match *n.* cerilla *f.;* fósforo *m.;*
  (sports) partido *m.*
match *v.t.* hacer juego (con)
match up *v.i.* coincidir
maternal *adj. (relative)*
  materno/a
mathematician *n.*
  matemático/a *m., f.*
mathematics *n.* matemáticas
  f., pl.
matriculation *n.* matrícula *f.*
matter *n.* cuestión *f.* **She's an**
  expert in matters of
  medieval history. Es una
  experta en cuestiones de
  historia medieval.
matter *v.t.* importar
mattress *n.* colchón *m.*
  foam mattress colchón de
  espuma
  sprung mattress colchón de
  muelles
mature *adj.* maduro/a
maturity *n.* madurez *f.*
maximum *n., adj.* máximo *m.;*
  máximo/a
May *n.* mayo *m.*
maybe *adv.* tal vez; quizás
mayonnaise *n.* mayonesa *f.*
mayor *n.* alcalde *m.,* alcaldesa
  f.

mayor's office *n.* alcaldía *f.*

meal *n.* comida *f.*

mean *adj.* *(person)* malo/a

means of communication *n.,* *pl.* medios *m.,* *pl.* de comunicación

means: by no means de ninguna manera, de ningún modo

measles *n.* sarampión *m.*

measure *v.t.* medir

measurement *n.* medición *f.;* medida *f.*

meat *n.* carne *f.*

mechanic *n.* mecánico/a *m., f.*

mechanic's workshop *n.* taller *m.* de mecánica

mechanism *n.* mecanismo *m.*

medal *n.* medalla *f.*

media *n.* medios *m., pl.* de comunicación

medical *adj.* médico/a

medical insurance *n.* seguro *m.* médico

medication *n.* medicamento *m.*

medicine *n.* medicina *f.*

medicine cabinet *n.* botiquín *m.*

mediocre *adj.* mediocre

meditate *v.i.* meditar

meditation *n.* meditación *f.*

medium *adj.* mediano/a

meet *v.t.* encontrar; *(each other)* encontrarse; conocerse **Where shall we meet?** ¿Dónde nos encontramos? **They met in Paris.** Se conocieron en París.

meeting *n.* reunión *f.; (political)*

n. mitin *m.*

megaphone *n.* megáfono *m.*

melon *n.* melón *m.*

melt *v.t.* derretir **The heat will melt the butter.** El calor derritirá la mantequilla.; *v.i.* derretirse **The ice cream melted.** El helado se derritió.

member *n.* miembro *m.*

membrane *n.* membrana *f.*

memorize *v.t.* memorizar

memory *n.* memoria *f.*

menopause *n.* menopausia *f.*

mental disorder *n.* trastorno *m.* mental

mental hospital *n.* manicomio *m.*

mentality *n.* mentalidad *f.*

menu *n.* menú *m.*

mercury *n.* mercurio *m.*

merit *n.* mérito *m.*

mess around: Don't mess around on the way to school. No te entretengas camino a la escuela.

message *n.* mensaje *m.; (telephone)* recado *m.*

messy *adj.* desarreglado/a

metabolism *n.* metabolismo *m.*

metabolize *v.t.* metabolizar

metal *n.* metal *m.*

metamorphosis *n.* metamorfosis *f.*

metaphor *n.* metáfora *f.*

metaphoric *adj.* metafórico/a

meteorite *n.* meteorito *m.*

meteorologist *n.* meteorólogo/a *m., f.*

meteorology *n.* metereología *f.*

method *n.* método *m.*

methodical *adj.* metódico/a
Mexican *n., adj.* mexicano/a *m., f.*
Mexico *n.* México *m.*
microphone *n.* micrófono *m.*
microscope *n.* microscopio *m.*
microwave *n.* microonda *f.*
microwave oven *n.* horno *m.* de microondas
middle age *n.* madurez *f.*
midnight *n.* medianoche *f.*
mild *adj. (taste)* suave
mile *n.* milla *f.*
milk *n.* leche *f.*
Milky Way *n.* Vía Láctea *f.*
mill *n.* molino *m.*
million *n.* millón *m.*
mind *n.* mente
  keep in mind tener en cuenta
mine *n.* mina *f.*
miner *n.* minero/a *m., f.*
mineral *n.* mineral *m.*
mining industry *n.* minería *f.*
miniskirt *n.* minifalda *f.*
minister *n. (government)* ministro/a *m., f.*
minority *n.* minoría *f.*
mint *n.* menta *f.*
minute *adj.* minúsculo/a
minute *n.* minuto *m.*
minute *adj. (object)* diminuto/a
mirror *n.* espejo *m.*
miscarriage *n.* aborto *m.* espontáneo
  have a miscarriage abortar
miser *n.* avaro/a *m., f.*
misfortune *n.* desgracia *f.*
Miss *n.* señorita *f.* (Srta.)
miss (someone) *v.t.* añorar (a

alguien)
missile *n.* misil *m.;* proyectil *m.*
missing *adj.* desaparecido/a
mistake *n.* equivocación *f.*
  make a mistake equivocarse
mistaken *adj.* equivocado/a
  be mistaken equivocarse
  You are mistaken in thinking that. Te equivocas si piensas eso.
mix *v.t.* mezclar
mixer *n.* batidora *(Spain) f.*
mobile *adj.* móvil
mobility *n.* movilidad *f.*
modem *n.* módem *m.*
modern *adj.* moderno/a
modernize *v.t.* modernizar
modest *adj. (person)* modesto/a; *(simple)* sencillo/a
modify *v.t.* modificar
moisturizer *n.* crema *n.* hidratante; humectante *m.*
molar *n.* muela *f.*
mold *n.* moho *m.*
mom *n.* mamá *f.,* mami *f.*
monarch *n.* monarca *m., f.*
monarchy *n.* monarquía *f.*
monastery *n.* monasterio *m.*
Monday *n.* lunes *m., sing.*
money *n.* dinero *m.*
  paper money billete *m.*
money order *n.* giro *m.* postal
monitor *n.* monitor *m.*
monk *n.* monje *m.*
monkey *n.* mono *m.*
monologue *n.* monólogo *m.*
month *n.* mes *m.*
monument *n.* monumento *m.*
mood: be in a good/bad mood

estar de buen/mal humor
moon *n.* luna *f.*
mop *n.* fregona *(Spain)* *f.;* trapeador *(L.A.)* *m.*
mop (the floor) *v.t.* trapear (el piso) *(L.A.);* fregar (el suelo) *(Spain)*
moral *n.* moral *f.*
morality *n.* moralidad *f.*
more *adj., adv.* más
  more . . . than más… que
  more than (+ *number*) más de (+ *number*)
moribund *adj.* moribundo/a
morning *n.* mañana *f.*
  in the morning de la mañana; por la mañana
morphology *n.* morfología *f.*
mortality *n.* mortalidad *f.*
mortality rate *n.* índice *m.* de mortalidad
mortgage *n.* hipoteca *f.*
mortgage *v.t.* hipotecar
mosque *n.* mezquita *f.*
mosquito net *n.* mosquitero *m.*
mother *n.* madre *f.*
mother-in-law *n.* suegra *f.*
motor *n.* motor *m.*
motorboat *n.* lancha *f.*
motorcycle *n.* moto *f.;* motocicleta *f.*
  go by motorcycle ir en moto
motorcycling *n.* motociclismo *m.*
motorcyclist *n.* motociclista *m., f.*
motorist *n.* automovilista *m., f.*
mountain *n.* montaña *f.*
mountain range *n.* cordillera *f.* (montañosa)

mountainside *n.* ladera *f.*
mouse *n.* ratón *m.*
mouth *n.* boca *f.; (river)* desembocadura *f.*
mouth-to-mouth resuscitation *n.* respiración *f.* boca a boca
move *n.* mudanza *f.*
move *v.i. (to a new place)* mudarse; *(from one place to another)* desplazarse
move forward *v.i.* avanzar
movement *n.* desplazamiento *m.*
movie *n.* película *f.*
  see movies ver películas
moviemaker *n.* cineasta *m., f.*
movie star *n.* estrella *f.* de cine
movie theater *n.* cine *m.*
mow *v.t. (lawn)* cortar
Mr. *n.* señor *m.* (Sr.)
Mrs. *n.* señora *f.* (Sra.)
much *adj., adv.* mucho/a
mud *n.* barro *m.;* fango *m.*
muffler *n. (car)* silenciador *m.*
mug *n.* taza *f.*
mug *v.t.* atracar
municipal *n.* municipal *m.*
murder *n.* asesinato *m.*
murderer *n.* asesino/a *m., f.*
muscle *n.* músculo *m.*
muscular *adj.* musculoso/a
museum *n.* museo *m.*
mushroom *n.* champiñón *m.*
music *n.* música *f.*
musical *adj.* musical
musician *n.* músico/a *m., f*
Muslim *n., adj.* musulmán *m.,* musulmana *f.*
mussel *n.* mejillón *m.*

must: It must be . . . Debe ser…

mustache n. bigote(s) m. (pl.)

mustard n. mostaza f.

mute adj. mudo/a

myopia n. miopía f.

myopic adj. miope

mysterious adj. enigmático/a; misterioso/a

mystery n. misterio m.; enigma m.
  a mystery novel una novela de misterio

N

nail n. clavo m.; (finger, toe) uña f.
  hit the nail on the head idiom dar en el clavo

nail file n. lima f.

name n. nombre m.
  be named llamarse
  in the name of a nombre de
  last name apellido m.
  My name is . . . Me llamo…
  What's your name? fam. ¿Cómo te llamas (tú)?, form. ¿Cómo se llama (usted)?

name v.t. ponerle nombre a

nap n. (afternoon) siesta f.

napkin n. servilleta f.

narrator n. narrador(a) m., f.

national adj. nacional

nationalism n. nacionalismo m.

nationalist adj. nacionalista

nationality n. nacionalidad f.

native adj. indígena

natural adj. natural

nature n. naturaleza f.

nature reserve n. parque m.

natural

naughty adj. travieso/a

nausea n. náusea f.

nauseate v.t. asquear, repugnar, dar asco

nauseating adj. asqueroso/a, repugnante

navel n. ombligo m.

navy blue n., adj. azul m. marino

near prep. cerca de

necessary adj. necesario/a
  It is necessary that . . . Hay que (+ inf.)…

necessity n. necesidad f.

neck n. cuello m.

necklace n. collar m.

nectarine n. nectarina f.

need v.t. faltar; necesitar

needle n. aguja f.

negative adj. negativo/a

neighbor n. vecino/a m., f.

neighborhood n. barrio m.

neither adv. tampoco
  neither . . . nor conj. ni… ni
  I eat neither meat nor fish. No como ni carne ni pescado.

nephew n. sobrino m.

nerve n. nervio m.; atrevimiento m.
  You've got some nerve! ¡Qué cara más dura tienes!

nervous adj. nervioso/a

nervous breakdown n. crisis f. nerviosa

network n. red f.

neuron n. neurona f.

never adv. nunca; jamás

new adj. nuevo/a; novato/a

What's new? ¿Qué hay de nuevo?

newlywed *n.* recién casado/a *m., f.*

news *n.* noticias *f., pl.;* actualidades *f., pl.*

newscast *n.* noticiero *m.*

newsletter *n.* boletín *m.* informativo

newspaper *n.* periódico *m.;* diario *m.*

next *adj.* próximo/a

nice *adj.* simpático/a; amable

nice person *idiom* buena gente

nickname *n.* apodo *m.*

niece *n.* sobrina *f.*

nieces and nephews *n., pl.* sobrinos *m., pl.*

night *n.* noche *f.*

at night *adv.* por la noche

night stand *n.* mesita *f.* de noche

nightmare *n.* pesadilla *f.*

nine hundred novecientos/as

nine nueve

nineteen diecinueve

ninety noventa

ninth noveno *m.;* noveno/a

nitrogen *n.* nitrógeno *m.*

no *adj.* ningún, ninguno/a(s)

no one *pron.* nadie

no *adv.* no

No entry (*sign*) Prohibido el paso

No problem. Ningún problema.

no way de ninguna manera

noise *n.* ruido *m.*

noisy *adj.* ruidoso/a

none *adj.* ningún, ninguno/a(s)

non-fattening *adj.* que no engorda

non-resident *n.* transeúnte *m., f.*

noon *n.* mediodía *m.*

nor *conj.* ni

Nordic *adj.* nórdico/a

north *n.* norte *m.*

to the north al norte

Northern European *n.* nórdico/a *m., f.*

nose *n.* nariz *f.*

not *adv.* no

not any *adj.* ningún, ninguno/a(s)

not anyone *pron.* nadie

not anything *pron.* nada

not bad at all nada mal

not either *adv.* tampoco

not ever *adv.* nunca; jamás

not very well no muy bien

notebook *n.* cuaderno *m.*

nothing *pron.* nada

I've nothing to say. No tengo nada que decir.

nothingness *n.* nada *f.*

notice *v.t.* notar; advertir

noun *n.* sustantivo *m.*

November *n.* noviembre *m.*

now *adv.* ahora

nowadays *adv.* hoy día

nucleus *n.* núcleo *m.*

number *n.* número *m.; (figure)* cifra *f.*

nun *n.* monja *f.*

nunnery *n.* convento *m.*

nurse *n.* enfermero/a *m., f.*

nursery school *n.* guardería *f.*

nutcracker *n.* cascanueces *m., sing.*

nutrition *n.* nutrición *f.*

nutritionist *n.* nutricionista *m.,
f.*

O

o'clock: It's . . . o'clock. Son
las...

oak tree *n.* roble *m.*

oar *n.* remo *m.*

obese *adj.* obeso/a

obesity *n.* obesidad *f.*

obey *v.t.* obedecer (c:zc)

objective *adj.* objetivo/a

objective *n.* meta *f.,* objetivo
m.

observant *adj.* observador(a)

observation *n.* observación *f.*

observatory *n.* observatorio *m.*

observe *v.t.* observar

obtain *v.t.* conseguir (e:i);
obtener

occupation *n.* ocupación *f.*

occur *v.i. (happen)* ocurrir,
suceder, pasar, realizarse;
(come to mind) ocurrir

ocean *n.* mar *m., f.;* océano *m.*

ocean liner *n.* transatlántico
m.

ocher *n.* ocre *m.*

October *n.* octubre *m.*

octopus *n.* pulpo *m.*

odor *n.* olor *m.*

of *prep.* de

   of course claro que sí; por
supuesto; *(idiom)* desde
luego

offend *v.t.* ofender

offer *n.* oferta *f.*

offer *v.t.* ofrecer (c:zc)

offering *n.* ofrenda *f.*

office *n.* oficina *f.; (medical)*
consultorio *m.*

often *adv.* a menudo

Oh! *interj.* ¡Ay!

oil *n.* aceite *m.;* petróleo *m.*

OK! *interj.* ¡Vale! *(Spain);* de
acuerdo

okay *adj.* regular

   It's okay. Está bien.

old *adj.* viejo/a; antiguo/a

   be . . . years old tener...
años

   How old are you? ¿Cuántos
años tienes?

   become old hacerse viejo/a

   grow old envejecer

old age *n.* vejez *f.*

older *adj.* mayor

   older brother/sister *n.*
hermano/a mayor *m., f.*

oldest *adj.* el/la mayor

old-fashioned *adj.* anticuado/a

olive *n.* aceituna *f.*

Olympic *adj.* olímpico/a

Olympic Games *n., pl.* Juegos
m., pl. Olímpicos

omelet *n.* tortilla (de huevo)
(Spain) f.

on *prep.* en; sobre

   on the dot en punto

   **on (the) one hand. . . on the
other hand. . .** por un lado…
por otro lado…

   on the other hand en cambio

on top of *prep.* encima de

once *adv.* una vez

oncologist *n.* oncólogo/a *m., f.*

one un, uno/a

   one of these days un día de
estos

one hundred cien(to)
one thousand mil
one way *n. (travel)* ida *f.*
onion *n.* cebolla *f.*
only *adj.* único/a
only *adv.* sólo, solamente
opaque *adj.* opaco/a
open *adj.* abierto/a
open *v.t.* abrir
  in the open air al aire libre
open-air dance *n.* verbena *f.*
opened *p.p.* abierto (*of* abrir)
opener *n.* abridor *m.*
opera *n.* ópera *f.*
operating room *n.* quirófano *m.*
operation *n.* operación *f.;*
  intervención *f.* quirúrgica
ophthalmologist *n.*
  oftalmólogo/a *m., f.*
opinion *n.* opinión *f.*
  express an opinion opinar
  in my opinion en mi opinión
opponent *n.* contrincante *m., f.*
opposite *prep.* en frente de
optimist *n.* optimista *m., f.*
optimistic *adj.* optimista
or *conj.* o
orange *adj.* anaranjado/a
orange *n.* naranja *f.*
orange tree *n.* naranjo *m.*
orchard *n.* huerta *f.*
orchestra *n.* orquesta *f.*
order *n.* orden *m.;*
  (commercial) encargo *m.*
  in order to (+ inf.) *prep.* para
  (+ *inf.*) ; a fin de (+ *inf.*)
  out of order descompuesto/a
  (L.A.); averiado/a *(Spain);*
  (sign) no funciona
order *v.t.* mandar*; (food)* pedir
  (e:i); encargar

orderly *adj.* ordenado/a
ordinal *adj.* ordinal
oregano *n.* orégano *m.*
organ *n.* órgano *m.*
organic *adj.* orgánico/a; *(food)*
  ecológico/a
organization *n.* organización *f.*
organize *v.t.* organizar
original *adj.* original
originality *n.* originalidad *f.*
ostrich *n.* avestruz *m.*
other *adj.* otro/a
ounce *n.* onza *f.*
out *adv.* fuera, afuera
out of stock *adj.* agotado/a
outline *v.t.* delinear
outrageous *adj.* escandaloso/a
outside *adv.* fuera
outskirts *n., pl.* afueras *f., pl.;*
  alrededores *m., pl.* **on the**
  outskirts of Barcelona en los
  alrededores de Barcelona
outstanding *adj.* sobresaliente,
  extraordinario, excepcional
oven *n.* horno *m.*
over *prep.* sobre
overcome *v.t.* superar
oversleep *v.i.* quedarse
  dormido
owl *n.* búho *m.*
own *adj.* propio/a
own *v.t.* poseer
owner *n.* dueño/a *m., f.*
oxygen *n.* oxígeno *m.*
oyster *n.* ostra *f.*

P

P.M. en la tarde, de la tarde
pacemaker *n.* marcapasos *m.,*
  sing.
pacifist *n., adj.* pacifista *m., f.*

pack (the suitcases) v.t. hacer las maletas; empacar
package n. paquete m.
padded adj. acolchado/a
page n. página f.
pain n. dolor m.
   have a pain in the (knee) tener dolor de (rodilla)
   What pain! ¡Qué dolor!
paint v.t. pintar
painter n. pintor(a) m., f.
painting n. pintura f.
pair n. par m.
pajamas n., pl. pijama (Spain) m.; piyama (L.A.) m.
palace n. palacio m.
palate n. paladar m.
paleontologist n. paleontólogo/a m., f.
paleontology n. paleontología f.
palm tree n. palmera f.
pan n. (frying) sartén f.
pancreas n. páncreas m.
panic attack n. ataque m. de nervios
panties n., pl. bragas (Spain.) f., pl.; pantaletas (Venezuela) f., pl.; calzones (L.A.) m., pl.
pantry n. despensa f.
pants n., pl. pantalones m., pl.
pantyhose n., pl. medias f., pl.
paper n. papel m.; (report) informe m.; (school essay) trabajo m.
paperback n. libro m. de bolsillo
parachute n. paracaídas m.
parachuting n. paracaidismo m.

parachutist n. paracaidista m., f.
parade n. desfile m.
paragraph n. párrafo m.
parakeet n. perico m.; periquito m.
Paralympics n., pl. Juegos m., pl. Paralímpicos
parasite n. parásito m.
Pardon me. Perdón.; (May I?) Con permiso.
parents n., pl. padres m., pl.; papás m., pl.
park n. parque m.
park v.t. estacionar
parking lot n. estacionamiento m.
parking n. estacionamiento m.
parking space n. estacionamiento m.
parole n. libertad f. condicional
parrot n. loro m.
parsley n. perejil m.
participate v.i. participar; (contest) concursar
participation n. participación f.; intervención f.
partner n. compañero/a m., f.; (business) socio/a m., f. (marriage, romance, sport) pareja f.
partnership n. asociación f.
   go into partnership (with) asociarse (con)
party n. fiesta f.; (political) partido m. (político)
party pooper n. aguafiestas m., f., sing.
pass v.t. pasar; (test) aprobar
   He passed the test. Aprobó

el examen.
pass (a vehicle) adelantar (a un vehículo)
pass away v. fallecer
pass on v. *(illness)* contagiar
passed *p.p.* pasado/a *(of pasar)*
passenger n. pasajero/a m., f.
passer-by n. transeúnte m., f.
passing grade n. aprobado m.
Passing prohibited *(sign)* Prohibido adelantar
passport n. pasaporte m.
past n., adj. pasado m.; pasado/a
pastime n. pasatiempo m.
pastry shop n. pastelería f.
paternal adj. *(relative)* paterno/a
path n. camino m.; sendero m.; *(of an object)* trayectoria f.
patience n. paciencia f.
patient n., adj. paciente m., f.
patio n. patio m.
patterned adj. *(fabric)* estampado/a
pay v.t. pagar
  pay attention atender; prestar atención
  pay in cash pagar al contado; pagar en efectivo
  pay in installments pagar a plazos
  pay the bill pagar la cuenta
pea n. arveja *(L.A.)* f.; chícharo *(Mexico)* m.; guisante *(Spain)* m.
peace n. paz f.
peach n. durazno *(L.A.)* m.; melocotón *(Spain)* m.
peak n. (mountain) cumbre m.,

cima f.; auge m.
pear n. pera f.
pedagogical adj. pedagógico/a
pedagogue n. pedagogo/a m., f.
pedagogy n. pedagogía f.
pedal n. pedal m.
pedantic adj. pedante
pedestrian n. peatón m.
pedicure n. pedicura f.
peel v.t. pelar
peeler n. pelapapas m., *sing.*
pen n. pluma f.; bolígrafo m.
pencil n. lápiz m.
penguin n. pingüino m.
penicillin n. penicilina f.
peninsula n. península f.
penitentiary n. penitenciaría f.
penknife n. navaja f.
pensioner n. pensionista m., f.
people n., pl. gente f., *sing.*
pepper n. *(black)* pimienta f.; *(bell)* pimiento m.
percentage n. porcentaje m.
perfect adj. perfecto/a
perfectionist adj. perfeccionista; detallista
perforate v.t. perforar
perform v.t. interpretar
perfume n. perfume m.
perfume shop n. perfumería f.
perhaps adv. quizás; tal vez
perimeter n. perímetro m.
period n. periodo m.; *(limited time)* plazo m., *(punctuation)* punto m.

permission *n.* permiso *m.*; consentimiento *m.*

permit *v.t.* permitir; consentir

persecution *n.* persecución *f.*
He suffered persecution for his ideas. Sufrió persecuciones por sus creencias.

persist *v.i.* persistir

persistent *adj.* persistente

person *n.* persona *f.*

personality *n.* personalidad *f.*

perspiration *n.* transpiración *f.*

perspire *v.i.* transpirar

pessimist *n.* pesimista *m., f.*

pessimistic *adj.* pesimista

pesticide *n.* pesticida *m.*

petal *n.* pétalo *m.*

petrified *adj.* petrificado/a

Ph.D. *n.* doctorado *m.; (title)* Dr. *m.*, Dra. *f.*

pharmacy *n.* farmacia *f.*

pharynx *n.* faringe *f.*

pheasant *n.* faisán *m.*

phenomenal *adj.* espectacular, extraordinario; increíble

phenomenon *n.* fenómeno *m.*

philately *n.* filatelia *f.*

philologist *n.* filólogo/a *m., f.*

philology *n.* filología *f.*

philosopher *n.* filósofo/a *m., f.*

philosophize *v.i.* filosofar

philosophy *n.* filosofía *f.*

phonetics *n.* fonética *f.*

phonology *n.* fonología *f.*

photocopier *n.* fotocopiadora *f.*

photocopy *v.t.* fotocopiar

photograph *n.* foto(grafía) *f.*
take photos tomar/sacar fotos

photosynthesis *n.* fotosíntesis *f., sing.*

physical *n.* chequeo *m.* (médico), revisión *f.* médica

physicist *n.* físico/a *m., f.*

physics *n.* física *f.*

physique *n.* tipo *m.*

pick up *v.t.* recoger

pick up boys/girls *v.i.* ligar

pickup truck *n.* camioneta *f.*

picture *n.* cuadro *m.*

picturesque *adj.* pintoresco/a

pie *n.* pastel *m.*

pig *n.* cerdo *m.*; puerco *m.*

pilgrim *n.* peregrino/a *m., f.*

pilgrimage *n.* peregrinación *f.*

pill *n.* pastilla *f.*; píldora *f.*

pillow *n.* almohada *f.*

pimple *n.* grano *m.*

pinch *n. (quantity)* pizca *f.*

pine forest *n.* pinar *m.*

pine tree *n.* pino *m.*

pineapple *n.* piña *f.*

pink *adj.* rosado/a

pipe *n.* tubo *m.*, caño *m.*; cañería *f.*, tubería *f.*

pit *n. (fruit)* hueso *m.*

pitcher *n.* jarra *f.*

pity *n.* lástima *f.*

place *n.* lugar *m.*

place *v.t.* poner; colocar

placing *n.* colocación *f.*

plagiarism *n.* plagio *m.*

plagiarize *v.t.* plagiar

plaid *adj.* de cuadros

plan (to do something) *v.* pensar *(+ inf.)*

plan *n.* plan *m.*
have plans tener planes

planet *n.* planeta *m.*

planetarium n. planetario m.
plant n. planta f.
  climbing plant enredadera f.
plantain n. plátano m.
plastic n. plástico m.
  made of plastic de plástico
plate n. plato m.
  license plate placa f.
plateau n. meseta f.
platter n. fuente f.
  platter of fried food n. fuente
  de fritada
play n. drama m.
play v.t. jugar (u:ue); (a
  musical instrument) tocar; (a
  role) hacer el papel de;
  (cards) jugar a (las cartas);
  (sports) practicar
  play hooky hacer novillos
  (Spain)
player n. jugador(a) m., f.
playwright n. dramaturgo/a m.,
  f.
plead v.i. rogar (o:ue), suplicar
pleasant adj. agradable
please interj. por favor
  be pleased (with)
  contentarse (con)
  Pleased to meet you. Mucho
  gusto.; Encantado/a (de
  conocerle).
pleasure n. gusto m.; placer m.
  It's a pleasure to . . . Gusto
  de (+ inf.)
  It's been a pleasure. Ha sido
  un placer.
  The pleasure is mine. El
  gusto es mío.
  What a pleasure to . . . !
  ¡Qué gusto (+ inf.)...

plot n. (story) argumento m.;
  (land) terreno m.
plot v.t. tramar
pluck v. (eyebrows) depilarse
plum n. ciruela f.
plumber n. fontanero/a (Spain)
  m., f.; plomero/a (L.A.) m., f.
plumbing n. fontanería (Spain)
  f.; plomería (L.A.) f.
pluralism n. pluralismo m.
plurality n. pluralidad f.
pocket n. bolsillo m.
podium n. podio m.
poem n. poema m.
poet n. poeta m., f.
poetry n. poesía f.
point n. punto m.
polemical adj. polémico/a
police n. policía f.
police officer n. policía m.,
  mujer f. policía
police station n. comisaría f.
  (de policía)
polish n. (shoe) brillo m. (para
  zapatos); (floor) abrillantador
  m. (para pisos/suelos)
polish v.t. abrillantar; encerar
polite adj. educado/a
politician n. político/a m., f.
politics n. política f.
polka dot n. lunar m.
polka-dot adj. de lunares
poll n. encuesta f.
pollen n. polen m.
pollinate v.t. polinizar
pollute v.t. contaminar
polluted adj. contaminado/a
  be polluted estar
  contaminado/a
pollution n. contaminación f.

169

water pollution
contaminación del agua

pomegranate *n.* granada *f.*

pond *n. (man-made)* estanque
m.; (natural) charca *f.*

pony tail *n.* cola *f.* de caballo

pool: swimming pool *n.*
piscina *f.;* alberca *(Mexico) f.*
indoor pool piscina
climatizada

poor *adj.* pobre
become poor empobrecerse
make poor empobrecer

poppy *n.* amapola *f.*

populate *v.t.* poblar

population *n.* población *f.*

porch *n.* porche *m.*

pork *n.* cerdo *m.*

pork chop *n.* chuleta *f.* de
cerdo

port *n.* puerto *m.*

portable *adj.* portátil

portable computer *n.*
computadora *f.* portátil

porter *n.* portero/a *m., f.*

position *n.* puesto *m.*

possession *n.* posesión *f.*

possessive *adj.* posesivo/a

possible *adj.* posible

post office *n.* correo *m.;*
correos *(Spain) m., pl.*

postcard *n.* postal *f.;* tarjeta *f.*
postal

poster *n.* cartel *m.*

postpone *v.t.* aplazar

postponement *n.* aplazamiento
m.

pot *n. (cooking)* olla *f.*

potato *n.* papa *(L.A.) f.;* patata
(Spain) f.

potato omelet *n.* tortilla *f.* de
patatas

potter *n.* ceramista *m., f.*

pottery *n.* cerámica *f.*

pound *n.* libra *f.*

pour *v.i.* llover a cántaros

poverty *n.* pobreza *f.*

power *n.* poder *m.;* potencia *f.*

power failure *n.* apagón *m.*

power steering *n.* dirección *f.*
asistida

powerful *adj.* poderoso/a

practice *n.* práctica *f.*

practice *v.t.* practicar;
entrenarse

prairie *n.* llanura *f.*

praise *n.* elogio *m.*

praise *v.t.* elogiar

prank *n.* travesura *f.*

prawn *n.* langostino *m.*

pray *v.i.* rezar

predator *n.* depredador *m.*

predatory *adj.* depredador(a)

prefabricate *v.t.* prefabricar

prefabricated *adj.*
prefabricado/a

prefer *v.t.* preferir (e:ie)

pregnant *adj.* embarazada

premiere *n. (film, play)* estreno
m.

preparations *n., pl.*
preparativos *m., pl.*

prepare *v.t.* preparar

preposition *n.* preposición *f.*

prescribe *v.t.* recetar

prescription *n.* receta *f.*

present *n. (gift)* regalo *m.;*
(time) presente *m.*

present *v.t.* presentar

presenter *n.* presentador(a) *m.*, *f.*

press *n.* prensa *f.*

pressure *n.* presión *f.*

be under a lot of pressure sufrir muchas presiones

pressure cooker *n.* olla *f.* a presión

pretend *v.t./v.i.* fingir; disimular

pretentious *adj.* pretencioso/a

pretty *adj.* bonito/a

prevent *v.t.* prevenir; impedir; evitar

prevention *n.* prevención *f.*

prey *n.* presa *f.*

price *n.* precio *m.*

What is the price? ¿Qué precio tiene?

pride *n.* orgullo *m.*

primitive *adj.* primitivo/a

print *v.t.* imprimir

printer *n. (machine)* impresora *f.*

prison *n.* prisión *f.;* cárcel *f.*

prisoner *n.* preso/a *m.*, *f.*

privacy *n.* intimidad *f.*

private *adj.* privado/a

prize *n.* premio *m.;* galardón *m.*

probable *adj.* probable

problem *n.* problema *m.*

prodigy *n.* prodigio/a *m.*, *f.*

produce *n.* frutas *f., pl.* y verduras *f., pl.*

produce *v.t.* fabricar

product *n.* producto *m.*

profession *n.* profesión *f.*

professor *n.* profesor(a) *m.*, *f.;* catedrático/a *m.*, *f.*

program *n.* programa *m.*

programmer *n.* programador(a) *m.*, *f.*

prohibit *v.t.* prohibir

prohibited *p.p.* prohibido (*of* prohibir)

project *v.t.* proyectar

projection *n.* proyección *f.*

prolific *adj.* prolífico/a

promote *v.i. (work)* ascender

promotion *n. (career)* ascenso *m.*

prone to *adj.* propenso/a a

pronoun *n.* pronombre *m.*

proof *n.* demostración *f.*

proposal *n.* propuesta *f.*

propose *v.t.* proponer

protect *v.t.* proteger

protection *n.* protección *f.*

protein *n.* proteína *f.*

protest *n.* protesta *f.*

protest *v.t.* protestar

Protestant *n., adj.* protestante *m.*, *f.*

proud *adj.* orgulloso/a

prove *v.t.* demostrar

provided that *conj.* con tal (de) que

provisions *n., pl.* provisiones *f., pl.;* víveres *m., pl.*

provocation *n.* provocación *f.*

provocative *adj. (dress)* atrevido/a

provoke *v.t.* provocar

psychiatrist *n.* psiquiatra *m.*, *f.*

psychiatry *n.* psiquiatría *f.*

psychologist *n.* psicólogo/a *m.*, *f.*

psychology *n.* psicología *f.*

puberty *n.* pubertad *f.*

publish *v.t.* publicar

Puerto Rican *n., adj.* puertorriqueño/a *m.*, *f.*

Puerto Rico n. Puerto Rico m.
pull v.t. halar (L.A.), jalar (L.A.);
  tirar (Spain)
  pull an all-nighter idiom
  quemarse las pestañas
  pull out all the stops loc.
  echar la casa por la ventana
  pull someone's leg idiom
  tomarle el pelo a alguien
pumpkin n. calabaza f.
punchbowl n. ponchera f.
punctual adj. puntual
punish v.t. castigar
punishment n. castigo m.
pupil n. (eye) pupila f.;
  (student) pupilo/a m., f.;
  alumno/a m., f.
purchase n. compra f.,
  adquisición f.
purchase v.t. comprar, adquirir
pure adj. puro/a
purple n., adj. morado m.;
  morado/a
purpose n. propósito m.
  on purpose adv. adrede; a
  propósito
purse n. bolsa f.
pursue v.t. perseguir
pursuit n. persecución f. **The
  police took off in pursuit of
  the fugitive.** La policía salió
  en persecución del fugitivo.;
  búsqueda f. **the pursuit of
  truth** la búsqueda de la
  verdad
push v.t. empujar
put v.t. poner; colocar
  put in a cast escayolar
  (Spain); enyesar (L.A.)
put p.p. puesto (of poner)
put off v. aplazar

put on v. (a performance)
  presentar; (clothing) ponerse
put out v.t. sofocar; extinguir
  **The firefighters put out the
  blaze.** Los bomberos
  extinguieron el incendio.
**put something over (on
  somebody)** idiom dar gato
  por liebre
put up v.t. (give lodging) alojar
put up with v. aguantar
puzzle n. rompecabezas m.,
  sing.
pyramid n. pirámide f.

Q

quail n. codorniz f.
qualify v.t./v.i. calificarse
quality n. calidad f.
quarrel n. pelea f.
quarrel v.i. pelearse; discutir
  **They always quarrel over
  money.** Siempre se pelean
  por el dinero.
quarter n. trimestre m.; cuarto
  m.
  quarter after (time) y cuarto;
  y quince **It's quarter after
  three.** Son las tres y
  cuarto/quince.
  quarter to menos cuarto;
  menos quince **It's quarter to
  five.** Son las cinco menos
  cuarto/quince.
queen n. reina f.
question v.t. cuestionar
question n. pregunta f.
quiet adj. tranquilo/a; callado/a
quit (doing something) v.t.
  (habit) dejar de (+ inf.)

R

rabbi *n.* rabino/a *m., f.*
rabbit *n.* conejo *m.*
race *n. (sport)* carrera *f.;* *(people)* raza *f.*
racecar *n.* carro *m.* de carreras
racism *n.* racismo *m.*
racist *adj.* racista
racket *n. (sport)* raqueta *f.*
radio *n. (medium)* radio *f.;* *(receiver)* radio *m.*
radish *n.* rábano *m.*
railroad *n.* ferrocarril *m.*
railroad crossing *n.* paso *m.* a nivel
rain *n.* lluvia *f.*
rain *v.imp.* llover (o:ue)
  It's raining. Llueve.
  rain cats and dogs *idiom* llover a cántaros
rain forest *n.* bosque *m.* tropical
rainbow *n.* arco *m.* iris
raincoat *n.* impermeable *m.*
raise *n. (salary)* aumento *m.* de sueldo
raise *v.t. (children, animals)* criar; *(money)* recaudar (fondos)
raisin *n.* pasa *f.*
rake *n.* rastrillo *m.*
rancher *n.* ganadero/a *m., f.*
ranching *n.* ganadería *f.*
randomly *adv.* al azar
  at random *adv.* al azar
ranger *n.* guarda *m., f.* forestal
raspberry *n.* frambuesa *f.*
rate *n.* índice *m.*
rattlesnake *n.* serpiente *f.* de cascabel
raw *adj. (food)* crudo/a
razor *n.* máquina *f.* de afeitar; rasuradora *f.*
reach *n.* alcance
  within arm's reach al alcance de la mano
reach *v.t.* alcanzar; llegar a; contactar, ponerse en contacto con
  reach a conclusion llegar a una conclusión
  reach an agreement llegar a un acuerdo
  How can I reach you? ¿Cómo puedo ponerme en contacto contigo?
react *v.i.* reaccionar
reaction *n.* reacción *f.*
read *v.t.* leer
read *p.p.* leído *(of* leer*)*
  read e-mail leer el correo electrónico
reader *n.* lector(a) *m., f.*
ready *adj.* listo/a
  get ready prepararse; arreglarse **He takes forever getting ready.** Tarda mucho en arreglarse.
real *adj.* auténtico/a
realistic *adj.* verosímil **His characters aren't realistic.** Sus personajes no son verosímiles.
realize *v.t.* darse cuenta de (que) **Gustavo realized he was alone.** Gustavo se dio cuenta de que estaba solo.
reap the benefits (of) *v.t.* disfrutar (de)

173

rearview mirror *n.* retrovisor *m.*

reason *n.* razón *f.*

reason *v.i.* razonar

receive *v.t.* recibir

receptionist *n.* recepcionista *m., f.; (hotel)* conserje *m., f.*

recess *n.* recreo *m.*

recipe *n.* receta *f.*

recital *n.* recital *m.*

recognition *n.* reconocimiento *m.*

recognize *v.t.* reconocer

recommend *v.t.* recomendar (e:ie)

record *n. (sport)* marca *f.;* récord *m.*

rectangle *n.* rectángulo *m.*

rectify *v.t.* rectificar

recycle *v.t.* reciclar

recycling *n.* reciclaje *m.*

red *n., adj.* rojo *m.;* rojo/a

Red Cross *n.* Cruz *f.* Roja

reddish *adj.* rojizo/a

red-haired *adj.* pelirrojo/a

reduce *v.t.* reducir
reduce stress/tension aliviar el estrés/la tensión

reduced *adj.* de rebaja

reef *n.* arrecife *m.*

referee *n.* árbitro/a *m., f.*

reference book *n.* libro *m.* de consulta

reflect *v.t. (light)* reflejar; *v.i.* **(on something)** reflexionar (sobre algo)

reform *n.* reforma *f.*

reform *v.t.* reformar

refreshing *adj.* refrescante

refrigerate *v.t.* refrigerar

refrigerator *n.* refrigerador *m.*

refund *n.* devolución *f.*

refusal *n.* negación *f.*

refuse *v.i.* negarse; *v.t.* negarse a (+ *inf.*)
He refused to answer. Se negó a contestar.

regarding to (con) respecto a

regards *n., pl.* recuerdos *m., pl.;* saludos *m., pl.*
Lila sends her regards. Lila manda saludos.

region *n.* región *f.*

register *v.i. (school)* matricularse; inscribirse **She intends to register for the astronomy class.** Pretende inscribirse en la clase de astronomía.

registration *n.* inscripción *f.; (education)* matrícula *f.*

registration number *n. (car)* matrícula *f.*

regret *v.t.* arrepentirse (de) (e:ie); lamentar

regular (customer) *n.* asiduo/a *m., f.*

regularization *n.* regularización *f.*

regulate *v.t.* regular; *(temperature, etc.)* graduar

rehearsal *n.* ensayo *m.*

rehearse *v.t.* ensayar

reign *v.i.* reinar

reinforce *v.t.* reforzar

reinforcement *n.* refuerzo *m.*

reject *v.t.* rechazar

rejection *n.* rechazo *m.*

rejoicing *n.* algarabía *f.*

rejuvenate *v.i.* rejuvenecer

rejuvenation *n.*
rejuvenecimiento *m.*
relationship *n.* relación *f.*
relative *adj., n.* relativo/a;
pariente *m., f.*
relax *v.i.* relajarse
relaxation *n.* relajación *f.*
relay race *n.* carrera *f.* de
relevos
release *v.t.* liberar; soltar;
poner en libertad
relief *n.* alivio *m.*
relieve *v.t. (pain)* aliviar
religion *n.* religión *f.*
religious *adj.* religioso/a
remain *v.i.* quedarse
remember *v.t./v.i.* recordar
(o:ue); acordarse (de) (o:ue)
remembrance *n.*
conmemoración *f.*
remote *adj.* alejado/a; lejano/a
remote control *m.* control *m.*
remoto
Renaissance *adj.* renacimento
m.
Renaissance artist *n.*
renacentista *m., f.*
renew *v.t.* renovar
renewal *n.* renovación *f.*
rent *n.* alquiler *m.*
rent *v.t.* alquilar
repeat *v.t.* repetir (e:i)
repellent *n.* repelente *m.*
replace *v.t.* reemplazar;
sustituir **They replaced the
sugar with honey.**
Sustituyeron el azúcar por la
miel.
report *n.* informe *m.;* reportaje
m.; boletín *m.;* denuncia *f.*

report *v.t. (crime)* denunciar
reporter *n.* reportero/a *m., f.*
repress *v.t.* reprimir
repression *n.* represión *f.*
reproduce *v.t.* reproducir **It's
difficult to reproduce the
results.** Es difícil reproducir
los resultados.; *(biology)*
reproducirse **Rabbits
reproduce quickly.** Los
conejos se reproducen
rápidamente.
reptile *n.* reptil *m.*
reputation *n.* reputación *f.;*
fama *f.*
have a good/bad reputation
tener buena/mala fama
have a reputation for tener
fama de
request *v.t.* pedir (e:i)
rescue *n.* rescate *m.;*
salvamento *m.*
rescue *v.t.* rescatar
research *v.t.* investigar
do research documentarse
researcher *n.* investigador(a)
m., f.
resentful *adj.* rencoroso/a
resentment *n.* rencor *m.*
reservation *n.* reservación *f.*
reserved *adj.* reservado/a
reservoir *n.* embalse *m.;*
pantano *m.*
reside *v.i.* residir
residence *n.* residencia *f.*
resident *n., adj.* residente *m., f.*
resign (from) *v.i.* renunciar (a)
resign *v.i.* dimitir
resignation *n.* dimisión *f.*
resist *v.t.* resistir

resistance *n.* resistencia *f.*
resolve *v.t.* resolver (o:ue)
resolved *p.p.* resuelto (*of* resolver)
resort *n.* *(coastal)* balneario *m.*
resource *n.* recurso *m.*
  natural resource recurso natural
respect *n.* respeto *m.*
respect *v.t.* respetar
respiration *n.* respiración *f.*
respiratory failure *n.* crisis *f.* respiratoria
responsibility *n.* responsabilidad *f.* ; deber *m.*
rest *n.* reposo *m.*
rest *v.i.* descansar; reposar **He had to rest for several weeks after the operation.** Tuvo que reposar por varias semanas después de la operación.
rest, the *n.* lo/los/las demás
restaurant *n.* restaurante *m.*
restore *v.t.* restaurar
restrain oneself *v.refl.* dominarse
result *n.* resultado *m.*
résumé *n.* curriculum *m.* (vitae); hoja *f.* de vida *(Colombia)*
retire (from work) *v.i.* jubilarse
retired person *n.* pensionista *m., f.;* jubilado/a *m., f.*
retirement pension *n.* pensión *f.*
return *n.* *(object)* devolución *f.*
return *v.i.* regresar; volver (o:ue); *v.t.* *(object)* devolver (o:ue)

return trip *n.* vuelta *f.*
returned *p.p.* vuelto (*of* volver)
rewind *v.t.* rebobinar
rewind button *n.* botón *m.* de rebobinado
  push the rewind button apriete el botón de rebobinado
rhetoric *n.* retórica *f.*
rhetorical *adj.* retórico/a
rheumatism *n.* reumatismo *m.*
rhinoceros *n.* rinoceronte *m.*
rhythm *n.* ritmo *m.;* compás *m.*
rib *n.* costilla *f.*
ribbon *n.* cinta *f.*
rice *n.* arroz *m.*
rich *adj.* rico/a
  get rich enriquecerse
  make rich enriquecer
riddle *n.* adivinanza *f.*
ridiculous *adj.* ridículo/a
right *n., adj.* *(direction)* derecha *f.;* derecho *m.;* derecho/a; correcto/a
  be right tener razón
  to the right a la derecha
  human rights derechos humanos
right? *interj.* ¿no?; ¿verdad?
right away *adv.* enseguida; en el acto
right here/there aquí/allí mismo
right now ahora mismo
ring *n.* anillo *m.;* sortija *f.;* *(boxing)* cuadrilátero *m.*
  wedding ring anillo de bodas
ring *v.t.* *(bell)* sonar (o:ue)
rise *n.* *(advance)* ascenso *m.*
rise *v.i.* ascender

river *n.* río *m.*

road *n.* camino *m.*

roar *n.* rugido *m.*

roar *v.i.* rugir

roast *n.* asado *m.*
  roast lamb *n.* asado de cordero

roasted *p.p.* asado/a (*of* asar)
  roast chicken *n.* pollo *m.* asado

rob *v.t.* robar

robber *n.* ladrón *m.*, ladrona *f.*

robbery *n.* atraco *m.;* robo *m.*

robe *n.* bata *f.*

rock *n.* roca *f.,* piedra *f.*

rock *v.t.* mecer

rocket *n.* cohete *m.*

rocking chair *n.* mecedora *f.*

role *n.* (*movie, theater*) papel *m.*
  leading role papel principal
  supporting role papel secundario

roller skating *n.* patinaje *m.* sobre ruedas

Roman *n., adj.* romano/a *m., f.*

Romanesque *adj.* románico/a

romantic *n., adj.* romántico/a *m., f.*

Romanticism *n.* romanticismo *m.*

room *n.* cuarto *m.;* habitación *f.*
  single room habitación individual

roommate *n.* compañero/a *m., f.* de cuarto

rooster *n.* gallo *m.*

root *n.* raíz *f.*

rope *n.* cuerda *f.*

rose *n.* rosa *f.*

rosebush *n.* rosal *m.*

rosemary *n.* romero *m.*

rough *adj.* (*surface, skin*) áspero/a

roulette *n.* ruleta *f.*

roundtrip *n., adj.* de ida y vuelta

roundtrip ticket *n.* pasaje *m.* de ida y vuelta

route *n.* ruta *f.*

routine *n.* rutina *f.*

row *n.* hilera *f.;* fila *f.*

row *v.i.* remar

rower *n.* remero/a *m., f.*

royal *adj.* real

royalty *n.* realeza *f.*

rubber *adj.* de goma

ruby *n.* rubí *m.*

rude *adj.* maleducado/a; grosero/a

rug *n.* alfombra *f.*

rugged *adj.* (*terrain*) accidentado/a

rule *v.t.* gobernar

rum *n.* ron *m.*

rumor *n.* rumor *m.*

run *v.t.* correr; *v.i.* (*business*) administrar

run away *v.* fugarse

run into *v.* (*have an accident*) chocar (con); (*meet accidentally*) darse con

run out *v.* (*supplies*) agotar(se)

run over *v.* derramarse

run over (someone with a vehicle) *v.* atropellar (a alguien con un vehículo)

rural *adj.* rural; campestre

rush *v.i.* apurarse

rust *n.* óxido *m.*

rust *v.i.* oxidarse

s

sacred *adj.* sagrado/a
sad *adj.* triste
sadness *n.* tristeza *f.*
saffron *n.* azafrán *m.*
saga *n.* saga *f.*
sage *n. (herb)* salvia *f.*
said *p.p.* dicho *(of* decir)
sail *n.* vela *f.*
sailboat *n.* velero *m.*
sailing *n.* vela *f.*
sake: for the sake of por
for the sake of love por amor
salad *n.* ensalada *f.*
salad bowl *n.* ensaladera *f.*
salary *n.* salario *m.;* sueldo *m.*
sale *n.* rebaja *f.*
salesperson *n.* vendedor(a) *m.,*
f.
salmon *n.* salmón *m.*
salt *n.* sal *f.*
salt shaker *n.* salero *m.*
salty *adj.* salado/a
same *adj.* mismo/a
be all the same dar lo mismo
It's all the same to me if she comes or not. Me da lo
mismo si viene o no.
sand *n.* arena *f.*
sandal *n.* sandalia *f.*
sandwich *n.* sándwich *m.*
sap *n.* savia *f.*
sardine *n.* sardina *f.*
Saturday *n.* sábado *m.*
sauce *n.* salsa *f.*
sauna *n.* sauna *f.*
sausage *n.* salchicha *f.*
sauté *v.t.* saltear, sofreír
save *v.t. (on a computer)*
guardar; *(money)* ahorrar;
salvar

savings *n.* ahorros *m., pl.*
savings account *n.* cuenta *f.*
de ahorros
saw *n.* sierra *f.*
saw *v.t.* serrar
say *v.t.* decir
You don't say! ¡No me
diga(s)!
say good-bye (to) despedirse
(de) (e:i)
saying *n.* dicho *m.;* refrán *m.*
scale *n.* balanza *f.;* báscula *f.*
scallop *n.* vieira *f.*
scalpel *n.* bisturí *m.*
scapula *n.* omoplato *m.*
scarcely *adv.* apenas
He can scarcely talk.
Apenas sabe hablar.
scarf *n.* bufanda *f.*
scent *n.* aroma *m.*
schedule *n.* horario *m.*
scheme *v.i.* tramar
scholarship *n.* beca *f.*
school *n.* escuela *f.*
school report *n.* boletín *m.* de
notas
science *n.* ciencia *f.*
science fiction *n.* ciencia *f.*
ficción
scientist *n.* científico/a *m., f.*
scissors *n.* tijeras *f., pl.*
scoreboard *n.* marcador *m.*
scorpion *n.* escorpión *m.*
scream *v.i.* gritar
screen *n.* pantalla *f.*
screenplay *n.* guión *m.*
screenwriter *n.* guionista *m., f.*
screw *n.* tornillo *m.*
screwdriver *n.* destornillador
m.

script *n.* guión *m.*
scriptwriter *n.* guionista *m., f.*
sculpt *v.t./v.i.* esculpir
sculptor *n.* escultor(a) *m., f.*
sculpture *n.* escultura *f.*
sea *n.* mar *m.;* océano *m.*
seafood *n.* mariscos *m., pl.*
　assorted seafood mariscada
　f.
seal *n.* foca *f.*
seaquake *n.* maremoto *m.*
search *n.* búsqueda *f.*
season *n.* estación *f.;*
　temporada *f.*
season *v.t. (salad)* aderezar,
　aliñar
seasoning *n.* aderezo *m.;* aliño
　m.
seat *n.* silla *f.;* asiento *m.*
seat belt *n.* cinturón *n.* de
　seguridad
seaweed *n.* alga (el) *f.*
second *n., adj.* segundo *m.;*
　segundo/a
secretary *n.* secretario/a *m., f.*
security guard *n.* guardia *m., f.*
　de seguridad
sedentary *adj.* sedentario/a
sediment *n.* sedimento *m.*
sedimentation *n.*
　sedimentación *f.*
seduce *v.t.* seducir
seducer *n.* seductor(a) *m., f.*
seductive *adj.* seductor(a)
seductress *n.* seductor(a) *m., f.*
see *v.t.* ver
　let's see a ver; veamos
　See you. Nos vemos.
　see (you) again volver a
　ver(te/lo/la)

See you later. Hasta la vista.;
　Hasta luego.
　See you soon. Hasta pronto.
　See you tomorrow. Hasta
　mañana.
see-through *adj.* transparente
seed *n.* semilla *f.;* grano *m.*
seem *v.i.* parecer
seen *p.p.* visto/a (*of* ver)
select *adj.* selecto/a
select *v.t.* seleccionar
self-employed worker *n.*
　autónomo/a *m., f.*
self-portrait *n.* autorretrato *m.*
self-taught *adj.* autodidacta
selfish *adj.* egoísta
selfishness *n.* egoísmo *m.*
sell *v.t.* vender
semantics *n.* semántica *f.*
semester *n.* semestre *m.*
seminar *n.* seminario *m.*
senate *n.* senado *m.*
send *v.t.* enviar, mandar
sense *n.* sentido *m.*
　common sense sentido
　común
sense of order *n.* sentido *m.*
　del orden
sensible *adj.* sensato/a
sensitive *adj.* sensible
sensitivity *n.* sensibilidad *f.*
sensory organs *n., pl.* órganos
　m., pl. de los sentidos
sentimental *adj.* sentimental
separate (from) *v.* separarse
　(de)
September *n.* septiembre *m.*
sequence *n.* secuencia *f.*
series circuit *n.* circuito *m.* en
　serie

179

serious *adj.* serio/a; *(illness, wound)* grave
serve *v.t./v.i.* servir (e:i)
service *n.* servicio *m.*
serving *n.* porción *f.*
set *adj. (price)* fijo/a
set *n. (theater)* decorado *m.*
set *v.t.* poner, colocar
  set the table poner la mesa
set (a world record) *v.* establecer (una marca mundial)
settle *v.i.* instalarse **He settled in front of the TV and didn't budge.** Se instaló ante la tele y no se movió.
settlement *n.* colonización *f.; (agreement)* resolución *f.*
settler *n.* colono/a *m., f.*
seven siete
seven hundred setecientos/as
seventeen diecisiete
seventh séptimo *m.;* séptimo/a
seventy setenta
sew *v.t./v.i.* coser
sewer *n.* cloaca *f.*
sewing machine *n.* máquina *f.* de coser
sexism *n.* sexismo *m.*
shame *n.* lástima *f.;* vergüenza *f.*
  It's a shame that . . . Es (una) lástima que (+ *subj.*)…
shame *v.t.* avergonzar
shameful *adj.* vergonzoso/a
shampoo *n.* champú *m.*
shape *n.* forma *f.*
  be in good shape estar en buena forma
  stay in shape mantenerse en forma

share *v.t.* compartir
shark *n.* tiburón *m.*
sharp *adv. (time)* en punto **It starts at 4:00 sharp.** Empieza a las cuatro en punto.
sharp curve *n.* curva *f.* peligrosa
shave *v.i.* afeitarse; *(legs)* depilarse
shaving cream *n.* crema *f.* de afeitar
shawl *n.* chal *m.*
shed *n.* cobertizo *m.*
sheep *n.* oveja *f.*
sheet *n.* sábana *f.; (paper)* hoja *f.*
shellfish *n.* mariscos *m. pl.*
sherry *n.* jerez *m.*
shift *n. (work)* turno *m.*
shift gears *v.t.* cambiar de marcha
shine *v.i.* brillar
ship *n.* barco *m.*
  go by ship ir en barco
shirt *n.* camisa *f.*
shiver *n.* escalofrío *m.*
shiver *v.i.* temblar; tener escalofríos
shock *n.* choque *m.,* impacto *m.*
shock absorber *n.* amortiguador *m.*
  electric shock *n.* descarga *f.* (eléctrica)
shoe *n.* zapato *m.*
  put one's shoes on calzarse
shoe size *n.* número *m.*
  take (wear) a shoe size calzar

shoe store *n.* zapatería *f.*
shoelace *n.* cordón *m.*
shoes *n.* calzado *m.*
shoot *v.t.* disparar; *(movies)* rodar
shooting *n.* rodaje *m.*
shooting star *n.* estrella *f.* fugaz
shop *n.* tienda *f.*
shop window *n.* escaparate *(Spain) m.;* vitrina *(L.A.) f.*
shopping mall *n.* centro *m.* comercial
shore *n.* orilla *f.* **The house is on the seashore.** La casa está a orillas del mar.
short *adj. (height)* bajo/a; *(length)* corto/a
  in short *loc.* en resumidas cuentas
short circuit *n.* cortocircuito *m.*
short cut *n.* atajo *m.*
shortage *n.* carencia *f.*
shortcoming *n.* deficiencia *f.*
shorts *n., pl.* pantalones *m., pl.* cortos
shot *n.* disparo *m.;* tiro *m.*
shot put *n. (sport)* lanzamiento *m.* de bala *(L.A.);* lanzamiento *m.* de peso *(Spain)*
should *(do something)* deber (+ *inf.*)
shoulder *n.* hombro *m.*
shoulder bag *n.* bolso *m.*
shovel *n.* pala *f.*
show *n.* espectáculo *m.*
show *v.t.* mostrar (o:ue)
shower *n.* ducha *f.*
shower *v.i.* ducharse
shrewd *adj.* astuto/a

shrimp *n.* camarón *(L.A.) m.;* gamba *(Spain) f.*
  marinated shrimp ceviche *m.* de camarón *m.*
shrub *n.* arbusto *m.*
shy *adj.* tímido/a
sick *adj.* enfermo/a
  be sick estar enfermo/a
  get sick enfermarse
sideburn *n.* patilla *f.*
sight *n. (senses)* vista *f.*
sight *v.t.* divisar
sightseeing: go sightseeing hacer turismo
sign *n. (board)* letrero *m.;* señal *f.*
sign *v.t.* firmar
signature *n.* firma *f.*
silence *n.* silencio *m.*
silk *n., adj.* seda *f.;* de seda
silky *adj.* sedoso/a
silly *adj.* tonto/a
silver *n., adj.* plata *f.;* plateado/a
silverware *n.* cubiertos *m., pl.*
similar *adj.* similar; semejante
simmer *v.t.* cocer a fuego lento
simple *adj.* sencillo/a, simple
sinagogue *n.* sinagoga *f.*
since *prep.* desde
sing *v.t.* cantar
singer *n.* cantante *m., f.*
single *adj.* soltero/a
single room *n.* habitación *f.* individual
singles *n. (sports)* individual *m.*
sink *n.* lavabo *m.;* lavamanos *m.;* (*kitchen*) fregadero (de la cocina) *m.*
sip *n.* sorbo *m.*

sir *n.* señor *m.* (Sr.)

sister *n.* hermana *f.*
younger sister hermana menor

sister-in-law *n.* cuñada *f.*

sit down *v.* sentarse (e:ie)

six seis

six hundred seiscientos/as

sixteen dieciséis

sixth sexto *m.*; sexto/a

sixty sesenta

size *n.* talla *f.*
What size do you take? ¿Qué talla lleva/usa?

skate *v.i.* patinar

skating *n.* patinaje *m.*

skating rink *n.* pista *f.* de patinaje

skeleton *n.* esqueleto *m.*

ski *v.i.* esquiar

ski cap *n.* gorro *m.* de lana

ski slope *n.* pista *f.* de esquí

skier *n.* esquiador(a) *m.*, *f.*

skiing *n.* esquí *m.*

skill *n.* habilidad *f.*

skillful *adj.* hábil

skimmed *adj. (dairy products)* descremado/a; desnatado/a

skin *n.* cutis *m.*; piel *f.*; *(on boiled milk)* nata *f.*

skinny *adj.* flaco/a

skirt *n.* falda *f.*

skull *n.* calavera *f.*; cráneo *m.*

sky *n.* cielo *m.*

sky blue *n., adj. (color)* azul *m.* celeste

skylight *n.* tragaluz *m.*

skyscraper *n.* rascacielos *m.*, *sing.*

sleep *n.* sueño *m.*

sleep *v.i.* dormir (o:ue)
fall asleep dormirse (o:ue)
I couldn't fall asleep last night. No pude dormirme anoche.
go to sleep dormirse (o:ue)

sleepy: be sleepy tener sueño

sleeping bag *n.* saco *m.* de dormir

sleeve *n.* manga *f.*

slender *adj. (person)* delgado/a, esbelto/a

slice *n.* trozo *m.*; rebanada *f.* **a slice of bread** una rebanada de pan; rodaja *f.* **sliced onions** rodajas de cebolla

slice *v.t.* cortar

slide *n. (photo.)* diapositiva *f.*

slim down *v.* adelgazar

slope *n.* ladera *f.* **The group ascended the northern slope.** El equipo subió por la ladera norte.

slot machine *n.* tragaperras *(Spain) f., sing.*; tragamonedas *(L.A.) f., sing.*

sloth *n.* perezoso *m.*

slow *adj.* lento/a; *adv.* despacio

small *adj.* pequeño/a

small intestine *n.* intestino *m.* delgado

smallpox *n.* viruela *f.*

smart *adj.* listo/a

smell *n. (sense)* olfato *m.*; olor *m.* **The smell of gasoline makes me sick.** El olor a gasolina me da asco.

smell (like) *v.i.* oler (a) **It smells like smoke here.**

Huele a humo aquí.
smile *n.* sonrisa *f.*
smile *v.i.* sonreír (e:i)
smiled *p.p.* sonreído (*of* sonreír)
smoggy: It's (very) smoggy. Hay (mucha) contaminación.
smoke *n.* humo *m.*
smoke *v.t./v.i.* fumar
  smoking section *n.* sección *f.* de fumadores
  no smoking section sección de no fumadores
smother *v.t. (fire)* sofocar
snack *n. (in the afternoon)* merienda *f.; (at a bar)* tapa *f.*
snack *v.i.* merendar
  have a snack (in the afternoon) merendar
snail *n.* caracol *m.*
snake *n.* serpiente *f.;* culebra *f.;* víbora *f.*
sneeze *v.i.* estornudar
snob *n.* esnob *m., f.*
snobbery *n.* esnobismo *m.*
snobbish *adj.* esnob
snore *n.* ronquido *m.*
snore *v.i.* roncar
snorkel *n.* esnórkel *m.*
snow *n.* nieve *f.*
snow *v.imp.* nevar (e:ie)
  It's snowing. Nieva.
so *adv.* tan; *(in such a way)* así
  It's so big. Es tan grande.
  and so on y así sucesivamente
so much *adv.* tanto
so that *conj.* para que
so-so *adv.* así así; regular
soap *n.* jabón *m.*

soap dish *n.* jabonera *f.*
soap opera *n.* telenovela *f.*
sob *n.* sollozo *m.*
sob *v.i.* sollozar
sober *adj.* sobrio/a
sobriety test *n.* prueba *f.* de la alcoholemia
soccer *n.* fútbol *m.*
soccer field *n.* campo *m.* de fútbol
soccer player *n.* futbolista *m., f.*
sociable *adj.* sociable
socialize *v.i.* socializar
society *n.* sociedad *f.*
sociologist *n.* sociólogo/a *m., f*
sociology *n.* sociología *f.*
sock *n.* calcetín *m.*
sodium *n.* sodio *m.*
sofa *n.* sofá *m.*
soft *adj. (to the touch)* suave; esponjoso/a
soft drink *n.* refresco *m.*
software *n.* programa *m.* de computación
soil *n.* tierra *f.*
solarium *n.* solario *m.*
solution *n. (to a problem)* resolución *f.*
solve *v.t.* resolver (o:ue); solucionar
some *pron., adj.* algún, alguno/a(s); unos/as
somebody *pron.* alguien
someone *pron.* alguien
somersault *n.* salto *m.* mortal; voltereta *f.*
something *pron.* algo
  something like that algo por el estilo

sometimes *adv.* a veces
son *n.* hijo *m.*
son-in-law *n.* yerno *m.*
song *n.* canción *f.*
soon *adv.* pronto
  as soon as en cuanto; tan pronto como
  as soon as possible lo antes posible
soprano *n.* soprano *m., f.*
sorbet *n.* sorbete *m.*
sorry: be sorry sentir(se) (e:ie); arrepentirse
  I'm extremely sorry. Mil perdones.
  I'm sorry. Lo siento.
soul *n.* alma (el) *f.*
soup *n.* sopa *f.; (broth)* caldo *m.*
  beef soup caldo de patas
sour *adj.* agrio/a
south *n.* sur *m.*
  to the south al sur
South American *n., adj.* sudamericano/a *m., f.*
souvenir *n.* recuerdo *m.*
spa *n.* balneario *m.*
space shuttle *n.* transbordador *m.*
Spain *n.* España *f.*
Spaniard *n.* español(a) *m., f.*
Spanish *n., adj.* español(a) *m., f.; (language)* español
spare time *n.* ratos *m., pl.* libres
spare tire *n.* rueda *f.* de recambio/repuesto
spark plug *n.* bujía *f.*
sparkling wine *n.* cava *m.*
sparrow *n.* gorrión *m.*

spatula *n.* espátula *f.*
speak *v.i.* hablar
Special Olympics *n., pl.* Olimpiadas *f., pl.* Especiales
specialist *n.* especialista *m., f.*
specialization *n.* especialización *f.*
specialize (in something) *v.i.* especializarse (en algo)
species *n.* especie *f.*
  protected species *n.* especie *f.* protegida
spectacular *adj.* espectacular
spectator *n.* espectador(a) *m., f.*
speech *n.* discurso *m.*
speed *n.* velocidad *f.*
speed limit *n.* velocidad *f.* máxima
spelling *n., adj.* ortografía *f.; ortográfico/a*
spend *v.t. (money)* gastar; *(time)* pasar
sphere *n.* esfera *f.*
spicy *adj.* picante
spider *n.* araña *f.*
spiderweb *n.* telaraña *f.*
spill *v.t.* derramar
spill over *v.* derramarse
spinach *n.* espinaca *f.*
spinal column *n.* columna *f.* vertebral
spine *n.* columna *f.* vertebral
spleen *n.* bazo *m.*
spoiled child *n.* niño/a *m., f.* mimado/a
spokesperson *n.* portavoz *m., f.*
sponge *n.* esponja *f.*
spongy *adj.* esponjoso/a
sponsor *n.* patrocinador(a) *m., f.*

sponsor *v.t.* patrocinar
spontaneous *adj.* espontáneo/a.
spoon *n.* cuchara *f.*
sport *n.* deporte *m.*
sporting *adj.* deportista
sporting goods *n., pl.* artículos *m., pl.* de deporte
sports car *n.* carro *m.* deportivo
sports center *n.* polideportivo *m.*
sports facilities *n., pl.* instalaciones *f., pl.* deportivas
sports-loving *adj.* deportivo/a
sportswear *n.* ropa *f.* deportiva
spouse *n.* esposo/a *m., f.*
sprain *n.* esguince
sprain (an ankle) *v.t.* torcerse (el tobillo)
sprained *adj.* torcido/a
  be sprained estar torcido/a
spread *v.t. (information)* divulgar; propagar **Some papers spread rumors.** Algunos periódicos propagan rumores.; propagarse **The rumor was spreading rapidly.** El rumor se propagaba rápidamente.; *(butter, etc.)* untar
spreading *n. (news, ideas)* divulgación *f.*
spring *n. (season)* primavera *f.; (coil)* muelle *m.,* resorte *m.; (water)* manantial *m.*
sprinkle *v.t. (sugar, etc.)* espolvorear

square *n.* cuadrado *m.; (town)* plaza *f.*
squat *v.i.* agacharse
squid *n.* calamar *m.*
squirrel *n.* ardilla *f.*
stable *n.* establo *m.*
stack *v.t.* apilar
stadium *n.* estadio *m.*
stage *n.* etapa *f.; (theater)* escenario *m.*
stained-glass window *n.* vidriera *f.* (de colores)
stainless steel *n.* acero *m.* inoxidable
stair *n.* escalón *m.;* peldaño *m.*
stairs *n.* escalera *f.*
stairway *n.* escalera *f.*
stammer *v.i.* tartamudear
stamp *n.* estampilla *(L.A.) f.;* sello *(Spain) m.*
stamp collecting *n.* filatelia *f.*
stand *v.i. (person)* estar parado *(L.A.);* estar de pie
stand in line *v.* hacer cola
stand out *v.* sobresalir
stand somebody up *v.* dejar a alguien plantado/a
star *n.* estrella *f.*
starry *adj.* estrellado/a
start *v.t. (vehicle)* arrancar; *(begin)* empezar (e:ie), comenzar (e:ie)
state *n.* estado *m.*
station *n. (train, bus)* estación *f.*
statue *n.* estatua *f.*
status: marital status estado *m.* civil

stay *n.* estancia *f.* **Our stay in La Coruña was magnificent.** Nuestra estancia en La Coruña fue magnífica.

stay *v.i.* quedarse; *(hotel)* alojarse

stay up all night *v.* trasnochar

steak *n.* bistec *m.*

steal *v.t.* robar

steam *n.* vapor *m.*

steel *n.* acero *m.*

steeplechase *n.* carrera *f.* de obstáculos

steering wheel *n.* volante *m.*

step *n.* etapa *f.;* paso *m.; (stair)* escalón *m.,* peldaño *m.*

stepbrother *n.* hermanastro *m.*

stepdaughter *n.* hijastra *f.*

stepfather *n.* padrastro *m.*

stepmother *n.* madrastra *f.*

stepsister *n.* hermanastra *f.*

stepson *n.* hijastro *m.*

stereo *n.* estéreo *m.*

sterile *adj.* estéril

sterilize *v.t.* esterilizar

stethoscope *n.* estetoscopio *m.*

stew *n.* guiso *m.*

stifling *adj. (heat)* sofocante, agobiante **The heat is stifling.** Este calor es agobiante.

still *adv.* todavía, aún

stingy *adj.* tacaño/a

stir *v.t.* remover

stock broker *n.* bolsista *m., f.*

stomach *n.* estómago *m. f.* **get an upset stomach** empacharse

stomach disorder *n.* trastorno *m.* estomacal

stone *n.* piedra *f.*

stool *n.* taburete *m.*

stop *v.i.* parar

stop *(doing something)* *v.* dejar de (+ *inf.*)

stop sign *n.* señal *m.* de alto

storage *n.* almacenamiento *m.*

store *n.* tienda *f.*

store *v.t.* almacenar

stork *n.* cigüeña *f.*

storm *n.* tormenta *f.*

story *n.* cuento *m.;* historia *f.*

stove *n.* estufa *f.*

straight *adj.* derecho/a; recto/a; *(hair)* lacio/a

straight *adv.* derecho **straight ahead** (todo) derecho

strain *v.t.* colar

strange *adj.* extraño/a **It's strange that . . .** Es extraño que (+ subj)…

straw *n.* paja *f.; (drinking)* pajita *f.,* popote *m.* **That's the last straw!** *loc.* ¡Esto es el colmo!

strawberry *n.* fresa *f.,* frutilla *(Ecuador) f.*

stream *n.* riachuelo *m.*

streamer *n.* serpentina *f.*

street *n.* calle *m.*

stress *n.* estrés *m.;* tensión *f.* **under stress** *adj.* estresado/a

stress *v.t.* destacar, enfatizar, recalcar

stressful *adj.* estresante

stretch *v.t.* estirar

stretcher *n.* camilla *f.*

stretching *n.* estiramiento *m.* **stretching exercises** *n., pl.*

ejercicios *m., pl.* de estiramiento
strike *n. (labor)* huelga *f.*
striker *n.* huelguista *m., f.*
stripe *n.* raya *f.*
striped *adj.* de rayas
stroke *n. (swimming)* estilo *m.*
stroll *v.i.* pasear
strong *adj.* fuerte
struggle (for; to + inf.) *v.* luchar (por; para + *inf.*)
stubborn *adj.* testarudo/a
student *n., adj.* estudiante *m., f.;* estudiantil
studious *adj.* estudioso/a
study *v.t./v.i.* estudiar
stuff *v.t. (culinary)* rellenar
stuff oneself *v.* hartarse
stuffed *adj.* relleno/a
   I love stuffed chilies. Adoro los chiles rellenos.
stuffed-up *adj.* congestionado/a
stuffing *n.* relleno *m.*
stunned *adj.* atontado/a
stupendous *adj.* estupendo/a
stutter *v.i.* tartamudear
style *n.* estilo *m.*
subject matter *n.* temática *f.*
subject *n. (university)* disciplina *f.;* tema *m.*
subjective *adj.* subjetivo/a
submarine *n.* submarino *m.*
substance *n.* sustancia *f.*
substitute *n.* sustituto/a *m., f.*
substitute *v.t.* sustituir
   He substituted coffe for tea. Sustituyó el café por el té.
subterranean *adj.* subterráneo/a

suburbs *n.* afueras *f., pl.*
subway *n.* metro *m.*
   go by subway ir en metro
subway station *n.* estación *f.* del metro
succeed *v.i.* triunfar
success *n.* éxito *m.*
   be successful tener éxito
successively *adv.* sucesivamente
such as [tal(es)] como
   She used words such as justice and freedom. Usó palabras (tales) como justicia y libertad.
suddenly *adv.* de repente
suffer *v.t.* sufrir
suffer from *v. (disease)* padecer de **He suffers from heart problems.** Padece del corazón.
   suffer from an illness sufrir una enfermedad
suffering *n.* padecimiento *m.*
sufficient *adj.* bastante
suffocation *n.* sofoco *m.*
sugar *n.* azúcar *m.*
sugar bowl *n.* azucarero *m.*
suggest *v.t.* sugerir (e:ie)
suggestion *n.* sugerencia *f.*
suicide *n.* suicidio *m.*
   commit suicide suicidarse
suit *n.* traje *m.*
suit *v.t. (clothes)* sentar
   That jacket suits you. Esa chaqueta te sienta bien.
suitable *adj.* apto/a
suitcase *n.* maleta *f.*
summer *n.* verano *m.*
summer *v.i.* veranear

She summers in the mountains. Veranea en las montañas.
summit n. cima f.
sumptuous adj. suntuoso/a
sun n. sol m.
sunbathe v.i. tomar el sol; tumbarse al sol
Sunday n. domingo m.
sunflower n. girasol m.
sunglasses n., pl. lentes m., pl. de sol; gafas f., pl. oscuras/negras
sunny adj. soleado/a
It's sunny. Hace sol.
sunrise n. salida f. del sol
sunset n. puesta f. de(l) sol
sunshade n. sombrilla f.
suntan lotion n. bronceador m.
suntanned adj. bronceado/a
supermarket n. supermercado m.
superstition n. superstición f.
superstitious adj. supersticioso/a
supervise v.t. supervisar
supplier n. suministrador(a) m., f.
supplies n., pl. provisiones f., pl.; víveres m., pl.
supply n. suministro m.
supply v.t. suministrar
support v.t. apoyar; sostener; soportar; respaldar
suppose v.t. suponer
Supreme Court n. Corte f. Suprema (L.A.); Tribunal m. Supremo (Spain)
sure adj. seguro/a
be sure estar seguro/a

surf v.i. (Internet) navegar (en)
surgeon n. cirujano/a m., f.
surgery n. cirugía f.
surprise n. sorpresa f.
What a surprise! ¡Qué sorpresa!
surprise v.t. sorprender
be surprised sorprenderse
He was surprised to see me. Se sorprendió al verme.
surrounding area n. alrededores m., pl.
survey n. encuesta f.
survival n. supervivencia f.
survivor n. superviviente m., f.
suspect v.t. sospechar
suspenders n., pl. tirantes m., pl.
suspense: in suspense adj. intrigado/a
suspension bridge n. puente f. colgante
suspicion n. sospecha f.
suspicious adj. sospechoso/a
swallow v.t./v.i. tragar
swamp n. pantano m.; ciénaga f.
swan n. cisne m.
swear v.t. jurar
sweat v.i. sudar
sweater n. suéter m.
sweaty adj. sudado/a
sweep (the floor) v.t. barrer (el piso/suelo)
sweet adj. dulce
sweets n., pl. dulces m., pl.
swim v.i. nadar
swimmer n. nadador(a) m., f.
swimming n. natación f.
synchronized swimming

natación sincronizada
swimming pool *n.* piscina *f.;*
alberca *(Mexico) f.*
symbiosis *n.* simbiosis *f.*
symbolize *v.t.* simbolizar
symphonic *adj.* sinfónico/a
symphony *n.* sinfonía *f.*
symphony orchestra *n.*
sinfónica *f.*
symptom *n.* síntoma *m.*
synonym *n.* sinónimo *m.*
synonymous *adj.* sinónimo/a
syntax *n.* sintaxis *f.*
syringe *n.* jeringa *f.*
syrup *n.* almíbar *m.*

T

table *n.* mesa *f.*
tablecloth *n.* mantel *m.*
tablespoon *n.* cuchara *f.*
tablet *n. (pill)* pastilla *f.*
tactful *adj.* diplomático/a
tactless *adj.* indiscreto/a
tail *n.* cola *f.*
tailor *n.* sastre *m.*
take *v.t.* llevar; tomar
take advantage of *v.*
aprovecharse de
take back *v.t.* devolver
take off *v. (clothes)* quitarse;
(airplane, rocket) despegar
  take off one's shoes
  descalzarse
take offense *v.* ofenderse
take out (the trash) *v.* sacar (la
basura)
take the risk *v.* arriesgarse
take up *v. (hobby)* aficionarse
talented *adj.* talentoso/a
talk *v.i.* hablar; conversar
talk show *n.* programa *m.* de

entrevistas
talkative *adj. (person)*
hablador(a); charlatán,
charlatana
tall *adj.* alto/a
tan *v.t.* broncear; *v.i.*
broncearse
tangerine *n.* mandarina *f.*
tangy *adj.* ácido/a
tank *n.* depósito *m.;* tanque *m.*
tape *n.* cinta *f.*
tape recorder *n.* grabadora *f.*
tapestry *n.* tapiz *m.*
target shooting *n.* tiro *m.* al
blanco
tart *adj.* ácido/a
taste *n. (senses)* gusto *m.*
taste *v.t.* probar (o:ue)
tasteless *adj.* soso/a
tasty *adj.* rico/a, sabroso/a
tax *n.* impuesto *m.*
taxi(cab) *n.* taxi *m.*
  go by taxi ir en taxi
tea *n.* té *m.*
  herbal tea *n.* infusión *f.* (de
  hierbas)
teabag *n.* bolsita *f.* de té
teach *v.t.* enseñar
teacher *n.* profesor(a) *m., f.;*
(elementary school)
maestro/a *m., f.*
team *n.* equipo *m.*
  technical team equipo de
  técnicos
teapot *n.* tetera *f.*
tear *n.* lágrima *f.*
tear gas *n.* gas *m.* lacrimógeno
technician *n.* técnico/a *m., f.*
teddy bear *n.* osito *m.* de
peluche

telecommuting *n.* teletrabajo *m.*

teleconference *n.* videoconferencia *f.*

telephone *n.* teléfono *m.*
cellular telephone teléfono celular
by phone por teléfono

telescope *n.* telescopio *m.*

television *n.* televisión *f.; (set)* televisor *m.*

temperament *n.* temperamento *m.*

temperature *n.* temperatura *f.*
take (someone's) temperature tomar la temperatura (a alguien)

temple *n.* templo *m.*

ten diez

tendency *n.* tendencia *f.*

tender *adj. (meat; loving)* tierno/a

tendon *n.* tendón *m.*

tennis *n.* tenis *m.*

tennis court *n.* pista *f.* de tenis

tennis player *n.* tenista *m., f.*

tennis shoes *n.* zapatillas *f., pl.* de deporte; zapatos *m., pl.* de tenis

tenor *n.* tenor *m.*

tension *n.* tensión *f.*

tent *n.* tienda *f.* (de campaña)

tenth décimo *m.;* décimo/a

terrace *n.* terraza *f.*

terrible *adj.* terrible

terrific *adj.* genial, fantástico, estupendo, chévere

terrorist *n., adj.* terrorista *m., f.*

terrorist attack *n.* atentado *m.* terrorista

test *n.* examen *m.;* prueba *f.;* evaluación *f.*
placement test prueba de nivel
aptitude test prueba de aptitud

test *v.t.* evaluar

thanks *interj.* gracias
Thank you. Gracias. **Thank you very much.** Muchas gracias. **Thank you very, very much.** Muchísimas gracias. **Thanks (a lot).** (Muchas) gracias. **Thanks again.** Gracias una vez más. **Thanks for everything.** Gracias por todo.

that *conj.* que

that which *conj.* lo que

that's why por eso

theater *n.* teatro *m.*

theft *n.* robo *m.*

thematic *adj.* temático/a

theme *n.* tema *m.*

then *adv. (afterward)* después; *(as a result)* entonces; *(next)* luego, pues

theorize *v.i.* teorizar

theory *n.* teoría *f.*

therapeutic *adj.* terapéutico/a

therapy *n.* terapia *f.*

there *adv.* allí

There is/are . . . Hay…

There is/are no . . . No hay…

therefore *adv.* por eso; por lo tanto

thermostat *m.* termostato

thesis *f.* tesis

thief *n.* ladrón *m.,* ladrona *f.*

thigh *n.* muslo *m.*

thin *adj.* delgado/a
thing *n.* cosa *f.*
think *v.t.* pensar (e:ie);
(believe) creer
  What do you think? *form.*
  ¿Qué le/les parece?
think about *v.* pensar en
third tercio *m.;* tercero/a
third-world country *n.* país *m.*
  tercermundista
thirst *n.* sed *f.*
  be thirsty tener sed
thirsty *adj.* sediento/a
thirteen trece
thirty treinta; *(minutes past the*
  hour) y treinta, y media
  It's six thirty. Son las seis y
  treinta/media.
This is he/she. *(on the phone)*
  Con él/ella habla.
thorn *n.* espina *f.*
thread *n.* hilo *m.*
threat *n.* amenaza *f.*
threaten *v.t.* amenazar
three tres
three hundred trescientos/as
thrilled *adj.* ilusionado/a
throat *n.* garganta *f.*
through *prep.* por; a través de
throw *n.* lanzamiento *m.*
throw *v.t.* echar; tirar; lanzar
throw away *v.t. (leftovers)*
  desechar, tirar
thunder *n.* trueno *m.*
Thursday *n.* jueves *m.*, *sing.*
thus *adv.* así
thyme *n.* tomillo *m.*
ticket *n. (show)* boleto *(L.A.)*
  m.; entrada *(Spain) f.; (trip)*
  pasaje

tidal wave *n.* maremoto *m.*
tie *n. (clothing)* corbata *f.;*
  (sports) empate *m.; (bond)*
  lazo *m.*, vínculo *m*
  family ties lazos familiares
tie *v.t.* atar; *(sports)* empatar
tiger *n.* tigre *m.*
tile *n. (ceramic)* azulejo *m.;*
  (floor) baldosa *f.; (roof)* teja *f.*
time *n.* tiempo *m.; (occasion)*
  vez *f.*
  We have time. Tenemos
  tiempo.
  We had a great time. Lo
  pasamos de película/super
  bien.
  What time is it? ¿Qué hora
  es?
  ahead of time con
  anticipación
  on time a tiempo
  one time una vez
  one more time una vez más
  many times muchas veces
time trial *n.* carrera *n.* contra
  reloj
timid *adj.* tímido/a
tinfoil *n.* papel *m.* de aluminio
tiny *adj.* minúsculo/a
tip *n.* propina *f.*
  leave a tip dejar una propina
tire *n.* llanta *f.;* neumático *m.*
tire oneself out *v.* cansarse
tired *adj.* cansado/a
  be tired estar cansado/a
tiredness *n.* cansancio *m.*
tissue *n. (anat.)* tejido *m.;*
  pañuelo *m.* de papel
title *n.* título *m.*
toad *n.* sapo *m.*

toast *n.* pan *m.* tostado; tostada *f.; (drinking)* brindis *m.*

toast *v.t.* tostar; *(drinking)* brindar (por)

toasted *adj.* tostado/a

toaster *n.* tostadora *f.*

today *adv.* hoy

toe *n.* dedo *m.* (del pie)

together *adj.* juntos/as

toiletry kit *n.* neceser *m.*

toilet paper *n.* papel *m.* higiénico

tolerance *n.* tolerancia *f.*

tolerant *adj.* tolerante

tolerate *v.t.* tolerar

tomato *n.* tomate *m.*

tomorrow *adv.* mañana

tongs *n., pl.* tenazas *f., pl.*

tonight *adv.* esta noche

tonsil *n.* amígdala *f.*

too *adv.* también

too much *adv.* demasiado; en exceso

tool *n.* herramienta *f.*

tooth *n.* diente *m.; (back)* muela *f.*
  pull a tooth sacar una muela
  I had a tooth pulled. Me sacaron una muela.

toothbrush *n.* cepillo *m.* de dientes

toothpaste *n.* pasta *f.* de dientes

toothpick *n.* mondadientes *m., sing.*; palillo *m.* (de dientes)

top *n.* cima *f.*

torch *n.* antorcha *f.*

tornado *n.* tornado *m.*

tortilla *n.* tortilla *f.*

toss *v.t.* tirar; mezclar

touch *n. (sense)* tacto *m.*

touch *v.t.* tocar

tour *n.* visita *f.* turística; viaje *m.*
  tour around an area excursión *f.*
  go on a tour hacer una excursión

tourism *n.* turismo *m.*

tourist *adj.* turístico/a

tourist *n.* turista *m., f.*

toward *prep.* hacia

towel *n.* toalla *f.*

towel bar *n.* toallero *m.*

tower *n.* torre *f.*

town *n.* pueblo *m.*

town square *n.* plaza *f.* mayor

toy *n.* juguete *m.*

toy store *n.* juguetería *f.*

track *n.* pista *f.; (sport)* pista de atletismo; *(railroad)* vía *f.*
  indoor track *n.* pista *f.* cubierta

track and field *n.* atletismo *m.*

trade *n.* oficio *m.*

tradition *n.* tradición *f.*

traffic *n.* circulación *f.*

traffic (in) *v.t.* traficar (en)

traffic jam *n.* atasco *m.;* embotellamiento *m.* (de tráfico) *(Spain)*

traffic sign *n.* señal *f.* de tráfico

traffic signal *n.* semáforo *m.*

tragedy *n.* tragedia *f.*

tragic *adj.* trágico/a

trail *n.* sendero *m.*

trailer *n.* caravana *f.*

trailhead *n.* sendero *m.*

train *n.* tren *m.*
  go by train ir en tren
train *v.i.* entrenarse
trainer *n.* monitor *m., f.*
training *n.* entrenamiento *m.*
traitor *n.* traidor(a) *m., f.*
trajectory *n.* trayectoria *f.*
transfer *n.* transferencia *f.*
transfusion *n.* transfusión *f.*
translate *v.t.* traducir
translation *n.* traducción *f.*
translator *n.* traductor(a) *m., f.*
transparent *adj.* transparente
transplant *n.* transplante *m.*
transport *v.t.* transportar
transportation *n.* transporte *m.*
trapshooting *n.* tiro *m.* al plato
trash *n.* basura *f.*
travel *v.i.* viajar; desplazarse
travel agency *n.* agencia *f.* de viajes
travel agent *n.* agente *m., f.* de viajes
travel document *n.* documento *m.* de viaje
traveler *n.* viajero/a *m., f.*
traveler's check *n.* cheque *m.* de viajero
treacherous *adj.* traicionero/a, traidor(a); peligroso/a
treachery *n.* traición *f.*
treason *n.* traición *f.*
treasure *n.* tesoro *m.*
tree *n.* árbol *m.*
trendy: be trendy ir a la moda
trial *n.* juicio *m.*
triangle *n.* triángulo *m.*
tribute *n.* homenaje *m.*
tricycle *n.* triciclo *m.*
trigger *n. (firearm)* gatillo *m.*
trigonometry *n.* trigonometría *f.*

trimester *n.* trimestre *m.*
trip *n.* viaje *m.;* desplazamiento *m.*
  go on a trip hacer un viaje
tripod *n.* trípode *m.*
triviality *n.* trivialidad *f.*
trivialize *v.t.* trivializar
trout *n.* trucha *f.*
truck *n.* camión *m.*
truck driver *n.* camionero/a *m., f.*
true *adj.* verdadero/a; cierto
true-to-life *adj.* verosímil
trunk *n.* baúl *m.; (car)* maletero *(Spain) m.; (live tree)* tronco *m.*
truth *n.* verdad *f.*
try *n.* intento *m.*
try *v.t.* intentar; probar (o:ue); *(to do something)* tratar de (+ *inf.*)
try hard *v.* esforzarse
try on *v. (clothes)* probarse (o:ue)
try out *v.t./v.i.* experimentar
t-shirt *n.* camiseta *f.*
tube *n.* tubo *m.*
tuberculosis *n.* tuberculosis *f.*
Tuesday *n.* martes *m., sing.*
tulip *n.* tulipán *m.*
tuna *n.* atún *m.*
tune up *v.t.* afinar
  out of tune *adj.* desafinado/a
tunnel *n.* túnel *m.*
turbine *n.* turbina *f.*
turkey *n.* pavo *m.*
turn *n.* giro *m.;* turno *m.*
turn *v.t./v.i.* doblar; girar **Turn left at the next corner.** Gira a la izquierda en la próxima esquina.

turn off *v.t.*
(electricity/appliance)
apagar

turn on *v.t.*
(electricity/appliance) poner,
encender

turn over *v.t. (tortilla, cup)*
voltear *(L.A.)*

turn signal *n. (car)* intermitente
m.

turquoise *n.* turquesa *f.*

turtle *n.* tortuga *f.*

tutor *n.* profesor(a) *m., f.*
particular

tweezers *n., pl.* pinzas *f., pl.*
(para depilar)

twelve doce

twenty veinte

twenty-eight veintiocho

twenty-five veinticinco

twenty-four veinticuatro

twenty-nine veintinueve

twenty-one veintiún,
veintiuno/a

twenty-seven veintisiete

twenty-six veintiséis

twenty-three veintitrés

twenty-two veintidós

twice *adv.* dos veces

twin *n.* mellizo/a *m., f.;*
gemelo/a *m., f.*

twisted *adj.* torcido/a
be twisted estar torcido/a

two dos

two hundred doscientos/as

two weeks *n., pl.* quincena *f.*

type *n.* especie *f.*

type *v.i.* escribir a máquina;
teclear

typewriter *n.* máquina *f.* de
escribir

typist *n.* mecanógrafo/a *m., f.*

U

**UFO (Unidentified Flying
Object)** *n.* OVNI *m.* (Objeto
Volador No Identificado)

ugly *adj.* feo/a

umbrella *n.* paraguas *m.*

umbrella stand *n.* paragüero
m.

umpire *n.* árbitro/a *m.*

unbearable *adj.* insoportable

unblock *v.t.* desatascar

uncertainty *n.* incertidumbre *f.*

uncle *n.* tío *m.*

under *adv.* bajo, debajo (de)

undergo *v.t. (test, examination)*
someterse a

underground *adj.*
subterráneo/a

underlined *adj.* subrayado/a

understand *v.t.* comprender;
entender (e:ie)

understanding *n.* comprensión
f.

underwear *n.* ropa *f.* interior
long underwear *n.*
calzoncillos *m., pl.* largos

undress *v.i.* desvestirse

unemployment *n.* desempleo
m.

unexpected *adj.* inesperado/a

unfair *adj.* injusto/a

unfavorable *adj.* desfavorable

unforgettable *adj.* inolvidable

unfortunate *adj.* desgraciado/a

unfortunately *adv.*
desafortunadamente;
desgraciadamente

unfriendly *adj.* antipático/a; arisco/a
ungrateful *adj.* desagradecido/a
unhappy *adj.* infeliz; desgraciado/a
United States *n., pl.* Estados *m., pl.* Unidos
universe *n.* universo *m.*
university *n.* universidad *f.*
unkempt *adj. (appearance)* desarreglado/a
unless *adv.* a menos que
unlikely *adj.* improbable, poco probable
  be unlikely that *(something will happen)* ser poco probable que (+ *subj.*) **It's unlikely that they will arrive on time.** Es poco probable que lleguen a tiempo.
unmarried *adj.* soltero/a
unnoticed *adj.* inadvertido/a
unpack *v.t.* desempacar
unpleasant *adj.* desagradable; *(person)* antipático/a
unresolved *adj.* pendiente
unsociable *adj.* insociable
unsuccessful *adj.* fracasado/a
unthinkable *adj.* impensable
until *adv.* hasta que
until *prep.* hasta
unusual *adj.* inusual, poco corriente; insólito/a
unwillingly *adv.* de mala gana
up *adv.* arriba
  up to date al día, al corriente
  bring someone up to date *idiom* poner a uno al día/al corriente

urgent *adj.* urgente
urinate *v.i.* orinar
urine *n.* orina *f.*
use *v.t.* usar
  make good use of aprovechar
useful *adj.* útil; práctico/a
usually *adv.* soler (o:ue) +*inf.*
  I usually study at night. Suelo estudiar por la noche.
utensil *n.* utensilio *m.*
uterus *n.* útero *m.*

V

vacation *n.* vacaciones *f., pl.*
  be on vacation estar de vacaciones
  go on vacation ir de vacaciones
vacationer *n. (summer)* veraneante *m., f.*
vacuum *v.i.* pasar la aspiradora
vacuum cleaner *n.* aspiradora *f.*
vain *adj.* presumido/a
valley *n.* valle *m.*
value *n.* valor *m.*
value *v.t.* valorar
vanilla *n.* vainilla *f.*
vapor *n.* vapor *m.*
variation *n.* variación *f.*
varied *adj.* variado/a
variety *n.* surtido *m.*
various *adj.* varios/as
vary *v.i.* variar
vase *n.* florero *m.*; jarrón *m.*
VCR *n.* videocasetera *f.*
veal *n.* ternera *f.*
vegetables *n., pl.* verduras *f., pl.*

vegetation *n.* vegetación *f.*
vehicle *n.* vehículo *m.*
vein *n.* vena *f.*
velodrome *n.* velódromo *m.*
velvet *n.* terciopelo *m.*
verb *n.* verbo *m.*
verisimilitude *n.* verosimilitud *f.*
vermillion *n.* bermellón *m.*
vermouth *n.* vermut *m.*
versatile *adj.* versátil
vertebra *n.* vértebra *f.*
vertebrate *n., adj.* vertebrado *m.;* vertebrado/a
very *adv.* muy
  Very good, thank you. Muy bien, gracias.
very much *adv.* muchísimo/a
vest *n.* chaleco *m.*
veterinarian *n.* veterinario/a *m., f.*
veterinary science *n.* veterinaria *f.*
vibrate *v.i.* vibrar
vibration *n.* vibración *f.*
video *n.* video *(L.A.) m.;* vídeo *(Spain) m.*
video(cassette) *n.* video(casete) *m.*
video camera *n.* cámara *f.* de video
video conference *n.* videoconferencia *f.*
view *n.* vista *f.*
village *n.* aldea *f.*
vinegar *n.* vinagre *m.*
violence *n.* violencia *f.*
visit *v.t.* visitar
  visit monuments visitar monumentos

visiting team *n. (sports)* equipo *m.* visitante
visitor *n.* visitante *m., f.*
vitamin *n.* vitamina *f.*
vocational training *n.* formación *f.* profesional
volcano *n.* volcán *m.*
volleyball *n.* vóleibol *m.*
volume *n.* volumen *m.*
voluntary *adj.* voluntario
volunteer *n.* voluntario/a *m., f.*
vomit *v.i.* vomitar
vote *n.* voto *m.*
vote *v.i.* votar
vulture *n.* buitre *m.*

W

waist *n.* cintura *f.*
wait for *v.i.* esperar
  be waiting estar pendiente
  I'm waiting for Woody to call me. Estoy pendiente de que Woody me llame.
waiter *n.* camarero *m.;* mesero *m.;* mozo *m. (L.A.)*
waitress *n.* camarera *f.;* mesera *f.;* moza *f. (L.A.)*
wake up *v.i.* despertarse (e:ie)
walk *v.i.* caminar
  take a walk pasear
walking stick *n.* bastón *m.*
walkman *n.* walkman *m.*
wall *n.* pared *f.;* muro *m.*
wallet *n.* cartera *f.*
walnut *n.* nuez *f.*
walnut tree *n.* nogal *m.*
want *v.t.* querer (e:ie)
war *n.* guerra *f.*
wardrobe *n.* ropero *m.;* vestuario *m.*

warm (oneself) up v. calentarse

warranty n. garantía f.

wart n. verruga f.

wash v.t. lavar; v.ref. (oneself) lavarse

  wash one's face/hands lavarse la cara/las manos

washing machine n. lavadora f.

wasp n. avispa f.

waste v.t. malgastar

wastebasket n. papelera f.

watch n. reloj m.

watch v.t./v.i. mirar

  watch television mirar (la) televisión

watch out interj. cuidado

water n. agua (el) f.

  drinking water agua potable

  fresh water agua dulce

  holy water agua bendita

  mineral water agua mineral

  salt water agua salada

water v.t. (plants) regar

water park n. parque m. acuático

waterfall n. catarata f.

watering can n. regadera f.

watermelon n. sandía f.

waterproof adj. impermeable

waterskiing n. esquí m. acuático

wave n. (water) ola f.; (physics, radio) onda f.

wax n. cera f.

wax v.t. encerar; (legs) depilarse

way n. manera f.; camino m.

weak adj. débil

weapon n. arma (el) f.

wear v.t. llevar; usar

  wear for the first time estrenar

wear oneself out v. fatigarse

weary adj. fatigado/a

weather n. tiempo m.

  It's good/bad weather. Hace buen/mal tiempo.

  What's the weather like? ¿Qué tiempo hace?

weaving n. tejido m.

Web site n. sitio m. (Web)

wedding n. boda f.

  wedding ring n. anillo m. de bodas

Wednesday n. miércoles m., sing.

week n. semana f.

  next week semana entrante, semana que viene

weekend n. fin m. de semana

weigh oneself v. pesarse

weight n. pesa f.

weightless adj. ingrávido/a

weightlifting n. (sport) halterofilia f.

welcome adj. bienvenido/a(s)

  You're welcome. (responding to thanks) ¡de nada!; ¡no hay de qué!

weld v.t. soldar

welding n. soldadura f.

well adv. bien

well n. pozo m.

well-being n. bienestar m.

well-known adj. conocido/a

  be well-known for tener fama de

well-mannered adj. educado/a

well-organized *adj.* ordenado/a

west *n.* oeste *m.*
  to the west al oeste

western *adj. (genre)* de vaqueros
  a western una (película) de vaqueros

wet *adj.* mojado/a

wet *v.t.* mojar
  get wet mojarse

whale *n.* ballena *f.*

wharf *n.* embarcadero *m.*

what *rel. pron.* lo que

what? *adj., pron.* ¿qué?
  What did you say? ¿Cómo?
  What's going on? ¿Qué pasa?
  What a . . . ! ¡Qué…!
  What a drag! *loc.* ¡Qué lata!

wheat *n.* trigo *m.*

wheel *n.* rueda *f.*

wheel chair *n.* silla *f.* de ruedas

wheelbarrow *n.* carretilla *f.*

when *adv., conj.* cuando

when? *adv.* ¿cuándo?
  when all's said and done *loc.* a fin de cuentas

where *prep.* donde

where? *adv. (destination)* ¿adónde?; *(location)* ¿dónde?
  Where are you from? *(fam.)* ¿De dónde eres (tú)?; *(form.)* ¿De dónde es (Ud.)?
  Where is . . .? ¿Dónde está...?

which? *adj., pron.* ¿cuál(es)?; ¿qué?

while *adv.* mientras

whim *n.* antojo *m.*; capricho *m.*

whine *v.i.* lloriquear

whisk *v.t.* batir

whisk *n.* batidor *m.*

whistle *n.* silbato *m.*

whistle *v.i.* silbar

white *n., adj.* blanco *m.*; blanco/a

who *pron.* que **Is there anyone who speaks English?** ¿Hay alguien que hable inglés?; quien(es)

who? *pron.* ¿quién(es)?
  Who is . . . ? ¿Quién es...?
  Who is calling? *(on telephone)* ¿De parte de quién?
  Who is speaking? *(on telephone)* ¿Quién habla?

whole *adj.* todo/a

whole-wheat bread *n.* pan *m.* integral

whose? *adj., pron.* ¿de quién(es)?

why? *adv.* ¿por qué?

wicker *n.* mimbre *m.*

widowed *adj.* viudo/a

wife *n.* esposa *f.*

wig *n.* peluca *f.*

wild *adj. (animal)* salvaje; *(plant)* silvestre

willingly *adv.* de buena gana

win *v.t.* ganar; vencer

wind *n.* viento *m.*
  It's (very) windy. Hace (mucho) viento.

window *n.* ventana *f.*; cristal *m.*

windshield *n.* parabrisas *m.*, *sing.*

windshield wiper *n.* limpiaparabrisas *m., sing.*
wine *n.* vino *m.*
  bottle of wine *n.* botella *f.* de vino
  red/white wine vino tinto/blanco
wine cellar *n.* bodega *f.*
wineglass *n.* copa *f.*
wink (one's eye) *v.t.* guiñar(le) (el ojo) (a alguien)
winter *n.* invierno *m.*
wire netting *n.* tela *f.* metálica
wisdom *n.* sabiduría *f.*
wisdom tooth *n.* muela *f.* del juicio
wise *adj.* sabio/a
wise person *n.* sabio/a *m., f.*
wish *n.* deseo *m.*
wish *v.t.* desear; esperar
  I wish (that) *interj.* Ojalá (que)
with *prep.* con
  with me conmigo
  with you *fam.* contigo
  with regard to con respecto a
withdrawn *adj. (person)* retraído/a
within *prep.* dentro de
without *conj.* sin que
without *prep.* sin
withstand *v.t.* soportar, resistir, aguantar
witness *n.* testigo *m., f.*
wolf *n.* lobo *m.*
woman *n.* mujer *f.*
womanizer *n.* donjuán *m.;* mujeriego *m.*
womb *n.* útero *m.*

wool *n.* lana *f.*
  made of wool de lana
wool cap *n.* gorro *m.* de lana
word *n.* palabra *f.*
work *n.* trabajo *m.; (of art, literature, music, etc.)* obra *f.*
work *v.i.* trabajar; funcionar
  not working *adj.* descompuesto/a
work out *v.i.* hacer gimnasia
workshop *n.* taller *m.; (mechanic's)* taller de mecánica
world *n.* mundo *m.*
worldwide *adj.* mundial
worm *n.* gusano *m.*
worried *adj.* preocupado/a; inquieto/a
worry (about) *v.* preocuparse (por); inquietar(se)
  Don't worry. No se/te preocupe/s.
worrysome *adj.* inquietante
worse *adj.* peor
worst *adj.* el/la peor, lo peor
  the worst *n.* el/la peor *m., f.* lo peor
worth *n.* valor *m.*
  be worth the trouble valer la pena
wound *n.* herida *f.*
wrap *v.t.* envolver
wretch *n.* desgraciado/a *m., f.*
wrist *n.* muñeca *f.*
write *v.t.* escribir
  write a letter/post card/e-mail message escribir una carta/una (tarjeta) postal/un mensaje electrónico
writer *n.* escritor(a) *m., f.*

written *p.p.* escrito/a (*of* escribir)
wrong *adj.* equivocado/a
  be wrong no tener razón
  What's wrong? ¿Qué pasa?

X
x-ray *n.* radiografía *f.*

Y
yam *n.* ñame *m.*
yard *n.* jardín *m.; patio m.*
year *n.* año *m.*
yearning *n.* añoranza *f.*
yeast *n.* levadura *f.*
yellow *n., adj.* amarillo *m.;* amarillo/a
yellowish *adj.* amarillento/a
yes *interj.* sí
  Yes, sure! ¡Sí, vale!
yesterday *adv.* ayer
yet *adv.* todavía
yield (the right of way) *v.* ceder el paso
yoga *n.* yoga *m.*
yogurt *n.* yogur *m.*
young *adj.* joven
young person *n.* joven *m., f.*
younger *adj.* menor
youngest *n.* el/la menor *m., f.*
youth *n.* juventud *f.*
youth hostel *n.* albergue *m.* juvenil
youthful *adj.* juvenil

Z
zebra *n.* cebra *f.*
zero *n.* cero *m.*
zipper *n.* cremallera *f.*
zoo *n.* zoológico *m.*
zoologist *n.* zoólogo/a *m., f.*

Expresiones útiles

The *Expresiones útiles* section of the **VISTAS Pocket Dictionary** puts at your fingertips a great variety of useful language organized according to situations similar to *Expresiones útiles* in your **VISTAS** textbook. This section of the dictionary provides numerous models of natural and expressive Spanish and covers all the conversational situations likely to come up as you progress through **VISTAS**.

To use *Expresiones útiles* for your class work, look for situations similar to those in the lesson you are studying, read through the section, copy out sentences and expressions that interest you, review them several times, and write new sentences modeled on them. Before you know it, you will find that you have acquired the new vocabulary, expressions, and language structures. *Expresiones útiles* can not only help you make yourself understood, it can help you express yourself, your opinions, and your personality in fluent and natural Spanish.

SALUDOS, PRESENTACIONES Y DESPEDIDAS

Buenos días.

¿Hay alguien?

¿Se puede pasar?

Pues claro, adelante.

Pasa./Pase./Pasen.

Es (todo) un placer conocerle.

El placer es mío.

Muchísimas gracias.

Quiero presentarle a la Sra. Paredes.

ENCUENTROS

¡Cuánto tiempo sin verte/verlo/verlos!

¡Qué alegría volver a verte!

¿Qué (te) cuentas?

Ha pasado mucho tiempo.

¡Cómo vuela el tiempo!

¿Cómo va la vida?

Bien, muy bien.

Todo va sobre ruedas.

¿Y tú, qué tal?

No me puedo quejar.

Me alegro de volver a verte.

Es estupendo verte otra vez.

GREETINGS, INTRODUCTIONS, AND FAREWELLS

Good morning.

Is anyone there?

May I come in?

Of course, come in.

Come in.

It's a (great) pleasure to meet you.

The pleasure is mine.

Thank you very much.

I would like you to meet Mrs. Paredes.

UPON MEETING

Long time no see!

How nice to see you again!

What's going on?/What's up?

What a long time it's been.

How time flies!

How's life?

Good, very good.

Everything's going smoothly.

How are things with you?

I can't complain.

I'm so glad to see you again.

It's great to see you again.

Igualmente.	Likewise./The same to you.
Lo mismo digo.	Same here.

EXPRESIONES CORTESES Y SERVICIALES

EXPRESSIONS OF COURTESY AND HELPFULNESS

Con permiso.	Excuse me.
Permítame.	Allow me.
¡A la orden!	At your service.
No hay de qué.	Don't mention it./You're welcome.
Con gusto.	With pleasure.
¡Para servirle!	At your service./You're welcome.
Perdone.	Pardon me./Excuse me.
Perdóneme.	Pardon me./Excuse me.
Sin falta.	By all means.
Ahora mismo.	Right away.
Al minuto.	Right away.
No faltaba más.	Of course./No problem.
¿Cómo no?	But of course./Sure.
Enseguida.	Right away.

EXPRESIONES DE TIEMPO

EXPRESSIONS OF TIME

¿A cuántos estamos? A doce de agosto.	What's the date? The twelfth of August.
¿A qué día estamos hoy? A seis.	What's the date today? The sixth.
¿Qué día es hoy? Miércoles veinticuatro.	What day is it? Wednesday, the twenty-fourth.
¡Uy, qué tarde es!	Oh, it's so late!
Se me ha hecho tarde.	I'm late.
¡Ya es mediodía!	It's already noon!

Tengo mucha prisa.	I'm in a big hurry.
¡Qué contratiempo! No tengo reloj.	What a nuisance! I don't have a watch.
¡Qué inconveniente!	How inconvenient!
Son las dos de la tarde.	It's two in the afternoon.
Son las tres de la madrugada.	It's three in the morning.
Es la una de la noche.	It's one in the morning.
Son las siete de la tarde.	It's seven in the evening.
¿Tiene (Ud.) hora, por favor?	Do you have the time, please?
¿Qué hora tiene?	What time do you have?
¿Me dice la hora?	Can you tell me the time?
¿Podría Ud. decirme qué hora es?	Could you please tell me what time it is?
Pasan diez minutos de las once.	It's ten minutes past eleven.
Llego justito.	I'm just in the nick of time.
Falta un cuarto para las dos.	It's a quarter to two.
Tengo tiempo de tomar un café.	I have time for a cup of coffee.
Es la una y media.	It's one thirty.
Aún es temprano.	It's still early.
Son las tres en punto.	It's three on the dot.
Aún falta una hora.	There's still an hour to go.
Son las seis menos cuarto.	It's a quarter to six.
No llego, no llego.	I'll never make it.
Se me/nos ha ido el día en tonterías.	I/We have fiddled away the entire day.
Son las cinco cuarenta y cinco.	It's five forty-five.
Ya llego tarde.	I'm already late.

¡Cómo vuela/pasa el tiempo!	How time flies!
El tiempo vuela.	Time flies.
¿Te das cuenta de lo rápido que pasa el tiempo?	You realize how fast time goes by?
¡Qué de prisa/despacio pasan las horas!	The hours pass so quickly/slowly!
Vamos, date prisa/apresúrate que llegamos tarde.	Let's go! Hurry up or we'll be late.
Siempre de prisa./Siempre con prisas.	Always in a hurry./Always in a rush.

DE VIAJE

TRAVELING

¡Por fin (nos) vamos de viaje!	At last we're going on a trip!
Nos vamos.	We're leaving.
Es hora de irse/partir.	It's time to leave.
¡Todos a bordo!	All aboard!
Vamos de excursión.	We're going on a field trip/day trip.
¡Vámonos!	Let's go!
Estamos listos.	We're ready.
Buen viaje.	Have a good trip/Bon voyage!
¡Que vaya bien!	Have a nice time!/Hope it goes well!
¡Que lo pases/pasen bien!	Have a nice time!/Hope it goes well!
¡Que disfrutes/disfruten!	Enjoy yourself/yourselves!
Nada de despedidas.	No goodbyes.
Feliz viaje y hasta la vuelta.	Have a nice trip. See you when you get back.

Nos vemos a la vuelta.	We'll see each other when you/we/I return.
¡Que se divierta/diviertan!	Have fun!
No olviden mandar una postal.	Don't forget to send a postcard.
A ver si nos escribes unas líneas.	Drop a line.

DE REGRESO

¡Estamos de vuelta!	We're back!
Aquí estamos, sanos y salvos.	Here we are, safe and sound.
Bienvenidos.	Welcome.
¡Qué alegría!	Great!/Wonderful!
¿Qué tal el viaje?	How was your trip?
Indescriptible. Inolvidable.	Indescribable. Unforgettable.
¿Cómo fue?	How was it?
Lo pasamos en grande.	We had a great time.
Lo pasamos super bien.	We had a terrific time.
No hay nada como volver a casa.	There's no place like home./It's great to be home.
Me alegro de que estés/estén de vuelta.	I'm glad you're back.
Me alegra volver a verte/verlo/verlos.	It's nice to see you again.
Ya te echaba de menos./Ya te extrañaba.	I missed you.
¿Me echaste de menos?/¿Me extrañaste?	Did you miss me?
Te eché muchísimo de menos./Te extrañé muchísimo.	I missed you a lot.
Pues claro que te extrañé.	Of course I missed you.

BACK HOME

Estamos impacientes por ver las fotos.	We can't wait to see the pictures.
Hogar, dulce hogar.	Home sweet home.

EN CLASE

Buenos días, clase.	Good morning, class.
Ahora voy a pasar lista.	Now I'll take the roll/attendance.
A ver… ¿Adams?	Let's see, Adams?
Presente.	Present./Here.
Ahora, presten atención.	Now pay attention.
Fíjense bien.	Pay attention.
¡Qué profe tan estupendo/a!	What a terrific professor!
La profesora de historia del arte es buenísima.	The Art History professor is great.
Sabe muchísimo y además explica muy bien.	She knows a lot and explains everything so well!
Sus clases son muy interesantes, y aprendo mucho.	Her classes are really interesting, and I learn a lot.
¡Qué profe tan pesado/a!	That professor is a pain in the neck!
Siempre habla de lo mismo.	He/She says the same thing over and over again.
¡Qué clase más/tan aburrida!	What a boring class!
El próximo semestre (no) voy a tomar geografía.	Next semester I'm (not) going to take geography.
Las fechas no son mi fuerte.	I don't have a head for dates.
Tengo ganas de que se acabe/termine el curso.	I can't wait until this course is over.
Yo también tengo ganas de ir de vacaciones.	I also want a vacation.

Tranquilo, hombre. Sólo faltan los exámenes finales.	Take it easy, man. Just the final exams are left.
Uf, no quiero ni pensarlo.	Ugh, I don't even want to think about it.
Tengo que presentar un trabajo el próximo martes.	I have to hand in a paper next Tuesday.
Es sobre la sociología de las masas.	It's on the sociology of the masses.
Tengo tanto/tantísimo trabajo.	I have so much work.
No sé por dónde empezar.	I don't know where to begin.
No te preocupes.	Don't worry.
Vas a sacar unas notas de fábula, como siempre.	You're going to get excellent grades, as always.
Ya lo verás.	You'll see.
Tú siempre apruebas todos los exámenes.	You always pass all your exams.
Y además con buena nota.	And with a good grade to boot.

DESPUÉS DE CLASE

AFTER CLASS

Ei, dormilón/dormilona, ¿de dónde sales?	Hey, sleepyhead, where have you been?
¿Dónde estabas esta mañana?	Where were you this morning?
¿Se te pegaron las sábanas?	Couldn't you drag yourself out of bed?
La clase de historia estuvo muy interesante; como siempre.	History class was very interesting, as always.
¡Anoche no pegué ojo.	I didn't sleep a wink last night.
Estoy/Voy atrasado/a en álgebra.	I'm behind in algebra.
Soy fatal para las matemáticas.	I'm lousy in math.

A mí se me dan muy bien las ciencias en general.	I do very well in science, in general.
Si necesitas ayuda, te hecho una mano.	If you need help, I'll give you a hand.
Laura es una sabihonda, ¡se cree que lo sabe todo!	Laura is a know-it-all; she thinks she knows everything!
Su nombre de pila es Eduardo; su apodo es Dudu.	His given name is Eduardo; his nickname is Dudu.
¿Por qué estudia tanto ese individuo?	Why does that guy study so much?
Quiere (llegar a) ser presidente.	He/she wants to be president some day.
Tiene fama de ambicioso.	He/she has a reputation for being ambitious.
No me digas. ¿En serio? ¿Me tomas el pelo?	You don't say. Seriously? Are you pulling my leg?
¿Cómo te fue el examen de química?… Fatal./Estupendo.	How was the chemistry exam?… Terrible./Great.
El examen fue pan comido.	The exam was a piece of cake.
Tengo que ponerme al día en biología.	I need to catch up in biology.
No quiero suspender otra vez.	I don't want to flunk again.
Los exámenes finales ya están cerca.	Final exams are getting close.
Sí, están a la vuelta de la esquina.	Yes, they're just around the corner.
No sé qué me pasa.	I don't know what's happening to me.
No me puedo concentrar.	I can't concentrate.
Estoy lleno/a de dudas.	I'm full of doubts.

209

No me gusta nada la computación. A mí tampoco.	I don't like computer science at all. Neither do I.
A mí se me dan muy bien los idiomas.	I do very well with languages.
¡Qué casualidad! A mí también.	What a coincidence! Me too.
¡Qué coincidencia! Compartimos el mismo interés por las lenguas.	What a coincidence! We share an interest for languages.
Tengo mucho interés en las lenguas clásicas.	I'm very interested in classical languages.
¡Genial! A mí me interesa muchísimo el latín.	Great! I'm really interested in Latin.
El único inconveniente es que no tengo con quién practicarlo.	The only drawback is that I don't have anyone to practice with.
¿Te importa dejarme los apuntes de literatura?	Would you mind lending me your literature notes?
En absoluto./Pues claro que no./Aquí los tienes./Aquí están.	Of course. /Of course not./Here you go./Here they are.
Espero que entiendas la letra.	I hope you can read my writing.
Tengo una letra horrible/ilegible.	My handwriting is terrible/illegible.
Pero están muy completos.	But they're very complete.

LA FAMILIA

YOUR FAMILY

¿Todos bien?	Is everyone well?
Sí, todos bien, gracias a Dios.	Yes, everyone's well, thank goodness.
¿Tienes muchos hermanos/ parientes/sobrinos?	Do you have a lot of brothers and sisters/relatives/nieces and nephews?
¿Dónde viven tus padres?	Where do your parents live?

¿Visitas muy a menudo a tus familiares/parientes?	Do you visit your family/relatives often?
¿Son tus padres muy mayores?	Are your parents very old?
¿Vives con tus padres?	Do you live with your parents?
¿Quién es mayor, tu padre o tu madre?	Who is older, your father or your mother?
¿A qué se dedica tu padre/madre?	What does your father/mother do for a living?
¿Qué estudia tu hermano mayor?	What does your older brother study?
¿Tienen bisnietos tus abuelos?	Do your grandparents have great-grandchildren?
¿Conoces a todos tus primos?	Do you know all your cousins?
¿Son tus padres de la misma nacionalidad?	Are your parents of the same nationality?
¿Hablan tus padres español?	Do your parents speak Spanish?
¿Te llevas bien con tus hermanos?	Do you get along well with your brothers and sisters?
¿Dónde se conocieron tus padres?	Where did your parents meet?
¿Tienes familiares en el extranjero?	Do you have relatives abroad?
¿Dónde nacieron tus padres?	Where were your parents born?
¡Qué dicha ver a toda la familia junta!	What good fortune to see the whole family together!
Con una familia tan grande, siempre hay de qué/con quién hablar.	With such a big family, there is always something to talk about/someone to talk to.

EL OCIO

¿Dónde vas a ir este sábado?

¿Vas a hacer algo especial el domingo?

¿Tienes algún pasatiempo favorito/preferido?

¿Cuál es tu pasatiempo favorito/preferido?

¿Qué haces después de clase?

¿Qué haces este fin de semana?

Creo que voy a ir al zoo.

La entrada es gratuita los fines de semana.

¿Puedes creerlo?

Y tú, ¿qué? ¿Vas a ir al cine este fin de semana?

Bah, ya estoy harto/a de ir al cine.

No hay ninguna película interesante.

¿Ves mucho la televisión?

¡Que va! Es terrible. Siempre hacen lo mismo.

Me gusta divertirme sin gastar mucho dinero.

Me gustan las actividades que no cuestan dinero.

LEISURE

Where are you going this Saturday?

Are you going to do anything special on Sunday?

Do you have a favorite pastime?

What is your favorite pastime?

What are you doing after class?

What are you doing this weekend?

I think I'll go to the zoo.

Admission is free on weekends.

Can you believe it?

What about you? Are you going to go to the movies this weekend?

I'm tired/sick of going to the movies.

There aren't any good (interesting) movies.

Do you watch a lot of television?

No way! It's awful. It's always the same thing.

I like to have fun without spending too much money.

I like activities that don't cost money.

Oye, ¿por qué no vienes conmigo al zoo?	Hey, why don't you come to the zoo with me?
Estupendo. ¡Decidido, pues!	Great. It's decided, then!
El domingo vamos los dos al zoo. ¡Y no se hable más!	On Sunday the two of us will go to the zoo. That's settled!
A partir de ahora voy a comprar la guía del ocio todas las semanas.	From now on I'm going to buy the city entertainment guide every week.
Quiero estar informado de todas las actividades que tienen lugar en la ciudad.	I want to know about all the activities that take place in the city.
No quiero perderme nada, sobre todo si es gratis.	I don't want to miss anything, especially if it's free.
Nos vemos en el zoo.	We'll see each other at the zoo.
¡Que se diviertan en el zoo!	Have a good time at the zoo!

EXPRESIONES DEL TIEMPO

WEATHER EXPRESSIONS

¡Qué buen día hace hoy!	What a nice day it is today!
Hoy hace un día espléndido.	It's a beautiful day today.
El cielo está totalmente despejado.	The sky is perfectly clear.
No hay ni una nube.	There's not a cloud in the sky.
El hombre del tiempo pronosticó lluvia para el fin de semana.	The weatherman predicted rain for the weekend.
Afortunadamente, ¡se equivocó!	Fortunately, he was wrong!
Me pregunto qué tiempo va a hacer mañana.	I wonder what the weather will be like tomorrow.
¡Últimamente el tiempo es tan variable!	The weather has been variable lately.
Sí, es imprevisible. No es fácil adivinar/predecir.	Yes, it's unpredictable. It's not easy to predict.

Mañana (dicen que) va a caer un aguacero.	Tomorrow (they say that) there will be a downpour.
Llueve a cántaros.	It's raining cats and dogs.
Y yo sin paraguas. ¡Qué contratiempo!	And me without an umbrella. How annoying!
No salgas sin paraguas.	Don't leave (go out) without an umbrella.
Si llueve y hace sol, va a salir el arco iris.	If it rains and the sun comes out, there will be a rainbow.
¡Qué emoción! Me fascinan los arco iris.	Cool! I love rainbows.
A ver si vemos uno bien grande.	Maybe we'll see a nice big one.
¡Qué lunes tan horrible!	What a horrible Monday!
Hace viento y hace frío.	It's windy and it's cold.
¡Qué día tan feo! Es feo con ganas.	What an awful day! It's awful and then some.
Hay mucha niebla y no se ve nada.	There's a lot of fog and you can't see anything.
Hoy hace un día para no salir de casa/para quedarse en casa.	Today is a nice day to stay home.
¡Que pase/tenga un buen día!	Have a nice day!
Igualmente.	Same to you.

EN LA AGENCIA DE VIAJES

AT THE TRAVEL AGENCY

Bueno, menos mal! Parece que hoy está abierto.	Okay, great! It looks like it's open today.
Quisiéramos dos pasajes para Octopulco, ida y vuelta.	We'd like two round-trip tickets to Octopulco.
En primera clase, por supuesto.	In first class, of course.
¿Cómo no?	But of course.

¿Para qué día?	For what day?
¿Cuándo quieren regresar?	When would you like to return?
Queremos hospedarnos en un hotel de cinco estrellas/hotel barato.	We'd like to stay in a five-star hotel/an inexpensive hotel.
¿Cuántos días van a quedarse?	How many days will you stay?
Nos vamos a quedar quince días.	We're going to stay two weeks.
¿Quieren alquilar un auto?	Do you want to rent a car?
No, no hace falta.	No, we don't need one.
La isla es pequeña. Podemos ir en bicicleta.	The island is small. We can get around by bike.
Aquí tienen sus pasajes.	Here are your tickets.

EN EL AEROPUERTO

AT THE AIRPORT

¿Dónde está la aerolínea Gavilán?	Where is Gavilán Airlines?
Vuelo 8778	Flight 8778
Destino Octopulco	To (destination:) Octopulco
¿Cancelado?… No, retrasado.	Canceled? . . . No, delayed.
Bueno, pues a esperar.	Okay, then we'll wait.
¡Estoy cansado/a de esperar en los aeropuertos!	I'm tired of waiting in airports!
¿Debemos facturar el equipaje ahora?	Should we check our luggage now?
Me olvidé el itinerario.	I forgot the itinerary.
Al menos es un vuelo directo, sin escalas.	At least it's a direct flight, without any stopovers.
¿Dónde está la tienda libre de impuestos?	Where is the duty-free shop?

215

Da igual. No tenemos tiempo. Ya vamos a embarcar.	It doesn't matter. We don't have time. We're going to board now.
Esta maleta pesa demasiado/es demasiado pesada.	This suitcase weighs too much/is too heavy.
Voy a buscar un carrito.	I'm going to look for a cart.
Yo prefiero viajar ligero de equipaje.	I prefer to travel light.
A la vuelta debemos pasar por la aduana.	On the way back we have to go through customs.
¿Algo que declarar?	Anything to declare?
No, nada.	No, nothing.

EN EL HOTEL

AT THE HOTEL

Bienvenidos al hotel Miramar.	Welcome to the Hotel Miramar.
Por fin llegamos.	Finally we're here.
¿Tuvieron un vuelo agradable?	Did you have a good flight?
¡Qué vuelo tan largo!	What a long flight!
Lo sentimos, pero el ascensor/el elevador no funciona hoy.	We're sorry, but the elevator is out of order today.
Deben subir por las escaleras.	You need to take the stairs.
Por suerte están Uds. en el primer piso.	Luckily you're on the second floor.
Ésta es la mejor habitación con vistas al mar.	This is the best room with an ocean view.
Esperamos que todo sea de su agrado.	We hope that everything will be to your liking.
Cualquier cosa que necesiten, llamen a recepción.	If you need anything, call the front desk.
Gracias por hospedarse en/elegir nuestro hotel.	Thank you for staying in/choosing our hotel.

Esperamos que tengan una estancia agradable.

We hope you have an enjoyable stay.

¡Que tengan una feliz estancia!

Have a nice stay!

EN LA PLAYA

AT THE BEACH

¡Qué belleza de paisaje!

What beautiful scenery!

Pues, espera a ver el atardecer.

Wait until you see the sunset.

Dicen que es de película.

They say it's fantastic.

¡Qué paz!

What peace!

¡Qué aire tan puro y fresco!

What pure, fresh air!

No hay nada como la brisa del mar.

There's nothing like a sea breeze.

¡Qué calor!

It's so hot!

Este verano no quiero quemarme.

This summer I don't want to get sunburned.

¡Cuánta gente!

What a lot of people!

Pensaba que veníamos a una isla desierta.

I though we were going to a desert island.

¡Qué tonto/a! Me olvidé el traje de baño.

How stupid! I forgot my bathing suit!

Hoy no me apetece hacer nada.

Today I'm not in the mood to do anything.

Voy a contemplar el paisaje y pasear por la orilla.

I'm going to contemplate the scenery and take a walk along the shore.

¿QUÉ ME PONGO PARA LA FIESTA DEL SÁBADO?

WHAT SHOULD I WEAR TO THE PARTY SATURDAY?

¡Qué problema!

What a problem!

No tengo nada que ponerme.

I don't have anything to wear.

Necesito renovar mi vestuario.

I need a new wardrobe.

217

No tengo nada que me guste.	I don't have anything that I like.
Estoy harta de ponerme siempre la misma ropa.	I'm tired of always wearing the same clothes.
Lo que necesitas es un cambio de imagen.	You need a new image.
Sí, tienes razón.	Yes, you're right.
Es justo lo que necesito.	It's just what I need.
¿Quieres ser mi asesor de imagen?	Would you like to be my image consultant?
Esta misma tarde voy a ir al centro a ver qué encuentro.	This afternoon I'm going to the mall/downtown to see what I can find.
Esta semana hay unas rebajas espectaculares.	This week there are some great discounts.
No me gustan los mercados; odio regatear.	I don't like markets; I hate to haggle.

EN LA TIENDA DE ROPA PARA DAMAS

IN THE WOMEN'S CLOTHING STORE

¡Cuánta variedad! ¡Cuánto colorido!	What variety! So many colors!
Va a ser difícil decidir.	It's going to be hard to decide.
Quiero un vestido bien llamativo.	I want an attractive dress.
Señorita, podría probarme este vestido.	Miss, may I try on this dress?
Naturalmente. El probador está al fondo a la derecha.	Of course. The fitting room is in the back to the right.
Uy, me queda un poco justo.	Aw, it's a little too small.
Necesito una talla más grande.	I need a bigger size.
¿Qué talla quiere?	What size do you want?
La mediana, por favor.	Medium, please.

Sí, éste me sienta bien/mejor.	Yes, this one fits me well/better.
¿Cuál te gusta más, el rojo o el negro?	Which do you like better, the red or the black?
El negro te va como anillo al dedo.	The black one suits you to a "T."
El color negro te favorece.	You look good in black.
Te ves más delgada.	It makes you look thinner.
Sí, el rojo no me sienta tan bien.	Yes, the red one doesn't fit me as well.
Te ves muy atractiva con ese vestido.	You look very attractive in that dress.
¡Y qué suave es!	And it's so soft!
¡Buena compra!	A good buy!
Ahora necesitas otro bolso.	Now you need another purse.
Ese bolso no va (bien) con el vestido.	This purse doesn't go (well) with this dress.
Y también unos zapatos a juego.	And also shoes to match.
Espérame, voy a pagar el vestido y nos vamos a una zapatería.	Wait, I'll pay for the dress, then we'll go to a shoe store.
¿Cuánto vale?	How much does it cost?
Uy, baratísimo.	Oh, really inexpensive/cheap.
¡Hoy es mi día de suerte!/¡Hoy estoy de suerte!	Today is my lucky day!
¿Vamos a la zapatería?	Shall we go to the shoe store?

EN LA TIENDA DE ROPA PARA CABALLEROS

IN THE MEN'S CLOTHING STORE

Necesito un traje bien elegante.	I need an elegant suit.
¿De qué color lo quiere?	What color would you like?

219

No sé… ¿Qué sugiere Ud.?	I don't know . . . What would you suggest?
Un color oscuro le quedará/sentará bien.	You'd look good in a dark color.
Venga por aquí, joven.	Come hear, young man.
¿Qué talla usa?	What size do you wear?
No sé, es mi primer traje.	I don't know. It's my first suit.
Bueno, Ud. debe usar la talla 52 para la chaqueta… y la talla 32 para los pantalones.	Well, you should wear a size 52 jacket . . . and size 32 pants.
A ver, pruébese este traje azul marino… ¿Qué tal?	Let's see. Try on this dark blue suit. What do you think?
Le queda perfecto.	It fits you perfectly.
Parece hecho a su medida.	It looks like it was made for you.
Ahora necesita una bonita camisa.	Now you need a nice shirt.
¿La prefiere blanca o azul?	Would you like white or blue?
¿Blanca?	White?
Muy bien. Tenga, pruébese ésta.	Okay. Here you are. Try on this one.
Es la talla 16.	It's size 16.
Sí, me gusta…¡Qué tela más fina!	Yes, I like it. . . . What nice material.
Ahora sólo falta el último toque… ¡la corbata!	Now all you need is the last touch . . .a tie!
¿Qué tal esta roja?	How about a red one?
Ni hablar… demasiado llamativa.	Don't even suggest it . . . too flashy.
Necesitamos un color más suave.	We need a more muted color.

Azul celeste… Confíe en mí.	Light blue . . . trust me.
Mire, pruébese ésta… Es de seda italiana.	Look, try this one on. It's Italian silk.
Está Ud. impecable.	You are impeccable.
Pues sí, parezco otra persona.	Yes, I look like another person.
No sabía que era tan guapo.	I didn't know I was so handsome.
Muchísimas gracias por su ayuda.	Thanks so much for your help.
¿Cuánto le debo?	How much do I owe you?
LA RUTINA DIARIA	DAILY ROUTINE
¿Necesitas simplificar tu vida?	Do you need to simplify your life?
¿A qué hora te levantas?	What time do you get up?
¿Qué es lo primero que haces al levantarte?	What's the first thing you do when you get up?
¿Desayunas en casa?	Do you have/eat breakfast at home?
¿Qué desayunas? ¿Tostadas con mantequilla?	What do you have/eat for breakfast? Toast with butter?
¿Desayunas lo mismo todos los días?	Do you have/eat the same thing for breakfast every day?
¿Te vistes antes de desayunar o desayunas primero y luego te vistes?	Do you get dressed before breakfast or do you eat breakfast first and then get dressed?
¿A qué hora sales de casa?	What time do you leave the house?
¿Cuánto tiempo necesitas para prepararte por la mañana?	How much time do you need to get ready in the morning?
¿Te gusta ir de prisa o te tomas las cosas con calma?	Do you like to be quick or do you take your time?
¿A qué hora almuerzas?	What time do you eat lunch?

221

¿Dónde? ¿Con quién?	Where? With whom?
¿Te gusta almorzar solo o acompañado/a?	Do you like to eat lunch alone or with other people?
¿Estudias, trabajas o haces las dos cosas?	Are you studying, working, or both?
¿Qué haces de las 3 a las 5 de la tarde?	What do you do from 3:00 to 5:00 in the afternoon?
¿Qué haces después de las clases/después del trabajo?	What do you do after class/after work?
¿A qué hora regresas a casa?	What time do you get home?
¿Llegas muy tarde a casa por la noche?	Do you get home very late at night?
¿Qué es lo primero que haces al llegar a casa?	What's the first thing you do when you get home?
¿A qué hora cenas?	What time do you eat/have dinner?
¿Qué haces después de cenar?	What do you do after dinner?
¿Cuántas veces al día te lavas los dientes?	How many times a day do you brush your teeth?
¿A qué hora te vas a dormir/te acuestas?	What time do you go to sleep/to bed?
¿Qué es lo último que haces antes de acostarte?	What is the last thing you do before going to bed?
¿Cuántas horas duermes?	How many hours do you sleep?
¿Crees que duermes pocas horas?	Do you think you don't get enough sleep?
¿Es necesaria la rutina?	Is routine necessary?
¿Estás contento/a con tu rutina?	Are you happy with your routine?
¿Pierdes mucho tiempo por las mañanas?	Do you waste a lot of time in the morning?

222

¿Cuál es tu secreto para ganar tiempo libre?	What is your secret for finding free time?

EN EL RESTAURANTE

AT THE RESTAURANT

¿Mesa para dos?	Table for two?
¡Qué ambiente más selecto!	What an exclusive place!
Este lugar es muy acogedor.	This place is very cozy.
Está decorado con mucho gusto.	This place is decorated in very good taste.
Sin duda es el restaurante más caro de la ciudad.	Without a doubt, this is the most expensive restaurant in the city.
Tiene fama de buenísimo… y de carísimo.	It is supposed to be excellent . . . and very expensive.
Todo el mundo habla muy bien de este sitio.	Everyone speaks very well of this place.
Los cubiertos son de plata.	The silverware is real silver.
A ver el menú.	Let's look at the menu.
Aquí tienen el menú.	Here's the menu.
Mmm, se me hace la boca agua.	Mmm, it makes my mouth water.
No sé qué pedir.	I don't know what to order.
¿Qué nos sugiere?	What do you suggest?
Pidan lo que más les guste.	Order whatever you like the best.
Todo es exquisito, sin excepción.	Everything is superb, without exception.
Esta carne está en su punto.	This meat is just right.
¡Qué ensalada más original!	What an original salad!
Sí, combina frutas y verduras.	Yes, it combines fruit and vegetables.
El aliño es divino.	The dressing is divine.

¿Nos trae la carta de vinos, por favor?	Would you bring us the wine list, please?
No me gusta el vino tinto; prefiero el vino blanco.	I don't like red wine; I prefer white wine.
Yo no puedo tomar vino de ningún color; enseguida me emborracho.	I can't drink wine of any color; it goes right to my head.
Tenemos una selección de postres que les va a encantar.	You're going to love our dessert selection.
¡Qué carta de postres más creativa!	What a creative dessert menu!
Tiremos la casa por la ventana.	Let's go all out.
Probémoslos todos.	Let's try everything.
Camarero/a, nos trae la cuenta (cuando pueda), por favor.	Waiter, please bring us the check (when you can).
¿Cuánto se debe?	How much is it?
Quédese con el cambio.	Keep the change.
Nos quedamos sin plata/dinero.	We're broke.
¡Qué velada más/tan agradable!	What a pleasant evening!
¿A quién vamos a recomendar este restaurante?	To whom are we going to recommend this restaurant?

EL ALMUERZO	LUNCH
¡A comer!	Lunch is ready!
¿Qué hay para comer?	What is there/do we have to eat?
¡Qué hambre tengo!	I'm so hungry!
Estoy muerto/a de hambre./Me muero de hambre.	I'm starved.
Tengo un hambre feroz.	I'm famished./I could eat a horse.
Yo me lo como todo.	I'll eat anything.

224

Pues yo no. Estoy harto/a de lentejas.	Well, not me. I'm tired of lentils.
¿Otra vez lo mismo?	The same thing again?
No tengo (nada de) hambre.	I'm not hungry (at all).
¡Mmm, qué bien huele!	Mmm, it smells good!
Este estofado sabe a gloria.	This casserole tastes heavenly.
Esta sopa quema.	This soup is burning hot.
¡Pues sopla!	So blow on it!
Por favor, me pasas la sal.	Please pass the salt.
¿Qué es esto rojo?	What's this red stuff?
Esta carne no me la como, está cruda.	I won't eat this meat, it's raw.
No me gusta este pescado, tiene muchas espinas.	I don't like this fish, it has lots of bones.
Esta salsa es demasiado picante/pica demasiado.	This sauce is too spicy.
¿Qué hay de postre?	What's for dessert?
Yo estoy lleno/a.	I'm full.
Claro, te comiste todo el pan.	Of course, you ate all the bread.
Voy a explotar.	I'm going to explode.
Mejor dejo el postre para la noche.	I'd better leave dessert until later tonight.
¡Coman, coman!	Eat up!
¡Buen provecho!/¡Que aproveche!	Enjoy your meal!

USEFUL EXPRESSIONS

CELEBRACIONES

CELEBRATIONS

Estamos de fiesta.	Let's celebrate!
¿Qué se celebra?	What is being celebrated?

USEFUL EXPRESSIONS

EL NACIMIENTO DE NUESTRO HIJO

Mi esposa dio a luz a nuestro tercer hijo.

¿Cuándo nació?

El 1º de enero.

¡Enhorabuena! ¡Felicidades!

¡Es un niño precioso!

EL CUMPLEAÑOS DE MI HERMANO JORGE

¿Cuántos años cumple?

Dieciocho. Ya es mayor de edad.

¡Cuántos amigos y amigas tiene tu hermano!

En esta fiesta no cabe ni un alfiler.

¡Muchísimas felicidades, Jorge!

¡Y que cumplas muchos más!

LA GRADUACIÓN DE MARGARITA

Es nuestra hija pequeña.

Se acaba de graduar en geología.

Estamos muy orgullosos de ella.

¡Felicidades!

¡Por un futuro brillante!

EL ANIVERSARIO DE BODAS DE MIS PADRES

¿Cuántos años hace que se casaron?

THE BIRTH OF OUR SON

My wife gave birth to our third child/son.

When was he born?

January first.

Congratulations!

What a beautiful child!

MY BROTHER JORGE'S BIRTHDAY

How old is he?

Eighteen. He's of legal age now.

Your brother has so many friends!

This party is packed.

Best wishes, Jorge!

And may you have many more!

MARGARITA'S GRADUATION

She's our youngest daughter.

She's just graduated with a degree in geology.

We're very proud of her.

Congratulations!

To a bright future!

MY PARENTS' ANNIVERSARY

How many years have they been married?

Cincuenta. Celebran sus bodas de oro.	Fifty. They are celebrating their golden anniversary.
Y aún se quieren como cuando eran novios.	They still love each other as much as they did when they were newlyweds.
¡Qué maravilla!	How wonderful!
¡Feliz aniversario!	Happy anniversary!
¡Y que celebren muchos más!	May you have many more!

LA BODA DE MI TÍA CAROLINA	*MY AUNT CAROLINA'S WEDDING*
¡Qué dicha!	What good fortune!
¡Que sean muy felices!	May they be very happy!
¡Que se besen los novios!	A kiss!
Un brindis por los recién casados.	A toast to the newlyweds.
¡Vivan los novios!	Long live the newlyweds!

DAR EL PÉSAME

GIVING CONDOLENCES

Estamos de luto.	We're in mourning.
¡Qué desgracia!	How unfortunate!
Murió Roberto.	Roberto died.
¡Qué lastima!	What a shame!
Pobre Roberto, era tan joven.	Poor Roberto, he was so young.
Estamos todos muy apenados/tristes.	We're all very sad.
Le acompaño en el sentimiento.	My thoughts are with you.
Reciba nuestro más sincero pésame.	Our deepest sympathies.
No sé qué decir.	I don't know what to say.
Sólo puedo llorar.	I can only cry.

Lo vamos a echar mucho de menos.	We're going to miss him very much.

EN EL CONSULTORIO

IN THE DOCTOR'S OFFICE

Me duele todo el cuerpo.	My whole body aches!
¿Cuál es el problema?	What is the problem?
¿Qué le pasa?	What's the matter?
¿Dónde le duele?	Where does it hurt?
¿Qué síntomas tiene?	What are your symptoms?
¿Cuáles son sus síntomas?	What are your symptoms?
¿Cómo se encuentra hoy?	How are you feeling today?
Mejor./Peor.	Better./Worse.
Doctor, parece que no mejoro.	Doctor, it seems like I'm not getting better.
¿Se encuentra mejor hoy?	Are you feeling better today?
Al contrario, cada día estoy peor.	No, just the opposite, every day I'm worse.
¿Qué dicen los resultados de los análisis?	What do the test results show?
Tiene Ud. el colesterol muy alto/por las nubes.	Your cholesterol is very high/sky-high.
¿Duele?	Does it hurt?
Sólo va a notar un pinchazo.	You'll only feel a pinch.
¿Me va a doler, doctor?	Will it hurt, doctor?
Esto le va a doler un poco.	This will hurt a little.
Ay, creo que me voy a desmayar.	Oh, I think I'm going to faint.
Me aterran las agujas.	I'm afraid of needles.
No va a sentir ningún dolor.	You won't feel any pain.

Le vamos a operar con anestesia local/general.	We'll operate with local/general anesthesia.
¡Qué valiente es Vicente!	Vicente is so brave!
¿Hay que operar?	Do you have to operate?
¿Me quedará cicatriz?	Will I have/it leave a scar?
¿Podré volver a andar?	Will I be able to walk again?
¿Cuánto dura el tratamiento?	How long will the treatment last?
Doctor, ¿puede recetarme algo para el dolor?	Doctor, can you prescribe me something for the pain?
Inyecciones no, por favor.	Please, no shots.
¿No hay otra solución?	There's no other solution?
Le recomiendo que siga el tratamiento al pie de la letra.	I recommend that you follow the treatment to the letter.
¿Qué efectos secundarios tiene este medicamento?	What are the side effects of this medication?
Produce vómito y somnolencia.	It causes vomiting and drowsiness.
¿Qué opciones tengo?	What options do I have?
¿Va a tomarme la presión?	Are you going to take my blood pressure?
Tiene Ud. la tensión muy alta/baja.	You have very high/low pressure.
¿Cuándo empezó a fumar?	When did you start smoking?
¿Cuántos años hace que fuma?	How many years have you been smoking?
Debe dejar de fumar YA.	You must stop smoking NOW.
Le aconsejo que deje de fumar cuanto antes.	I advise you to stop smoking immediately.
El tabaco perjudica la salud.	Tobacco jeopardizes your health.

Durante el embarazo no debe fumar ni consumir alcohol.	While you're pregnant, you shouldn't smoke or drink alcohol.
Debe Ud. ver a un especialista.	You need to see a specialist.
Es una enfermedad muy grave.	It's a very serious illness.
Conocemos los síntomas, pero no las causas.	We are familiar with the symptoms, but not the causes.
El pronóstico es grave/favorable.	The prognosis is serious/good.
Lo que yo necesito es reposo indefinido.	What I need is a prolonged rest.

LA COMUNICACIÓN TELEFÓNICA

TELEPHONING

¿Con quién hablo?	With whom am I speaking?
Soy el vecino de al lado…	I'm the next-door neighbor.
¿Quién es? ¿Quién?	Who is it? Who?
Hable más fuerte. No oigo/no oigo nada.	Please, speak up. I can't hear you/a thing.
Soy Juan, tu vecino.	It's Juan, your neighbor.
Te importaría bajar el volumen del radio, por favor.	Would you mind turning the radio down, please?
¿Podría hablar con el director?	May I speak with the director?
Por favor, me pone con el Sr. Ramos.	May I speak with Mr. Ramos, please?
¿De parte de quién? ¿Quién lo llama?	May I tell him/ask who's calling?
Dígale que lo llama Ruti, su primo.	Tell him that his cousin Ruti is calling.
Espere un momentito, ahora pongo.	Just a minute, here he is.
No cuelgue por favor, ahora paso.	Don't hang up, please; here he is.

Oiga, el Sr. Ramos salió a almorzar.	Oh, Mr. Ramos is out to lunch.
¿Quiere dejar un mensaje?	Would you like to leave a message?
No, yo vuelvo a llamar mañana.	No, I'll call back tomorrow.
Dígale que me llame, por favor.	Tell him to call me, please.
¿Quiere que le devuelva la llamada cuando regrese?	Would you like me to have him call you when he gets back?
Pues sí. Gracias.	Yes, thanks.
Mire, mi número es el 001-1100.	My number is 001-1100.
¿Es éste el 010-0110?	Is this 010-0110?
Lo siento, se ha equivocado de número.	I'm sorry, you have the wrong number.
Disculpe.	Oh, excuse me./I'm sorry.
Vuelva a marcar.	Try dialing again.
Estoy esperando una llamada importante.	I'm expecting an important call.
¡Ese teléfono no para de sonar!	That phone won't stop ringing/is ringing off the hook!
¿Quieres hacer el favor de contestar el teléfono?	Would you please answer the phone?
¿Cómo? ¿No tienes contestador automático?	What? You don't have an answering machine?
Señora, tiene una llamada a cobro revertido. ¿Acepta Ud. la llamada?	Ma'am, you have a collect call. Will you accept the call?
Hago un sinfín de llamadas de larga distancia e internacionales.	I make a ton of long distance and international calls.

La factura del teléfono me cuesta cada mes una fortuna/un dineral.	My phone bill costs a fortune each month.
Ring, riiiing,… riiiiiiing. No contestan.	Ring, ring, riiiing. No answer.
Parece que la línea está ocupada.	It seems that the line is busy.
Llama/e a la operadora.	Call the operator.
¿A qué número llama?	What number are you calling?
Ay, olvidé el número.	Oh, I forgot the number.
Llame a información. Marque el 003.	Call information. Dial 003.
Para más información, llame al 1-800-289-1948.	For more information, call 1-800-289-1948.
Las líneas están abiertas 24 horas al día, siete días a la semana.	The lines are open 24 hours a day, seven days a week.

LOS APARATOS

MECHANICAL DEVICES

¿Cómo funciona esto?	How does this thing work?
¿Y me preguntas a mí?	You're asking me?
¡Qué sé yo!	What do I know?
¿Y a mí me lo preguntas?	You're asking me?
No tengo ni (la más mínima) idea.	I have no idea./I haven't the foggiest idea.
Las máquinas me asustan.	Machines frighten me.
Las instrucciones me aburren.	Instructions bore me.
¿No hay una versión abreviada?	Isn't there a shorter version?
¿Cuándo viene el técnico a arreglar la antena?	When is the repair man coming to fix the antenna?

Hace semanas que no funciona el televisor.	It's been weeks since the television worked.
Me vuelvo loco/a sin la caja tonta.	I'm going crazy without the idiot box.
Creo que quiero una computadora portátil.	I think I want a laptop.
Están de moda.	They are in style.
Son prácticas, ¿no?	They're practical, aren't they?
¿Cómo se pone en marcha este trasto?	How do you get this thing/piece of junk to work?
Esta máquina de coser funciona a las mil maravillas.	This sewing machine works like a dream.
No sé qué haría sin ella.	I don't know what I would do without it.
En fin, ¿qué más?	So, what else?

LOS AUTOMÓVILES

CARS

¿Necesito carro?	Do I need a car?
A lo mejor me compro uno de segunda mano.	Maybe I should get a used one.
Cuanto más barato sea, mejor, ¿no?	The cheaper the better, no?
Total, ¿qué más da? Se va a estropear/descomponer igual.	Bah, what does it matter? It will break down just the same.
Al menos si me cuesta barato, no me preocupo tanto.	At least if it's cheap, I won't worry too much.
Un carro puede durar muchos años si lo cuidas bien.	A car can last many years if you take good care of it.
Creo que voy a vender mi carro viejo y me voy a comprar uno nuevo.	I think I'll sell my old car and buy a new one.

233

Pero no puedo tomar una decisión sin ton ni son.	But I can't make a decision willy nilly.
Esto es un asunto serio.	This is a serious matter.
Debo pensarlo bien.	I should think it over well.
A ver, ¿qué tipo de carro me conviene más?	Let's see, what kind of car is best for me?
¿Uno automático o uno de marchas?	An automatic or manual transmission?
¿Uno deportivo o uno familiar?	A sports car or a family car?
¿Uno de lujo o uno todo terreno?	A luxury car or an all-terrain vehicle?
¿Cuánto dinero me quiero gastar?	How much money do I want to spend?
¿Qué es lo más importante a la hora de comprar un carro?	What is the most important thing when it comes time to buy a car?
¿Cuál es mi máxima necesidad/prioridad?	What is my top priority?
¿Una carretera sin baches?	A road without potholes?
Pero pensándolo bien/mejor, ¿para qué necesito yo un carro?	But, on second thought, what do I need a car for?
¿Qué sé yo de mecánica?	What do I know about mechanics?

LAS AVERÍAS	*BREAKDOWNS*
Otra vez al mecánico.	To the mechanic again.
Este carro es un tremendo dolor de cabeza.	This car is a big headache.
Se estropea/descompone cada dos por tres.	It breaks down all the time.
Cuando no es una cosa es otra.	If it's not one thing, it's another.
El mes pasado eran los frenos.	Last month it was the brakes.

Hace dos meses, el cambio de marchas.	Two months ago, the gear shift.
Ayer, el intermitente delantero izquierdo.	Yesterday, the front left directional signal.
Ya te digo, me da más problemas que alegrías/satisfacciones.	I'm telling you, it's more trouble than it's worth.
Cada reparación me cuesta una fortuna/un ojo de la cara.	Every repair costs a fortune/an arm and a leg.
Además, es dificilísimo encontrar un buen mecánico en quien poder confiar.	And it's so hard to find a good, trustworthy mechanic.
Encontrar un buen mecánico es como buscar una aguja en un pajar.	Finding a good mechanic is like finding a needle in a haystack.
Ahora llevo el tubo de escape colgando y, cuando llueve, no hay quien lo ponga en marcha.	Now my exhaust pipe is hanging, and when it rains the car won't start.

EN LA CARRETERA

ON THE HIGHWAY

Iba yo conduciendo tan tranquilo/a y me paró la policía.	I was just driving along and the police pulled me over.
Me paró la policía de tráfico…	The traffic cop stopped me…
Aparentemente, por ir demasiado despacio.	Apparently, for driving too slowly.
La velocidad límite era de 65 millas por hora.	The speed limit was 65 miles per hour.
Yo iba a 15 millas por hora.	I was going 15 miles per hour.
Le dije que no tenía gasolina.	I told him that I didn't have gas.
El policía se hizo el sordo y me puso una multa.	The policeman didn't listen and gave me a fine.
Fue inútil discutir.	It was pointless to argue about it.

Me pregunto quién la va a pagar.	I'm wondering who is going to pay it.
¿Dónde hay una estación de servicio?	Where is there a service station?
Necesito llenar el tanque/el depósito.	I need to fill the tank.

UNA VIVIENDA DESASTROSA

A DISASTROUS HOUSE

¡Esta casa es un desastre!	This house is a disaster!
¡Qué casa, madre mía! Un frigorífico en invierno y un horno en verano.	What a house! A refrigerator in the winter and an oven in the summer.
Las luces se encienden y se apagan cuando les da la gana.	The lights turn on and off when they feel like it.
¿Electrodomésticos? ¿Para qué?	Appliances? For what?
Por la noche hay que tener las velas preparadas.	At night we have to have candles ready.
Siempre hay que estar prevenido (por lo que pueda pasar).	You always have to be prepared (for what may happen).
Ninguna puerta cierra bien; ninguna ventana abre bien.	None of the doors close tight; none of the windows open easily.
Las paredes son de papel.	The walls are like paper.
No existe la intimidad.	There is no privacy.
El gato que tenía se ha mudado.	The cat I had has moved.
La ropa sale de la lavadora tal y como estaba.	The clothes come out of the washing machine the same as they went in.
Las goteras inundan el altillo.	The leaks flood the attic.
El día que llueve es todo un espectáculo.	When it rains, it's a show.

No queda pintura en la fachada.	There's no paint left on the outside.
Y esta escalera de caracol es una pesadilla a cualquier hora del día.	And this spiral staircase is a nightmare at any time of day.
Las sorpresas no faltan viviendo en tal casa.	We have no lack of surprises living in such a house.
¿Por qué no vienen Uds. mañana?	Why don't you come over tomorrow?

LA VIVIENDA PERFECTA

THE PERFECT HOUSE

¡Qué ilusión me hace tener una casa!	How I'd love to own a house!
Una casa bien grande, con jardín y con terraza.	A fairly large house, with a garden and a patio.
Siempre he querido ser ama de casa.	I have always wanted to be a housewife.
Limpiar, ordenar y lavar a todas horas del día.	Cleaning, straightening up, and washing at all hours of the day.
Cantar y cantar mientras preparo la comida.	Singing and singing while I prepare the meals.
Tener una cocina moderna y práctica a la vez.	I'd have a kitchen that was both modern and practical.
Tener electrodomésticos de todos los colores y tamaños.	I'd have appliances of all shapes and colors.
Pues no son sólo trastos; algunos te echan una mano.	They're not just pieces of junk; some help you out.
Y con un lavaplatos, todo está limpio y ordenado.	And with a dishwasher, all is clean and organized.
¡Qué maravilla! ¡Qué sueño de vida!	How wonderful! What a dream of a life!

MEDIO AMBIENTE Y ECOLOGÍA

ENVIRONMENT AND ECOLOGY

Parece que la contaminación de la atmósfera crece a un ritmo alarmante.

It seems that air pollution is growing at an alarming rate.

El dióxido de carbono es cada vez más abundante en la atmósfera.

There is more and more carbon dioxide in the atmosphere.

La sequía es un grave problema en muchos países de África.

Drought is a serious problem in many African countries.

Las aguas de los ríos, océanos y mares están cada vez más contaminadas.

Rivers, oceans, and seas are becoming more and more polluted.

El agujero de la capa de ozono sigue creciendo.

The hole in the ozone layer keeps growing.

Los incendios forestales y las inundaciones están a la orden del día.

Forest fires and floods are everyday events.

PREGUNTAS SOBRE ECOLOGÍA

ENVIRONMENTAL QUESTIONS

¿Está en peligro la vida en la Tierra?

Is life on earth in danger?

¿A quién afecta la destrucción del medio ambiente?

Who does the destruction of the environment affect?

¿Qué predicen los científicos para dentro de cincuenta años?

What do scientists predict for the next fifty years?

¿Qué consecuencias puede tener el calentamiento global de la Tierra?

What can the consequences of global warming be?

¿Es posible que se deshielen los casquetes polares?

Is it possible that the polar caps will melt?

¿Crees que hay solución a los problemas actuales de contaminación?

Do you think there's a solution to the current pollution problems?

¿Cuáles son las condiciones medioambientales óptimas que garantizan la existencia de los seres vivos en la Tierra?

What are the optimal environmental conditions that guarantee the existence of living beings on earth?

¿Qué medidas se pueden tomar para poner marcha atrás al problema de la contaminación atmosférica? ¿Y de la contaminación del agua?

What measures can be taken to reverse the problem of atmospheric pollution? And of water pollution?

¿Qué medidas generales se pueden adoptar para conservar la naturaleza?

What general measures can be adopted to conserve nature?

¿Qué países producen más basura? ¿Cuáles consumen más recursos naturales?

What countries produce the most garbage? Consume more natural resources?

¿Perteneces a alguna organización dedicada a la conservación del medio ambiente?

Do you belong to an organization dedicated to environmental conservation?

¿Crees que son exagerados los datos sobre el calentamiento global del planeta?

Do you think the global warming data is exaggerated?

¿Crees que es todo una farsa? ¿Una exageración de los Verdes?

Do you think it is all a farce? An exaggeration of the Green Party?

¿Cómo afecta la tala de árboles al ecosistema?

How does the cutting of trees affect the ecosystem?

¿Cuáles son en tu opinión las principales causas del creciente deterioro medioambiental?

In your opinion, what are the main causes of the increasing environmental degradation?

¿De qué modo colaboras tú en la conservación de la naturaleza?

In what way do you help in the conservation of nature?

¿Quién tiene la culpa del deterioro medioambiental? ¿Hay algún culpable?

Whose fault is environmental degradation? Is anyone at fault?

DAR Y PEDIR DIRECCIONES

GIVING AND ASKING DIRECTIONS

¿Por dónde se va al centro?

How do I get downtown?

Sigan todo recto/derecho hasta el final de esta calle.

Keep going straight until you get to the end of this street.

Luego doblen/giren a la derecha.

Then turn right.

Anden tres cuadras y ya están en pleno centro.

Go three blocks and you'll be right downtown.

¿Señor, sabe cómo llegar al Museo Nacional de Arte Contemporáneo?

Sir, do you know how to get to the National Museum of Contemporary Art?

Está en la otra punta de la ciudad.

It's on the other side of the city.

Está demasiado lejos para ir andando.

It's too far to walk.

Tienen que tomar el metro.

You need to take the subway.

Tomen la línea roja en dirección Colinas.

Take the red line towards Colinas.

Deben bajarse en la última parada.

You should get off at the last stop.

Luego deben tomar la línea amarilla en dirección Paseo Coral.

Then you need to take the yellow line towards Paseo Coral.

Y bajarse en la penúltima parada.

Get off at the next-to-last stop.

Todo el trayecto les tomará casi una hora y cuarto.

The whole trip should take about an hour and a quarter.

Al salir del metro verán el Museo Nacional justo enfrente.	When you get out of the subway, you'll see the National Museum right in front of you.
¿Señora, le importaría decirnos cómo llegar al Ayuntamiento?	Ma'am, would you mind telling us how to get to City Hall?
Es que somos turistas y queremos verlo todo.	We're tourists and we want to see everything.
Es mejor que no vayan andando.	It's better not to walk.
Les recomiendo que tomen un taxi.	I recommend that you take a taxi.
¡Qué paciencia tiene con nosotros la gente de esta ciudad!	The people in this city are so patient with us!
Creo que debemos dejar de preguntar.	I think we should stop asking questions.
Esta ciudad es monstruosa, gigantesca y complicada.	This city is monstrous, gigantic, and complicated.
Y una de dos, o compramos un mapa o tomamos un autobús turístico.	One or the other: do we buy a map or take a tour bus?
Si es que queremos llegar a algún sitio.	If we want to get anywhere.
¿Qué opinas?	What do you think?
Me parece buena la idea del autobús turístico.	I think the tour bus idea is a good idea.

PREGUNTAS SOBRE NUTRICIÓN

QUESTIONS ABOUT NUTRITION

¿Cuántas calorías tiene este plato preparado?	How many calories does this prepared meal have?
¿Qué porcentaje de sodio tiene una lata de frijoles?	What percentage of sodium does a can of beans have?

¿Cuántos gramos de azúcar suele tener más o menos un jugo envasado?	How many grams of sugar, more ore less, does a container of juice have?
¿Qué alimentos son ricos en Vitamina A?	What foods are rich in Vitamin A?
¿Es verdad que el aceite de hígado de bacalao contiene Vitamina D?	Is it true that cod liver oil has Vitamin D?
¿Es verdad que la falta de hierro en la sangre causa anemia?	Is it true that a lack of iron in the blood causes anemia?
¿Para qué es importante la Vitamina C?	What is Vitamin C important for?
¿Por qué necesita el cuerpo vitaminas y minerales?	Why does the body need vitamins and minerals?
¿Es bueno ingerir fibra para evitar el estreñimiento?	Is it good to eat fiber to avoid constipation?
¿Por qué es mejor comer pan integral que pan blanco?	Why is it better to eat whole-wheat bread than white bread?
¿Qué alimentos son esenciales para llevar una dieta equilibrada?	What foods are essential to a balanced diet?
¿Qué alimentos deben ingerirse diariamente?	What foods should you eat daily?
¿Qué alimentos deben consumirse con moderación?	What foods should you eat in moderation?
¿Qué desventajas tiene la dieta vegetariana?	What drawbacks does a vegetarian diet have?
¿Qué ventajas tiene la dieta mediterránea?	What advantages does a Mediterranean diet have?
¿Qué alimentos constituyen la base de la dieta mediterránea?	What are the basic foods in a Mediterranean diet?
¿Qué dieta proporciona mayores ventajas para la salud?	What diet offers the most health advantages?

¿Qué es el colesterol?	What is cholesterol?
¿Qué alimentos son ricos en colesterol?	What foods are high in cholesterol?
¿Qué alimentos contienen elevados índices de colesterol?	What foods have high amounts of cholesterol?
¿Cuáles son los inconvenientes de la comida rápida?	What are the drawbacks of fast food?
¿Qué tipo de alimentación favorece el buen funcionamiento del organismo?	What kind of nutrition promotes the proper functioning of the body?
¿Qué sustancias son perjudiciales para la salud?	What substances are harmful to your health?
¿Qué comían nuestros antepasados?	What did our ancestors eat?
¿Cómo han evolucionado los hábitos alimenticios a lo largo de la historia?	How have nutritional habits evolved throughout history?

PREGUNTAS SOBRE LA FORMA FÍSICA Y MENTAL

QUESTIONS ABOUT PHYSICAL AND MENTAL WELL-BEING

¿Es el estar en forma una moda o un estilo de vida?	Is being in shape a fashion or a lifestyle?
¿Hasta qué punto es importante estar en forma?	How important is it to be in shape?
¿Qué es aconsejable hacer para mantenerse en forma?	What activities are advisable for staying in shape?
¿Qué es recomendable hacer para perder peso?	What is recommended for losing weight?
¿Hasta qué punto es importante mantener un peso adecuado?	How important is it to maintain enough weight?
¿Por qué es aconsejable realizar algún tipo de actividad física?	Why is it advisable to keep up some kind of physical activity?

¿Es la obesidad una cuestión estética o un grave problema de salud?	Is obesity an issue of appearance or a serious health problem?
¿Qué inconvenientes presenta para la salud el estilo de vida de los países industrializados?	What disadvantages does the lifestyle of industrialized countries have to health?
¿Qué es el estrés?	What is stress?
¿Qué papel juega el estrés en la salud de la sociedad actual?	What role does stress play in the health of society today?
¿En qué medida puede afectar el medio ambiente a la salud?	To what extent can the environment affect health?
¿Qué condiciones medioambientales son perjudiciales para la salud?	What environmental conditions are hazardous to our health?
¿Me preocupa lo que como/bebo?	Should I worry about what I eat/drink?
¿Qué hago para mantenerme en forma?	What can I do to stay in shape?
¿Vigilo mi peso?	Should I watch my weight?
¿Soy un fanático/una fanática de la nutrición?	Am I a nutrition fanatic?
¿Qué me preocupa más, el número de calorías que ingiero al día o el valor nutritivo de los alimentos que tomo?	What should I worry about more, the number of calories I take in every day or the nutritional value of the foods I eat?
¿Quiero vivir cien años? ¿Por qué?	Do I want to live a hundred years? Why?

PREGUNTAS SOBRE EL FUTURO LABORAL

QUESTIONS ABOUT YOUR FUTURE IN THE WORKPLACE

¿Qué piensas hacer cuando te gradúes?	What do you think you'll do after you graduate?

¿Piensas en el futuro o vives al día?	Do you think about the future, or do you live day to day?
¿Has pensado seriamente en tu futuro?	Have you thought seriously about your future?
¿De qué color lo ves?	And how do you see it?/What do you think it will be like?
¿Eres optimista o más bien pesimista?	Are you an optimist or a pessimist?
¿Te gustan los retos?	Do you like challenges?
¿Te interesa correr riesgos?	Are you interested in taking risks?
¿Cuál es tu profesión/trabajo ideal?	What is your ideal job/profession?
¿Qué buscas en un trabajo? ¿Y en un jefe o jefa?	What do you look for in a job? And in a boss?
¿Qué alicientes crees que ofrece el mundo del trabajo?	What incentives/attractions do you think the working world offers?
¿Quieres ganar mucho dinero?	Do you want to earn a lot of money?
¿Podrías vivir sin dinero?	Could you live without money?
¿Qué tipo de trabajo buscas?	What kind of job are you looking for?
¿En qué tipo de ambiente laboral sueñas?	What kind of work atmosphere are you thinking about?
¿Estás impaciente por salir de la universidad e incorporarte al mundo laboral?	Are you eager to leave school and enter the working world?
¿Eres una persona responsable?	Are you a responsible person?
¿Crees que trabajar es más interesante que estudiar?	Do you think working is more interesting than studying?

245

¿Has asistido ya a alguna entrevista de trabajo?	Have you gone on a job interview yet?
¿Cuáles consideras tus puntos fuertes?	What do you consider your strong points to be?
¿Cuáles crees que son tus puntos débiles?	What do you think your weak points are?
¿Buscas un trabajo creativo, de atención al público o de dirección?	What kind of job are you looking for, a creative one, one where you have to work with the public, or a managerial one?
¿Buscas un trabajo vocacional o uno puramente lucrativo?	Are you looking for a job you love, or just one that will make a lot of money?
¿Para qué tipo de trabajo crees que estás mejor preparado?	For what type of job do you think you are best prepared?
¿Qué crees que puedes ofrecer?	What do you think you have to offer?
¿Qué esperas recibir a cambio?	What do expect to get in return?
¿Cuál es tu meta u objetivo principal?	What is your main goal or objective?
¿Hasta dónde quieres llegar?	How far do you want to go?
¿Qué estás dispuesto/a a arriesgar para conseguirlo?	What are you willing to risk to get there?
¿Qué precio estás dispuesto/a a pagar?	What price are you willing to pay?
¿Cuáles serían tus prioridades?	What would your priorities be?
¿Estarías interesado/a en trabajar horas extras?	Would you be interested in working extra hours?
En caso afirmativo, ¿esperarías algo a cambio?	If so, would you expect something in return?
¿Por qué cualidades te gustaría ser recordado?	For what qualities would you like to be remembered?

246

¿Cómo te gustaría pasar a la historia?	How would you like to go down in history?
¿O prefieres vivir tranquilo/a y pasar desapercibido/a?	Or do you prefer to live quietly and go unnoticed?

LAS ARTES

THE ARTS

¿Para qué sirve el arte?	What is art for?
¿Qué significa el término artista?	What does the term "artist" mean?
¿Para qué usa el arte el/la "artista"?	What does an artist use art for?
¿Cuál es la misión del/de la artista?	What is the artist's mission?
¿Son los artistas egocentristas?	Are artists egocentric/self-centered?
¿Son realistas los artistas?	Are artists realists?
¿Envidias la vida del/de la artista?	Do you envy the life of an artist?
¿Tienes tú madera de artista?	Do you have what it takes to be an artist?
¿Qué significa la expresión "trabajar por amor al arte"?	What does the expression "to work for the love of art" mean?
¿Por qué llaman al cine el séptimo arte?	Why do they call film the seventh art?
¿Crees que una imagen vale más que mil palabras?	Do you think a picture is worth a thousand words?
¿Te gusta ver películas extranjeras en versión original subtitulada?	Do you like to see foreign films in the original language with subtitles?
¿Cómo expresas lo que piensas, lo que sientes, lo que quieres, lo que te gusta?	How do you express what you think, feel, want, and like?

¿Eres aficionado/a a la pintura?	Are you a painting aficionado?
¿Estás familiarizado/a con el surrealismo? ¿Y con el cubismo?	Are you familiar with surrealism? With cubism?
¿Qué otras tendencias artísticas conoces? ¿Cuáles te interesan más? ¿Por qué?	What other artistic movements do you know about? Which ones interest you the most? Why?
¿Te gusta o te gustaría coleccionar objetos de arte?	Do you or would you like to collect works of art?
¿Pagarías cincuenta millones de dólares por un original de Picasso?	Would you pay fifty million dollars for a Picasso original?
¿Eres amante de la música?	Are you a music lover?
¿A qué sentidos seduce la música?	Which senses does music affect?
¿Qué se necesita para disfrutar del arte?	What do you need to enjoy art?
¿Hace falta un sexto sentido?	Do you need a sixth sense?
¿Sin cuál de los cinco sentidos no podrías vivir?	Which of the five senses could you not live without?
¿Qué tipo de música está de moda entre la juventud actual?	What kind of music is popular with today's youth?
Y por último, la pregunta del millón, ¿Beatles o Rolling Stones?	And finally, the million-dollar question, the Beatles or the Rolling Stones?

PREGUNTAS SOBRE LAS ACTUALIDADES

QUESTIONS ABOUT CURRENT EVENTS

¿Estás al día?	Are you up to date?
¿Qué dicen hoy los periódicos?	What do the newspapers say today?
¿Has leído las últimas noticias?	Have you read the latest news?

248

¿Te interesa la política? ¿Por qué?	Are you interested in politics? Why?
¿Estás al día de lo que pasa en tu país? ¿Y en el resto del mundo?	Are you up to date with what's happening in your country? And in the rest of the world?
¿Qué temas sociales y políticos te preocupan?	What social and political topics concern you?
Si fueras político/a, ¿qué medidas tomarías para solucionar los actuales problemas medioambientales?	If you were a politician, what measures would you take to solve the current environmental problems?
¿Sigues de cerca la actualidad (política)?	Do you follow current events/politics closely?
¿Lees las noticias internacionales?	Do you read international news?
¿Te interesa la política exterior?	Does foreign politics interest you?
¿Te crees todo lo que lees en los periódicos?	Do you believe everything you read in the newspapers?
¿Te consideras una persona bien informada?	Do you consider yourself well-informed?
¿Crees que estamos bien informados?	Do you think we are well-informed?
¿Cómo es posible digerir tanta información?	How can one take in so much information?
En tu opinión, ¿qué cualidades debe tener un buen político/una buena política?	In your opinion, what qualities should a good politician have?
¿Qué harías si fueras presidente de los Estados Unidos?	What would you do if you were president of the United States?
¿Cuáles crees que son las principales causas de la violencia?	What do you think the principal causes of violence are?

¿Qué opinas de las campañas electorales/publicitarias?	What do you think of electoral/publicity campaigns?
¿Crees que los políticos tienen demasiado poder?	Do you think politicians have too much power?
¿Crees que el poder corrompe?	Do you think that power corrupts?
¿Qué opinas de la sociedad actual?	What do you think about present-day society?
¿Cómo valoras los últimos avances de la técnica?	What do you think of/How do you rate the latest technical advances?
¿Ha avanzado el ser humano al mismo ritmo que la tecnología?	Have human beings advanced at the same rate as technology?
¿Qué avances positivos se lograron a lo largo del siglo XX?	What positive advances were made over the course of the 20th century?
¿Qué cuestiones te gustaría ver resueltas en el siglo XXI?	What issues would you like to see resolved in the 21st century?
¿Confías en los líderes políticos de tu país?	Do you trust the political leaders of your country?
¿Qué papel crees que juega el dinero en la sociedad actual?	What role do you think money plays in present-day society?
¿Hasta qué punto crees que los medios de comunicación influyen en la visión que tenemos del mundo?	To what extent do you think that the media influence our world view?
¿Crees que está bien repartida la riqueza del planeta?	Do you think the wealth of the planet is well distributed?
¿Hay problemas de discriminación en tu ciudad y/o país?	Are there discrimination problems in your city and/or country?
¿Crees que vivimos en un mundo justo y solidario?	Do you think we live in a just and supportive world?

¿Qué medidas tomarías para
que el mundo fuera un lugar
mejor para todos?

What measures would you take
so that the world would be a better place for everyone?

¿Quién tiene la última palabra?

Who has the last word?

251

Verb conjugation tables

The verb lists

The list of verbs below and the model-verb tables that start on page 256 show you how to conjugate every verb taught in **VISTAS**. Each verb in the list is followed by a model verb that is conjugated according to the same pattern. The number in parentheses indicates where in the tables you can find the conjugated forms of the model verb. If you want to find out how to conjugate **divertirse**, for example, look up number 33, **sentir**, the model for verbs that follow the **i:ie** stem-change pattern.

abrazar (c) like cruzar (37)
abrir like vivir (3)
aburrir(se) like vivir (3)
acabar de like hablar (1)
acampar like hablar (1)
acompañar like hablar (1)
aconsejar like hablar (1)
acordarse (o:ue) like contar (24)
acostarse (o:ue) like contar (24)
adelgazar (c) like cruzar (37)
afeitarse like hablar (1)
ahorrar like hablar (1)
alegrarse like hablar (1)
aliviar like hablar (1)
almorzar (o:ue) like contar (24) *except* (z:c)
alquilar like hablar (1)
anunciar like hablar (1)
apagar (gu) like llegar (41)
aplaudir like vivir (3)
apreciar like hablar (1)
aprender like comer (2)
apurarse like hablar (1)
arrancar (qu) like tocar (43)
arreglar like hablar (1)
asistir like vivir (3)

aumentar like hablar (1)
ayudar(se) like hablar (1)
bailar like hablar (1)
bajar(se) like hablar (1)
bañarse like hablar (1)
barrer like comer (2)
beber like comer (2)
besar(se) like hablar (1)
brindar like hablar (1)
bucear like hablar (1)
buscar (qu) like tocar (43)
caber (4)
caer(se) (5)
calentarse (e:ie) like pensar (30)
calzar (c) like cruzar (37)
cambiar like hablar (1)
caminar like hablar (1)
cantar like hablar (1)
casarse like hablar (1)
celebrar like hablar (1)
cenar like hablar (1)
cepillarse like hablar (1)
cerrar (e:ie) like pensar (30)
chocar (qu) like tocar (43)
cobrar like hablar (1)
cocinar like hablar (1)
comenzar (e:ie) like empezar (26)
comer (2)

How to use the verb tables

In the tables you will find the infinitive, past and present participles, and all the simple forms of each model verb. The formation of the compound tenses of any verb can be inferred from the table of compound tenses, pages 256–259, either by combining the past participle of the verb with a conjugated form of **haber** or combining the present participle with a conjugated form of **estar**.

compartir like vivir (3)
comprar like hablar (1)
comprender like comer (2)
comprometerse like comer (2)
comunicarse (qu) like tocar (43)
conducir (c:zc) (6)
confirmar like hablar (1)
conocer (c:zc) (35)
conseguir (e:i)
  like seguir (32)
conservar like hablar (1)
consumir like vivir (3)
contaminar like hablar (1)
contar (o:ue) (24)
controlar like hablar (1)
correr like comer (2)
costar (o:ue) like contar (24)
creer (y) (36)
cruzar (c) (37)
cubrir like vivir (3)
cuidar like hablar (1)
cumplir like vivir (3)
dañar like hablar (1)
dar(se) (7)
deber like comer (2)
decidir like vivir (3)
decir (e:i) (8)
declarar like hablar (1)
dejar like hablar (1)

depositar like hablar (1)
desarrollar like hablar (1)
desayunar like hablar (1)
descansar like hablar (1)
describir like vivir (3)
descubrir like vivir (3)
desear like hablar (1)
despedirse (e:i) like pedir (29)
despertarse (e:ie)
  like pensar (30)
destruir (y) (38)
dibujar like hablar (1)
disfrutar like hablar (1)
divertirse (e:ie) like sentir (33)
divorciarse like hablar (1)
doblar like hablar (1)
doler (o:ue) like volver (34) *except*
  past participle is regular
dormir(se) (o:ue) (25)
ducharse like hablar (1)
dudar like hablar (1)
durar like hablar (1)
echar like hablar (1)
elegir (e:i) like pedir (29) *except* (g:j)
emitir like vivir (3)
empezar (e:ie) (26)
enamorarse like hablar (1)

encantar like hablar (1)
encontrar(se) (o:ue) like contar (24)
enfermarse like hablar (1)
engordar like hablar (1)
enojarse like hablar (1)
enseñar like hablar (1)
ensuciar like hablar (1)
entender (e:ie) (27)
entrenarse like hablar (1)
entrevistar like hablar (1)
enviar (envío) (39)
escalar like hablar (1)
escribir like vivir (3)
escuchar like hablar (1)
esculpir like vivir (3)
esperar like hablar (1)
esquiar (esquío) like enviar (39)
establecer (c:zc) like conocer (35)
estacionar like hablar (1)
estar (9)
estornudar like hablar (1)
estudiar like hablar (1)
evitar like hablar (1)
explicar (qu) like tocar (43)
explorar like hablar (1)
faltar like hablar (1)
fascinar like hablar (1)
firmar like hablar (1)
fumar like hablar (1)
funcionar like hablar (1)
ganar like hablar (1)
gastar like hablar (1)
graduarse (gradúo) (40)
guardar like hablar (1)
gustar like hablar (1)
haber (hay) (10)
hablar (1)
hacer (11)
importar like hablar (1)
imprimir like vivir (3)
informar like hablar (1)
insistir like vivir (3)
interesar like hablar (1)
invertir (e:ie) like sentir (33)
invitar like hablar (1)

ir(se) (12)
jubilarse like hablar (1)
jugar (u:ue) (28)
lastimarse like hablar (1)
lavar(se) like hablar (1)
leer (y) like creer (36)
levantar(se) like hablar (1)
limpiar like hablar (1)
llamar(se) like hablar (1)
llegar (41) (gu)
llenar like hablar (1)
llevar(se) like hablar (1)
llover (o:ue) like volver (34) *except* past participle is regular
luchar like hablar (1)
mandar like hablar (1)
manejar like hablar (1)
mantener(se) (e:ie) like **tener** (20)
maquillarse like hablar (1)
mejorar like hablar (1)
merendar (e:ie) like pensar (30)
mirar like hablar (1)
molestar like hablar (1)
montar like hablar (1)
morir (o:ue) like dormir (25)
mostrar (o:ue) like contar (24)
mudarse like hablar (1)
nacer (c:zc) like conocer (35)
nadar like hablar (1)
navegar (gu) like llegar (41)
necesitar like hablar (1)
negar (e:ie) like pensar (30) *except* (g:gu)
nevar (e:ie) like pensar (30)
obedecer (c:zc) like conocer (35)
obtener (e:ie) like tener (20)
ocurrir like vivir (3)
odiar like hablar (1)
ofrecer (c:zc) like conocer (35)
oír (13)
olvidar like hablar (1)
pagar (gu) like llegar (41)
parar like hablar (1)
parecer (c:zc) like conocer (35)
pasar like hablar (1)

pasear like hablar (1)
patinar like hablar (1)
pedir (e:i) (29)
peinarse like hablar (1)
pensar (e:ie) (30)
perder (e:ie) like entender (27)
pescar (qu) like tocar (43)
pintar like hablar (1)
planchar like hablar (1)
poder (o:ue) (14)
ponchar like hablar (1)
poner(se) (15)
practicar (qu) like tocar (43)
preferir (e:ie) like sentir (33)
preguntar like hablar (1)
preocuparse like hablar (1)
preparar like hablar (1)
presentar like hablar (1)
prestar like hablar (1)
probar(se) (o:ue) like contar (24)
prohibir like vivir (3)
proteger (42)
publicar (qu) like tocar (43)
quedar(se) like hablar (1)
querer (e:ie) (16)
quitar(se) like hablar (1)
recetar like hablar (1)
recibir like vivir (3)
reciclar like hablar (1)
recoger like proteger (42)
recomendar (e:ie) like pensar (30)
recordar (o:ue) like contar (24)
reducir (c:zc) like conducir (6)
regalar like hablar (1)
regatear like hablar (1)
regresar like hablar (1)
reír(se) (e:i) (31)
relajarse like hablar (1)
renunciar like hablar (1)
repetir (e:i) like pedir (29)
resolver (o:ue) like volver (34)
respirar like hablar (1)
revisar like hablar (1)
rogar (o:ue) like contar (24) *except* (g:gu)

romper(se) like comer (2)
saber (17)
sacar (qu) like tocar (43)
sacudir like vivir (3)
salir (18)
saludar(se) like hablar (1)
seguir (e:i) (32)
sentarse (e:ie) like pensar (30)
sentir(se) (e:ie) (33)
separarse like hablar (1)
ser (19)
servir (e:i) like pedir (29)
solicitar like hablar (1)
sonar (o:ue) like contar (24)
sonreír (e:i) like reír(se) (31)
sorprender like comer (2)
subir like vivir (3)
sudar like hablar (1)
sufrir like vivir (3)
sugerir (e:ie) like sentir (33)
suponer like poner (15)
temer like comer (2)
tener (e:ie) (20)
terminar like hablar (1)
tocar (43) (qu)
tomar like hablar (1)
torcerse (o:ue) like volver (34) *except* (c:z)
toser like comer (2)
trabajar like hablar (1)
traducir (c:zc) like conducir (6)
traer (21)
transmitir like vivir (3)
tratar like hablar (1)
usar like hablar (1)
vender like comer (2)
venir (e:ie) (22)
ver (23)
vestirse (e:i) like pedir (29)
viajar like hablar (1)
visitar like hablar (1)
vivir (3)
volver (o:ue) (34)
votar like hablar (1)

Regular verbs: simple tenses

	Infinitive	INDICATIVE			
		Present	Imperfect	Preterite	Future
1	hablar	hablo	hablaba	hablé	hablaré
		hablas	hablabas	hablaste	hablarás
	Participles:	habla	hablaba	habló	hablará
	hablando	hablamos	hablábamos	hablamos	hablaremos
	hablado	habláis	hablabais	hablasteis	hablaréis
		hablan	hablaban	hablaron	hablarán
2	comer	como	comía	comí	comeré
		comes	comías	comiste	comerás
	Participles:	come	comía	comió	comerá
	comiendo	comemos	comíamos	comimos	comeremos
	comido	coméis	comíais	comisteis	comeréis
		comen	comían	comieron	comerán
3	vivir	vivo	vivía	viví	viviré
		vives	vivías	viviste	vivirás
	Participles:	vive	vivía	vivió	vivirá
	viviendo	vivimos	vivíamos	vivimos	viviremos
	vivido	vivís	vivíais	vivisteis	viviréis
		viven	vivían	vivieron	vivirán

All verbs: compound tenses

PERFECT TENSES					
INDICATIVE					
Present Perfect		Past Perfect		Future Perfect	
he		había		habré	
has		habías		habrás	
ha	hablado	había	hablado	habrá	hablado
hemos	comido	habíamos	comido	habremos	comido
habéis	vivido	habíais	vivido	habréis	vivido
han		habían		habrán	

INDICATIVE	SUBJUNCTIVE		IMPERATIVE
Conditional	Present	Past	
hablaría	hable	hablara	
hablarías	hables	hablaras	habla (no hables)
hablaría	hable	hablara	hable
hablaríamos	hablemos	habláramos	hablemos
hablaríais	habléis	hablarais	hablad (no habléis)
hablarían	hablen	hablaran	hablen
comería	coma	comiera	
comerías	comas	comieras	come (no comas)
comería	coma	comiera	coma
comeríamos	comamos	comiéramos	comamos
comeríais	comáis	comierais	comed (no comáis)
comerían	coman	comieran	coman
viviría	viva	viviera	
vivirías	vivas	vivieras	vive (no vivas)
viviría	viva	viviera	viva
viviríamos	vivamos	viviéramos	vivamos
viviríais	viváis	vivierais	vivid (no viváis)
vivirían	vivan	vivieran	vivan

PERFECT TENSES

INDICATIVE	SUBJUNCTIVE	
Conditional Perfect	Present Perfect	Past Perfect
habría	haya	hubiera
habrías	hayas	hubieras
habría $\}$ hablado	haya $\}$ hablado	hubiera $\}$ hablado
habríamos $\}$ comido	hayamos $\}$ comido	hubiéramos $\}$ comido
habríais vivido	hayáis vivido	hubierais vivido
habrían	hayan	hubieran

PROGRESSIVE TENSES

INDICATIVE

Present Progressive		Past Progressive		Future Progressive	
estoy		estaba		estaré	
estás		estabas		estarás	
está	hablando	estaba	hablando	estará	hablando
estamos	comiendo	estábamos	comiendo	estaremos	comiendo
estáis	viviendo	estabais	viviendo	estaréis	viviendo
estan		estaban		estarán	

Irregular verbs

	Infinitive	INDICATIVE			
		Present	Imperfect	Preterite	Future
4	caber	**quepo**	cabía	**cupe**	**cabré**
		cabes	cabías	**cupiste**	**cabrás**
	Participles:	cabe	cabía	**cupo**	**cabrá**
	cabiendo	cabemos	cabíamos	**cupimos**	**cabremos**
	cabido	cabéis	cabíais	**cupisteis**	**cabréis**
		caben	cabían	**cupieron**	**cabrán**
5	caer(se)	**caigo**	caía	**caí**	caeré
		caes	caías	**caíste**	caerás
	Participles:	cae	caía	**cayó**	caerá
	cayendo	caemos	caíamos	**caímos**	caeremos
	caído	caéis	caíais	**caísteis**	caeréis
		caen	caían	**cayeron**	caerán
6	conducir	**conduzco**	conducía	**conduje**	conduciré
	(c:zc)	conduces	conducías	**condujiste**	conducirás
	Participles:	conduce	conducía	**condujo**	conducirá
	conduciendo	conducimos	conducíamos	**condujimos**	conduciremos
	conducido	conducís	conducíais	**condujisteis**	conduciréis
		conducen	conducían	**condujeron**	conducirán

PROGRESSIVE TENSES

		SUBJUNCTIVE	
Conditional Progressive		**Present Progressive**	**Past Progressive**
estaría estarías estaría estaríamos estaríais estarían } hablando comiendo viviendo		esté estés esté estemos estéis estén } hablando comiendo viviendo	estuviera estuvieras estuviera estuviéramos estuvierais estuvieran } hablando comiendo viviendo

	SUBJUNCTIVE		IMPERATIVE
Conditional	**Present**	**Past**	
cabría	quepa	cupiera	
cabrías	quepas	cupieras	cabe (no **quepas**)
cabría	quepa	cupiera	**quepa**
cabríamos	quepamos	cupiéramos	**quepamos**
cabríais	quepáis	cupierais	cabed (no **quepáis**)
cabrían	quepan	cupieran	**quepan**
caería	caiga	cayera	
caerías	caigas	cayeras	cae (no **caigas**)
caería	caiga	cayera	**caiga**
caeríamos	caigamos	cayéramos	**caigamos**
caeríais	caigáis	cayerais	caed (no **caigáis**)
caerían	caigan	cayeran	caigan
conduciría	conduzca	condujera	
conducirías	conduzcas	condujeras	conduce (no **conduzcas**)
conduciría	conduzca	condujera	**conduzca**
conduciríamos	conduzcamos	condujéramos	**conduzcamos**
conduciríais	conduzcáis	condujerais	conducid (no **conduzcais**)
conducirían	conduzcan	condujeran	**conduzcan**

		INDICATIVE			
	Infinitive	Present	Imperfect	Preterite	Future
7	dar	**doy**	daba	**di**	daré
		das	dabas	**diste**	darás
	Participles:	da	daba	**dio**	dará
	dando	damos	dábamos	**dimos**	daremos
	dado	dais	dabais	**disteis**	daréis
		dan	daban	**dieron**	darán
8	decir (e:i)	**digo**	decía	**dije**	**diré**
		dices	decías	**dijiste**	**dirás**
	Participles:	**dice**	decía	**dijo**	**dirá**
	diciendo	decimos	decíamos	**dijimos**	**diremos**
	dicho	decís	decíais	**dijisteis**	**diréis**
		dicen	decían	**dijeron**	**dirán**
9	estar	**estoy**	estaba	**estuve**	estaré
		estás	estabas	**estuviste**	estarás
	Participles:	está	estaba	**estuvo**	estará
	estando	estamos	estábamos	**estuvimos**	estaremos
	estado	estáis	estabais	**estuvisteis**	estaréis
		están	estaban	**estuvieron**	estarán
10	haber	**he**	había	**hube**	**habré**
		has	habías	**hubiste**	**habrás**
	Participles:	**ha**	había	**hubo**	**habrá**
	habiendo	**hemos**	habíamos	**hubimos**	**habremos**
	habido	**habéis**	habíais	**hubisteis**	**habréis**
		han	habían	**hubieron**	**habrán**
11	hacer	**hago**	hacía	**hice**	**haré**
		haces	hacías	**hiciste**	**harás**
	Participles:	hace	hacía	**hizo**	**hará**
	haciendo	hacemos	hacíamos	**hicimos**	**haremos**
	hecho	hacéis	hacíais	**hicisteis**	**haréis**
		hacen	hacían	**hicieron**	**harán**
12	ir	**voy**	**iba**	**fui**	iré
		vas	**ibas**	**fuiste**	irás
	Participles:	**va**	**iba**	**fue**	irá
	yendo	**vamos**	**íbamos**	**fuimos**	iremos
	ido	**vais**	**ibais**	**fuisteis**	iréis
		van	**iban**	**fueron**	irán
13	oír (y)	**oigo**	oía	**oí**	oiré
		oyes	oías	**oíste**	oirás
	Participles:	**oye**	oía	**oyó**	oirá
	oyendo	**oímos**	oíamos	**oímos**	oiremos
	oído	**oís**	oíais	**oísteis**	oiréis
		oyen	oían	**oyeron**	oirán

	SUBJUNCTIVE		IMPERATIVE
Conditional	**Present**	**Past**	
daría	**dé**	**diera**	
darías	des	**dieras**	da (no des)
daría	**dé**	**diera**	**dé**
daríamos	demos	**diéramos**	demos
daríais	deis	**dierais**	dad (no deis)
darían	den	**dieran**	den
diría	**diga**	**dijera**	
dirías	**digas**	**dijeras**	di (no **digas**)
diría	**diga**	**dijera**	**diga**
diríamos	**digamos**	**dijéramos**	**digamos**
diríais	**digáis**	**dijerais**	decid (no **digáis**)
dirían	**digan**	**dijeran**	**digan**
estaría	**esté**	**estuviera**	
estarías	**estés**	**estuvieras**	está (no **estés**)
estaría	**esté**	**estuviera**	**esté**
estaríamos	estemos	**estuviéramos**	estemos
estaríais	**estéis**	**estuvierais**	estad (no **estéis**)
estarían	**estén**	**estuvieran**	**estén**
habría	**haya**	**hubiera**	
habrías	**hayas**	**hubieras**	
habría	**haya**	**hubiera**	
habríamos	**hayamos**	**hubiéramos**	
habríais	**hayáis**	**hubierais**	
habrían	**hayan**	**hubieran**	
haría	**haga**	**hiciera**	
harías	**hagas**	**hicieras**	haz (no **hagas**)
haría	**haga**	**hiciera**	**haya**
haríamos	**hagamos**	**hiciéramos**	**hayamos**
haríais	**hagáis**	**hicierais**	haced (no **hayáis**)
harían	**hagan**	**hicieran**	**hayan**
iría	**vaya**	**fuera**	
irías	**vayas**	**fueras**	ve (no **vayas**)
iría	**vaya**	**fuera**	**vaya**
iríamos	**vayamos**	**fuéramos**	**vayamos**
iríais	**vayáis**	**fuerais**	id (no **vayáis**)
irían	**vayan**	**fueran**	**vayan**
oiría	**oiga**	**oyera**	
oirías	**oigas**	**oyeras**	oye (no **oigas**)
oiría	**oiga**	**oyera**	**oiga**
oiríamos	**oigamos**	**oyéramos**	**oigamos**
oiríais	**oigáis**	**oyerais**	oíd (no **oigáis**)
oirían	**oigan**	**oyeran**	**oigan**

			INDICATIVE		
	Infinitive	**Present**	**Imperfect**	**Preterite**	**Future**
14	poder (o:ue)	**puedo**	podía	**pude**	podré
		puedes	podías	**pudiste**	podrás
	Participles:	**puede**	podía	**pudo**	podrá
	pudiendo	podemos	podíamos	**pudimos**	podremos
	podido	podéis	podíais	**pudisteis**	podréis
		pueden	podían	**pudieron**	podrán
15	poner	**pongo**	ponía	**puse**	pondré
		pones	ponías	**pusiste**	pondrás
	Participles:	pone	ponía	**puso**	pondrá
	poniendo	ponemos	poníamos	**pusimos**	pondremos
	puesto	ponéis	poníais	**pusisteis**	pondréis
		ponen	ponían	**pusieron**	pondrán
16	querer (e:ie)	**quiero**	quería	**quise**	querré
		quieres	querías	**quisiste**	querrás
	Participles:	**quiere**	quería	**quiso**	querrá
	queriendo	queremos	queríamos	**quisimos**	querremos
	querido	queréis	queríais	**quisisteis**	querréis
		quieren	querían	**quisieron**	querrán
17	saber	**sé**	sabía	**supe**	sabré
		sabes	sabías	**supiste**	sabrás
	Participles:	sabe	sabía	**supo**	sabrá
	sabiendo	sabemos	sabíamos	**supimos**	sabremos
	sabido	sabéis	sabíais	**supisteis**	sabréis
		saben	sabían	**supieron**	sabrán
18	salir	**salgo**	salía	salí	**saldré**
		sales	salías	saliste	**saldrás**
	Participles:	sale	salía	salió	**saldrá**
	saliendo	salimos	salíamos	salimos	**saldremos**
	salido	salís	salíais	salisteis	**saldréis**
		salen	salían	salieron	**saldrán**
19	ser	**soy**	**era**	**fui**	seré
		eres	**eras**	**fuiste**	serás
	Participles:	**es**	**era**	**fue**	será
	siendo	**somos**	**éramos**	**fuimos**	seremos
	sido	**sois**	**erais**	**fuisteis**	seréis
		son	**eran**	**fueron**	serán
20	tener (e:ie)	**tengo**	tenía	**tuve**	**tendré**
		tienes	tenías	**tuviste**	**tendrás**
	Participles:	**tiene**	tenía	**tuvo**	**tendrá**
	teniendo	tenemos	teníamos	**tuvimos**	**tendremos**
	tenido	tenéis	teníais	**tuvisteis**	**tendréis**
		tienen	tenían	**tuvieron**	**tendrán**

	SUBJUNCTIVE		IMPERATIVE
Conditional	Present	Past	
podría	pueda	pudiera	
podrías	puedas	pudieras	puede (no puedas)
podría	pueda	pudiera	pueda
podríamos	podamos	pudiéramos	podamos
podríais	podáis	pudierais	poded (no podáis)
podrían	puedan	pudieran	puedan
pondría	ponga	pusiera	
pondrías	pongas	pusieras	pon (no pongas)
pondría	ponga	pusiera	ponga
pondríamos	pongamos	pusiéramos	pongamos
pondríais	pongáis	pusierais	poned (no pongáis)
pondrían	pongan	pusieran	pongan
querría	quiera	quisiera	
querrías	quieras	quisieras	quiere (no quieras)
querría	quiera	quisiera	quiere
querríamos	queramos	quisiéramos	queramos
querríais	queráis	quisierais	quered (no queráis)
querrían	quieran	quisieran	quieran
sabría	sepa	supiera	
sabrías	sepas	supieras	sabe (no sepas)
sabría	sepa	supiera	sepa
sabríamos	sepamos	supiéramos	sepamos
sabríais	sepáis	supierais	sabed (no sepáis)
sabrían	sepan	supieran	sepan
saldría	salga	saliera	
saldrías	salgas	salieras	sal (no salgas)
saldría	salga	saliera	salga
saldríamos	salgamos	saliéramos	salgamos
saldríais	salgáis	salierais	salid (no salgáis)
saldrían	salgan	salieran	salgan
sería	sea	fuera	
serías	seas	fueras	sé (no seas)
sería	sea	fuera	sea
seríamos	seamos	fuéramos	seamos
seríais	seáis	fuerais	sed (no seáis)
serían	sean	fueran	sean
tendría	tenga	tuviera	
tendrías	tengas	tuvieras	ten (no tengas)
tendría	tenga	tuviera	tenga
tendríamos	tengamos	tuviéramos	tengamos
tendríais	tengáis	tuvierais	tened (no tengáis)
tendrían	tengan	tuvieran	tengan

		INDICATIVE			
	Infinitive	**Present**	**Imperfect**	**Preterite**	**Future**
21	traer	**traigo**	traía	**traje**	traeré
		traes	traías	**trajiste**	traerás
	Participles:	trae	traía	**trajo**	traerá
	trayendo	traemos	traíamos	**trajimos**	traeremos
	traído	traéis	traíais	**trajisteis**	traeréis
		traen	traían	**trajeron**	traerán
22	venir (e:ie)	**vengo**	venía	**vine**	**vendré**
		vienes	venías	**viniste**	**vendrás**
	Participles:	**viene**	venía	**vino**	**vendrá**
	viniendo	venimos	veníamos	**vinimos**	**vendremos**
	venido	venís	veníais	**vinisteis**	**vendréis**
		vienen	venían	**vinieron**	**vendrán**
23	ver	**veo**	**veía**	vi	veré
		ves	**veías**	viste	verás
	Participles:	ve	**veía**	vio	verá
	viendo	vemos	**veíamos**	vimos	veremos
	visto	veis	**veíais**	visteis	veréis
		ven	**veían**	vieron	verán

Stem changing verbs

		INDICATIVE			
	Infinitive	**Present**	**Imperfect**	**Preterite**	**Future**
24	contar (o:ue)	**cuento**	contaba	conté	contaré
		cuentas	contabas	contaste	contarás
	Participles:	**cuenta**	contaba	contó	contará
	contando	contamos	contábamos	contamos	contaremos
	contado	contáis	contabais	contasteis	contaréis
		cuentan	contaban	contaron	contarán
25	dormir (o:ue)	**duermo**	dormía	dormí	dormiré
		duermes	dormías	dormiste	dormirás
	Participles:	**duerme**	dormía	**durmió**	dormirá
	durmiendo	dormimos	dormíamos	dormimos	dormiremos
	dormido	dormís	dormíais	dormisteis	dormiréis
		duermen	dormían	**durmieron**	dormirán
26	empezar	**empiezo**	empezaba	**empecé**	empezaré
	(e:ie) (c)	**empiezas**	empezabas	empezaste	empezarás
		empieza	empezaba	empezó	empezará
	Participles:	empezamos	empezábamos	empezamos	empezaremos
	empezando	empezáis	empezabais	empezasteis	empezaréis
	empezado	**empiezan**	empezaban	empezaron	empezarán

	SUBJUNCTIVE		IMPERATIVE
Conditional	Present	Past	
traería	**traiga**	**trajera**	
traerías	**traigas**	**trajeras**	trae (no **traigas**)
traería	**traiga**	**trajera**	**traiga**
traeríamos	**traigamos**	**trajéramos**	**traigamos**
traeríais	**traigáis**	**trajerais**	traed (no **traigáis**)
traerían	**traigan**	**trajeran**	**traigan**
vendría	**venga**	**viniera**	
vendrías	**vengas**	**vinieras**	ven (no **vengas**)
vendría	**venga**	**viniera**	**venga**
vendríamos	**vengamos**	**viniéramos**	**vengamos**
vendríais	**vengáis**	**vinierais**	venid (no **vengáis**)
vendrían	**vengan**	**vinieran**	**vengan**
vería	**vea**	**viera**	
verías	**veas**	**vieras**	ve (no **veas**)
vería	**vea**	**viera**	**vea**
veríamos	**veamos**	**viéramos**	**veamos**
veríais	**veáis**	**vierais**	ved (no **veáis**)
verían	**vean**	**vieran**	**vean**

	SUBJUNCTIVE		IMPERATIVE
Conditional	Present	Past	
contaría	**cuente**	contara	
contarías	**cuentes**	contaras	**cuenta** (no **cuentes**)
contaría	**cuente**	contara	**cuente**
contaríamos	contemos	contáramos	contemos
contaríais	contéis	contarais	contad (no **contéis**)
contarían	**cuenten**	contaran	cuenten
dormiría	**duerma**	**durmiera**	
dormirías	**duermas**	**durmieras**	**duerme** (no **duermas**)
dormiría	**duerma**	**durmiera**	**duerma**
dormiríamos	**durmamos**	**durmiéramos**	**durmamos**
dormiríais	**durmáis**	**durmierais**	dormid (no **durmáis**)
dormirían	**duerman**	**durmieran**	**duerman**
empezaría	**empiece**	empezara	
empezarías	**empieces**	empezaras	**empieza** (no **empieces**)
empezaría	**empiece**	empezara	**empiece**
empezaríamos	**empecemos**	empezáramos	**empecemos**
empezaríais	**empecéis**	empezarais	empezad (no **empecéis**)
empezarían	**empiecen**	empezaran	**empiecen**

			INDICATIVE		
	Infinitive	Present	Imperfect	Preterite	Future
27	entender (e:ie)	**entiendo**	entendía	entendí	entenderé
		entiendes	entendías	entendiste	entenderás
		entiende	entendía	entendió	entenderá
	Participles:	entendemos	entendíamos	entendimos	entenderemos
	entendiendo	entendéis	entendíais	entendisteis	entenderéis
	entendido	**entienden**	entendían	entendieron	entenderán
28	jugar (u:ue) (gu)	**juego**	jugaba	**jugué**	jugaré
		juegas	jugabas	jugaste	jugarás
		juega	jugaba	jugó	jugará
	Participles:	jugamos	jugábamos	jugamos	jugaremos
	jugando	jugáis	jugabais	jugasteis	jugaréis
	jugado	**juegan**	jugaban	jugaron	jugarán
29	pedir (e:i)	**pido**	pedía	pedí	pediré
		pides	pedías	pediste	pedirás
		pide	pedía	**pidió**	pedirá
	Participles:	pedimos	pedíamos	pedimos	pediremos
	pidiendo	pedís	pedíais	pedisteis	pediréis
	pedido	**piden**	pedían	**pidieron**	pedirán
30	pensar (e:ie)	**pienso**	pensaba	pensé	pensaré
		piensas	pensabas	pensaste	pensarás
	Participles:	**piensa**	pensaba	pensó	pensará
	pensando	pensamos	pensábamos	pensamos	pensaremos
	pensado	pensáis	pensabais	pensasteis	pensaréis
		piensan	pensaban	pensaron	pensarán
31	reír(se) (e:i)	**río**	reía	**reí**	reiré
		ríes	reías	**reíste**	reirás
	Participles:	**ríe**	reía	**rió**	reirá
	riendo	**reímos**	reíamos	**reímos**	reiremos
	reído	**reís**	reíais	**reísteis**	reiréis
		ríen	reían	**rieron**	reirán
32	seguir (e:i) (gu)	**sigo**	seguía	seguí	seguiré
		sigues	seguías	seguiste	seguirás
		sigue	seguía	**siguió**	seguirá
	Participles:	seguimos	seguíamos	seguimos	seguiremos
	siguiendo	seguís	seguíais	seguisteis	seguiréis
	seguido	**siguen**	seguían	**siguieron**	seguirán
33	sentir (e:ie)	**siento**	sentía	sentí	sentiré
		sientes	sentías	sentiste	sentirás
	Participles:	**siente**	sentía	**sintió**	sentirá
	sintiendo	sentimos	sentíamos	sentimos	sentiremos
	sentido	sentís	sentíais	sentisteis	sentiréis
		sienten	sentían	**sintieron**	sentirán

	SUBJUNCTIVE		IMPERATIVE
Conditional	Present	Past	
entendería	**entienda**	entendiera	
entenderías	**entiendas**	entendieras	**entiende** (no **entiendas**)
entendería	**entienda**	entendiera	**entienda**
entenderíamos	entendamos	entendiéramos	entendamos
entenderíais	entendáis	entendierais	entended (no **entendáis**)
entenderían	**entiendan**	entendieran	**entiendan**
jugaría	**juegue**	jugara	
jugarías	**juegues**	jugaras	**juega** (no **juegues**)
jugaría	**juegue**	jugara	**juegue**
jugaríamos	**juguemos**	jugáramos	**juguemos**
jugaríais	**juguéis**	jugarais	jugad (no **juguéis**)
jugarían	**jueguen**	jugaran	**jueguen**
pediría	**pida**	**pidiera**	
pedirías	**pidas**	**pidieras**	**pide** (no **pidas**)
pediría	**pida**	**pidiera**	**pida**
pediríamos	**pidamos**	**pidiéramos**	**pidamos**
pediríais	**pidáis**	**pidierais**	pedid (no **pidáis**)
pedirían	**pidan**	**pidieran**	**pidan**
pensaría	**piense**	pensara	
pensarías	**pienses**	pensaras	**piensa** (no **pienses**)
pensaría	**piense**	pensara	**piense**
pensaríamos	pensemos	pensáramos	**pensemos**
pensaríais	penséis	pensarais	pensad (no **penséis**)
pensarían	**piensen**	pensaran	**piensan**
reiría	**ría**	**riera**	
reirías	**rías**	**rieras**	**ríe** (no **rías**)
reiría	**ría**	**riera**	**ría**
reiríamos	**riamos**	**riéramos**	**riamos**
reiríais	**riáis**	**rierais**	reíd (no **riáis**)
reirían	**rían**	**rieran**	**rían**
seguiría	**siga**	**siguiera**	
seguirías	**sigas**	**siguieras**	**sigue** (no **sigas**)
seguiría	**siga**	**siguiera**	**siga**
seguiríamos	**sigamos**	**siguiéramos**	**sigamos**
seguiríais	**sigáis**	**siguierais**	seguid (no **sigáis**)
seguirían	**sigan**	**siguieran**	**sigan**
sentiría	**sienta**	**sintiera**	
sentirías	**sientas**	**sintieras**	**siente** (no **sientas**)
sentiría	**sienta**	**sintiera**	**sienta**
sentiríamos	**sintamos**	**sintiéramos**	**sintamos**
sentiríais	**sintáis**	**sintierais**	sentid (no **sintáis**)
sentirían	**sientan**	**sintieran**	**sientan**

		INDICATIVE			
	Infinitive	Present	Imperfect	Preterite	Future
34	volver (o:ue)	**vuelvo**	volvía	volví	volveré
		vuelves	volvías	volviste	volverás
	Participles:	**vuelve**	volvía	volvió	volverá
	volviendo	volvemos	volvíamos	volvimos	volveremos
	vuelto	volvéis	volvíais	volvisteis	volveréis
		vuelven	volvían	volvieron	volverán

Verbs with spelling changes only

		INDICATIVE			
	Infinitive	Present	Imperfect	Preterite	Future
35	conocer	**conozco**	conocía	conocí	conoceré
	(c:zc)	conoces	conocías	conociste	conocerás
		conoce	conocía	conoció	conocerá
	Participles:	conocemos	conocíamos	conocimos	conoceremos
	conociendo	conocéis	conocíais	conocisteis	conoceréis
	conocido	conocen	conocían	conocieron	conocerán
36	creer (y)	creo	creía	**creí**	creeré
		crees	creías	**creíste**	creerás
	Participles:	cree	creía	**creyó**	creerá
	creyendo	creemos	creíamos	**creímos**	creeremos
	creído	creéis	creíais	**creísteis**	creeréis
		creen	creían	**creyeron**	creerán
37	cruzar (c)	cruzo	cruzaba	**crucé**	cruzaré
		cruzas	cruzabas	cruzaste	cruzarás
	Participles:	cruza	cruzaba	cruzó	cruzará
	cruzando	cruzamos	cruzábamos	cruzamos	cruzaremos
	cruzado	cruzáis	cruzabais	cruzasteis	cruzaréis
		cruzan	cruzaban	cruzaron	cruzarán
38	destruir (y)	**destruyo**	destruía	destruí	destruiré
		destruyes	destruías	destruiste	destruirás
	Participles:	**destruye**	destruía	**destruyó**	destruirá
	destruyendo	destruimos	destruíamos	destruimos	destruiremos
	destruido	destruís	destruíais	destruisteis	destruiréis
		destruyen	destruían	**destruyeron**	destruirán
39	enviar	**envío**	enviaba	envié	enviaré
	(envío)	**envías**	enviabas	enviaste	enviarás
		envía	enviaba	envió	enviará
	Participles:	enviamos	enviábamos	enviamos	enviaremos
	enviando	enviáis	enviabais	enviasteis	enviaréis
	enviado	**envían**	enviaban	enviaron	enviarán

	SUBJUNCTIVE		IMPERATIVE
Conditional	Present	Past	
volvería	**vuelva**	volviera	
volverías	**vuelvas**	volvieras	**vuelve** (no **vuelvas**)
volvería	**vuelva**	volviera	**vuelva**
volveríamos	volvamos	volviéramos	**volvamos**
volveríais	volváis	volvierais	volved (no **volváis**)
volverían	**vuelvan**	volvieran	**vuelvan**

	SUBJUNCTIVE		IMPERATIVE
Conditional	Present	Past	
conocería	**conozca**	conociera	
conocerías	**conozcas**	conocieras	conoce (no **conozcas**)
conocería	**conozca**	conociera	**conozca**
conoceríamos	**conozcamos**	conociéramos	**conozcamos**
conoceríais	**conozcáis**	conocierais	conoced (no **conozcáis**)
conocerían	**conozcan**	conocieran	**conozcan**
creería	crea	**creyera**	
creerías	creas	**creyeras**	cree (no **creas**)
creería	crea	**creyera**	**crea**
creeríamos	creamos	**creyéramos**	**creamos**
creeríais	creáis	**creyerais**	creed (no **creáis**)
creerían	crean	**creyeran**	**crean**
cruzaría	**cruce**	cruzara	
cruzarías	**cruces**	cruzaras	cruza (no **cruces**)
cruzaría	**cruce**	cruzara	**cruce**
cruzaríamos	**crucemos**	cruzáramos	**crucemos**
cruzaríais	**crucéis**	cruzarais	cruzad (no **crucéis**)
cruzarían	**crucen**	cruzaran	**crucen**
destruiría	**destruya**	**destruyera**	
destruirías	**destruyas**	**destruyeras**	destruye (no **destruyas**)
destruiría	**destruya**	**destruyera**	**destruya**
destruiríamos	**destruyamos**	**destruyéramos**	**destruyamos**
destruiríais	**destruyáis**	**destruyerais**	destruid (no **destruyáis**)
destruirían	**destruyan**	**destruyeran**	**destruyan**
enviaría	**envíe**	enviara	
enviarías	**envíes**	enviaras	**envía** (no **envíes**)
enviaría	**envíe**	enviara	**envíe**
enviaríamos	**enviemos**	enviáramos	**enviemos**
enviaríais	**enviéis**	enviarais	enviad (no **enviéis**)
enviarían	**envíen**	enviaran	**envíen**

	Infinitive	INDICATIVE			
		Present	Imperfect	Preterite	Future
40	graduarse	**gradúo**	graduaba	gradué	graduaré
	(gradúo)	**gradúas**	graduabas	graduaste	graduarás
	Participles:	**gradúa**	graduaba	graduó	graduará
	graduando	**graduamos**	graduábamos	graduamos	graduaremos
	graduado	**graduáis**	graduabais	graduasteis	graduaréis
		gradúan	graduaban	graduaron	graduarán
41	llegar (gu)	llego	llegaba	**llegué**	llegaré
		llegas	llegabas	llegaste	llegarás
	Participles:	llega	llegaba	llegó	llegará
	llegando	llegamos	llegábamos	llegamos	llegaremos
	llegado	llegáis	llegabais	llegasteis	llegaréis
		llegan	llegaban	llegaron	llegarán
42	proteger (j)	**protejo**	protegía	protegí	protegeré
		proteges	protegías	protegiste	protegerás
	Participles:	protege	protegía	protegió	protegerá
	protegiendo	protegemos	protegíamos	protegimos	protegeremos
	protegido	protegéis	protegíais	protegisteis	protegeréis
		protegen	protegían	protegieron	protegerán
43	tocar (qu)	toco	tocaba	**toqué**	tocaré
		tocas	tocabas	tocaste	tocarás
	Participles:	toca	tocaba	tocó	tocarás
	tocando	tocamos	tocábamos	tocamos	tocaremos
	tocado	tocáis	tocabais	tocasteis	tocaréis
		tocan	tocaban	tocaron	tocarán

	SUBJUNCTIVE		IMPERATIVE
Conditional	Present	Past	
graduaría	**gradúe**	graduara	
graduarías	**gradúes**	graduaras	**gradúa** (no **gradúes**)
graduaría	**gradúe**	graduara	**gradúe**
graduaríamos	**graduemos**	graduáramos	**graduemos**
graduaríais	**graduéis**	graduarais	graduad (no **graduéis**)
graduarían	**gradúen**	graduaran	**gradúen**
llegaría	**llegue**	llegara	
llegarías	**llegues**	llegaras	llega (no **llegues**)
llegaría	**llegue**	llegara	**llegue**
llegaríamos	**lleguemos**	llegáramos	**lleguemos**
llegaríais	**lleguéis**	llegarais	llegad (no **lleguéis**)
llegarían	**lleguen**	llegaran	**lleguen**
protegería	**proteja**	protegiera	
protegerías	**protejas**	protegieras	protege (no **protejas**)
protegería	**proteja**	protegiera	**proteja**
protegeríamos	**protejamos**	protegiéramos	**protejamos**
protegeríais	**protejáis**	protegierais	proteged (no **protejáis**)
protegerían	**protejan**	protegieran	**protejan**
tocaría	**toque**	tocara	
tocarías	**toques**	tocaras	toca (no **toques**)
tocaría	**toque**	tocara	**toque**
tocaríamos	**toquemos**	tocáramos	**toquemos**
tocaríais	**toquéis**	tocarais	tocad (no **toquéis**)
tocarían	**toquen**	tocaran	**toquen**

Sección de consulta
Reference Section

MATERIAS	ACADEMIC SUBJECTS
la administración de empresas	business administration
la agronomía	agriculture
el alemán	German
el álgebra	algebra
la anatomía	anatomy
la antropología	anthropology
la arqueología	archaeology
la arquitectura	architecture
el arte	art
la astronomía	astronomy
la biología	biology
la bioquímica	biochemistry
la botánica	botany
el cálculo	calculus
el chino	Chinese
las ciencias políticas	political science
la computación	computer science
las comunicaciones	communications
la contabilidad	accounting
la danza	dance
el derecho	law
la economía	economics
la educación	education
la educación física	physical education

la enfermería	nursing
el español	Spanish
la filosofía	philosophy
la física	physics
el francés	French
la geografía	geography
la geología	geology
el griego	Greek
el hebreo	Hebrew
la historia	history
la informática	computer science
la ingeniería	engineering
el inglés	English
el italiano	Italian
el japonés	Japanese
el latín	Latin
las lenguas clásicas	classical languages
las lenguas romances	romance languages
la lingüística	linguistics
la literatura	literature
las matemáticas	mathematics
la medicina	medicine
el mercadeo	marketing
la música	music
los negocios	business
el periodismo	journalism

el portugués	Portuguese
la psicología	psychology
la química	chemistry
el ruso	Russian
los servicios sociales	social services
la sociología	sociology
el teatro	theater
la trigonometría	trigonometry
la zoología	zoology

LOS ANIMALES — ANIMALS

la abeja	bee
la araña	spider
la ardilla	squirrel
el ave (f.), el pájaro	bird
la ballena	whale
el burro	donkey
la cabra	goat
el caimán	alligator
el camello	camel
la cebra	zebra
el ciervo, el venado	deer
el cocodrilo	crocodile
el cochino, el cerdo, el puerco	pig
el conejo	rabbit
el coyote	coyote

la culebra, la serpiente, la víbora	snake
el elefante	elephant
la foca	seal
la gallina	hen
el gallo	rooster
el gato	cat
el gorila	gorilla
el hipopótamo	hippopotamus
la hormiga	ant
el insecto	insect
la jirafa	giraffe
el lagarto	lizard
el león	lion
el lobo	wolf
el loro, la cotorra, el papagayo, el perico	parrot
la mariposa	butterfly
el mono	monkey
la mosca	fly
el mosquito	mosquito
el oso	bear
la oveja	sheep
el pato	duck
el perro	dog
el pez	fish
la rana	frog

el ratón	mouse
el rinoceronte	rhinoceros
el saltamontes, el chapulín	grasshopper
el tiburón	shark
el tigre	tiger
el toro	bull
la tortuga	turtle
la vaca	cow
el zorro	fox

EL CUERPO HUMANO Y LA SALUD

THE HUMAN BODY AND HEALTH

El cuerpo humano

The Human Body

la barba	beard
el bigote	mustache
la barriga, la panza, la guata	belly, tummy
la boca	mouth
el brazo	arm
la cabeza	head
la cadera	hip
la ceja	eyebrow
el cerebro	brain
la cintura	waist
el codo	elbow
el corazón	heart
la costilla	rib
el cráneo	skull

el cuello	neck
el dedo	finger
el dedo del pie	toe
la espalda	back
el estómago	stomach
la frente	forehead
la garganta	throat
el hombro	shoulder
el hueso	bone
el labio	lip
la lengua	tongue
la mandíbula	jaw
la mejilla	cheek
el mentón, la barba	chin
la muñeca	wrist
el músculo	muscle
el muslo	thigh
las nalgas, el trasero, las asentaderas	buttocks
la nariz	nose
el nervio	nerve
el oído	(inner) ear
el ojo	eye
el ombligo	navel, belly button
la oreja	(outer) ear
la pantorrilla	calf

el párpado	eyelid
el pecho	chest
la pestaña	eyelash
el pie	foot
la piel	skin
la pierna	leg
el pulgar	thumb
el pulmón	lung
la rodilla	knee
la sangre	blood
el talón	heel
el tobillo	ankle
el tronco	torso, trunk
la uña	fingernail
la uña del dedo del pie	toenail
la vena	vein

LOS CINCO SENTIDOS	*THE FIVE SENSES*
el gusto	taste
el oído	hearing
el olfato	smell
el tacto	touch
la vista	sight

LA SALUD	*HEALTH*
el accidente	accident
alérgico/a	allergic
el antibiótico	antibiotic

la aspirina	aspirin
el ataque cardiaco, el ataque al corazón	heart attack
el cáncer	cancer
la cápsula	capsule
la clínica	clinic
congestionado/a	congested
el consultorio	doctor's office
la curita	adhesive bandage
el/la dentista	dentist
el/la doctor(a), el/la médico/a	doctor
el dolor (de cabeza)	(head)ache, pain
embarazada	pregnant
la enfermedad	illness, disease
el/la enfermero/a	nurse
enfermo/a	ill, sick
la erupción	rash
el examen médico	physical exam
la farmacia	pharmacy
la fiebre	fever
la fractura	fracture
la gripe	flu
la herida	wound
el hospital	hospital
la infección	infection
la inyección	injection

el insomnio	insomnia
el jarabe	(cough) syrup
mareado/a	dizzy, nauseated
el medicamento	medication
la medicina	medicine
las muletas	crutches
la operación	operation
el/la paciente	patient
el/la paramédico/a	paramedic
la pastilla, la píldora	pill, tablet
los primeros auxilios	first aid
la pulmonía	pneumonia
los puntos	stitches
la quemadura	burn
el quirófano	operating room
la radiografía	X-ray
la receta	prescription
el resfriado	cold (illness)
la sala de emergencia(s)	emergency room
saludable	healthy, healthful
sano/a	healthy
el seguro médico	medical insurance
la silla de ruedas	wheelchair
el síntoma	symptom
el termómetro	thermometer
la tos	cough

la transfusión	transfusion
la vacuna	vaccination
la venda	bandage
el virus	virus
cortar(se)	to cut (oneself)
curar	to cure, to treat
desmayar(se)	to faint
enfermarse	to get sick
enyesar	to put in a cast
estornudar	to sneeze
guardar cama	to stay in bed
hinchar(se)	to swell
internar(se) en el hospital	to check into the hospital
lastimarse (el pie)	to hurt (one's foot)
mejorar(se)	to get better; to improve
operar	to operate
quemar(se)	to burn
respirar (hondo)	to breathe (deeply)
romperse (la pierna)	to break (one's leg)
sangrar	to bleed
sufrir	to suffer
tomarle la presión a alguien	to take someone's blood pressure
tomarle el pulso a alguien	to take someone's pulse
torcerse (el tobillo)	to sprain (one's ankle)
vendar	to bandage

EXPRESIONES ÚTILES PARA LA CLASE

USEFUL CLASSROOM EXPRESSIONS

PALABRAS ÚTILES

USEFUL WORDS

ausente	absent
el departamento	department
el dictado	dictation
la conversación, las conversaciones	conversation(s)
la expresión, las expresiones	expression(s)
el examen, los exámenes	test(s)
la frase	sentence
la hoja de actividades	activity sheet
el horario de clases	class schedule
la oración, las oraciones	sentence(s)
el párrafo	paragraph
la persona	person
presente	present
la prueba	quiz
siguiente	following
la tarea	homework

EXPRESIONES ÚTILES

USEFUL EXPRESSIONS

Abra(n) sus libros.	Open your book(s).
Cambien de papel.	Change roles.
Cierre(n) su(s) libro(s).	Close your books.
¿Cómo se dice ___ en español?	How do you say ___ in Spanish?
¿Cómo se escribe ___ en español?	How do you write ___ in Spanish?

¿Comprende(n)?	Do you understand?
(No) comprendo.	I (don't) understand.
Conteste(n) las preguntas.	Answer the questions.
Continúe(n), por favor.	Continue, please.
Escriba(n) su nombre.	Write your name.
Escuchen la cinta (el disco compacto).	Listen to the tape (compact disc).
Estudie(n) la lección tres.	Study lesson three.
Haga(n) la actividad (el ejercicio) número cuatro.	Do activity (exercise) number four.
Lea(n) la oración en voz alta.	Read the sentence aloud.
Levante(n) la mano.	Raise your hand(s).
Más despacio, por favor.	Slower, please.
No sé.	I don't know.
Páse(n)me los exámenes.	Pass me the tests.
¿Qué significa ___?	What does ___ mean?
Repita(n), por favor.	Repeat, please.
Siénte(n)se, por favor.	Sit down, please.
Siga(n) las instrucciones.	Follow the instructions.
¿Tiene(n) alguna pregunta?	Do you have any questions?
Vaya(n) a la página dos.	Go to page two.

COUNTRIES & NATIONALITIES

PAÍSES Y NACIONALIDADES (GENTILICIOS)

NORTH AMERICA	**NORTEAMÉRICA**	
Canada	**Canadá**	canadiense
Mexico	**México**	mexicano/a
United States	**Estados Unidos**	estadounidense

CENTRAL AMERICA	**CENTROAMÉRICA**	
Belize	**Belice**	beliceño/a
Costa Rica	**Costa Rica**	costarricense
El Salvador	**El Salvador**	salvadoreño/a
Guatemala	**Guatemala**	guatemalteco/a
Honduras	**Honduras**	hondureño/a
Nicaragua	**Nicaragua**	nicaragüense
Panama	**Panamá**	panameño/a

THE CARIBBEAN	**EL CARIBE**	
Cuba	**Cuba**	cubano/a
Dominican Republic	**República Dominicana**	dominicano/a
Haiti	**Haití**	haitiano/a
Puerto Rico	**Puerto Rico**	puertorriqueño/a

SOUTH AMERICA	**AMÉRICA DEL SUR**	
Argentina	**Argentina**	argentino/a
Bolivia	**Bolivia**	boliviano/a
Brazil	**Brasil**	brasileño/a
Chile	**Chile**	chileno/a
Colombia	**Colombia**	colombiano/a

Ecuador	**Ecuador**	**ecuatoriano/a**
Paraguay	**Paraguay**	**paraguayo/a**
Peru	**Perú**	**peruano/a**
Uruguay	**Uruguay**	**uruguayo/a**
Venezuela	**Venezuela**	**venezolano/a**
EUROPE	*EUROPA*	
Armenia	**Armenia**	**armenio/a**
Austria	**Austria**	**austríaco/a**
Belgium	**Bélgica**	**belga**
Bosnia	**Bosnia**	**bosnio/a**
Bulgaria	**Bulgaria**	**búlgaro/a**
Croatia	**Croacia**	**croata**
Czech Republic	**República Checa**	**checo/a**
Denmark	**Dinamarca**	**danés, danesa**
England	**Inglaterra**	**inglés, inglesa**
Estonia	**Estonia**	**estonio/a**
Finland	**Finlandia**	**finlandés, finlandesa**
France	**Francia**	**francés, francesa**
Germany	**Alemania**	**alemán, alemana**
Great Britain (United Kingdom)	**Gran Bretaña (Reino Unido)**	**británico**
Greece	**Grecia**	**griego/a**
Hungary	**Hungría**	**húngaro/a**
Iceland	**Islandia**	**islandés, islandesa**
Ireland	**Irlanda**	**irlandés, irlandesa**
Italy	**Italia**	**italiano/a**

Latvia	**Letonia**	**letón, letona**
Lithuania	**Lituania**	**lituano/a**
Netherlands (Holland)	**Países Bajos (Holanda)**	**holandés, holandesa**
Norway	**Noruega**	**noruego/a**
Poland	**Polonia**	**polaco/a**
Portugal	**Portugal**	**portugués, portuguesa**
Romania	**Rumania**	**rumano/a**
Russia	**Rusia**	**ruso/a**
Scotland	**Escocia**	**escocés, escocesa**
Serbia	**Serbia**	**serbio/a**
Slovakia	**Eslovaquia**	**eslovaco/a**
Slovenia	**Eslovenia**	**esloveno/a**
Spain	**España**	**español(a)**
Sweden	**Suecia**	**sueco/a**
Switzerland	**Suiza**	**suizo/a**
Ukraine	**Ucrania**	**ucranio/a, ucraniano/a**
Wales	**Gales**	**galés, galesa**
Yugoslavia	**Yugoslavia**	**yugoslavo/a**
ASIA	*ASIA*	
Bangladesh	**Bangladesh**	**bangladesí**
Cambodia	**Camboya**	**camboyano/a**
China	**China**	**chino/a**
India	**India**	**indio/a**
Indonesia	**Indonesia**	**indonesio/a**

Iran	**Irán**	iraní
Iraq	**Iraq, Irak**	iraquí
Israel	**Israel**	israelí
Japan	**Japón**	japonés, japonesa
Jordan	**Jordania**	jordano/a
Korea	**Corea**	coreano/a
Kuwait	**Kuwait**	kuwaití
Lebanon	**Líbano**	libanés, libanesa
Malaysia	**Malaisia**	malaisiano/a
Pakistan	**Pakistán**	pakistaní
Russia	**Rusia**	ruso/a
Saudi Arabia	**Arabia Saudí**	saudí
Singapore	**Singapur**	singapurés, singa-puresa
Syria	**Siria**	sirio/a
Taiwan	**Taiwán**	taiwanés, taiwanesa
Thailand	**Tailandia**	tailandés, tailandesa
Turkey	**Turquía**	turco/a
Vietnam	**Vietnam**	vietnamita
AFRICA	*ÁFRICA*	
Algeria	**Argelia**	argelino/a
Angola	**Angola**	angolano/a
Cameroon	**Camerún**	camerunés, camerunesa
Congo	**Congo**	congolés, congolesa
Egypt	**Egipto**	egipcio/a
Equatorial Guinea	**Guinea Ecuatorial**	ecuatoguineano

Ethiopia	**Etiopía**	etíope
Ivory Coast	**Costa de Marfil**	ivoriano/a
Kenya	**Kenia, Kenya**	keniano/a
Libya	**Libia**	libio/a
Mali	**Malí**	malinqués, malinquesa
Morocco	**Marruecos**	marroquí
Mozambique	**Mozambique**	mozambicano
Nigeria	**Nigeria**	nigeriano/a
Rwanda	**Ruanda**	ruandés, ruandesa
Somalia	**Somalia**	somalí
South Africa	**Sudáfrica**	sudafricano/a
Sudan	**Sudán**	sudanés, sudanesa
Tunisia	**Tunicia, Túnez**	tunecino/a
Uganda	**Uganda**	ugandés, ugandesa
Zambia	**Zambia**	zambiano/a
Zimbabwe	**Zimbabue**	zimbabuense
AUSTRALIA AND THE PACIFIC	*AUSTRALIA Y EL PACÍFICO*	
Australia	**Australia**	australiano/a
New Zealand	**Nueva Zelanda**	neozelandés, neozelandesa
Philippines	**Filipinas**	filipino/a

288

MONEDAS DE LOS PAÍSES HISPANOS

CURRENCIES OF SPANISH-SPEAKING COUNTRIES

PAÍS *Country*	*MONEDA* *Currency*
Argentina	el peso
Bolivia	el boliviano
Chile	el peso
Colombia	el peso
Costa Rica	el colón
Cuba	el peso
Ecuador	el sucre, el dólar estadounidense
El Salvador	el colón, el dólar estadounidense
España	la peseta, el euro
Guatemala	el quetzal, el dólar estadounidense
Honduras	el lempira
México	el nuevo peso
Nicaragua	el córdoba
Panamá	el balboa, el dólar estadounidense
Paraguay	el guaraní
Perú	el sol
Puerto Rico	el dólar estadounidense
República Dominicana	el peso
Uruguay	el peso
Venezuela	el bolívar

EXPRESIONES Y REFRANES

EXPRESIONES Y REFRANES CON PARTES DEL CUERPO

EXPRESSIONS & SAYINGS

EXPRESSIONS & SAYINGS WITH PARTS OF THE BODY

A cara o cruz	Heads or tails
A corazón abierto	Open heart
A lo hecho, pecho	What's done is done./Don't cry over spilled milk.
A ojos vistas	Clearly, visibly
Al dedillo	Like the back of one's hand
Choca esos cinco.	Put it there!/Give me five!
Codo con codo	Very closely/Cheek by jowl
Con las manos en la masa	Red handed
Costar (algo) un ojo de la cara	To cost an arm and a leg
De rodillas	On one's knees
Duro de oído	Hard of hearing
En cuerpo y alma	In body and soul
En la punta de la lengua	On the tip of one's tongue
Darle a la lengua	To chatter/To gab
En un abrir y cerrar de ojos	In a blink of the eye
Entrar por un oído y salir por otro	In one ear and out the other
Estar con el agua al cuello	To be up to one's neck with/in
Estar para chuparse los dedos	To be delicious/To be finger-licking good
Hablar entre dientes	To mutter/To speak under one's breath
Hablar por los codos	To talk a lot
Hacer la vista gorda	To turn a blind eye on something

Hombro con hombro	Shoulder to shoulder
Llorar a lágrima viva	To sob/To cry one's eyes out
Metérsele (a alguien) algo entre ceja y ceja	To put an idea in someone's head
Mirar por encima del hombro	To look down on someone
No pegar ojo	Not to be able to sleep/To stay up all night
No tener corazón	Not to have a heart
No tener dos dedos de frente	Not to have an ounce of common sense
Ojos que no ven, corazón que no siente	Out of sight, out of mind
Perder la cabeza	To lose one's head
Quedarse con la boca abierta	To be thunderstruck
Romper el corazón	To break someone's heart
Tener buen/mal corazón	Have a good/bad heart
Tener un nudo en la garganta	Have a knot in your throat
Tomarse algo a pecho	To take something too seriously
Venir como anillo al dedo	To fit like a charm/To suit perfectly

EXPRESIONES Y REFRANES CON ANIMALES	*EXPRESSIONS & SAYINGS WITH ANIMALS*
A caballo regalado no le mires el diente.	Don't look a gift horse in the mouth.
Comer como un cerdo	To eat like a pig
Cuando menos se piensa, salta la liebre.	Things happen when you least expect it.
Es una mosquita muerta.	Butter wouldn't melt in his/her mouth.

Llevarse como el perro y el gato	To fight like cats and dogs
Perro ladrador, poco mordedor.	His/her bark is worse than his bite.
¿Quién le pone el cascabel al gato?	Who will bell the cat?
Ser una tortuga	To be a slowpoke

EXPRESIONES Y REFRANES CON ALIMENTOS

EXPRESSIONS AND SAYINGS WITH FOOD

Agua que no has de beber, déjala correr.	If you're not interested, don't ruin it for everybody else.
Al pan, pan y al vino, vino.	Not to mince words
Como agua para chocolate	Ready to explode/At the boiling point
Con pan y vino se anda el camino.	Things never seem as bad after a good meal.
Contigo pan y cebolla.	You are all I need.
Dame pan y dime tonto.	I don't care what you say, as long as I get what I want.
Descubrir el pastel	To have one's head in the clouds
Dulce como la miel	Sweet as honey
Estar en el ajo	To be in the know
Estar en la higuera	To take the lid off something
Estar más claro que el agua	To be clear as a bell
Ganarse el pan	To earn a living/To earn one's daily bread
No hay miel sin hiel.	There's no rose without a thorn./There's always a catch.
No sólo de pan vive el hombre.	Man doesn't live by bread alone.

Pan con pan, comida de tontos.	Variety is the spice of life./All work and no play makes Jack a dull boy.
Ser agua pasada	To be water under the bridge
Ser más bueno que el pan	To be gorgeous
Temblar como un flan	To shake/tremble like a leaf

EXPRESIONES Y REFRANES CON COLORES

EXPRESSIONS AND SAYINGS WITH COLORS

Estar verde	To be inexperienced/wet behind the ears
Poner los ojos en blanco	To roll one's eyes
Ponerle a alguien un ojo morado	To give someone a black eye
Ponerse rojo de ira	To turn red with anger.
Ponerse rojo	To turn red/To blush
Ponerse verde de envidia	To be green with envy
Quedarse en blanco	To go blank
Verlo todo de color de rosa	See the world through rose-colored glasses.

REFRANES

SAYINGS

A buen entendedor, pocas palabras bastan.	A word to the wise is sufficient.
Ande o no ande, caballo grande.	Bigger is always better.
A quien madruga, Dios le ayuda.	The early bird catches the worm.
Cuídate, que te cuidaré.	Take care of yourself, and then I'll take care of you.
De tal palo tal astilla.	A chip off the old block.
Del dicho al hecho hay mucho trecho.	Easier said than done.

Dime con quién andas y te diré quién eres.	A man is known by the company he keeps.
El saber no ocupa lugar.	You can never know too much.
Lo que es moda no incomoda.	No discomfort is too great in the name of fashion.
Más vale maña que fuerza.	Brains is better than brawn.
Más vale prevenir que curar.	Prevention is better than cure.
Más vale solo que mal acompañado.	Better alone than with a bad companion.
Más vale tarde que nunca.	Better late than never.
Mucho ruido y pocas nueces.	All talk and no action.
No es oro todo lo que reluce.	All that glitters is not gold.
Poderoso caballero es don Dinero.	Money talks.
Por la boca muere el pez.	Talking too much can be dangerous.
Vale más una imagen que mil palabras.	A picture is worth a thousand words.

COMMON FALSE FRIENDS

False friends are Spanish words that look similar to English words but have very different meanings. While recognizing the English relatives of unfamiliar Spanish words you encounter is an important way of constructing meaning, there are some Spanish words whose similarity to English words is deceptive. Here is a list of some of the most common Spanish false friends.

actualmente ≠ actually

actualmente = nowadays, currently

actually = **de hecho, en realidad, en efecto**

aprobar ≠ approve

aprobar = to pass (an exam)

approve = **consentir, estar de acuerdo**

argumento ≠ argument

argumento = plot

argument = **discusión, pelea**

armada ≠ army

armada = navy

army = **ejército**

asistir ≠ assist

asistir = to attend, to go to

assist = **ayudar, colaborar**

balde ≠ bald

balde = pail, bucket

bald = **calvo/a**

batería ≠ battery

batería = drum set

battery = **pila**

bravo ≠ brave

bravo = wild, fierce

brave = **valiente**

cándido/a ≠ candid

cándido/a = innocent

candid = **sincero/a**

carbón ≠ carbon

carbón = coal

carbon = **carbono**

casual ≠ casual

casual = coincidental

casual = **informal, despreocupado/a**

casualidad ≠ casualty

casualidad = coincidence

casualty = **víctima**

colegio ≠ college

colegio = school

college = **universidad**

collar ≠ collar

collar = necklace

collar = **cuello (de camisa)**

comprensivo/a ≠ comprehensive

comprensivo/a = understanding

comprenhensive = **completo, extensivo**

constipado ≠ constipated

estar constipado/a = to have a cold

to be constipated = **estar estreñido/a**

crudo/a ≠ crude

crudo/a = raw, undercooked

crude = **burdo/a; grosero/a**

desgracia ≠ disgrace

desgracia = misfortune

disgrace = **deshonra, vergüenza**

divertir ≠ divert

divertirse = to enjoy oneself

to divert = **desviar**

educado/a ≠ educated

educado/a = well-behaved

educated = **culto/a, instruido/a**

embarazada ≠ embarrassed

estar embarazada = to be pregnant

to be embarrassed = **tener vergüenza**

eventualmente ≠ eventually

eventualmente = possibly

eventually = **finalmente, al final**

éxito ≠ exit

éxito = success

exit = **salida**

físico/a ≠ physician

físico/a = physicist

physician = **médico/a**

fútbol ≠ football

fútbol = soccer

football = **fútbol americano**

lectura ≠ lecture
lectura = reading
lecture = **conferencia**

librería ≠ library
librería = bookstore
library = **biblioteca**

máscara ≠ mascara
máscara = mask
mascara = **rímel**

molestar ≠ to molest
molestar = to bother, to annoy
molest = **abusar**

oficio ≠ office
oficio = trade, occupation
office = **oficina**

rato ≠ rat
rato = while
rat = **rata**

realizar ≠ realize
realizar = to do
to realize = **darse cuenta**

red ≠ red
red = net
red = **rojo**

remover ≠ remove
remover = to stir; to turn over
remove = **sacar, quitar**

revolver ≠ revolver
revolver = to stir; to rummage through
revolver = **revólver**

sensible ≠ sensible
sensible = sentitive
sensible = **sensato/a, razonable**

suceso ≠ success
suceso = event
success = **éxito**

sujeto ≠ subject
sujeto = fellow, guy
subject = **tema, asunto**

LOS ALIMENTOS

FOODS

FRUTAS

FRUITS

la aceituna	olive
el aguacate	avocado
el albaricoque, el damasco	apricot
la banana, el plátano	banana
la cereza	cherry
la ciruela	plum
el dátil	date
la frambuesa	raspberry
la fresa, la frutilla	strawberry
el higo	fig
el limón	lemon, lime
el melocotón, el durazno	peach
la mandarina	tangerine
el mango	mango
la manzana	apple
la naranja	orange
la papaya	papaya
la pera	pear
la piña	pineapple
el pomelo, la toronja	grapefruit
la sandía	watermelon
las uvas	grapes

VEGETALES	*VEGETABLES*
la alcachofa	artichoke
el apio	celery
la arveja, el guisante	pea
la berenjena	eggplant
el brócoli	broccoli
la calabaza	squash, pumpkin
la cebolla	onion
el champiñón, la seta	mushroom
el col, el repollo	cabbage
el coliflor	cauliflower
los espárragos	asparagus
las espinacas	spinach
los frijoles, las habichuelas	beans
las habas	lima beans
las judías verdes, los ejotes	string beans, green beans
la lechuga	lettuce
el maíz, el choclo, el elote	corn
la papa, la patata	potato
el pepino	cucumber
el pimentón	bell pepper
el rábano	radish
la remolacha	beet
el tomate, el jitomate	tomato
la zanahoria	carrot

EL PESCADO Y LOS MARISCOS	*FISH AND SHELLFISH*
la almeja	clam
el atún	tuna
el bacalao	cod
el calamar	squid
el cangrejo	crab
el camarón, la gamba	shrimp
la langosta	lobster
el langostino	prawn
el lenguado	sole, flounder
el mejillón	mussel
la ostra	oyster
el pulpo	octopus
el salmón	salmon
la sardina	sardine
la vieira	scallop
LA CARNE	*MEAT*
la albóndiga	meatball
el bistéc	steak
la carne de res	beef
el chorizo	hard pork sausage
la chuleta de cerdo	pork chop
el cordero	lamb
los fiambres	cold cuts; food served cold
el filete	fillet
la hamburguesa	hamburger

el hígado	liver
el jamón	ham
el lechón	suckling pig; roasted pig
el pavo	turkey
el pollo	chicken
el puerco	pork
la salchicha	sausage
la ternera	veal
el tocino	bacon

OTRAS COMIDAS	*OTHER FOODS*
el ajo	garlic
el arroz	rice
el azúcar	sugar
el batido	milkshake
el budín	pudding
el cacahuete, el maní	peanut
el café	coffee
los fideos	noodles, pasta
la harina	flour
el huevo	egg
el jugo, el zumo	juice
la leche	milk
la mermelada	marmalade; jam
la miel	honey
el pan	bread
el queso	cheese

la sal	salt
la sopa	soup
el té	tea
la tortilla	omelet (Spain); tortilla (Mexico)
el yogur	yogurt

CÓMO DESCRIBIR LA COMIDA	*WAYS TO DESCRIBE FOOD*
a la plancha, a la parrilla	grilled
ácido/a	sour
al horno	baked
amargo/a	bitter
caliente	hot
dulce	sweet
duro/a	tough
frío/a	cold
frito/a	fried
fuerte	strong, heavy
ligero/a	light
picante	spicy
sabroso/a	tasty
salado/a	salty

DÍAS FESTIVOS

Enero
Año Nuevo (1)
Día de los Reyes Magos (6)
Día de Martin Luther King, Jr.

Febrero
Día de San Blas (Paraguay) (3)
Día de San Valentín, Día de los Enamorados (14)
Día de los Presidentes
Carnaval

Marzo
Día de San Patricio (17)
Nacimiento de Benito Juárez (México) (21)

Abril
Semana Santa
Pésaj
Pascua
Declaración de la Independencia de Venezuela (19)
Día de la Tierra (22)

HOLIDAYS

January
New Year's Day
Three Kings Day (Epiphany)
Martin Luther King, Jr. Day

February
St. Blas Day (Paraguay)
Valentine's Day
Presidents' Day
Carnival (Mardi Gras)

March
St. Patrick's Day
Benito Juárez's Birthday (Mexico)

April
Holy Week
Passover
Easter
Declaration of Independence of Venezuela
Earth Day

Mayo	May
Día del Trabajo (1)	Labor Day
Cinco de Mayo (5) (Mexico)	Cinco de Mayo (May 5th)
Día de las Madres	Mother's Day
Independencia Patria (Paraguay) (15)	Independence Day (Paraguay)
Día Conmemorativo	Memorial Day
JUNIO	*JUNE*
Día de los Padres	Father's Day
Día de la Bandera (14)	Flag Day
Día del Indio (Perú) (24)	Native People's Day
JULIO	*JULY*
Día de la Independencia de los Estados Unidos (4)	Independence Day (United States)
Día de la Independencia de Venezuela (5)	Independence Day (Venezuela)
Día de la Independencia de la Argentina (9)	Independence Day (Argentina)
Día de la Independencia de Colombia (20)	Independence Day (Colombia)
Nacimiento de Simón Bolívar (24)	Simón Bolívar's Birthday
Día de la Revolución (Cuba) (26)	Revolution Day (Cuba)
Día de la Independencia del Perú (28)	Independence Day (Peru)

AGOSTO
Día de la Independencia de Bolivia (6)

Día de la Independencia del Ecuador (10)

Día de San Martín (Argentina) (17)

Día de la Independencia del Uruguay (25)

SEPTIEMBRE
Día del Trabajo (EE. UU.)

Día de la Independencia de Costa Rica, El Salvador, Guatemala, Honduras y Nicaragua (15)

Día de la Independencia de México (16)

Día de la Independencia de Chile (18)

Año Nuevo judío

Día de la Virgen de las Mercedes (Perú) (24)

OCTUBRE
Día de la Raza (12)

Noche de Brujas (31)

AUGUST
Independence Day (Bolivia)

Independence Day (Ecuador)

San Martín Day (anniversary of his death)

Independence Day (Uruguay)

SEPTEMBER
Labor Day (U. S.)

Independence Day (Costa Rica, El Salvador, Guatemala, Honduras, Nicaragua)

Independence Day (Mexico)

Independence Day (Chile)

Jewish New Year

Day of the Virgin of Mercedes (Peru)

OCTOBER
Columbus Day

Halloween

NOVIEMBRE	*NOVEMBER*
Día de los Muertos (2)	All Souls Day
Día de los Veteranos (11)	Veterans' Day
Día de la Revolución Mexicana (20)	Mexican Revolution Day
Día de Acción de Gracias	Thanksgiving
Día de la Independencia de Panamá (28)	Independence Day (Panama)

DICIEMBRE	*DECEMBER*
Día de la Virgen (8)	Day of the Virgin
Día de la Virgen de Guadalupe (México) (12)	Day of the Virgin of Guadalupe (Mexico)
Januká	Chanukah
Nochebuena (24)	Christmas Eve
Navidad (25)	Christmas
Año Viejo (31)	New Year's Eve

NOTE: In Spanish, dates are written with the day first, then the month. Christmas Day is **el 25 de diciembre**. In Latin America and in Europe, abbreviated dates also follow this pattern. Halloween, for example, falls on 31/10. You may also see the numbers in dates separated by periods: 14.2.01. When referring to centuries, roman numerals are always used. The 16th century, therefore, is **el siglo XVI**.

PESOS Y MEDIDAS

LONGITUD

El sistema métrico
Metric system

milímetro	**= 0,001 metro**	= 0.039 inch
millimeter	= 0.0001 meter	
centímetro	**= 0,01 metro**	= 0.39 inch
centimeter	= 0.01 meter	
decímetro	**= 0,1 metro**	= 3.94 inches
decimeter	= 0.1 meter	
metro		= 39.4 inches
meter		
decámetro	**= 10 metros**	= 32.8 feet
dekameter	= 10 meters	
hectómetro	**= 100 metros**	= 328 feet
hectometer	= 100 meters	
kilómetro	**= 1.000 metros**	= .62 mile
kilometer	= 1,000 meters	

WEIGHTS & MEASURES

LENGTH

El equivalente estadounidense
U.S. equivalent

U.S. system
El sistema estadounidense

Metric equivalent
El equivalente métrico

inch		= 2.54 centimeters
pulgada		**= 2,54 centímetros**
foot	= 12 inches	= 30.48 centimeters
pie	**= 12 pulgadas**	**= 30,48 centímetros**
yard	= 3 feet	= 0.914 meter
yarda	**= 3 pies**	**= 0,914 metro**
mile	= 5,280 feet	= 1.609 kilometers
milla	**= 5.280 pies**	**= 1,609 kilómetros**

SUPERFICIE

El sistema métrico
Metric system

metro cuadrado
square meter

SURFACE AREA

El equivalente estadounidense
U.S. equivalent

= 10.764 square feet

área	= **100 metros cuadrados**	
are	= **100 square meters**	= 0.025 acre
hectárea	= **100 áreas**	
hectare	= **100 ares**	= 2.471 acres

U.S. system
El sistema estadounidense

Metric equivalent
El equivalente métrico

yarda cuadrada = 9 pies cuadrados = 0,836 metros cuadrados
square yard = 9 square feet = 0.836 square meters

acre = 4.840 yardas cuadradas = 0,405 hectáreas
acre = 4,840 square yards = 0.405 hectares

CAPACIDAD

El sistema métrico
Metric system

CAPACITY

El equivalente estadounidense
U.S. equivalent

mililitro	= **0,001 litro**	
mililiter	= 0.001 liter	= 0.034 ounces
centilitro	= **0,01 litro**	
centiliter	= 0. 01 liter	= 0.34 ounces
decilitro	= **0,1 litro**	
deciliter	= 0.1 liter	= 3.4 ounces
litro		
liter		= 1.06 quarts
decalitro	= **10 litros**	
dekaliter	= 10 liters	= 2.64 gallons

| **hectolitro** | = | **100 litros** | |
| hectoliter | = | 100 liters | = 26.4 gallons |

| **kilolitro** | = | **1.000 litros** | |
| kiloliter | = | 1,000 liters | = 264 gallons |

| *U.S. system* | | *Metric equivalent* |
| ***El sistema estadounidense*** | | ***El equivalente métrico*** |

| ounce | | | = 29.6 milliliters |
| **onza** | | | = 29,6 mililitros |

| cup | = | 8 ounces | = 236 milliliters |
| **taza** | = | **8 onzas** | = **236 mililitros** |

| pint | = | 2 cups | = 0.47 liters |
| **pinta** | = | **2 tazas** | = **0,47 litros** |

| quart | = | 2 pints | = 0.95 liters |
| **cuarto** | = | **2 pinta** | = **0,95 litros** |

| gallon | = | 4 quarts | = 3.79 liters |
| **galón** | = | **4 cuartos** | = **3,79 litros** |

PESO   *WEIGHT*

El sistema métrico   **El equivalente estadounidense**
Metric system   U.S. equivalent

| **miligramo** | = | **0,001 gramo** | |
| **milligram** | = | **0.001 gram** | |

| **gramo** | | | |
| gram | | | = 0.035 ounce |

| **decagramo** | = | **10 gramos** | |
| dekagram | = | 10 grams | = 0.35 ounces |

| **hectogramo** | = | **100 gramos** | |
| hectogram | = | 100 grams | = 3.5 ounces |

| **kilogramo** | = | **1.000 gramos** | |
| kilogram | = | 1,000 grams | = 2.2 pounds |

**tonelada
(métrica)** = **1.000 kilogramos**

metric ton = 1,000 kilograms = 1.1 tons

U.S. system
El sistema estadounidense

Metric equivalent
El equivalente métrico

ounce
onza

= 28.35 grams
= 28,35 gramos

pound
libra

= 16 ounces
= **16 onzas**

= 0.45 kilograms
= 0,45 kilogramos

ton
tonelada

= 2,000 pounds
= **2,000 libras**

= 0.9 metric tons
= 0,9 toneladas métricas

Temperatura

Grados centígrados
Degrees Celsius

To convert from Celsius to Fahrenheit, multiply by 9/5 and add 32.

Temperature

Grados Fahrenheit
Degrees Fahrenheit

To convert from Fahrenheit to Celsius, subtract 32 and multiply by 5/9.

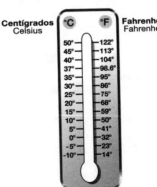

Centígrados
Celsius °C   °F   Fahrenheit
Fahrenheit

50°—122°
45°—113°
40°—104°
37°—98.6°
35°—95°
30°—86°
25°—75°
20°—68°
15°—59°
10°—50°
5°—41°
0°—32°
-5°—23°
-10°—14°

NOMBRES DE PILA ESPAÑOLES

SPANISH PERSONAL NAMES

Note: Not all Spanish names have English equivalents.

NOMBRES FEMENINOS	WOMEN'S NAMES
Alba	Elba
Alicia	Alice, Alicia
Amanda	Amanda
Ana	Ann, Anne
Araceli (Celi)	
Asunción (Asun)	
Asunta	
Aurora	Aurora, Dawn
Beatriz (Bea, Beti, Biata)	Beatrice
Belén	
Berta	Bertha
Blanca	Blanche
Carlota	Charlotte
Carolina (Carol)	Caroline
Catarina (Cati)	Catherine, Catharine
Cecilia	Cecile
Celia	Celia
Claudia	Claudia
Consuelo	
Diana	Diane
Dorotea	Dorothy
Elena	Helen, Ellen

Elia	
Elvira	Elvira
Emilia	Emily
Encarna	
Ester	Esther
Estrella	Stella, Estelle
Eva	Eve
Gemma	
Gertrudes	Gertrude
Gloria	Gloria
Inés	Inez
Irene	Irene
Isabel	Elizabeth
Josefa	
Josefina (Pepi, Fina)	Josephine
Juana	Joan, Joanne, Jane
Judith	Judith
Julia	Julia, Julie
Julieta	Juliet, Juliette
Laura	Laura
Leonor	Leonore
Lidia	Lydia
Lourdes	
Luisa	Louise
Manuela (Manola, Manoli)	
Margarita (Marga)	Margaret

María	Mary, Marie
Marta	Martha
Mercedes (Merche)	
Mónica	Monica, Monique
Montserrat (Montse)	
Noelia	
Norma	Norma
Olga	Olga
Paloma	
Patricia (Pati)	Patricia
Paula	Paula
Raquel	Rachel
Rocío	
Rosa	Rose
Rosalía	Rosalie
Rosana	Rosana, Roseanne
Rosario	
Sandra	Sandra
Sara	Sarah
Silvia	Sylvia
Sofía	Sophia
Sonia	Sonya
Susana (Susi)	Susan
Teresa	Theresa
Verónica	Veronica
Victoria (Vicki)	Victoria

Violeta	Violet
Zoe	Zoe
NOMBRES MASCULINOS	*MEN'S NAMES*
Alberto	Albert
Alejandro	Alexander
Álex	Alex
Alfonso	Alphonse
Alfredo	Alfred
Andrés	Andrew
Ángel	
Antonio (Toni)	Anthony
Aquiles	Achilles
Arturo	Arthur
Augusto	August
Bernardo	Bernard
Camilo	
Carlos	Charles
César	
Cristiano	Christian
Cristóbal	Christopher
Damián	Damian
David	David
Diego	James
Eduardo	Edward
Emilio	Emil
Enrique	Henry, Eric

Ernesto	Ernest
Esteban	Stephen
Eugenio	Eugene
Evaristo	
Federico (Fede)	Frederick
Felipe	Philip
Fernando	
Francisco (Paco)	Francis
Gerardo	Gerard
Gregorio	Gregory
Guillermo	William
Gustavo	Gustav
Ignacio (Nacho)	Ignatius
Jaime	James
Javier (Javi)	Xavier
Jeremías	Jeremiah, Jeremy
Jesús	
Joaquín	
Jorge	George
José (Pepe)	Joseph
Juan	John
Julián	Julian
Julio	Julius
Justino	Justin
León	Leo, Leon
Leonardo	Leonard

Lucas	Luke
Luis	Louis
Manolo	
Manuel	
Marcelo	Marcel
Marcos	Mark
Mariano	
Miguel	Michael
Oscar (Óscar)	Oscar
Pablo	Paul
Patricio	Patrick
Pedro	Peter
Rafael (Rafa)	Raphael
Raimundo	Raymond
Ramón	Raymond
Ricardo	Richard
Roberto	Robert
Santiago	James
Sebastián	Sebastian
Sergio	Serge
Simón	Simon
Sixto	
Teodoro	Theodore
Tomás	Thomas
Vicente	Vincent

COMPOUND WOMEN'S NAMES

In Spanish-speaking countries women frequently have names that are a combination of **María** and another name, as in **María Dolores** or **Ana María**, for example. Women with such names are rarely known as **María** but are addressed using the second name in the combination or a nickname derived from both names. **María del Carmen**, therefore, might be called **Carmen** or perhaps **Maricarmen**. Below are listed common combinations with **María**, followed by nicknames derived from them.

Note: **María** is not strictly a woman's name in the Spanish-speaking world. Some men's names contain **María**. **José María**, for example, is a common name.

María Ana (Ana, Mariana)

María Antonia (Antonia, Tonia, Toñi)

María Concepción (Concha)

María Cristina (Cristina, Cris, Tina)

María de los Ángeles (Ángeles, Mariángeles)

María del Carmen (Carmen, Maricarmen, Mámen)

María del Mar (Marimar)

María Dolores (Dolores, Mariló, Loles, Lola, Lolita)

María Elena (Elena)

María Eugenia (Eugenia, Maru, Genia)

María Inmaculada (Inma)

María Isabel (Isabel, Isa, Maribel, Mabel)

María Luisa (Luisa, Marilú)

María Nieves (Nieves, Marinieves)

María Pilar (Pilar, Pili, Maripili, Mapi)

María Reyes (Reyes, Marireyes)

María Rosa (Marisa)

María Soledad (Marisol)

María Teresa (Teresa, Tere, Maritere, Maite)

Ana María (Ana, Anamari)

Ángela María (Ángela)

Eva María (Eva)

Rosa María (Rosa, Rosamari)

COMPOUND MEN'S NAMES

José Manuel (Josema)

José María (Josema, Chema)

José Miguel

Juan Antonio

Juan Carlos (Juanca)

Juan José (Juanjo)

Juan Luis (Juanlu)

Juan Manuel (Juanma)

Juan Pablo (Juanpa)

Miguel Ángel

NÚMEROS

NÚMEROS ORDINALES

primero/a	1º/1ª
segundo/a	2º/2ª
tercero/a	3º/3ª
cuarto/a	4º/4ª
quinto/a	5º/5ª
sexto/a	6º/6ª
séptimo/a	7º/7ª
octavo/a	8º/8ª
noveno/a	9º/9ª
décimo/a	10º/10ª

FRACCIONES

$\frac{1}{2}$	un medio, la mitad
$\frac{1}{3}$	un tercio
$\frac{1}{4}$	un cuarto
$\frac{1}{5}$	un quinto
$\frac{1}{6}$	un sexto
$\frac{1}{7}$	un séptimo
$\frac{1}{8}$	un octavo
$\frac{1}{9}$	un noveno
$\frac{1}{10}$	un décimo
$\frac{2}{3}$	dos tercios
$\frac{3}{4}$	tres cuartos
$\frac{5}{8}$	cinco octavos

NUMBERS

ORDINAL NUMBERS

first	1st
second	2nd
third	3rd
fourth	4th
fifth	5th
sixth	6th
seventh	7th
eighth	8th
ninth	9th
tenth	10th

FRACTIONS

one half	
one third	
one fourth (quarter)	
one fifth	
one sixth	
one seventh	
one eighth	
one ninth	
one tenth	
two thirds	
three fourths (quarters)	
five eighths	

DECIMALES		*DECIMALS*	
un décimo	0,1	one tenth	0.1
un centésimo	0,01	one hundredth	0.01
un milésimo	0,001	one thousandth	0.001

OCUPACIONES

el/la abogado/a	lawyer
el actor, la actriz	actor
el/la administrador(a)	administrator
el/la agente de bienes raíces	real estate agent
el/la agente de seguros	insurance agent
el/la agricultor(a)	farmer
el/la arqueólogo/a	archaeologist
el/la arquitecto/a	architect
el/la artesano/a	artisan
el/la auxiliar de vuelo	flight attendant
el/la basurero/a	garbage collector
el/la bibliotecario/a	librarian
el/la bombero/a	firefighter
el/la cajero/a	bank teller, cashier
el/la camionero/a	truck driver
el/la cantinero/a	bartender
el/la carnicero/a	butcher
el/la carpintero/a	carpenter
el/la científico/a	scientist
el/la cirujano/a	surgeon

OCCUPATIONS

el/la cobrador(a)	bill collector
el/la cocinero/a	cook, chef
el/la comprador(a)	buyer
el/al consejero/a	counselor, advisor
el/la contador(a)	accountant
el/la corredor(a) de bolsa	stockbroker
el/la diplomático/a	diplomat
el/la diseñador(a)	designer
el/la electricista	electrician
el/la empresario/a de pompas fúnebres	funeral director
el/la especialista en dietética	dietician
el/la fotógrafo/a	photographer
el hombre/la mujer de negocios	businessperson
el/la intérprete	interpreter
el/la juez	judge
el/la maestro/a	elementary school teacher
el/la marinero/a	sailor
el/la obrero/a	manual laborer
el/la obrero/a de la construcción	construction worker
el/la optometrista	optometrist
el/la panadero/a	baker
el/la paramédico/a	paramedic
el/la peluquero/a	hairdresser
el/la piloto	pilot
el/la pintor(a)	painter

el/la político/a	politician
el/la plomero/a	plumber
el/la psicólogo/a	psychologist
el/la quiropráctico/a	chiropractor
el/la redactor(a)	editor
el/la reportero/a	reporter
el/la sastre	tailor
el/la secretario/a	secretary
el/la supervisor(a)	supervisor
el/la técnico/a	technician
el/la terapista físico/a	physical therapist
el/la vendedor(a)	sales representative
el/la veterinario/a	veterinarian